Contents

Series Editor's Preface

We live in a global age. We inhabit a world that has become radically interconnected, interdependent, and communicated in the formations and flows of the media. This same world also spawns proliferating, often interpenetrating, "global crises."

From climate change to the war on terror, financial meltdowns to forced migrations, pandemics to world poverty, and humanitarian disasters to the denial of human rights, these and other crises represent the dark side of our globalized planet. Their origins and outcomes are not confined behind national borders and they are not best conceived through national prisms of understanding. The impacts of global crises often register across "sovereign" national territories, surrounding regions, and beyond, and they can also become subject to systems of governance and forms of civil society response that are no less encompassing or transnational in scope. In today's interdependent world, global crises cannot be regarded as exceptional or aberrant events only, erupting without rhyme or reason or dislocated from the contemporary world (dis)order. They are endemic to the contemporary global world, deeply enmeshed within it. And so too are they highly dependent on the world's media.

The series Global Crises and the Media sets out to examine not only the media's role in the *communication* of global threats and crises but also how the media can enter into their *constitution,* enacting them on the public stage and thereby helping to shape their future trajectory around the world. More specifically, the volumes in this series seek to: (1) contextualize the study of global crisis reporting in relation to wider debates about the changing flows and formations of world media communication; (2) address how global crises become variously communicated and contested in the media around the world; (3) consider the possible impacts of global crisis reporting on public awareness, political action, and policy responses; (4) showcase the very latest research findings and discussion from leading authorities in their respective fields of inquiry; and (5) contribute to the development of positions of theory and debate that deliberately move beyond national parochialisms and/or geographically disaggregated research agendas. In these ways the specially commissioned books in the Global Crises and the Media series aim to provide a sophisticated and empirically engaged understanding of the media's role in global crises and thereby contribute to academic and public debate about some of the most significant global threats, conflicts and contentions in the world today.

Migrations and the Media, edited by Kerry Moore, Bernhard Gross and Terry Threadgold, expertly meets this series brief. The movement of people around the globe both is an index of and a contributing factor to accelerating processes of economic, political and cultural globalization. It can also be construed and is experienced by many in terms of 'crisis.' The United Nations High Commission for Refugees (UNCHR), for example, confronting the new global challenges posed by the changing nature of migration in the 21st century, talks of the need for a 'new paradigm.' 'Today', says UNCHR, 'people do not just flee persecution and war but also injustice, exclusion, environmental pressures, competition for scarce resources and all the miserable human consequences of dysfunctional states' (UNCHR, 2007). Forced migrations today involve internally displaced peoples as well as international people flows. It is often the rural poor, for example, who are forced off their lands to make way for dams, agricultural and industrial developments or new cities in the name of 'progress' and 'the national interest'—projects which invariably benefit national elites. *Un*natural disasters and climate change are also beginning to propel movements of people both intra-nationally and internationally, tendencies widely predicted to rise exponentially in the years ahead. And human trafficking by criminal gangs, including women and children for sexual exploitation and the illegal transportation of migrants across national borders, are also characteristic features of contemporary forced migration. Globally more and more countries are experiencing the arrival of migrants from diverse countries and backgrounds, and migration has become increasingly politicized as policies of border control are tightened in the name of national (but not 'human(e)') security.

Migrations and the Media critically intervenes into this most pressing of contemporary human concerns and does so on the basis of in-depth research and inter-disciplinary academic thinking. The editors together with an international line-up of contributing authors incisively interrogate the media's roles, representations and responsibilities in respect of migrations and migrants, examining not only how media report *on* but also discursively *construct* and thereby *intervene* within the 'crisis' of migration in different national and global contexts. How do contemporary media contribute discursively to the problematisation of migrants, undermining their claims for recognition and compounding their sense of dislocation? Have media sought to communicate something of the lived realities of asylum seekers and refugees, granting them a voice and situating their plight in relation to endemic global processes or discourses of human rights? This book critically unravels the ways in which media have become powerfully involved in global and national discourses of migration and how this registers in the political field and conditions the circumstances of life for those increasing numbers of migrants in the world today.

Simon Cottle, Series Editor

UNCHR. (2007). World Refugee Day: Displacement in the 21st Century. A New Paradigm. (http://www.unch.org/cgi-bin/texis/vtx/events?id=3e7f46e04 accessed 19.10.09)

Acknowledgments

This book would not have been possible without the help of numerous people and institutions. An extra special thanks to Simon Cottle for coming to our MeCCSA conference presentation at JOMEC in 2008, for asking us to contribute to his book series and for all of his encouragement and invaluable advice since then. Thank-you to our contributors for being so willing to write and re-write their chapters as requested. We would also like to thank our many friends and colleagues at Cardiff University School of Journalism, Media and Cultural Studies and at the University of the West of England Faculty of Arts, Creative Industries and Education for their enthusiasm and support for the book along the way, and to Paul Bowman for reading early drafts of some of our own contributions to the volume. Finally, we would especially like to thank Mary Savigar and Sophie Appel at Peter Lang for their understanding, assistance and patience in guiding us through the various stages of editing and production.

Introduction to Migrations and the Media

Kerry Moore

What's in a Crisis?

Migration is a subject rarely absent from news headlines or political agendas. Every day people want to move to countries that cannot or do not want to grant them entry. Some have to move from their places of origin because of political conflict, war or natural disasters. As this book nears completion, many examples of such stories populate the news media around the world as emergencies and longer-term "migration crises". These include the reporting of "one of the biggest human crises on the globe" (ABC news anchor Diane Sawyer), as refugees fleeing long-running war and famine in Somalia struggle to survive en route to and at camps in Kenya (Harding, 2011; Muir, 2011). They also include coverage of illegal immigration, "one of the most contentious debates in American politics" (Harris, 2011), in the United States, as Arizona made international news headlines by signing controversial Senate Bill 1070 into law. The Arizona bill was reported by the *New York Times* to be "the broadest and strictest immigration measure in generations", and was pronounced by Governor Jan Brewer to be "another tool for our state to use as we work to solve a crisis we did not create and the federal government has refused to fix" (Archibold, 2010). In April 2011, the Obama administration's injunction to block some of the key provisions of 1070 has been successfully upheld in the courts (Reuters, 2011). In June 2011, the US immigration debate was represented from a very different perspective by journalist Jose Antonio Vargas, whose self-disclosure as an undocumented immigrant has drawn media attention to a personal story of the crises attending such a status and the case against stringent new anti-immigration laws and for the legal recognition of sections of the already-resident undocumented population in the United States[1] (Mirkinson, 2011; Vargas, 2011).

These two contemporary migration stories begin to indicate something of the heterogeneity of meaning possible in the term "migration crisis". It may include the experiences of those who are readily recognised and admitted by the authorities as refugees, or who somehow make it across national borders in other ways, only to find they are not necessarily welcomed in encounters with already-resident communities. In addition, "crisis" may well describe the experiences of those who are trafficked against their will to work, for example, in the sex industry or who find themselves trapped in other conditions of highly exploitative, or forced labour akin to slavery. If these latter examples are migration "crisis narratives", however, they are rarely given priority in news agendas. Instead, what are far more likely to take precedence in migration news, as previous media research and many of the contributions to this book would suggest, are the national interests of states and the powers they are able to exercise in controlling undesirable immigration.

Crisis Management of the "Undesirable"

In a neoliberal world order, social theorist Zygmunt Bauman argues, "uncertainty and anguish born of uncertainty" are the "staple products" of globalisation (Bauman, 2004, p. 66). Under the forces of neoliberal globalisation, the governments of nation states have altered the orientation of their policy strategies. As McNevin contends, state powers have "reformulated their priorities away from the protection of citizens and towards integration with a global economy and sources of global capital" (McNevin, 2006, p. 139). Citizens relationships to the state, their forms of political belonging and once comparatively stable social identities and relationships have been disturbed and fragmented by such changes. In turn, the sovereign power of liberal democratic state authorities have been seriously reduced, such that "the most they can do", according to Bauman:

> ...is to refocus it on objects within reach; shift it from the objects they can do nothing about to those they can at least make a show of being able to handle and control. Refugees, asylum seekers, immigrants—the waste products of globalisation—fit the bill perfectly. (Bauman, 2004, p. 66)

Such defensive modalities of politics, in the terms of Ghassan Hage, reflect a "deficit of hope" in modern Western democracies, where politicians endeavour to, "reassert a sense of governmental power over the nation through their worrying" (Hage, 2003, p. 2). Indeed, what Hage identifies as the expression of defensive, or "paranoid" forms of nationalism may help to account for the popularity of policies tightening national border controls around the West and their intensification in an era of globalisation (Andreas, 2000; Moses, 2006; Snyder, 2000). From this perspective, perhaps it is unsurprising that migration crisis is more likely to refer to something imperative that wealthy "receiving" nations "manage" (see for example, Gross in this volume) or to be represented as a possible "index of national crisis" (Clarke, 2008).

Especially since the "war on terror" has positioned national security and the fear of "threatening cultural others" as pre-eminent concerns, alternative and perhaps more ethical perspectives for making sense of migration seem, as Cohen notes, to have been "effectively silenced", at least within the dominant public discourses of wealthy "receiving" countries (Cohen, 2006; Moore, in this volume). In this context, as Altheide asserts of news crises more generally, "fear" has played an important ideological role, defining migration crises and serving certain material interests: "to bump along those claims so that leaders can take political action against 'external enemies' or 'internal enemies'" (Altheide, 2002, p. 12). Nation-states have cooperated at an international level in their efforts to regulate migration flows, to define and separate "desirable" from "undesirable" migrants and to deter the latter from reaching their shores. Information sharing between states, electronic borders and other, increasingly sophisticated technologies of surveillance and securitisation, serve to control the physical movement of migrants across as well as within national borders. The bureaucracy of immigration systems, and internalisation of border controls which regulate the provision of legal, social and welfare services, have produced new regimes of control—criminalising certain categories of migrant and presenting further impediments to the free movement and survival of the unwelcome. In addition, measures to externalise borders have been designed to manage migration, for example in so called "transit processing centres" and "regional protection zones" in regions closer to migrants' countries of origin in the South (Klepp, 2010; Weber & Bowling, 2004). Australia's "Malaysia refugee exchange programme" is one of the latest manifestations of policies to manage and control undesirable migrants by exporting the business end of the filtering process away from Western nation-state territorial boundaries (Martin & Veness, 2011). These technologies of control of migration often remain unquestioned and are rarely radically scrutinised or subjected to critique by reporters in the pressured conditions of journalistic practice (see for example, Harris, in this volume). Nonetheless, they may play a highly determining role in the dominant news discourses surrounding the coverage of migration crises, and moreover, in important transformations of the normal mode of governance of liberal democratic states, as will be explored further below.

Migration Crisis Coverage and the "Arab Spring"

An important part of the ongoing coverage of the so-called "Arab Spring" has been the alarming reports of many people crossing borders to seek sanctuary from the armed conflict and insecurities of ongoing political antagonisms and violence. The news media rubric "Arab Spring", potentially limiting in many ways, has provided a shorthand terminology for classifying the migration news associated with the uprisings in 2011 including the revolutions in Tunisia and Egypt; the civil war in Libya; and conflicts between the people and authorities in Bahrain, Yemen, Syria and other neighbouring countries. The internal and international political contexts of these uprisings have been distinct and diverse, conditioning complex patterns of migration and displacing peoples in and between countries in the region. Some of this complexity has been captured in the "Arab Spring" migration coverage reported in the mainstream English-language media. Yet, as media research of asylum and immigration news content has repeatedly demonstrated, some migration stories appear far more likely to have been told by journalists than others, and some themes familiar to publics in wealthy, refugee-receiving countries have emerged in the coverage (Bleasdale, 2008; Buchanan, Grillo, & Threadgold, 2003; Clarke, 1998; Danso & McDonald, 2001; Gross, Moore, & Threadgold, 2007; Kaye, 2001; Speers, 2001). For example, the scale of population movements and/or rising numbers of migrants crossing borders have constituted a clear focus, although the accuracy of figures and scale of the "refugee crisis" remain in dispute (see for example, Ulack, 2011 and posted responses).

More particularly, much of the focus upon a "refugee crisis" in both the quality and tabloid press has highlighted large numbers of "boat people" arriving from North African countries on the Italian Mediterranean island of Lampedusa.[2] Some reports have reported the suffering experienced by "boat people" themselves. (for example, the *Irish Times*, 2011), including coverage drawn by the presence of actress, Angelina Jolie who visited Lampedusa as a UNHCR advocate—an example of celebrity advocacy that Chouliaraki (in this volume) argues is not unproblematic as a genre of humanitarian news (UNHCR, 2011). By contrast, in the *Economist*'s 11th April: THE NEXT EUROPEAN CRISIS: BOAT PEOPLE and the *Daily Express*'s, 3rd June: CRISIS TALKS IN FIGHT TO STEM MIGRANT HORDES (Allen, 2011), for example, "boat people" are represented as a significant problem, framed, moreover, as potentially opportunist migrant workers rather than genuinely flee-ing conflict. Such suspicions seem to heighten the news value of migration sto-ries. They articulate an imperative to identify and control "undesirable" migrants, and promote a culture of disbelief that has become a sedimented ele-ment of dominant media and policy discourses surrounding asylum seekers in the West (Sassen, 1999; Souter, 2011). Indeed a "commonsense" hostility to-wards certain kinds of migrant as a threat to the economic stability, well-being and security of wealthy "receiving societies" has become an enduring character-istic of migration as a hot news topic in recent years, and often linked with wider social, cultural or political "crises" (Gross, et al., 2007; Lynn & Lea, 2003; Threadgold, 2006; Tyler, 2006).

Charged with the responsibility to manage these "crises", policy makers across Europe, North America and Australasia have instituted increasingly re-strictive measures designed to police borders and control immigration (Buonfino, 2004; Nevins, 2007; Schuster, 2005; Weber & Bowling, 2004). In their efforts to outflank anti-immigrant politics of the far-right, mainstream politicians have proposed and instituted new laws intended to symbolise a "tough stance" and to further restrict and regulate the movement and rights of asylum seekers and other migrants (Bloch & Schuster, 2005; Fekete, 2005; Ticktin, 2005). Taking place on the edge of "Fortress Europe", the news media coverage of "Arab Spring" migration has clearly touched upon some important aspects of these politics. The representation of a migration crisis has not just re-ferred to political and/or humanitarian concerns about the numbers of people making dangerous crossings of the Mediterranean Sea to Europe, but arguably has been more fundamentally concerned with questioning the capacity of the normal legal and political systems of European nations to exercise sovereign power over forces that potentially exceed their control. Indeed, the news cover-age has focused upon questions of national power and sovereignty, relationships between nation-states and the reputations of EU political leaders. In March 2011, the Italian Prime Minister Silvio Berlusconi sought to placate his domestic audience by promising a rapid dispersal of migrants from the island of Lampe-dusa, as the newspaper *Corriere Della Sera* reported: "BERLUSCONI PLEDGES TO CLEAR LAMPEDUSA IN TWO OR THREE DAYS" (Watson, 2011). Reports of a diplomatic "border crisis" then emerged when President Nicholas Sarkozy of France, fearing the Italian policy to issue temporary residence permits would enable migrants to extend their journeys across the EU's internal national borders, called for a suspension of the Schengen agreement.[3] Indeed, such has been the gravity of the "crisis" for European politicians[4]—essentially a crisis in maintaining what Balibar (2006) has referred to as the "south Mediterranean fence"—that the migration of "boat people" has been reported as having been encouraged and promoted by Muammar Gaddafi as a valuable "weapon" against his European opponents (see for example, Squires & McElroy, 2011).[5]

The importance of this "crisis" might also be traced in reports in May 2011 of over 60 migrants having died after their boat ran into trouble in the Mediterranean, its distress calls allegedly ignored by European military in clear contravention of maritime law (Shenker, 2011). Although not a unique tragedy, with many lives having been lost making this treacherous journey in recent months and years, the incongruity between to failure to rescue on the one hand, and NATO justifications for military intervention in Libya on humanitarian grounds on the other, is particularly striking. Arguably, however, these events seem less incongruous in the context of the routines that have developed for policing and surveillance of the external Mediterranean borders of "Fortress Europe" in recent years, including measures that have seemed to suspend, compromise or fail to take into account existing international human rights laws and obligations to which EU states are signatory (Hamood, 2008; Klepp, 2010). In this, there have been striking resonances between aspects of this "refugee crisis" and previous "boat people" controversies such as the August 2001 "Tampa affair" during the era of Australian Prime Minister John Howard's "Pacific Solution" (see for example, Gale, 2004; O'Doherty & Augoustinos, 2008; Tazreiter, 2003; Ward, 2002) and subsequent controversies in that region and elsewhere (McKay, Thomas, & Warwick Blood, 2011; Pugh, 2004).

Such radical policies and attendant administrative practices instituted by these and other liberal democratic states suggest a concerning trend towards what Agamben has termed "states of exception" in the global management of migration (see, for example Ticktin, 2005 on practices in France). These unusual extensions of sovereign power, historically enacted in times of perceived emergency or crisis, make exceptions to, and thus displace the normal, limited authority of the existing legal order (Agamben, 2005). However, states of exception have become, Agamben contends, a "paradigm of government today", with important consequences for the condition of democracy and the rule of law in liberal nation-states. The "juridical procedures and deployments of power" of these exceptional contexts can be seen to produce undesirable migrants as what Agamben terms *Homo Sacer*, or bare life, human beings potentially "so completely deprived of their rights and prerogatives that no act committed against them could appear any longer as a crime" (Agamben, 1998, p. 97).

This brief and limited exploration of Arab Spring migration news narratives merely scratches the surface of the coverage that has surrounded these issues to date and its social or political significance. What it may illustrate at least, however, is that accepting the classification of migration as a "crisis" too easily or uncritically perhaps masks more than it reveals; that the representation of "crisis" can serve as an element within much wider and complex discourses concerned with globalisation, national identity and sovereignty; and may or may not be concerned with issues that are beyond the power of national politicians to control. However, it is also important to note that the journalistic reporting of migration stories has neither necessarily simply reproduced the "crisis narratives" of the dominant political discourse nor those directly useful to politicians seeking to justify exceptional measures.

Theorising, Representing and Reporting Migration Crises

This book aims to critically examine, both theoretically and empirically, the diverse roles played by the global news media in reporting migration and those of "migration crises" shaping news media discourses.

Research in migration studies and its cognate fields has developed a variety of newly theorised conceptions of human spaces, movements and identities, as well as of polities, sovereignty and governance. Engaging some of the most important political, social and cultural issues facing contemporary societies in what Castles and Miller have termed an "age of migration" (Castles & Miller, 2003), this scholarship presents radical conceptual challenges to a range of "fixed" or "settled" relationships between the local, the national and the international. Meanwhile, media studies continues to critically engage and theorise key developments within and between post-industrial societies of "the north" and emerging economies of "the south", addressing questions of power operating within diverse fields of communications: political, cultural and social. Media scholars highlight increasingly complex communication systems, their ideological or discursive processes and relations within and between local and global contexts.

Both migration studies and media studies are centrally concerned with questions
of identity and social relations, each scrutinises the formation and maintenance
of communities, institutions and the operation of power transnationally and internationally. Both scholarly areas have been fundamentally concerned with
movement, mobility and networks; each with the transformation, flows and reproduction of information and ideas across borders, and with social change. In
many ways, migration and media studies are already implicitly interlinked and
mutually constitutive. Yet rarely has scholarship from these important fields of
study critically engaged one another explicitly and systematically. The collection
of chapters in this book seeks to address this, aiming to bridge some of the gaps
between media and migration research.

The chapters that follow bring together a range of contemporary research
from the broad interdisciplinary fields of migration studies and journalism, media and cultural studies, focusing upon the global reporting of migration to critically explore the mediation of a range of migration issues in a diverse range of
international contexts. We have assembled work from international researchers
working on a variety of forced migration and other migration topics, including:
asylum seeking and refugees; human trafficking and smuggling; "climate refugees"; undocumented and economic migrants; the genres of humanitarian reporting; and the discourse of election debates; as well as the rights and
responsibilities of journalism; and the presuppositions and pressures upon journalists working in this area. In different ways, the contributions theorise the
mechanisms and meanings involved in the interactions between these areas and
the media in the context of contemporary global patterns of migration, as well
as their possible impacts upon policy making and public discourse. The book
prioritises the examination of key contemporary political, cultural and social issues and debates with which migration is entwined, bringing together work
which develops existing and new conceptual understanding of how migration is
represented and constructed as "a crisis" and articulated within news narratives
in relation to areas such as the politics of national identity and difference, globalisation, cultural belonging and otherness; social cohesion, integration or exclusion; xenophobia, racist hostility, stigma and stereotyping. Institutional
restraints and established journalistic practices may, in fact, contribute to the reaffirmation of highly questionable commonsense understandings of migration *as*
"a crisis." The reproduction of such an understanding may not necessarily be a
deliberate, conscious undertaking of journalistic reporting. To address this, the

collection also includes analyses of the *reporting practices* through which migration coverage is produced.

The book is organised into three distinct, but inter-related sections: Section One: Migration Reporting and the Discursive Construction of Crisis; Section Two: Crisis Reporting and the Representation of Migration; and Section Three: The Management of Migration and Journalistic Practice. While each of the book's sections are inter-related and complementary, a section introduction is included at the beginning of each to serve as a guide to the key themes and objectives explored, as well as providing a summary of each chapter and its relation to others in the section. A final Conclusion chapter by Terry Threadgold incorporates a comprehensive critical commentary upon the issues explored by each of the chapters included in the collection.

Notes

1. This includes, for example, the DREAM Act (Development, Relief and Education for Alien Minors), a nearly 10-year-old immigration bill that would offer a route to permanent legal residency for undocumented immigrants who have been successfully educated in the US.

2. They also recall earlier crises such as those Vietnamese "boat people" from the mid-1970s—Cold War-era refugees whose plight perhaps appeared to map onto a far more simple political terrain where humanitarian responses of the West could be held to signify ideological values clearly contrasting with those of Communism, yet who were nonetheless subject to stereotyping and social/political hostilities in North America, Australasia and Europe (see for example: Baer, 1982; Threadgold, 2006).

3. A detailed explanation of the Schengen Agreement, subsequent developments and related EU border management measures can be found at: http://europa.eu/legislation _summaries/justice_freedom_security/free_movement_of_persons_asylum_immigrati on/l33020_en.htm

4. See for example: Chebil, 2011 for France-Italy relations; Day, 2011 on EU passport control policy; and Jamieson, 2011 for concerns about migrants reaching Britain.

5. Previously, controversial agreements between Libya and Italy, reaffirmed in the 2008 "Friendship, Partnership and Cooperation Treaty" (and which were being further strengthened in the EU-Libya Framework Agreement, dropped in February 2011) existed to cooperate on policing the Mediterranean borders of the EU (Amnesty International, 2010; Back, 2009). Since 2000, agreements had developed to allow Italy to return migrants intercepted at sea to Libya, the detention and deportation of migrants as well as Italian/EU funding of border policing and Libyan surveillance patrols the north African Mediterranean coastal waters. (Hamood, 2008)

Section One—Migration Reporting and the Discursive Construction of Crisis

We begin with a collection of four chapters that, in quite different ways, offer rich and rewarding conceptual frameworks through which to critically explore the relationship between migration and the media. Influenced by theoretical paradigms ranging from neo-pragmatism to post-Marxism, Hegelian dialecticism to Foucault, and exploring a variety of examples and contexts, these chapters nonetheless share a commitment to examining how migration or migrants are constructed in discourse and to critically exploring the social significance or consequences of those constructions.

First, Lilie Chouliaraki's chapter presents a compelling argument for closely examining the humanitarian discourses through which refugee issues are often reported, with respect to the emphases they place upon the Western self and the forms of solidarity with refugee "others" they appear to promote. Chouliaraki alerts us to the importance of questioning "our" place in the humanitarian and post-humanitarian discourses that often accompany journalistic reporting of plights of others, including refugee crises. The chapter not only provides an insightful analysis of such reportage, but a conceptual framework through which to radically critique morally comforting, and too easy, assumptions about refugee news reported through a humanitarian lens. The chapter also encourages more reflexive forms of thinking to open new possibilities for political solidarity and journalistic discourse that do not marginalise injustice and refugee experiences.

While Chouliaraki's chapter theorises the potential for confronting injustice within humanitarian approaches to reporting migration, Harald Bauder's chapter also attends to the political possibilities opened by a specific form of migration reporting. Bauder focuses in particular upon exploring "crisis", and how it may function within migration debates as a moment of change or "transformation", discursively and materially. Drawing upon a Marxian notion of crisis and a Hegelian theory of dialectics in his analyses of the immigration debate in Germany and Canada, Bauder identifies three key dialectical dimensions shaping migration reporting (journalistic balance, discursive-material practices, and migrant-national identity formation), and traces some key themes of "crisis" within the news coverage (terrorism, economics, and humanitarian stories). For Bauder, "crisis is an integral part of dialectical process. In fact, crises constitute transformative moments that initiate dialectical progression" although such moments remain "highly contingent on the national contexts in which these debates occur."

Bernhard Gross also explores the role of "crisis" in migration debate, sharing with Bauder a focus upon the importance of the political context as well as the construction of "the nation" in representing migration crisis. In the heightened competitive context of Britain's first televised General Election leadership debate, Gross demonstrates how the shifting referents invoked in distinguishing "us" from "them", "inside" from "outside" led to a shifting and often ambivalent definition of "migration crisis". Gross offers a compelling case for the expediency of such an interpretative context for politicians seeking electoral advantage through an alignment with the concerns of "us real people" on immigration, yet constrained by limitations of their own power and the sovereignty of the British state. He also raises very important questions about the role of journalistic processes of selection in enabling and facilitating the immigration discussions of the televised election debate.

Finally, Kerry Moore's chapter, like those of Bauder and Gross, is concerned to identify and analyse the dynamics of reporting migration that are central to the construction of migration crises. Moore draws upon post-Marxist discourse theory to demonstrate how dominant ideas surrounding migration, and in particular those surrounding asylum, can change. In focusing upon the contingency and shifting status of human rights, Moore shares with Chouliaraki and Bauder a concern to critically analyse expressions of humanitarianism within migration reporting. The chapter examines the rhetorical function of such expressions in the arguments of national politicians whose purpose has been primarily to "talk tough" about, and to restrict immigration rather than to confront the injustices faced by refugees. As universal ideals of human rights have been repositioned in various ways as a "potential threat to the stability, well-being and security of the British nation" Moore contends, new forms of "commonsense" on asylum have become possible in Britain, including the association of asylum and human rights with the threat of terrorism. While the apparent contradiction with continuing claims that Britain has a "proud history" on human rights has played a "necessary structural function" in reproducing the dominant securitising discourses surrounding asylum, it has not been subjected to the critical scrutiny of the news media that it should have received.

CHAPTER ONE

Between Pity and Irony—Paradigms of Refugee Representation in Humanitarian Discourse

Lilie Chouliaraki

Introduction

Humanitarian appeals, where population displacements are portrayed through our own emotions about them, and celebrity advocacy, where refugees' lives are narrated through a celebrity's confessions about her own life, tell us much more than the cause they seek to communicate. They tell us something important about the ways in which we represent the world beyond ourselves as a cause for our action. It is this humanitarian discourse on refugees that I critically discuss in this chapter.

This is a discourse, I propose, that responds to existing concerns about the moral deficit of "common humanity" as a justification for solidarity, by moving away from the refugee and towards the self as the primary object of our cognition and emotion—a move that I have elsewhere described as a shift from a humanitarian discourse of pity to a post-humanitarian discourse of irony.[1] Despite its problematisation of "common humanity", I argue, irony ultimately fails to address the key critique of pity: its de-humanisation of the refugee. This is because, rather than reflexively engaging with the complex politics of population displacement, the discourse of irony replaces a morality of universalism, where solidarity signals our moral obligation to the human species, with an opposing, yet structurally equivalent, morality of contingency, where solidarity signals our distrust of all moral obligation but the obligation to oneself. What remains excluded from both "paradigms" of humanitarian discourse is the question of politics, which would situate the refugee as an actor in her/his historical context, treating her/his suffering as a consequence of a complex field of interests and confronting us with the question of why we should act upon it and how.

I begin with a review of the critique of traditional refugee representations as a politics of pity in order to show how such critique has opened up the discursive space for alternative articulations of solidarity as irony to emerge (Section 1. The Representation of Refugees as a Politics of Pity). Drawing upon specific examples of two key UNHCR communication genres, appeals and celebrity advocacy, I then proceed to show how the representational practices of irony shift the justification for solidarity with refugees from human suffering to personal self-fulfilment (Section 2. "Post-Humanitarianism": The Communication of Solidarity as Self-Communication). Far from a purely philosophical affair, I argue, this discursive shift is co-nascent with the increasing "instrumentalisation" of solidarity in the global humanitarian market, which de-politicises human vulnerability and turns the imperative to act on distant others into a matter of consumerist self-gratification (in Section 3. Solidarity as Irony: A Critique of Post-Humanitarianism). In conclusion, I suggest that a discourse of reflexive solidarity may be able to challenge the logic of the market and encourage a new, politicised engagement with the refugee as an "other" with her/his own humanity (in Section 4. Beyond Pity and Irony: Towards a Reflexive Solidarity).

The Representation of Refugees as a Politics of Pity

Public discourse, in the spheres of humanitarianism, journalism and policy-making, construes the refugee as a fundamentally ambivalent figure that is, simultaneously, a *sufferer* of geo-political conflict and a *threat* to the Westphalian, nation-based global order (Nyers, 1999; Gross, Moore & Threadgold, 2007). As a sufferer, the refugee raises the moral claim to cosmopolitan solidarity, whilst, as a threat, the refugee is implicated in regulative discourses that seek to reinstate the normalcy of the national order of things.

It is this ambivalence, particularly (but not exclusively) as it is articulated in humanitarian discourse, that has resulted in two distinct critiques of representation: a critique of negative representation that focuses on the "speechless" refugee and a critique of positive representation that focuses on the "utopian" agency of the refugee. Whilst both strategies of representation, in different ways, seek to resolve the ambivalence of the refugee as an ethico-political signifier, they converge in that they appeal to "common humanity" as the moral justification for acting upon her/his suffering. By so doing, both strategies of representation situate the refugee within a discursive regime of pity—a regime of representation that aspires to mobilise concern for the other on the grounds of her/his human vulnerability rather than on the grounds of a principle of justice (Boltanksi, 1999; Chouliaraki, 2004). What the problematisation of refugee representation in humanitarian discourse throws into relief, therefore, is precisely the inadequacy of pity to ultimately humanise refugees and, thereby, to legitimise claims to solidarity among Western publics.

The critique of negative representation takes its starting point on the traditional iconography of displaced populations as masses of destitute, on-the-move populations that, without a territorial attachment, are negatively defined as "those who do not belong" (Malkki, 1996). Two features characterise these negative representations: the photorealistic imagery of refugees, which seeks to portray the raw truth of their destitution, and their lack of voice, which defines their identity as primarily bodily beings devoid of political subjectivity. Both features, critics claim, contribute to the de-humanisation of refugees. Photorealistic imagery, on the one hand, represents refugees in terms of their vulnerability alone, thereby reducing their complex experience of displacement to immediate, corporeal needs (Rajaram, 2002). Such imagery also tends to portray this vulnerability as a collective attribute of the social category of the "refugee", thereby further depriving each individual refugee of her/his own quality of humanity (Nyers, 1999). The lack of voice, on the other, reflects the status of refugees as stateless people that have been degraded to the status of "sub-citizens": once-citizens that have now no legitimacy to articulate political will or rational argument (Hyndman, 2000). At the same time, by being denied the right to belong to a territorially bounded body politic, critics say, not only do refugees lose their right to articulate legitimate claims about their own destiny but, by trespassing borders and seeking protection in other countries, they further disrupt the nation-based global order: from "speechless emissaries" they become a potential threat (Malkki, 1995).

De-humanisation, in the negative critique, is then the consequence of a politics of representation that appeals to our "common humanity", reflected as this is in the hopeless destitution of the refugee's body, yet ultimately reduces the historical conditions of her/his displacement into "bare life": "it takes only a glance," says Agamben,

at the recent publicity campaigns to gather funds for the refugees from Rwanda to realize that human life is exclusively considered...as bare life—which is to say, as life that can be killed but not sacrificed—and that only as such is it made into the object of aid and protection. (1998, p. 133–134)

It is this critique of corporeal "common humanity" as the basis for our solidarity with refugees that the strategy of positive representation attempts to respond to, albeit without success.

Born, indeed, out of an increasing scepticism towards the photorealism of vulnerability in traditional refugee iconographies, positive representation is associated with the interventionist project of humanitarianism, which emphasises the importance of agency in the portrayal of refugees as human beings "like us" (Way, 2009). Two features characterise these positive representations: a *photorealistic imagery* of optimism that portrays refugees as active and hopeful, rather than as masses of destitute bodies, and the *attribution of voice*, which, in enabling them to speak, portrays refugees as endowed with a subjectivity that goes beyond their bodily needs.

Yet, positive representation has not been immune to critique, as both these features are also accused of de-humanising refugees. The photorealism of agency, on the one hand, is seen to conceal the truth of refugee lives, insofar as it seeks to portray such lives as spaces where sovereign choices can be made, when, in fact, none is possible.

In so doing, as critics put it, photorealism situates the refugee within a beautified narrative of identity that, whilst changing little (if anything) in the refugees' own condition of existence, fits neatly with the Western altruistic imagination: "there is", as Sandvik puts it, "something unsettling about the manner in which individuals in arguably desperate or dangerous situations are attributed agency…as token participants performing for a global audience" (2010, p. 294). The attribution of voice, on the other hand, noble in its intention to empower refugees as it may be, ultimately also contributes to their dehumanisation, insofar as their voice is inevitably controlled by the Western aid institutions that bring it into publicity and, hence, used to serve their needs. Perceived, again, as a potential threat that, if left unregulated, may go beyond the Western boundaries of political legitimacy, the voice of refugees obeys an institutional methodology of listening that is interested only in "outlining material needs [so as] to contribute to the efficiency and relevance of aid delivery" (Rajaram, 2002, p. 257).

De-humanisation, then, in the critique of positive representation, takes its starting point on the refugee's own testimonial voice so as to argue that, instead of construing the refugee as a human being "like us", such voice associates the refugee with a "utopian" view of agency as hopeful self-determination, which distorts the reality of violent displacement and domesticates the radical difference of the refugee in a familiar Western imagination.

In conclusion, what both strategies of representation, negative and positive, throw into relief is the inadequacy of the regime of pity to humanise the refugee. This is because, by relying upon the tropes of powerless vulnerability and hopeful self-determination, pity perpetuates the construal of the refugee as an ambivalent figure (at once a sufferer and a threat) and ultimately fails to provide a legitimate justification upon which we are called to feel for and act upon her/his plight. It is in the context of this failure of pity to sustain a legitimate claim for solidarity that we should situate the emerging shift in the representation of refugees away from "common humanity" and towards the self as the new morality of humanitarianism.

The Representation of Refugees in Post-Humanitarian Discourse

The assumption that informs the study of changes in humanitarian discourse is that, by investigating the emerging strategies of refugee representation, we may learn something important about the moral claims of solidarity that these strategies articulate and the implications of their moral claims for our capacity to engage in acts of solidarity. Let me now discuss, in turn, the representational strategies of two key humanitarian genres in the most influential global governance institution today, the United Nations: humanitarian appeals and celebrity advocacy.

Humanitarian Appeals

The United Nations humanitarian appeals increasingly rely on strategies of textual playfulness that create a distance from the Western lifestyles of (relative) privilege and urge us to reflect on global issues, such as the question of refugees, not through moral argumentation but through the affective estrangement that these forms of distance enable.[2]

A recent animation, the UN's *"What If…"* appeal in sand drawing animation, illustrates this point.[3] This two-minute text combines artful visualisations of refugee experience, smoothly and swiftly re-configuring sand images of bombings, tearful eyes, human bodies, walking traces and UNHCR refugee camps, with the voiceover of a refugee, Adut Dau Atem—a "former refugee from southern Sudan who spent 8 years in UNHCR's Kakuma refugee camp before coming to Australia in 2002."[4]

The appeal introduces the cause of the UNHCR, by reference to the self: "What makes you, you?" the voiceover asks, whilst "scrabble" letters compose the word "you" on screen: "your friends, your family, your dreams, your passions, how you see the world." Having established the Western self as the imaginary subject of this story, the voiceover shifts to the question "What if one ordinary day people you don't know took it all away?" and the sand drawing begins with the image of bombings, turned into tearful eyes then into a human figure of vulnerability, "what if you were only little?" and confusion, "who are you now?" The narrative concludes by following refugee footsteps in their long walk towards a UNHCR camp: "Who are they? They give us food, shelter and protection. Now I am a refugee." This shift in the use of pronoun from "you" to "I", towards the end of the campaign, accomplishes the symbolic work of estrangement: a minor act of de-familiarisation, whereby the experience of vulnerability and confusion we are momentarily called to imagine, in the "you", now returns to its proper subject, the "I" of the refugee, and is given a name: "I am Adut and this is my story".[5] As the UNHCR logo is sand drawn, in the last sequence of the appeal, the voice changes into a native Australian accent and the structure of address shifts, once again, back to the "you": "because sometimes it is important to work out what you stand for…It's a way to share your good life. It's a win win."

Two textual choices are dominant in this appeal: the aesthetics of sand animation and the refugee voiceover. *Sand animation aesthetics*, part of a broader range of playful textualities in recent humanitarian appeals, addresses the suspicion towards the aesthetics of photorealism and its de-sensitising impact on Western publics (also known as compassion fatigue), by problematising the act of representing the humanity of the refugee itself. Yet, in so doing, it simultaneously also turns the context of displacement into a piece of indigenous art: minimalist, transient, fictional. *The refugee voiceover*, at the same time, upholds the principle of positive representation, by using the voice of a refugee, with its authentic Somalian accent, and by providing the name of the speaker, Adut. Yet, the content of this voiceover is less about the refugee's own experience of displacement and more about our own imaginary trauma, "who are you now?" as the minimalist narrative of Adut invites us to suspend our zone of comfort and contemplate on how the experience of displacement might have felt for us.

What these two key features, the aestheticisation of the visual and the de-familiarisation of the linguistic, tentatively point to is the emergence of a new humanitarian discourse, which abandons the de-humanising effects of the past and moves towards more self-reflexive strategies of representation, yet they both ultimately re-centre this discourse around the subjectivity of the Western actor. It is, after all, the "you" structure of address that dominates Adut's story and it is the pleasurable experience of an evocative "sand" aesthetics of displacement that carries the truth of refugee experience.

Even though the replacement of photorealism by artful textualities can be explained as a response to the failure of pity to represent the humanity of refugees, this change in the representational strategies of appeals must also be associated with the market logic that today informs organisational responses to compassion fatigue—what Hopgood refers to as the recent "commodification" of the moral authority of humanitarianism (2008, p. 99). Reflected in the language of the Australian voiceover, which signifies commitment to the cause of refugees in lifestyle terms, as a "way of sharing your good life" and, most tellingly, in corporate terms, as in "it is a win win," this commodification of moral authority introduces the logic of self-centred utilitarianism at the heart of humanitarian discourse. Indeed, the idea that the market can remedy the moral tensions of solidarity might have been met with fierce scepticism in the past, yet, today, it enjoys not only wide acceptance but even celebration—as former UN secretary-general Kofi Annan put it, in his launch of the UN Global Compact initiative: "Let us choose to unite the power of the market with the authority of universal ideals."[6]

Celebrity Advocacy

The commodification of the UN communication strategies, however, is nowhere illustrated more clearly that in its enthusiastic re-invigoration of celebrity advocacy—a humanitarian genre with a history of success associated with major Hollywood icons, such as Audrey Hepburn (1988–1993) and, more recently, Angelina Jolie (2001–present).[7] The advocacy of such star figures has always relied upon an ambivalent performativity of humanitarian discourse, which combines "impersonation", the celebrity's personal testimony of the suffering of others, with "personification", the infusion of such testimony with the celebrity's own distinct star aura.[8]

What differentiates contemporary from past articulations of advocacy, however, is the tendency of the former to privilege a "confessional" communicative structure of celebrity. Unlike the strict formality of earlier forms of celebrity advocacy, I argue, this is a performativity that rests upon "intimacy at a distance"—a key feature of today's popular culture that refers to our increasing mediated access to the intimate sphere of celebrity lives, rendering this sphere an inherent aspect of their public personae (Thompson, 1995). In celebrity discourse, this difference is reflected in the performativity of personification, which is about giving voice to "those who cannot speak for themselves," as Hepburn puts it, through the celebrity's own account of their suffering.

Hepburn's personification, as I have argued elsewhere, builds upon a public persona that places her Hollywood aura at the service of her professional role as a UNICEF Ambassador (Chouliaraki, 2011). Hepburn, for instance, hardly ever spoke about her film-related career or her private life—though she occasionally drew upon her experience as a recipient of UNICEF aid in post-WWII Europe. This strategy of "de-celebritisation", that is of the conscious self-effacement of her celebrity status, meant that Hepburn prioritised the voicing of the experience of suffering others, making them the focus of her narratives. Here is an example:

> I am very impressed by *the people of Ethiopia*. By *their* beauty, by *their* dignity, by *their* patience and by *their* enormous desire, (their) enormous will to help themselves. *They* are not just sitting here waiting, *their* patience is a patience that is coming partly from *their* religion and partly from *their* characters for dealing with *their* lot the best they can... (UNICEF Press Conference on Ethiopia, 1988, emphasis added).[9]

Grounded as it inevitably is on the "I" of her own testimony, the consistent use of "their" focalises, nonetheless, Hepburn's account around the qualities, *"their beauty, dignity, patience, desire, will"*, and agency, *"they are not just sitting around dealing with their lot,"* of the Ethiopian people.

Compared to this strictly professional performance of UN's Ambassadorial humanitarianism, Jolie's contemporary discourse is radically personalised. This is because, I argue, her performance draws upon a more complex public persona, which deliberately fuses the celebrity's UNHCR-related work with her private life as the mother of children adopted from developing countries *and* with her professional life as a human rights films actress and as an entrepreneurial activist of development projects around the world (Littler 2008). This strategy of "hyper-celebritisation", in turn, situates the celebrity's own sense of self at the heart of her account of vulnerable others. Here is an example of the language Jolie uses in her narrative of the experience of refugees:

> The refugees *I* have met and spent time with have profoundly *changed my life*. The eight-year-old who saved her brother *taught me* what it is to be brave. The pregnant woman in Pakistan *taught me* what it is to be a mother. And the paralyzed boy who was shot in the back with his big smile *showed me* the strength of an unbreakable spirit. So today, World Refugee Day, *I thank them for letting me* into their lives (UNHCR World Refugee Day, 2009, emphasis added).[10]

Unlike Hepburn's account, which uses her voice so as to convey a sense of agency for the Ethiopian sufferers, the key feature of Jolie's representational strategy is to co-articulate the humanitarian and the private in one hybrid text and, thereby, to evoke the experience of refugees only as a contribution to her own personal development—reflected as this is in the repeated structure of *"the eight-year-old taught me; the pregnant woman taught me; the paralyzed boy showed me."* By placing the refugees at the heart of her own confessional narrative, further framed within in a highly emotional body language, this strategy of representation ultimately re-centres their voice, which celebrity is supposed to speak for us, around the celebrity's own voice about them. An important consequence of this confessional performativity is that it is the emotional interiority of the celebrity, or her humanity, that we are now asked to identify with as moral actors, rather than the suffering others as others with their own humanity.[11]

This hybrid textuality of the "hyper-celebrity" is not simply a discursive construct, but should be understood as a further instrumentalisation move in the humanitarian field. Contemporary celebrity advocacy seems to move away from the subordination of the Hollywood brand to that of the UN, as in Hepburn's case, and strives instead to build powerful brand alliances between the two, with important benefits for both parties—a "win-win" situation, again, where the UNHCR maximises its visibility whilst Jolie legitimises her public image as a humanitarian. A magnet of massive public attention as it may be, this market strategy, nonetheless, has a significant cost insofar as, in the process, it denies refugees the legitimacy of their own voice (Sandvik 2010).[12] Solidarity

becomes, instead, a practice of voyeuristic altruism, which intensifies our engagement with the pleasures of show business whilst it reproduces the moral
distance between "us" and "them": "when most people think of the UN now,"
as a UN employee puts it,

> they think of Angelina Jolie on a crusade, not the work that goes on in the
> field...celebrity is at the heart of every UNICEF campaign and the association is being
> sold incredibly cheap.[13]

In conclusion, the artful story-telling of campaigns and the hybrid performativity of celebrity are but two of the multiple representational strategies of
post-humanitarian discourse—a discourse that abandons "common humanity"
and turns to the Western self, be this an ordinary spectator or an extraordinary
star, as the moral justification for engaging with the cause of refugees. What
characterises this discourse, as we saw, is its aspiration to resolve the ambivalence of the refugee, suspended between suffering and threat, by representing
this figure in innovative ways and by replacing the universal morality of the human species with the contingent morality of the "I". This shift may appear to be
a creative response to the generalised disaffection of Western publics towards
institutional calls to solidarity.[14] Yet, insofar as it reduces the communication of
solidarity to self-communication, situating the traumatic or confessional self at
the heart of its discourse, irony risks substituting the public justification of solidarity with narcissistic self-expression. Let me now elaborate on this point, by
theorising post-humanitarian discourse as a neo-liberal version of solidarity that
today articulates a particular cultural sensibility—the culture of irony.

Solidarity as Irony

The post-humanitarian textualities of the UN, animated appeals and confessional celebrity, are a response to previous realistic imageries of refugees,
speechless or agentive, and to the dispassionate style of earlier forms of celebrity advocacy. Even though these historical genres of pity have traditionally
appealed to the morality of "common humanity", they have, at the same time,
been criticised for de-humanising the vulnerable "other" and for naturalising,
rather than problematising, the power relations of humanitarianism between the
West and the "rest". The discourse of pity, as Tomlinson would put it, belongs
to a:

vision of technocratic, Enlightenment universalism, largely untroubled by concerns of cultural difference…and populated by orderly, rational, co-operative moral agents who had transcended all cultural particularity. (2010, p. 35)

It is this distrust towards "universalism" that informs the communicative ethos of the new genres of humanitarianism. What they intend to do is challenge the "truth" of suffering that pity represents and draw attention, instead, to the act of representing the many "truths" of suffering as itself a part of their appeal to act upon it. In this way, post-humanitarian genres transform the "universal" morality of pity into a morality of contingency—one that, according to Rorty, "combines commitment with a sense of contingency about (our) own commitment" (1989, p. 61). Turning, thus, distrust from problem into promise for a renewed commitment to solidarity, the morality of contingency further situates post-humanitarianism within a specific cultural sensibility, the culture of "irony" (Rorty 1989).

Grounded as it may be on contingency, the culture of irony nonetheless differs from the radical relativism of postmodern culture in that it recognises in human suffering that minimal, yet crucial, moral claim to other people that remains irreducible to any language game and defines the nature of sociality in our culture. The ironic discourse of solidarity, in this sense, flourishes within a world of situated meanings and values not in the form of a "universal" truth, but in the form of stories of suffering that, by way of "sentimental education," mundanely cultivate the virtue of "being kind to others as *the only social bond that is needed*" (Rorty, 1989, p. 93, emphasis added).

However, this profound shift in the epistemological basis of solidarity away from the moral justification of distant action as action on suffering humanity and towards a reliance on our own "truths" as a justification for such action should not only be seen as a shift in discourse. It is, as I mentioned earlier, also an ambivalent political project, firmly grounded on the politics of advanced liberalism and its aggressive instrumentalisation of spheres of action that have hitherto remained outside the remit of global capitalism[15]. The corporate appropriation of solidarity refers, in this context, to the increasingly managerial practices that regulate the communicative structure of humanitarianism with a view to increasing its economic efficiency in a globally competitive media market.[16] This corporate process signals, according to Calhoun, "the end of the humanitarian field...as it came to be conceived over a longish history and as it flourished especially in the four decades after 1968" (2010, p. xx). [17]

Whereas the instrumentalisation of the communicative structure of solidarity is evident in the commodification of its textual strategies, discussed in the previous section, the instrumentalisation of the proposals to solidarity action can be identified in the individuated ways by which Western publics are today asked to engage with refugees: the online activism of campaigns, evident in the invitation to join the UNHCR's website (part of the linguistic text of the appeal) and the confessional ethos of UN advocacy that turns commitment into fandom. Far from claiming that these proposals exhaust the responses of their publics in fully predictable ways, a question open to empirical research, they do indicate that ironic solidarity responds to the challenges of compassion fatigue, by replacing an ethos of conviction to a cause with a closer-to-life altruism of the everyday.

Two properties of solidarity define the discourse of irony: solidarity as *private choice*, which treats our action towards refugees as public but keeps the justification of such action private; and solidarity as *self-fulfilment*, which, consequently, construes our action on refugees as the realisation of our own humanity whilst keeping the humanity of the refugee out of view. Dialectically related to one another, these two properties of ironic solidarity are informed by an instrumental logic of market consumerism that subordinates the political question of population displacement as injustice to a de-politicised practice of sentimental self-expression.

Solidarity as Private Choice

The contingent morality of animated stories and celebrity emotions originates in the subjectivist epistemology of neo-pragmatism (Rorty, 1989). As there is no knowledge outside the self, neo-pragmatism claims, there can be no moral appeal to solidarity beyond the stories *we* produce so as to imagine ourselves as altruistic actors within our own communities of belonging.

It is Rorty's figure of the "liberal ironist" that best exemplifies the subjectivism of this moral discourse (1989, p. 15). Much like the post-humanitarian activist who expresses solidarity with distant others from the comfort of her living room, the liberal ironist treats what Rorty calls the "vocabulary of justice" as a private matter, which enables the ironist to both remain sceptical of any claims as to the justification of solidarity and, simultaneously, to engage in solidarity action on vulnerable others as part of her own project of moral self-fulfilment. Whilst, therefore, the imperative to reduce suffering marks the liberal's commitment to the public realm of solidarity, the question of justification that informs this moral imperative is treated as inherently un-resolvable in the public realm and, hence, as belonging to the private realm of the ironist (Rorty, 1989, pp. 73–95).

Insofar as it turns the morality of solidarity into a private affair that concerns no one but ourselves, irony further privileges the cultural dimension of solidarity, self-expressive stories that speak to our commitment to refugees, over the political dimension of solidarity, argumentative stories that help us understand and judge the conditions of vulnerability. This is because, if it is through our own stories of suffering that we become accustomed to a "vocabulary of justice" rather than through the argumentative justification of justice (the latter being a cause of scepticism rather than commitment), then solidarity cannot but be a matter of "training the soul" rather than a matter of critically engaging with questions of vulnerability as injustice.

It is precisely this view of solidarity as sentimental education that dominates the post-humanitarian genres I examined earlier. What the introspection of campaigns and the confessional ethos of celebrity demonstrate is that, by ceasing to rely on the justification for action on vulnerable others, ironic solidarity becomes today a matter of crafting artful stories that situate the self at the heart of their communicative structure.

This does not mean that the vocabulary of justice is absent from these genres. Far from it. It could be argued, in fact, that it is the very proliferation of this vocabulary that enables these genres to emerge, in the first place. The elliptical communication of humanitarian animation, for instance, presupposes our familiarity with a vocabulary of justice and taps in on our already existing awareness of displaced populations as a cause for action, whilst the entrepreneurial activism of Jolie rests on criticisms of Hepburn's de-politicised Good Samaritanism, which prioritised the alleviation of suffering at the expense of questions of development.

Even though these systematic references to a vocabulary of justice could be seen as performing what Benhabib calls a series of "democratic iterations," that is, a chain of moral claims that catalyse debate and action in the mediated public realm (2007, p. 31), they do not, in fact, constitute a resource for the exercise of judgment. What renders judgment marginal to the communication of ironic solidarity is the fact that these iterations are textually implicit. Their references to justice are fully embedded in the story-telling conventions of the post-humanitarian genres and, therefore, are always formulated as subordinate to the dominant reference to a "vocabulary of the self" as the only legitimate source of knowledge on the world.

As a consequence, rather than providing us with the resources to judge the predicament of refugees as a cause for our action, these genres present us with shortcuts to judgment, hinting to a vocabulary of justice, but ultimately engaging with corporate persuasion: the "win-win" message of appeals and Jolie's performativity, herself a mega-brand of the film industry, increases the authority of the Hollywood star system. This marginalisation of judgment, in turn, allows no space for accounts of humanitarianism that may touch on solidarity as a project of social change; by being prevented, as McCarthy puts it, "from even thinking…the thought that the basic structures of society might be inherently unjust in some way, that they might work to the systematic disadvantage of certain social groups" (1990, p. 367), solidarity as self-distance favours a complacent view of culture populated by self-expressive ironists and devoid of visions of social change.

Solidarity as Self-Fulfilment

Online activism and celebrity fandom are some of the key proposals to solidarity available in the post-humanitarian genres. In their refusal to engage our capacity for judgment, these proposals speak to the liberal ironist—a figure suspicious of the moral "truth" of suffering, yet harbouring a visceral sense of care towards vulnerable others. At the absence of argumentative justification, however, how do these genres appeal to solidarity as a meaningful practice for the Western actor? They do so, I argue, by construing solidarity as a matter of self-fulfilment.

This is evident in campaign slogans, which focus on the promise to enhance our social consciousness through estrangement from our everyday lifestyle ("*What if?*") and in the entrepreneurial individualism of celebrity, whose activism is hailed as the most effective model of solidarity today.[18] If, then, personal choice is responsible for keeping the justification of solidarity private, self-fulfilment is further responsible for construing this private choice as a matter of a personally rewarding moral life.

However, insofar as solidarity is presented as a matter of self-gratification, rather than (also) as an act oriented towards those who would benefit from it, the communication of solidarity ceases to be about educating Western publics into the sensibilities of empathy and responsibility towards refugees. Under conditions of global market competition, the communication of solidarity becomes, ultimately, an effort to seduce publics into "empathetically" identifying with the better brand—be this the UN, AI or Oxfam. The tearful celebrity and UN's *'What if...?'* campaign, in this context, are sentimental discourses of the humanitarian market, whose value lies not in showing us how to relate to the world beyond "us" but "in the attempt of one will to align the attitudes, feelings, preferences and choices of another with its own" (McIntyre, 2006 [1981], p. 24).

To the extent that we are addressed as primarily sentimental publics, whose personal preference for a cause depends on the marketing strategy of a campaign or the star appeal of a celebrity, ironic solidarity treats us more as a means to the accomplishment of certain ends—sign, donate or buy online—and less as ends in ourselves—as citizens who may engage with the cause of refugees because we feel committed to do so. In the ironic solidarity of self-fulfilment, as McIntryre would put it, "others are always means, never ends" (p. 24).

Yet, solidarity as self-fulfilment does not only instrumentalise Western publics. It also construes refugees as "annihilated" figures, who have no voice of their own (Silverstone, 2007). Campaigns aestheticise the visual presence of refugees whilst using their voice as a vehicle for Western experience, and celebrity appropriates their suffering in her own confessional performativity of emotion. Even though they may employ a rhetoric of dignity, these representational choices fail to construe refugees as historical beings who struggle to come to terms with their own predicament and, hence, as figures who can legitimately invite our emotion and action.

As a consequence, the post-humanitarian genres may aim at resolving the ambivalence of the refugee between suffering and threat, yet, ultimately, they distribute the quality of humanity unequally among its communicative figures. Whilst their promises to self-fulfilment over-humanise the Western actor, be this a celebrity or an ordinary media user, their silencing of refugees dehumanises those who already lie outside Western centres of power and visibility.

Ironic solidarity is, in this sense, an ethnocentric solidarity that encourages identification with others like "us" but employs strategies of annihilation in the
sphere of transnational politics. Instead of enabling us to hear their voice, it
treats refugees as voiceless props that evoke responses of self-expression, but
cannot in themselves become anything more than shadow figures in someone
else's story.

In summary, the discourse of irony reflects the instrumentalisation of solidarity, under conditions of neo-liberalism. As market practices are increasingly
infusing non-economic spheres of activity with a corporate rationality, solidarity
becomes a practice of self-expression, which treats the imperative to act on
refugees and other vulnerable populations as a matter of free choice at the service of our moral self-fulfilment. In so doing, however, ironic solidarity reduces
us to sentimental publics with little capacity for judgment, whilst it also reduces
vulnerable others to voiceless figures without humanity.

Beyond Pity and Irony: Towards a Reflexive Solidarity

Pity and irony, I have argued in this chapter, are the two key historical discourses of humanitarianism, neither of which manages to sustain a legitimate
appeal to action towards refugees. Pity is associated with a solidarity of "universalism", which operates on a morality of "common humanity" that sup-
presses the difference between "us" and the refugee, whilst irony is associated
with a solidarity of contingency, which, by turning the Western self into the
source of morality, reproduces an equally misleading difference between these
two parties. Both discourses, I have argued, have proved to be unproductive
proposals for solidarity.

The alternative, I suggest, should be a reflexive discourse of solidarity that
starts by treating the imperative to act towards refugees as a matter of public
judgment rather than private preference. This means that, *contra* irony, we need
to be explicit about the social values, notably social justice, that inform our solidarity towards displaced populations as a public act. It also means that, *contra*
pity, we do not treat the meaning of these values as "universal" truths, for there
may indeed be many "truths" to justice and many manifestations of responsibility that could serve the project of solidarity. Reflexive solidarity should, therefore, make the public values of solidarity explicit as the object of our collective
deliberation and judgment, so that such values re-galvanise the moral sensibili-

ties of Western publics towards other-oriented, rather than self-oriented, expressions of solidarity.

At the same time, we also need to be able to imagine the refugee as an "other" with her/his own humanity. This means that, *contra* irony, the refugee should be portrayed as having a voice of her/his own: as an agent who is endowed with her/his right to have a voice precisely because, rather than despite, being deprived of territorial belonging. It also means that, *contra* pity, this other is represented neither through stereotypes of destitution, as in traditional portrayals of poverty as famine, nor through stereotypes of individual sovereignty, as in positive, yet misleading, representations of self-determination. A more complex and, perhaps, a more discomforting representation of refugees can today become possible, precisely because of the multiplicity of new media genres that are available to us. Rather than using these new media genres primarily as means for self-expression, we should, therefore, re-think the ways in which current economies of global communication may be used to facilitate our moral imagination, by encouraging more plural and dialogic encounters with these others.

Whereas some genres might prove to be less conducive to this process, for instance celebrity or advertising, others may prove to be powerful vehicles of reflexive solidarity—the broader media ecology of convergent journalism, for instance, documentaries or independent films. The potential (albeit not fully realised) for such encounters is present in BBC's *Road to Refuge* website[19], which, despite its Western bias, combines a series of links on the historical, legal and political contexts of population displacements with testimonial narratives and refugee portraits as well as interactive platforms that facilitate dialogue between UNHCR and Western publics; what is missing, but could have been included, is, again, the voice of refugees themselves in direct interactions with these publics. Despite this crucial omission, what this instance of journalism shows is that, far from requiring a fundamental transformation of the economic relations of global capitalism, reflexive solidarity resides instead in subtle but crucial rearticulations of current practices of representation that break with corporate genres of persuasion or seduction and introduce judgment and empathy as crucial resources for our engagement with refugees as moral and political subjects—as others with their own humanity.

Conclusion

In this chapter, I have engaged with a critical analysis of the humanitarian discourse of the United Nations on refugees, so as to sketch out a typology of its key paradigms of solidarity: "pity" and "irony". Both paradigms, I have argued, are unable to resolve the inherent ambivalence of refugee representation between suffering and threat and, therefore, fail to humanise the refugee—to represent her/him as a vulnerable figure subject to historical conditions of injustice, yet able to articulate her/his own with political will.

Focusing on a critique of irony, I have shown that, even though it has emerged as a promising response to pity and its universal morality of "common humanity", irony is itself a manifestation of the consumerist morality of neoliberalism and, therefore, unable to put forward a morally acceptable proposal of solidarity. This is because the focus of ironic morality on the Western self tends to associate solidarity with self-empowerment whilst keeping the refugee outside the remit of our judgment and imagination. I have, in response, formulated the contours of an alternative vision of reflexive solidarity—a solidarity that is neither about the sharing of the same humanity for all nor the sharing of our own feelings for refugees but about the communication of human vulnerability as a political question of injustice that can become the object of our collective reflection, emotion and action.

Notes

1. For theoretical elaborations of the term "post-humanitarianism" see Chouliaraki (2010, 2011).
2. For substantial empirical evidence on this tendency see Chouliaraki (2010), Vestergaard (2010), and Sandvik (2010).
3. Sand animation written and directed by Sophie Weldon (Ambassador of UNHCR Australia). Voice over by Adut Dau Atem and Sophie Weldon. Music by Elroy Finn. Produced by Liquid Animation. Available at: http://www.youtube.com/watch?v=g3AXfaZq44E
4. Short biography available at http://www.unrefugees.org.au/about-us/special-representatives/adut-dau-atem
5. For the concept of estrangement see Orgad (2011)
6. Available at: htttp://www.unglobalcompact.org
7. UN celebrity advocacy took a new impetus as a spearheading communication strategy towards the attainment of the Millenium goals; as Koffi Annan put it: "You [celebrities]

are here because you want those people to know more about the hardship of others, and because you want to encourage them to do something about it… Whenever you put your name to a message, you raise awareness far and wide, among policymakers and among millions of people who elect them. … Our chances of breaking through the barrier of indifference are vastly improved when we have people like you in our corner and for our cause" (UN Press Release SG/SM/7595; October 23, 2000)

8. For the mechanism of impersonation/personification in the public performativity of celebrity, see King (2006 [1985], p. 230–235; 244–246). For an analysis of the performativity of humanitarian celebrity, in particular, along these lines see Chouliaraki (2011).

9. Available at: http://www.youtube.com/watch?v=W7V6OQcu5ZY&NR=1

10. http://www.youtube.com/watch?v=iPAuNl4cSpU&NR=1&feature=fvwp

11. For the confessional in the realm of celebrity altruism see Illouz (2003) on the therapeutic sentimentalism of Oprah Winfrey; t'Hardt and Tindall (2008) on Geldof's anger; Littler (2008) on Jolie's tearful appearances.

12. For further critiques of commodification in contemporary celebrity advocacy see Marks and Fischer (2002); Dieter and Kumar (2008); de Waal (2008).

13. McDougall G. (2006). For critical accounts of the celebritization of UN advocacy see Cooper (2007).

14. For public disaffection with humanitarianism see Cohen (2001); for a gerenalised distrust of politics see Hay (2007).

15. For an account of the distinction between liberalism and advanced liberalism or neoliberalism see Lemke (2001). As he puts it, the key transformation of advanced or neoliberalism lies precisely in the generalization of the economic logic beyond the sphere of economic activity with a view to accomplishing two things: "First, the generalization functions as an analytical principle in that it investigates non-economic areas and forms of action in terms of economic categories…and…Second, the economic matrix…it enables a critical evaluation of governmental practices by means of market concept." (2001, p. 198)

16. For the commodification of the humanitarian field see Cottle and Nolan (2007) and Cottle (2009).

17. For a discussion of instrumentalisation as a complex process that combines the appropriation of humanitarianism by a market logic with the subordination of humanitarian ends to a military logic of a realpolitik diplomacy, see Calhoun (2010).

18. For a discussion on celebrity entrepreneurialism, or 'celanrthopy', as part of philanthrocapitalism, a CSR-type solidarity that is based on harnessing the creativity of major corporations to find solutions to the problems of global poverty see Bishop and Green (2008, pp. 194–213).

19. Available at http://news.bbc.co.uk/hi/english/static/in_depth/world/2001/road_to_refuge/persecution/story.stm

CHAPTER TWO

Immigration Dialectic in the Media and Crisis as Transformative Moment

Harald Bauder

Introduction

The debate of immigration in the media involves a series of interlocking and nested dialectics. These dialectics are characterised by the juxtaposition of contradictory positions, the connection between media discourse and material practices towards immigration, and the interrelationship between immigration and national identity. In this chapter, I examine the role of crisis as a transformative moment in the context of these dialectics.

Both traditional settler societies and historically ethnic nations are subject to these dialectics. I use Canada and Germany as representative countries of settler and ethnic nations. Although the dialectical principle operates in both countries, the contents and nature of the dialectics are very different (Bauder, 2011). Variable material histories and geographical circumstances, and different national identities and attitudes towards newcomers situate immigration debates in Canada and Germany in very particular material contexts. Due to these contingencies, crisis can be expected to perform differently as a catalyst of transformation in Canadian and German media debates.

Crisis, in the context of this chapter refers to conditions and their consequences, which the media portrays as unacceptable. In the particular debates that I examine, crisis involves the humanitarian consequences of war, the threat of terrorism, and anxieties associated with rising unemployment. These crises harbour the potential to change fundamentally the media debate of immigration and affect the dialectics of this debate, in particular the material practices towards immigration and the relationship between immigration and national identity.

In the empirical investigation, I analyse the contents of five Canadian and five German daily newspapers to explore the impact of crisis on immigration debate in the media. I am especially interested in the debate of legal immigration reforms that occurred roughly at the same time in both countries. This focus enables me to correlate discursive media practices with the corresponding material immigration legislation.

The remainder of the chapter is organised into four sections. In the next section below, I develop three dialectical dimensions of media debate of immigration, and I discuss the role of crisis in the context of these dialectical dimensions. Second, I briefly introduce the research context of the empirical analysis and explain how I obtained the data. The third section contains the results of my analysis and discusses the role of humanitarian, terrorist and economic crises as transformative moments in the Canadian and German debates. Finally, I interpret these results in light of Canada's and Germany's identities as a long-established settler society and a historically ethnic nation respectively.

Dialectics and Crisis

Media debate of immigration involves at least three dialectical "dimensions" (Wodak, 2001). The first dimension refers to the journalistic practice of presenting opposing viewpoints. This dialectical dimension constitutes a journalistic method of discovery that articulates pro and con positions on a particular topic and aspires to "balanced" reporting by including contradictory viewpoints (Merrill, 1989). Although individual articles, op-eds and letters to the editor may present one-sided viewpoints, media coverage as whole tends to present multiple perspectives of an issue. For example, the Canadian and German media discuss the positive and negative impacts of immigration on the national economy (e.g., Bauder, 2008d, 2008e; Wengeler, 2000).

The second dialectical dimension encapsulates the relationship between discursive practices and material circumstances. This dimension lies at the core of "critical discourse analysis", which seeks to understand the way in which the practice of language generates material effects and vice versa (e.g., Fairclough and Wodak, 1997; Wodak et al. 1999). In the context of media reporting on immigration, the media may reproduce and cultivate stereotypes, for example, of Muslim immigrants that reinforce the material exclusion of corresponding immigrant groups from society (Beck-Gernsheim, 2007).

The third dialectical dimension relates to a Hegelian process of identity formation. This dialectical dimension describes the interdependence between national and immigrant identities. In the context of media reporting of immigration, national identity serves as a reference point for the debate of immigration.

Immigrants are often the negation of the national self. For example, the representation of immigrants as Muslim fundamentalist and backward Others implies that the national self is enlightened and progressive (Beck-Gernsheim, 2007; Bauder and Semmelroggen, 2009). In a legal context, Catherine Dauvergne (2005) shows how the admission of refugees in need represents the receiving nation as compassionate. In addition, if refugees flee violence and political persecution, the country accepting these asylum seekers and refugees acquires an identity of being peaceful, safe and democratic. Furthermore, in a settler society, like Canada, these refugees are expected to become citizens, dispensing of their role as Other and becoming part of the national self. In the context of Hegelian dialectics, this process can be described as sublation (*Aufhebung*) (Hegel, 2005 [1807]), whereby two seemingly opposing identities of the refugee Other and the national self merge into a new identity. In settler societies, immigrants "replenish" the nation (Honig, 2001). This Hegelian immigration-nation dialectic is reflected in the manner in which the media reports on immigration (Bauder, 2011).

The argument I am pursuing in this chapter expands on the dialectical understanding of immigration debate in the media. In particular, I discuss the notion of crisis and its relevance in this debate. According to Marxian thought, crisis reveals important contradictions that are irresolvable under existing conditions; the pursuit to overcome a crisis perpetuates the dialectical process. Karl Marx, for example, argued that economic crisis reveals the inherent contradictions of capitalism and thus leads to revolutionary change (Marx, 2001 [1867]; Marx and Engels, 1953). According to such views, crisis is an integral part of dialectical process. In fact, crises constitute transformative moments that initiate dialectical progression.

Crises can be objective, material conditions as well as social constructions and interpretations of events. As a social construction, a crisis can be a mechanism to initiate political changes that otherwise would be impossible or difficult to implement (Hay, 1996). For example, Sean Hier and Joshua Greenberg (2002) documented how the media constructed a crisis of Canada's immigration system based on the arrival of the relatively small number of 599 undocumented Chinese migrants at the Canadian west coast in 1999. The media's reporting of a crisis led to concrete policy responses and political interventions by the Canadian state. In this case, the discursive construction of a crisis facilitated the progression of the second dialectical dimension, whereby discursive media practice produced concrete, material outcomes.

In the discussion below, I explore the role of crisis in the second dialectical dimension, linking discursive practice and material circumstances, and the third dialectical dimension of Hegelian identity formation in the context of media reporting on immigration. In particular, I investigate whether and how the perception of crisis relates policy and legal change, and whether and how crisis constitutes a transformative moment in the immigration-nation dialectic.

Research Context

The analysis draws on an empirical investigation of reporting in the newsprint media on legal immigration reforms in Canada and Germany. By analysing the reporting of *legal* immigration reforms rather than general representations of immigration, I reference my analysis of immigration debate in the material context of the law and the concrete political process of law making. With this approach, I am able to infer linkages between discursive practices and material outcomes. In addition, this approach bridges other research that either examined the legislative debate and legal practice (e.g., Dauvergne, 2005; Takle, 2007; Bauder & Semmelroggen, 2009) or general media representations of immigrants (e.g., Mahtani, 2001; Wengeler, 2003).

The Canadian media engaged in a debate of immigration reform between 1996 and 2004. This debate was initiated by the release of the report *Not Just Numbers: A Canadian Framework for Future Immigration* by the Immigration Legislative Review Advisory Group (1997). After a series of follow-up reports, including a critique by the United Nations High Commission for Refugees, the debate culminated in the passage of the *Immigration and Refugee Protection Act* in 2001. Between 2002 and 2004, regulations of the new immigration law were fine-tuned and new initiatives were implemented, including mandatory permanent residency cards for immigrants and a Safe Third Country Agreement with the United States.

In Germany, a legal reform involving foreigners and immigration occurred roughly at the same time as in Canada. The German government initiated the debate in the year 2000, with a German "Greencard", designed to provide foreign information-technology workers temporary access to the German labour market.[1] This initiative was followed by the establishment of the so-called

Süßmuth-Commission—named after its chair, Rita Süßmuth, a former President of Parliament—to develop the guiding principles of Germany's first immigration law (*Zuwanderungsgesetz*). Political negotiations stretched over several
years. The new law passed parliament in 2004 and took effect in 2005 (Bendel,
2004).

The fact that both Canada and Germany almost simultaneously engaged in
legal immigration reform enables a comparison between the national media debates of these reforms. In both countries, I developed a sample of articles published in the daily newsprint media that reported on the legal immigration
reforms. The Canadian sample contains 490 articles from the *Calgary Herald*,
National Post, Toronto Star, Halifax Herald and *Vancouver Sun*, which cover the debate of Canadian immigration reform between 1996 and 2004. The German
sample, covering the debate of the immigration law between 2000 and 2004
contains 609 articles from *Bild Zeitung, Frankfurter Allgemeine Zeitung, Süddeutsche
Zeitung, Stuttgarter Zeitung* and *Tageszeitung*. Detailed descriptions of the principle
characteristics of these debates are published elsewhere (Bauder, 2008b, 2008c).
Of interest in the discussion below is how representations of crisis have influenced the law and perpetuated the immigration-nation dialectic in both countries.

Crisis as Productive Moment

In this section, I examine three different crises that were addressed in the immigration debates in Canada and Germany: humanitarian crisis, the crisis of terrorism, and economic crisis. I examine the role of each of these crises in the
dialectic of discursive practice, material law and national identity.

Humanitarian Crisis

Humanitarian immigration refers to the admission of refugees and asylum seekers. In both Canadian and German media debate, the circumstances of refugees
and asylum seekers negate the national self. In particular, the conditions of political persecution and violence that exist in the country of origin constitute the
counter-image of a national self that upholds political freedom and peace. By
protecting refugees and asylum seekers, the nation demonstrates its commitment to these principles of liberal democracy (Bauder, 2008a, 2009).

While many refugee and asylum cases and their admission may be a matter of routine administrative processes (Dauvergne, 2005), the media also reported on refugee flows originating from places where humanitarian crises rage. An example is the humanitarian crisis resulting from the Kosovo War in the late 1990s. The Canadian *National Post* reported that the "humanitarian crisis" in Kosovo requires swift actions regarding refugee admission:

> The massive airlift of Kosovo refugees has split NATO countries as the alliance scrambles to cope with the humanitarian crisis caused by the air assault on Yugoslavia.
>
> While some allies, such as the United States, Canada, Norway, and Germany, have been quick to accept some 100,000 ethnic Albanians driven from their homes by Serb forces, others have been critical of the plan.
>
> Canada's Immigration Minister, Lucienne Robillard, said yesterday that the 5,000 exiled Kosovar refugees who will be airlifted to Canada, beginning this weekend, will be able to claim permanent residency once they arrive. (Fife, 1999a)

The humanitarian crisis of the Kosovo War prompted the Canadian government not only to airlift roughly 5,000 Kosovar refugees to Canada but also to fast-track another 2,250 under the Kosovo Family Reunification program. The representation of crisis resulted in an ad-hoc response by the Canadian government.

The Canadian government and media reporting, however, did not only discuss the refugees' need for protection. It also established a clear distinction between the deserving refugees and the "war criminals" responsible for the humanitarian crisis. In a separate article, the same *National Post* reporter supported the government's actions to ban senior officials of the Milosevic regime from entering Canada:

> "Canada will not become a sanctuary for war criminals or people involved in atrocities," Ms. Robillard said. "This is consistent with our government's commitment to Canadians and the international community to address war criminals and crimes against humanity." (Fife, 1999b)

The distinction between deserving and undeserving refugees is a common rhetorical practice in the Canadian media (Bauder, 2011). By advocating both, the admission of deserving refugees and the denial of protection to war criminals, the press constructs an image of Canada as both compassionate and tough on the perpetrators of humanitarian crimes. The humanitarian crisis in Kosovo presented the opportunity to construct a positive national identity for Canada.

In Germany after World War II, the right to asylum was initially enshrined in Article 16 of the Constitutional Law of the Federal Republic of Germany to recognise the importance of protection from political persecution in light of the country's own record of atrocities under the Nazi-regime. Article 16, however, was changed in the early 1990s due to increasing hostility towards asylum seekers among the German population. This change resulted in a drastic decline of refugee applications and acceptance rates. Unlike in Canada, where refugees obtain legal immigrant status and qualify for citizenship after three years of residence, in Germany refugees and asylum seekers are not considered future Germans but foreigners who were supposed to be repatriated as soon as the situation in their country of origin permits the return.

In the sampled media articles of the German immigration law, the discussion of refugees and asylum seekers was not linked to any humanitarian crisis that existed in another part of the world. Rather than projecting a sense of crisis, the German debate addressed the moral and legal obligations towards refugees and asylum seekers in relatively sober and matter-of-fact language. For example, newsprint articles repeatedly mentioned the "C" in the names of the two conservative parties, the Christian Democratic Union and the Christian Social Union, in juxtaposition to the apparent lack of compassion among conservative politicians towards refugees and asylum seekers. The debate of the humanitarian aspect of immigration law in Germany is characterised by calm and inward-looking discussion rather than a sense of urgency associated with the need to cope with humanitarian crisis.

Crisis of Terrorism

The "terrorist" is the ultimate representation of the enemy of freedom and democracy. Terrorism can thus be interpreted as the negation of the free and democratic national self. In this context, one could expect that the media represented the airplane attacks of September 11, 2001, in New York and Washington as a terrorism "crisis" that constituted a critical moment in the formation of national identity. The scholarly literature on immigration seems to support such an interpretation and has emphasised the importance of "9/11" in framing immigration as a potential terrorism and security threat (e.g., Dauvergne, 2007; Tsoukala 2008a, 2008b).

The association of immigration with terrorism also occurred in the Canadian and German debates of immigration law. In Canada, however, the attacks of "9/11" were not the catalytic event that changed the nature of media debate of immigration. Immigration had been linked to danger and a threat to Canadian national security long before September 2001 (Bauder, 2008b). For example, between 1999 and 1998, all sampled Canadian newspapers reported on the case of Mahmoud Es-Sayy Jaballah, a refugee and alleged member of al-Jihad, a group blamed for the 1998 embassy bombings in Kenya and Tanzania. The reporting on this case generally represented Jaballah as a terrorism threat and national security risk. Another case that circulated through the press between 1999 and 2001, referred to the legal proceedings involving alleged Tamil Tiger fund-raiser Manickavasagan Suresh and former Iranian intelligence officer Manour Ahani. In May 2001, the *Vancouver Sun* commented on the case and suggested that Canada is a "base camp" for terrorism (Tibbetts, 2001). In July 2001, the *National Post* ran the headline "Scale up the war against terrorism" and, in the associated article, called for an amendment to immigration law enabling the detention of "arrivals who arouse terrorism-related suspicions" (Landy, 2001). Similar calls were repeated in a subsequent article published prior to 9/11 (Bell, 2001). In the Canadian press, the "crisis" of 9/11 was not the transforming moment in the immigration-nation dialectic.

In the German media debate of immigration, a much more important event than 9/11 was the Madrid train bombings of March 11, 2004. Until this event, the German media paid relatively little attention to the dangers of immigration. In fact, a separate analysis revealed that the theme of danger—emanating from terrorism or other factors—played only a minor role in the debate of the immigration law. With the Madrid attacks, the association of immigration with danger skyrocketed (Bauder, 2008c). In particular, the media linked immigration to Muslim extremism and framed immigration as a security threat.

Emblematic of the transformation of the German media debate is the case of Metin Kaplan. Kaplan was self-proclaimed caliph and the leader of a Cologne-based religious movement, which the German government had declared anti-constitutional (*verfassungsfeindlich*) and therefore illegal. Furthermore, Kaplan had been convicted by a court of instigating the murder of a rival cleric and was to be deported to Turkey to serve a life-sentence in prison for planning attacks against the Turkish state. After the Madrid attacks and in light of Kaplan's immanent deportation the press used Kaplan's case to construct an association between immigration, Muslim extremism and terrorism. The media called Kaplan a "hate preacher" (*Hassprediger*), who supposedly turns his immigrant followers into terrorists.

The Madrid attacks served as the catalytic event that facilitated the association between immigration and terrorism, and the increasing scepticism towards the identity of Germany as an immigration country that had developed in the 1990s. The *Tageszeitung*, for example, reports that the strong "feeling of threat (*Bedrohungsempfinden*) among the people" renders the law that facilitates new immigration without strict security provisions unacceptable (Weikert, 2004). The increasing fear of terrorism after Madrid contributed to the revival of Germany's identity as a non-immigrant country.

The discursive association between immigration, Muslim extremism and national security subsequently shaped the immigration law. After the German Federal Constitutional Court had ruled that a previous vote on the immigration law in 2002 did not follow proper parliamentary procedure, the law was back in parliament for debate. In October 2003, a parliamentary committee was established to negotiate a compromise on the contents of the new law. The law that was eventually passed and that took effect in January 2005 does not facilitate new immigration to Germany of any significant magnitude. Instead, it effectively blocks new immigration and instead focuses on the integration of foreigners and immigrants already in Germany.

In a German context, the 2004 attack of Madrid can be interpreted as a "crisis" that constituted a critical moment in the immigration-nation dialectic. This crisis affected the material practices enacted by the immigration law as well as national identity.

Economic Crisis

The economic utility of immigration has been an important theme of immigration policy and debate in both Canada and Germany. In Canada, economic considerations are the most important criteria for selecting immigrants. For example, since 1995 the majority of immigrants have entered Canada under the "Economic Class", which assesses immigrants based on the human capital they bring to the Canadian labour market or their willingness to invest in the Canadian economy or to start a Canadian business (Citizenship and Immigration Canada, 2009). The assumption that immigration should make a contribution to Canada's national economy is generally not questioned by the media (Bauder, 2008e). In fact, the media reports more frequently on the link between immigration and crime, violence and terrorism or humanitarian aspects of Canadian immigration policy than on economic aspects of immigration. Apparently, the taken-for-granted assumption that immigration should make an economic contribution is less interesting to the media than other, more contested issues of immigration policy (Bauder, 2008b).

As an uncontroversial issue, the economic aspect of immigration debate has been relatively robust in light of the cyclical fluctuations of the Canadian economy and labour market. While the media debated how the selection of immigrants could be improved to maximise the economic utility of immigration to the Canadian economy, the economic objective of immigration is generally not questioned. In this way, the economic theme of Canadian immigration debate is "one-dimensional" (Marcuse, 1964); it does not involve the position that economic immigration to Canada should be prevented. During the study period, economic crisis—or the perception of it—has not played a role in changing this characteristic of the debate.

In the German media, the debate of the economic utility of immigration was fundamentally different in nature than in the Canadian media. Economic considerations were the most frequent theme of discussion in the debate of immigration policy (Bauder, 2008c). In addition, the debate juxtaposed two opposing positions. The first position suggests that the immigration of highly skilled workers and IT specialists is a necessity for the German economy to remain globally competitive. Immigration of these workers should therefore be enabled by the new immigration law. The second position proposes that the immigration of workers has a negative impact on the labour market for native workers and is a burden on the welfare system (Bauder, 2008d).

The paradigm that Germany has become an immigration country that can benefit from the infusion of highly skilled labour featured prominently in the media throughout the study period. For example, in 2001, the *Frankfurter Allgemeine Zeitung* reported how the president of a Frankfurt-based consulting company "appeals to the federal government to use the planned immigration law to drastically reduce the employment barriers for foreign workers in Germany" (Bröll, 2001, p. 19). The idea that immigration is essential to maintain economic prosperity also extended into the later phases of the debate. In 2004, for example, an article in the *Süddeutsche Zeitung* suggested that "growth opportunities would be wasted if the demand for skilled workers is not sufficiently met" through immigration (Beise, 2004, p. 19).

Interestingly, this position did not suggest that a crisis exists that requires a corresponding legislative response, but rather that a crisis may be imminent if the reforms were not implemented. The case of Indonesian immigrant Hariato Wijaya illustrates this point. Wijaya was the first recipient of the German Greencard, and the media celebrated his pioneering role. After the delay in the immigration law, which was supposed to enable Wiljaya to permanently stay in Germany, Mr. Wijaya decided to leave Germany and emigrate to the USA. In response to this decision, the *Frankfurter Allgemeine Zeitung* ran the headline "Germany kicks out smart heads" (Schmidt, 2004, p. 42); the *Tageszeitung* lamented that Wijaya's "taxes will...flow into the American state coffer" (Spannbauer, 2003, p. 8); and the *Süddeutsche Zeitung* regretted the loss of human capital (Prantl, 2004, p. 4). The reporting on Wijaya's case suggested that without the immigration of skilled labour, the economic future of Germany was uncertain.

A different perspective of "crisis" is represented by the second position that immigration is a burden on German workers and citizens. This position gained strength as unemployment figures steadily increased throughout the study period. In 2002, the *Frankfurter Allgemeine Zeitung* published an interview in which a high-ranking conservative politician questions "whether we can afford an army of unemployed and get people from abroad" (Euler & Schwan, 2002, p. R1). In 2004, the *Frankfurter Allgemeine Zeitung* reported how even the main governing party that had supported the immigration of skilled workers changed it opinion: "With 4.6 million unemployed, even the SPD could not find an acceptable reason to let the negotiations fail on this point [to insist on the points system to select skilled workers]" (Dietrich, 2004, p. 1). The idea that immigrants compete with Germans for the same jobs was sometimes accompanied by the rhetoric of "immigration into the welfare system", suggesting that immigrants who cannot find jobs in a tight labour market will eventually be a financial burden rather than an economic asset. The *Süddeutsche Zeitung* further reports about a study by the Institute for Labour Market and Employment Research (*Institut für Arbeitsmarkt- und Berufsforschung*), which illustrates that "many of the skilled workers attracted [by the Greencard] have long become unemployed" (Jacobi, 2003, p.

1). The position that immigration damages German workers and the welfare system challenged the paradigm that Germany has become an immigration country, and contests the very identity of Germany as an immigrant nation.

The rise of unemployment rates above nine percent in 2003 and exceeding the ten percent threshold in 2004 can be interpreted as a "crisis" that nourished the position that immigration of skilled workers should be blocked. The *Frankfurter Allgemeine Zeitung* (2003, p. 12) spoke explicitly of the "crisis" in the IT-Sector and the labour market which "caused seven percent of the foreign specialists with a Greencard to register as unemployed". This crisis accelerated precisely during the period in which the debate of immigration to Germany reignited after the German Constitutional Court nullified the first vote about the immigration law in 2002. The version of the immigration law that emerged from this debate and that was passed into law in 2004 effectively blocks the immigration of workers to Germany. In particular, the Canadian-style points system that was supposed to enable the immigration of skilled workers was dropped from the law. Apparently, the perception of an unemployment crisis affected the material context of the immigration law.

Conclusion

That crisis can be a discursive construction aimed to achieve political goals is not lost on the media. For example, in the context of the arrival of Chinese refugees by boat on Canada's west coast in 1999, Lorne Waldman of the *Toronto Star* remarks:

> Reform Party critics and others are demanding that Parliament take immediate action to change Canada's so-called "lax" immigration laws to prevent further occurrences. But is there really a crisis? Does Canada need changes in the legislation? Or is the problem really one of critics of the system using this opportunity to whip up hysteria to further their own agendas? (Waldman, 1999, p. 1)

Waldman concludes that the social construction of crisis should not be used to criticise or dismantle Canada's existing immigration system. The above analysis illustrated that similar events, such as the attacks in New York and Madrid, had varied impacts on media debate of immigration in Canada and Germany. Whether crisis serves as a transformative moment in these debates is highly contingent on the national contexts in which these debates occur.

In respect to the second dialectical dimension that encapsulates the relationship between discursive practices and material circumstances, the reporting of a crisis in the Canadian media had little influence on the reform of immigration law and the way Canada generally regulates immigration. Although the humanitarian crisis in Kosovo triggered an ad-hoc response from the Canadian government, I could not discern from the media debate a longer-term effect on immigration law.

In the German context, the perception of crisis played a much more prominent role in shaping the immigration law. In particular, the German media linked the terrorism crisis after the 2004 attacks in Madrid to immigration debate. In addition, it constructed immigration as a liability to the German workers and welfare system in light of an emerging unemployment crisis. Both terrorism and unemployment crises resulted in increasing scepticism towards immigration in the media. This scepticism is also reflected in the immigration law, which passed parliament shortly after these crises occurred and which has prevented any significant new immigration to Germany and into the German labour market.

The perception of crisis also affected the manner in which the media constructed national identity. In Canada, the Kosovo crisis and the ad-hoc response by the government projected an image for the nation as compassionate towards innocent victims of war and as tough on war criminals. In Germany, the crisis of terrorism and unemployment were catalytic events for the media to portray Germany as a non-immigrant nation. This transformation of national identity is significant since a redefinition of German identity away from ethnic to immigrant nation seems to have occurred in the late 1990s (Meier-Braun, 2002). The establishment of the Süßmuth Commission and the effort to create Germany's first immigration law reflected this new identity (Zinterer, 2004). The perception of immanent terrorism and unemployment crises, however, challenged this identity.[2]

The comparison between Canadian and German media debate of immigration reform illustrates that the perception of crisis played different roles in both national contexts. Canada has a long history of immigration and has placed immigration at the very core of its national identity. This established identity is relatively robust against perceptions of crisis. While crises may trigger ad-hoc responses from government, they are unlikely to shape long-term policies or affect Canada's established national identity as an immigrant nation.

Conversely, Germany had long defined itself as an ethnic nation; the realisation that Germany is an immigration country is relatively recent. Accordingly, national identity in respect to immigration was relatively unstable during the study period and vulnerable to perceptions of crisis linked to immigration. In fact, crises were the key transformative moments of the immigration debate in the German media.

Notes

1. German citizenship legislation was reformed in an earlier initiative in 1999.
2. I have argued elsewhere that Germany did not return to its former national identity of an ethnic nation, but rather that the media projected in the later phases of the immigration debate a new identity of Germany as an "integration" country (Bauder, 2011).

CHAPTER THREE

Controlled Conditions—an Analysis of the Positioning of Migration during the Prime Ministerial Debates for the 2010 UK General Election

Bernhard Gross

Introduction

In 2010 for the first time in a UK general election, the candidates for Prime Minster of the three major parties, Gordon Brown for Labour, David Cameron for the Conservatives and Nick Clegg for the Liberal-Democrats, faced each other in a series of three television debates in front of a carefully selected audience supposed to represent the British electorate. After opening statements by each of the candidates—again—carefully selected members of the audience posed—again—carefully selected questions to the panel. This aspect of selection represents the link through which the debates can be defined as the outcome of a journalistic production process. This chapter will start out with a consideration of the rules that governed the debate to establish the role journalists played in shaping its content. The actual content in relation to migration will then be analysed in relation to Britain as a nation state. The chapter concludes by returning to the role of journalists, this time by analysing a particular exchange within the debates. Though Britain's status as a multi*cultural* and multi*national* state raises specific issues, the argument illustrates a dynamic of wider applicability: current discourses of nation state and migration render the latter as permanent source of crisis for the former.

The Rules of the Debate

So how does journalism fit into what was overtly presented as a series of exchanges between members of the public and the candidates as well as between the candidates? A closer look at the processes that led to these exchanges highlights the pivotal role journalistic activity played in them. As highlighted above

the interaction between members of the public and the three politicians under-
went several stages of selection. The composition of the audience and the question schedule were negotiated and codified before the debate. The result was a
76-point document called *Prime Ministerial Debates—Programme Format* (All Parties, 2010) that addressed the following issues: audience selection (points 1 to
13); audience role (14–40); structure of the programme (41–57); role of the
moderator (58–64); themes (65.1–65.3); set (66–68); audience cutaways (69–76).
Rather than going through all the points I want to highlight a few because they
are indicative of the journalistic component in the debate.

First of all, although well-established journalists served as moderators in all
three debates—Alastair Stewart in the first debate on ITV 1 (Gardiner, 2010),
Adam Boulton in the second debate on Sky News (McAndrew, 2010) and
David Dimbleby (Pearl, 2010) in the final debate on BBC 1—their role during
the broadcast was restricted to ensuring that the candidates stuck to the rules
and to calling on members of the audience to pose their questions. As outlined
above, the latter aspect was the result of a carefully calibrated pre-production
process of selection, the first step of which was audience composition. Recruit-
ing conducted by ICM, had to follow a strict weighting in terms of voting preference. Broadcasters were only allowed to recruit a small number of additional
audience members. The overall objective in terms of the role of the audience, as
set out in rule 14, was "to ensure maximum debate between the party leaders—
the distinctive characteristic of these programmes—while allowing the audience's voices to be heard directly posing questions." However, being included in
the audience did not automatically confer a right or even the opportunity to be
heard. Being heard was dependent on a screening process conducted by an editorial panel—staffed by the respective broadcaster for each debate—and ruled
by a number of aspects addressed in points from the audience role, structure of
the programme and themes sections of the *Programme Format*. Whilst editorial
independence was explicitly assured (rule 33), the selection process was closely
determined by the rules. The first section of each debate was to focus on a particular main theme: domestic affairs in the first, international affairs in the second, economic affairs in the third. The second, un-themed section rule 30 stated
that "a maximum of two questions will be selected on a single subject." For
both sections the editorial panel had various elements to consider, for which
rule 32 provides an interesting insight. Among the considerations listed there
"voters' interest" is the only one that indicates the public's point of view as an

unqualified starting point of question selection. "Prominence of certain issues", "parties' policies on election issues" and prime ministerial issues, on the other hand, represent selection criteria that start with party programmes and political institutions, thus the relevance and "selectability" of a question depends on the extent it reflects these programmes and institutions. The topic of migration was selected by each panel.

Incidentally, the audience question of concern here is the very first from the very first debate broadcast live on ITV 1 on 15 April 2010. In the two subsequent debates it featured in the un-themed sections, both of which I will look at briefly after examining in more details this Q & A exchange of the first debate. Through a close analysis of it, I intend to argue that migration in this context is discursively positioned not as a momentary crisis in the face of a specific challenge but as a permanent and existential crisis for the nation state.

The First and Third Debate

One of the regular presenters of ITV 1 *News*, Alastair Stewart, moderated this historic programme—the first ever such General Election debate. To begin the candidate-audience interaction, Stewart called on one Gerard Oliver. Oliver, according to the moderator a retired toxicologist from Cheshire, asked the candidates: "Good evening. What key elements for a fair, workable immigration policy need to be put in place to actually make it work effectively?"

The obvious point of connection between Oliver's question and the themes of this book can of course be found in the fact that both are about migration. However, this is merely a starting point and the relevance runs much deeper than surface-level. Oliver does more than mention migration. The way he phrases his question indicates a set of assumptions that begins to discursively position the phenomenon of the movement of people across space—*begins*, because it is only in the responses from the candidates that the discursive framework of this phenomenon is more fully revealed. To start with Oliver's question, it is the term "immigration" that begins to define the phenomenon by determining the characteristics of the space and thus producing this space, to use Lefebvre's term (1991 [1974]), through which people move not as *open* space, as the term "migration" would suggest, but as *bounded* spaces, as territories. When migrants cross these boundaries they become *im*-migrants. These bounded spaces are defined further, as "immigration" denotes a specific direction of movement: from a space that is defined as outside to a bounded space that is defined as inside. Combining the terms "immigration" and "policy" introduces another definitional degree. Now, the inside space is defined not only as bounded but also as controlled. It is turned into an administrative unit within which policy is to be enforced. The aspect of enforcement, of the legitimate application of force within it, allows defining this territory as a state in Weberian terms:

> a state is a human community that (successfully) claims the *monopoly of the legitimate use of physical force* within a given territory. ... The state is considered the sole source of the "right" to use violence. (Weber, 1948 [1918], p. 78 original emphasis)

To reiterate: Oliver defines the phenomenon of migration as a movement from a generic outside space to a specific bounded and controlled inside space, a state territory. Considering the addressees of the question suggests that Oliver assigns *sole* responsibility for policy implementation to the British Prime Minister and his government, this allows for the conclusion that Oliver's question produces a specific space, the British state. It would be premature to make further inferences about the nature of the British state, if for instance it could be characterised as national. As Agnew and Corbridge (1995, p. 83) point out, a territorial state is not necessarily a nation state. There is little in Oliver's question that goes beyond the territorial. Further definition of the state will have to wait until the analysis of the candidates' responses. Instead, the next analytical step turns towards the overt content of Oliver's query.

By posing the question, Oliver suggests that the current immigration policy does not work effectively. His expectation that the future Prime Minister should do something about it, also suggests that Oliver considers this state of affairs to be problematic. In other words, he offers a set of definitions: migration as immigration and space as divided into a generic outside space in difference to a specific inside state territory; he also offers a diagnosis of a situation: immigration policy as problematic, and asks the candidates for a solution, a remedy to the situation. However, it is important to note here that he casts the situation and not the phenomenon as problematic. This is an important distinction that I will come back to later in the chapter. Oliver defines migration as immigration, but does not offer a value judgement on immigration itself. The problem he diagnoses is not with immigration, but with immigration policy, i.e., the way government handles immigration. His suggestions that there should be a "fair,

workable immigration policy" that "work[s] effectively" do not in themselves allow for conclusions to be drawn as to his opinion about immigration. "Fair" to
whom or to what? "Effective" in achieving what outcome? If Oliver had given
an indication as to how these questions could be answered, how fairness and effectiveness could be judged, the situation would be different. However, he does
not supply any such points of reference. Once Oliver had posed the question,
the terms and targets of fairness and effectiveness were open to the interpretation of the three candidates.

The format of the debate allowed for each candidate to give a response to
an audience question first, before they could engage with each other. The candidates responded in the following order: Brown, Cameron, Clegg (see transcripts available online for details.) It is worth considering these initial responses
in some detail here, as they not only indicate the candidates' lines of interpretation of Oliver's question but also further develop the definitional layers of space
and state. In their responses all three accept Oliver's definition of immigration
and the definition of space this entails. Although, Cameron and Clegg acknow-
ledge that migration can occur in the opposite direction, too, i.e., from the inside to the outside, this does not question the underlying division of space into
bounded territories. In this context Clegg's reference to exit controls implies an
emphasis on boundaries, an aspect that will be picked up later. It is important to
mention here though that boundaries play an important role in the context of
state formation. They are "social and political constructs…whose establishment
is a manifestation of power" (Paasi, 2001, p. 17). Moreover, Brown and Clegg
explicitly evoke the inside space that is only implied in the questioner's use of
the term "immigration" by first calling it "the country" and later in Brown's
case "Britain". All three also accept the responsibility Oliver charged them with
and suggest that they have the power to do something about the problem—
although it is worth pointing out that both Brown and Cameron reference another administrative, quasi-state space, the European Union (EU). In terms of
spatial definition the EU indicates that the outside space can be differentiated
three spatial categories: EU space, "new countries joining the EU" and outside-
EU space. It can also be read as an implied acknowledgement of the limits of
their power. Their own responses suggest the tension, which they have to negotiate throughout the debate, between their projection of themselves as "unre-
strained" leaders of the nation-state and their actual far more restrained
position—the result of the difference between the presumed and actual degree

of sovereignty of the contemporary nation-state, more of which later. Overall, the three candidates share a similar understanding of space and migration with Oliver. However, they differ from Oliver in another important aspect: their definition of what actually constitutes the problem.

All three, but Brown and Cameron more so than Clegg, shift the focus of Oliver's diagnosis from immigration policy to immigration itself. Also, all three decide to interpret the measurement of fairness and effectiveness, left open by Oliver, in a single direction. The "pressure" Brown and Cameron mention towards the beginning of their respective responses is in their view directly caused by immigration not by immigration policy. They do return to the policy aspect, but only after asserting immigration as the actual problem. Clegg's response, on the other hand, remains focussed on policy. In fact, he even challenges Brown's and Cameron's shifts in focus. Their responses could be taken as exactly the kinds of "tough talking on immigration" Clegg has in mind. However, though Clegg avoids joining in their tough talk, he too interprets Oliver's question along the same lines as his colleagues: fairness and effectiveness of policy are to be measured by their impact on an Us evoked by the use of We by all three. Brown's response merits a closer look in this respect.

For one, by being the first to respond Brown sets the parameters against which the other two can be measured. As Clegg's response indicates, his co-debaters could have challenged Brown immediately had they wanted to do so, even within the constricted format of the debate. Also, in his response Brown moves beyond an unspecified We and explicitly relates the pronoun to Britain as well as a specific set of people. Finally, the relationship between these two elements—Britain and these people—as presented by Brown, hints at a further characteristic of the state space introduced by Oliver. These people are defined in difference to another set of people. On the one hand, *these* people are the people that Brown listened to and who feel the pressure caused by immigration. On the other hand, there are *those* people who "come from abroad". One set is present and established on the inside; the other kind is coming in from abroad, the outside. Yet again, the outside space is not defined with any more specificity. The inside, however, is and not just in name.

As already discussed, Brown evokes the space as Britain and he evokes an established set of people that are located within it. In the final sentence of his statement he moves beyond locating these people within space to redefining the space through them. When Brown says "We are a tolerant, we are a diverse country…" not only does he position himself as part of these people through the use of the first person plural, he also equates these people with this space he calls a country. These people do more than live *in* this space; these people *are* this space; these people *are* the state prescribed by this space. In Brown's words these people *are* Britain. The twofold definition of Britain as a state as well as a people suggests that Brown conceives of it as a particular kind of state, a nation-state. A number of definitions of nation exist, but I want to draw on one by Renan:

> No, it is no more the land than the race that makes a nation. Man is everything in the formation of that sacred thing which we call the people. Nothing of a material nature suffices for it. A nation is a spiritual principle, the result of profound historical complications, a spiritual family, not a group determined by the configuration of the soil. (Renan, 2001 [1882], p. 174)

Renan emphasises the importance of people in the make-up of a nation without resorting to notions of an essentialised, biologically determined race. Also, when it comes to what constitutes a people, Renan emphasises the historicity of this unit, which allows for change in the make-up of a people over time. These are important points, as debates of nationhood beyond the racial definition often centre on a national culture as the element that brings a people together and how such a culture may have come about. While scholars in the primordialist (cf. Smith, 1989) tradition accept that national cultures are ultimately constructed, they argue that nations are founded on pre-existing cultures, which are often described as ethnic cultures. Modernist scholars, on the other hand, (cf. Gellner, 1983; Hobsbawm, 1990) argue that even if there are pre-existing elements within a national culture, its composition is not the result of a continuous, gradual development but the outcome of a comparatively abrupt introduction in the interests of a particular class (cf. Pecora, 2001 for a discussion of the different approaches). Either way, culture can be seen in Renan's terms as the outcome of "profound historical complications". Returning to Brown, he, too, explicitly rejects a racially constituted "We the people" when he describes it as tolerant and diverse. Initially, these characteristics might suggest a rejection of a unifying culture and a national definition of Britishness and instead an avowal of multiple cultures. However, such an avowal conforms with a particular contemporary formation of nationalism, what Fortier (2005, pp. 560-561) calls with specific reference to Britain a "multiculturalist nationalism":

that is, the reworking of the nation as inherently multicultural. Multiculturalism is generally considered in relation to specific national settings, but the predominant theory is
that diversity is a disruptive, extraneous element causing a crisis of the nation, conceived
as founded on monoculturalism. But in multiculturalist nationalism, there is a shift away
from linear narratives of nations moving from monoculture to multiculture...

It is important to note that "multiculturalist nationalism" does not necessarily result in the inclusion of everyone, as Brown clearly highlights. Though he
evokes Britain as a multicultural nation, he also establishes limits to its diversity
and tolerance straight away through his setting up of two kinds of people. Neither Cameron nor Clegg challenge Brown's claim, which is not to say that they
repeat it. Cameron's use of the term "people", for instance, is more generic in
that it refers to a number of persons. But in phrases such as "we should have
transitional controls so they can't all come here at once" and "So that we only
send immigrants to those places where they can be coped" made by Cameron
and Clegg respectively, they evoke a similar categories of inclusion and exclusion, of a resident populace, a nation, on the inside and immigrants who remain
excluded.

More will be said later on about British multiculturalism and challenges to
conceiving of Britain as a nation state. However, at this point the focus is on the
specific content of the candidates' responses to Oliver. Drawing on Renan allows reading Brown's evocation of We as an evocation of a nation. Drawing on
Fortier explains the politicians' definition of diversity and tolerance as national
characteristics. However, it is important to remember Weber's definition of
state before concluding that Brown conceives of Britain as a nation-state. As
mentioned above, Brown accepts Oliver's definition of space and by accepting
responsibility to regulate immigration into this space he claims the right to legitimate violence within this territory. It is the overlap of these two elements
under the auspices of a nation, territory and state sovereignty that define the
modern nation-state, a status Brown claims for Britain. While it might not be
surprising that the Prime Minister of a state would make such a claim, it is important to highlight how migration is appropriated in the process.

When migration reappears in the second and third debates, it does so in a
similar discursive framework. In the second debate migration was raised in a
question by Bethlehem Negessi, who asked: "I'm an immigrant, and I have been
in the UK for 13 years. I recognise that immigration is becoming a problem in

the country. What new measures would you introduce in order to make the system more fair?"

In the third debate Radley Russell raised the issue when he asked: "Are the politicians aware that they have become removed from the concerns of the real people, especially on immigration, and why don't you remember that you are there to serve us, not ignore us?"

Both questions raise some interesting points about the way they are worded as well as how they came to be selected. Though second in actual sequence, it is Russell's question I will briefly address, to conclude this section, as it is more closely related to what has been said so far. To explain the inclusion of Russell's question, I suggest, one has to consider a particular event during the campaign in the week preceding the final debate. During that week Gordon Brown was caught out calling Gillian Duffy, a woman he had met in a regular-voter-on-the-street encounter, a bigot because of her views on immigration. That he did not do so to her face but after their conversation as he was being driven away added to the media outrage that followed. The issue dominated the election news for several days. Russell's question reflects both elements of the coverage: politicians out of touch with the electorate in general and on the issue of migration in particular. Compared to the first debate the question is more overtly critical of migration, but this is couched in a concern about politicians' common touch. The criticism is directed at the politicians rather than immigrants. It implies an "us real people" vs. immigration dichotomy, although the second dichotomy between "us real people" vs. "you ignorant politicians" is much stronger and the focus of the question. However, in their initial responses to the question, all three candidates focussed very much on the migration issue itself (see transcripts). Rather than addressing the question whether they were in fact out of touch, they try to realign themselves with the "us real people" of the first dichotomy by emphasising it over the second.

While Russell's question as well as the candidates' responses provides further evidence for the evocations of the nation in the context of migration, it is Negressi's question that allows for a closer analysis of the role of journalism in this process. I will return to Negressi's in the conclusion to this chapter. Right now I will further examine the notion of *a* nation in relation to Britain. Above I have introduced the concept of the nation state by citing Lefebvre in relation to space and state territoriality, Weber in relation to state, and Renan, Gellner and Smith in relation to nation. I have also begun to relate their respective concepts to the specifics of the British state. However, as its full name, the United King-dom of England, Scotland, Wales and Northern Ireland suggests, it is a state comprised of a set of distinct components generating a dynamic that cannot be explained by reference to multiculturalism alone.

To be British–National identity
in a Multinational and Multicultural State

All three candidates develop their arguments about immigration and immigra-tion policy on the basis of a shared understanding of space and people as de-fined by the national. They not only add the specificity of the national in response to Oliver's question, they also recast immigration as the problem. The political elites in the UK as represented by the prime ministerial candidates from the three major parties see themselves as part of a British nation that is faced with this problem. In fact, I would suggest that they recast immigration not merely as a problem for the nation but as a challenge to its cohesion. However, they implicitly assume the existence of cohesion among the non-immigrant populace—something which is debateable.

Colley (1992, p. 5) calls Great Britain and British nationalism "an invention forged above all by war". For her it was war with France that shaped this nation from the late 17th century to the mid 19th century. Before that time, though al-ready under the control of the same ruler, the Irish, English, Scots and Welsh had not developed into a British nation. Putting the confrontations and con-flicts of the era at the centre of British national identity formation, Colley con-cludes that the peoples inhabiting the British Isles "came to define themselves as a single people not because of any political or cultural consensus at home, but rather in reaction to the Other beyond their shores." (p. 6) Of course, it would be remiss to deny that others have reached different conclusions about the formation of British nationalism. Nairn (1981), for instance, in his influen-tial collection of essays that make up *The Break-up of Britain* defines nationalism in general as "the joint product of external pressures and an internal balance of class forces" (p. 41). In relation to the development of British nationalism, he suggests that it "suffered far less from external pressures and threats than any other" (p. 42). Though placing the emphasis on the internal dimension in his analysis, Nairn still considers the external dimension important and cites warfare as of particular relevance in the formation of British nationalism (p. 42). Both

Nairn and Colley, with their arguments about the past, the origin and development of British nationalism, intend to illuminate the present. Nairn, identifies an overall backwardness and uneven development within Britain as the reason behind the "territorial disintegration" and "threat of secession" (1981, p. 14), the break-up of Britain. Colley explains "a revival of internal divisions" (1992, p. 7) and a subsequent, though gradual unravelling of Britishness with the fact that former points of external conflict have disappeared or at least diminished well below the level of large-scale warfare threatening the integrity of British territory. While I believe an internal dimension to be important—whether necessarily in Nairn's terms of class struggle is another matter—it is Colley's argument about the external dimension that I want to pursue here further.

First of all, however, it has to be noted the British state still exists, as does a sense of Britishness. Survey data provides evidence for the latter, though it also shows an increasing importance of other, disaggregated British national identities, i.e., English, Scottish, Welsh and Irish, and a complex set of attitudes towards Britishness (Bechhofer & McCrone, 2007, 2008). To Kumar (2010, p. 475) this indicates that:

> one may still think of oneself as British, but with a decreasing sense of its salience in one's life and a diminishing commitment to the political entity of Britain. It is almost as if, for significant sections of the population, Britishness is becoming a residual legacy of the glory days of British power and prestige.

The resurgence of these nationalities that for a time were, though never entirely subsumed into but 'nested' (Miller, 2001) within a British nation, highlights not only that contemporary Britain needs to be understood as a multinational state, but also that the idea of the multicultural nation state already needs further attention. As mentioned above "multicultural nationalism" attempts to accommodate one dimension of multiplicity specific to the British context that challenges the notion of a British nation. However, the acceptance of diversity under the auspices of multiculturalism does not mean that minority and majority communities are on an equal footing in the national We; as "minorities' ethnicity is understood as otherness, foreignness, from 'mainstream' British culture" (Fortier, 2005, p. 371). This limitation echoes New Labour's move away from an unqualified support for multiculturalism to an increasing emphasis on social cohesion, based on "belonging given by loyalty and adherence to central hegemonic, so called British, values" (Yuval-Davis et al., 2005, p.

528). A similar line has been pursued by the Conservative Liberal-Democrat coalition government since the election, as evidenced by Prime Minister David Cameron's claim in a speech in February 2011 that state multiculturalism had failed. So while diversity is accepted, "in order to be welcomed in the national fold, [members of ethnic minorities] must deracinate themselves" (Fortier, 2005, p. 571) and conform to these "British values." As Yuval-Davis et al. (2005, p. 521) point out multicultural policies are, "aimed almost exclusively towards communities of immigrants from ex-New Commonwealth and Pakistan countries" established before the 1981 Nationality Act further restricted "privileged rights of settlement of non-patrial ex-colonial settlers." Diversity and tolerance are not aims pursued for their own sake nor is multicultural nationalism, but rather they are the outcome of "historical complications"; they are a consequence of Britain's imperial past.

In targeting the level of what are defined as ethnic communities, this kind of multiculturalism sets Britain up as a nation comprised of a number of specific immigrant ethnic minority communities and a settled majority community. The latter is supposed to embody the "British values" the minority groups ultimately have to accept to become more or less fully recognised. The exact nature of these values, however, is unclear and attempts by New Labour and in particular Gordon Brown to establish a coherent and normative set of British characteristics remain contested (Bechhofer & McCrone, 2007, p. 251). Partly, this difficulty stems from the achievements of multiculturalism as a challenge to a dominant mono-culture; at least equally important, though, is another dynamic already mentioned above: the challenge to this mono-culture from within. Whereas in the context of multiculturalism the majority culture is considered as one coherent unit, outside this context it is considered to be comprised of at least four parts: England, Scotland, Wales and (Northern) Ireland. While the political debate over challenges to the *social* cohesion of the British nation tends to focus on multiculturalism (see for instance Cameron's speech on the alleged failure of state multiculturalism mentioned above), it is the resurgence of these nations that may actually challenge the very cohesion of the UK as a unitary state unit, because, as Miller (2001, p. 307) points out:

> the component nationalities have most of the properties of independent nations,…the Scots in Britain have a claim to self-determination which Muslims, say, in Britain do not,…

Considering the twofold dynamics of multiculturalism and multinationalism, it appears difficult to sustain a contemporary and mutually re-enforcing British identity/British nation state pairing. In light of the challenge of multinationalism but also relevant in relation to multiculturalism, Aughey (2010, p. 350) suggests foregrounding a sense of allegiance to the British state as a multinational democracy over a sense of allegiance demanding a "common identity (a sort of British nationalism) and identities demanding exclusive allegiance (varieties of sub-British nationalism)." However, considering the political discourse as evidenced in the responses from the prime ministerial debate, a common identity with "a sort of British nationalism" seems to remain the goal. Clearly, this evidence is selective and narrow, but especially in Gordon Brown's response it highlights an underlying understanding of Britain as a nation state.

To (re)forge the nation, to come back to Colley's argument, a new outside threat has to be defined: immigration. As Cohen (2000, p. 576) argues in *The Incredible Vagueness of Being British/English*: "Migration policy remains a national function (who is included and who is excluded here takes a literal form)." Cohen's argument rests on a specific understanding of identity and how it is constructed:

> A method for analysing an identity cannot start from the crease and move the boundary or migrate from the core to the periphery, as there is no kernel and no core. Instead, the fuzzy edges of an identity are where the action is and where the answers lie. We know who we are by agreeing who we are not. Others judge us as we judge others. The Other cannot be separated from the Self.

To engage here fully in a discussion of collective identity formation on a state level would lead too far from the focus of this chapter; instead I only want to pick up on the aspect of boundary to highlight the special predicament of the contemporary nation-state and the almost reflexive response to migration it engenders.

Migration and Territoriality in the Era of Globalisation

Barth (1998 [1969], p. 15), based on his analysis of how communities come to understand themselves as ethnic groups, has called for a focus on "the ethnic boundary that defines the group, not the cultural stuff that it encloses". His emphasis is on social boundaries, though he acknowledges that, "they may have territorial counterparts". In fact, a claim to territory, a "territorial homeland" as

Miller describes it, with territorial boundaries, is a key aspect of the discourse that turns an ethnic group into a nation. In the case of a nation-state the boundary is turned into a fixed, administrative border, the territorial homeland into a territory, which allows for nations to assert power within it. Taylor (2003, p. 101) calls this spatial assertion of the nation *territoriality*: "a form of behaviour that uses a bounded space, a territory, as the instrument for securing a particular outcome." For Taylor (2003, p. 102) modern states have four main functions: "states wage war, they manage the economy, they give national identity, and they provide social services", all of which the state tries to achieve through "strategies of territoriality". Taylor's argument is similar to Giddens' (1987, p. 120) concept of the modern state as "a bordered power-container", but with an even stronger focus on territory and boundary, as he returns to boundary as *the* strategy of territoriality (Taylor, 2003, p. 101): "By controlling access to a territory through boundary restrictions, the content of a territory can be manipulated and its character designed." However, and this is where territoriality turns into a predicament, absolute sovereign control over what is perceived to be national territory and thus over what is going on within its boundaries is an illusion. To mistake this illusion for fact means to fall into what Agnew (1994) calls a "territorial trap". Together with Corbridge, Agnew (1995, p. 100) argues that "Social, economic and political life cannot be contained within the territorial boundaries of states through the methodological assumption of 'timeless space'." Far from eternally fixed in time and space "the territorial state and its power" is "dependent on the interaction between global and local (including state-territorial) processes of political economic structuration" (p. 91), which produces a) changing territorial formations but more importantly b) entirely non-territorial-based power structures over time. So while this interaction between the global and the local may have been conducive to the territorial nation state there is no guarantee that it will remain so. In fact Hurrelmann et al. (2007) speak of a golden age of the territorial nation state between the late 19th century and the 1970s. Since then aspects of power the territorial nation state used to control have been transferred to private actors and international institutions. At the same time as power is escaping from the nation state container, the container in terms of territory itself appears to remain intact. It *appears* intact because a closer look reveals that, as Lefebvre (2003 [1978], p. 92) points out, the apparent physical inviolability of territory hides its increasing hollowness, as "Flows traverse borders with the impetuosity of rivers." This phenomenon of deterritorialisation, of course, has been defined as an integral part of the process of contemporary globalisation (cf. Bauman, 2007, p. 2). And yet, as Calhoun (2007, p. 171) asserts "Globalization has not put an end to nationalism...Nationalism still matters, still troubles many of us, but still organizes something considerable in who we are." In fact, as Calhoun acknowledges, nationalism often reasserts itself in reaction to the process of globalisation. Calhoun (2008) explicitly positions himself in opposition to the likes of Ulrich Beck. In the face of the same dynamic Beck (2005, p. 115) calls for a "cosmopolitan realism", because

> the points at which domestic state power struggles, inter-state power struggles and non-state power struggles dovetail with one another can no longer be located within the frame of reference of either 'national' or 'international' arenas.

To Calhoun (2008, p. 443), however, this cosmopolitan perspective remains based on "class position and privileged citizenship" and ignores the necessity of other forms of belonging—often national—as a basis of democracy and of "actual social action" for most.

Returning to Cohen's suggestion of migration policy as a "national function", I also draw on Bauman's (2007, p. 14) argument about a shift in what the territorial nation state can provide its citizens in response to the challenges of globalisation and in the hope to maintain its legitimacy: "The spectre of social degradation against which the social state swore to insure its citizens is being replaced in the political formula of the 'personal safety state'..." Bauman lists a number of threats against which the "personal safety state" appears to defend its citizens. And yet in his view migration has a special role to play. Parallel to Barth's focus on the boundary in relation to ethnic group formation, Cohen's similar focus in relation to national identity formation and finally Colley's analysis of British identity formation in relation to an external threat, Bauman (2007, p. 85) suggests that:

> The latent function of the barriers at the border, ostensibly erected against 'false asylum seekers' and 'merely economic' migrants, is to fortify the shaky, erratic and unpredictable existence of the insiders.

This strategy only works while the border is still intact not just as an imagined line around a territory but also as an actual barrier. In this context it is worth remembering Clegg's emphasis on border controls in his response to Oliver's question. It is also worth pointing to an immediate limitation of this strategy acknowledged by Brown as well as Cameron in their responses. By virtue of being part of the EU the barrier has already become fairly easy to cross for most EU citizens. Though Brown's and Cameron's rhetoric starts to unravel from the inside, overall all three politicians still follow an argumentative line that traces the strategies and dynamics outlined by Barth, Bauman, Cohen and Colley. In their one-sided emphasis on fairness and effectiveness of immigration policy to the benefit of the UK none of the three responses addresses global inequalities, thus are positioned well beyond Calhoun's reformulation, towards a reactionary nationalism. However, it is interesting to note that at the same time of evoking the nation through immigration, the candidates highlight the nation's contingency. If the nation is so easily threatened in its essence by immigration, as their comments suggest, it cannot be particularly sturdy. Playing the populist move of talking tough on immigration turns out to be predicated on emphasising the fragility of the national construct. As pointed out at the beginning of this chapter, though Britain's status as a multi*cultural* and multi*national* state raises specific issues, the argument illustrates a dynamic of wider applicability: current discourses of   nation state and migration render the latter as permanent source of crisis for the former.

Conclusion

After having analysed how the three candidates talked about migration and how this relates to wider issues of migration and the British nation, I will conclude this chapter by returning to the role journalists played in shaping this content by looking at the way migration was raised as an issue in the second debate. As mentioned above, in this debate Negessi asked:

> I'm an immigrant, and I have been in the UK for 13 years. I recognise that immigration is becoming a problem in the country. What new measures would you introduce in order to make the system more fair?

In difference to Russell's, there is no timely event that would explain the inclusion of this question in the debate. This is the more surprising, as in essence Negessi's question is a repeat of Oliver's question in the first debate. Only this time, the questioner already frames migration as a problem for the candidates.

The reason for repeating the question can be interpreted in several ways: not all viewers watch all three debates hence a certain overlap is justified; migration is an issue that voters are concerned about; migration is an issue that features in the parties' election manifestos; the candidates need a second chance to clarify their positions about migration; migration is an issue the editorial panel judged to be important. There are probably several reasons more. Still, it is striking that the two questions so closely resemble each other and yet also differ from each other at the same time. What is also striking is who the election panel selected to deliver it. Choosing a self-identified immigrant in the role of the-one-who-puts-his-finger-on-the-problem avoids suspicions of anti-immigrant bias. I do not suggest that there is anti-immigrant bias. But considering the question selection process and the fact that audience members have to stick to the agreed question, I do suggest that all information contained in the question can be considered important and that strategic decisions were made by the panel as to who would ask a specific question and how the question would be phrased. The fact that Negessi identifies himself as an immigrant adds nothing to the question itself, i.e., the candidates should be able to respond to it in exactly the same way without this additional piece of information—in fact parts of their initial responses closely resemble those from the first debate (see transcript)—so why let him add it?

The reason I raise this question, is not to suggest that these issues might not be of genuine concern to the audience and this particular audience member, but to emphasise that (1) the audience present at the debate was a highly constructed representation of the British public, and (2) the questions individual audience members asked had undergone a journalistic process of selection. Though they may have been authors and originators in Goffman's terms (1981) of their submitted questions, at the point of delivery during the debate, the members of the audience had been reduced to mere animators, a role embodied in rule 38: "The audience members will be restricted to asking the selected questions." The questions are meant to be if not representative in quantitative terms then at least illustrative in qualitative terms of the British public, as judged by the editorial panel. Through this process of journalistic filtering audience members in general and those who ask a question in particular turn into parts within a script fit for the emerging dramaturgy of a prime ministerial debate in which everybody has their role play. The audience's role is to be the British public, the British nation. It is cast in this role by the journalists—the panel behind the scenes represented on stage by the moderator. The latter acts out his own role: a conduit between the nation and its leaders; apparently not in charge of either but making sure that both keep to the rules. However, considering the influence journalists had over the selection process, I would argue that not only were they in control of the audience on the night, they were in control of this representation of the British nation in preparation for the night and to a substantial degree consequently shaped the positioning of migration during these debates.

CHAPTER FOUR

"Asylum Crisis", National Security and the Re-articulation of Human Rights

Kerry Moore

Introduction

The dominant public discourses surrounding asylum in the UK since the early 1990s have been characterised by an underlying suspicion of, and often an outright hostility towards, asylum seekers. During the period of New Labour's term in office (1997–2010) this antagonism was clearly evident in both mainstream political and news media representations (Bailey & Harindranath, 2005; Buchanan, Grillo, & Threadgold, 2003; Coole, 2002; Gross, Moore, & Threadgold, 2007; ICAR, 2004; Kaye, 1998, 2001; Saxton, 2003; Speers, 2001; Thomson, 2003). In the early 2000s, the dominant discourse focused upon the magnitude of asylum as a growing "problem." Headlines announced that so-called, "bogus asylum seekers" were seeking to penetrate UK borders,[1] and repeatedly implied that asylum claims merely served to camouflage ulterior motives for migration. News narratives routinely associated asylum with unreasonable pressures upon social resources, typically characterising asylum seekers as "scrounging" off the welfare state, being granted unjustified benefits, free care on the National Health Service and jumping queues for social housing (Cohen, 2003, 2006a; Cohen, Humphries, & Mynott, 2002; Jordan & Brown, 2006). Asylum seekers were constructed not just as a mass of undeserving and duplicitous "intruders", but as a group who simply did not belong and yet were somehow allowed to defy the rules, or at least to avoid the conditions to which "ordinary Britains" were subject. Such press coverage articulated both particular and generalised suspicions of asylum seekers, reproducing a "culture of disbelief" (and perhaps also what Souter has recently termed a "culture of denial") about asylum claims (ICAR, 2008; Souter, 2011; Threadgold, 2006; Weber & Gelsthorpe, 2000). Concomitantly, asylum discourse positioned the British state as manipulated and compromised—emasculated by the supposed "abuse" of its immigration system and its failure to deal with an "asylum crisis" (Moore, 2010).

In this chapter, I will explore one of the key dynamics in the articulation of an "asylum crisis" in the UK since 1997, focusing upon mainstream national news media and political representations of asylum seekers and the asylum system. In particular, I investigate how asylum has been associated with national security issues as a matter of "common sense". In this, I contend, "asylum crisis" discourses have contributed to the re-positioning of "human rights" in British political culture and the re-articulation of liberal democratic values as a potential threat to the stability, well-being and security of the British nation. The analysis is primarily informed by Laclau and Mouffe's post-Marxist discourse theory—a theoretical approach that has not been greatly utilised or developed in journalism and media studies but which, I hope to demonstrate, can offer a very rewarding framework through which to investigate the relationships between migration and the media.

Asylum Crisis Discourse Through a Post-Marxist Lens

In Laclau and Mouffe's anti-foundationalist and anti-essentialist approach, the social (i.e., political identities, social relations, economic or cultural structures) is regarded as a complex terrain of conflict interwoven with discursive struggles to constitute, maintain and/or challenge hegemonic formations. In this, the social is considered neither naturally nor objectively intelligible—indeed, nothing exists *meaningfully* outside of discourse (Laclau & Mouffe, 1985). So, while discourse is concerned with the way in which language takes on a characteristic expression for the operation of different paradigms, restricting what can be meaningfully said or thought about a particular topic, it also determines "how ideas are put into practice and used to regulate the conduct of others" such that, "all practices have a discursive aspect" (Hall, 1997, p. 44). This role in determining conduct and practices means that it is not only language and ideas, but also identities, social relations and institutional practices that can be analysed as continuously made, remade and regulated through discourse. For example, the discourses through which the figure of the "refugee" is rendered meaningful as an object for policy discussion and public debate in Britain not only determines the range of ideas and practices which seem appropriate to associate with refugees, but also how the settled population are conditioned to think of themselves and their society. As discourse is understood as, "an articulatory practice which constitutes and organises social relations", it does not merely reflect, but actively constructs "truths" about asylum and refugee issues—what we understand as the social reality of Britain's relationship with asylum. In this way it defines and reproduces the objects of our knowledge (Laclau & Mouffe, 1985, p. 105).

Several concepts developed in Laclau and Mouffe's work are particularly useful for my analysis of political and news media discourse. Each relates to the *contingency* of discursive structures—a formal characteristic, central to Laclau and Mouffe's anti-essentialist political philosophy, that signals that possibilities for change remain even in an area, such as asylum, that appears sedimented with strongly negative assumptions and hostile news narratives. The contingency of discourses means that all identity, including those of social agents, social relations and ideas, (ideas which, for example, may function at any moment in time as "common sense"), cannot be seen as timelessly fixed or determined in any necessary way. Instead, every discourse is always overdetermined (there is always a multitude of alternative meanings possible for any signifier—a "constant overflowing of every discourse by the infinitude of the field of discursivity") and constituted through a process of *articulation* (Laclau & Mouffe, 1985, p. 113). Whilst meaning is produced through the differences between signs, those relations of difference shift and change depending upon the context of their use, with all discourses, in principle, potentially open to disarticulation and re-articulation (Laclau, 1996a). As such, as I will explore in further detail below, whilst a set of very powerful and positive connotations have been attached to the term "human rights" in twentieth-century politics (articulating human rights as an ideal to which respectable liberal democratic regimes should ascribe—a symbol of their humanitarian "goodness") this does not mean that alternative meanings have been precluded. Indeed, the meaning of the signifier "human rights" is constructed in relation to its social, political or cultural context and, as with all identities, its "regularities merely consist of the relative and precarious forms of fixation which accompany the establishment of a certain order" (Laclau & Mouffe, 1985, p. 98). According to discourse theory, all identities are continuously reproduced and always conditioned by a, "politics of identity, a politics of position, which has no absolute guarantee in an unproblematic, transcendental *law of origin*" (Hall, 1990, p. 226). Moreover, a person might hold multiple or even seemingly contradictory identities that are dependent upon the social context, adopting apparently different behaviours or attitudes for different social interactions, or when subject to different social forces. For example, a politician may advocate the promotion of human rights in general, but in an ap-

parently contradictory move, ardently support measures that would seriously restrict the right to asylum in the UK according to the policy line of his or her
party. As I will explore in the next section, such a contradiction has played a key
role in "asylum crisis" politics and its reporting in the national press.

Re-articulating a "Proud Tradition" on Human Rights

Within the dominant discourse, the representation of asylum as a serious problem or "crisis" facing the British state on the one hand, and the very identity of
the British state on the other have seemingly been conditional upon the frequently expounded "proud tradition" of Britain in welcoming and providing
sanctuary to deserving refugees. Such statements often seem to accompany new
proposals to further restrict the rights of, rather than extend protections to, asylum seekers (Cohen, 2003, 2006a, 2006b). As Ghassan Hage has noted in the
Australian context, it is particularly striking that the supposedly liberal or anti-
racist "credentials" of mainstream politicians, commentators or "the State" are
most ardently asserted at the very moment when "othering" is articulated with
most force (Hage, 2003). Similarly, "a discourse of national *tolerance*", in Britain,
as Pitcher observes, has been, "mobilized in the area of asylum and immigration
to defend exclusionary practices against the charge of racism" (Pitcher, 2009, p.
41-2).

During the height of the most sensationalist of news coverage in the run up
to the 2001 General Election when, as Richardson and Franklin note, "there
were widespread reported claims of an "asylum crisis" affecting/afflicting Britain", the anti-racist credentials of the British state were especially in evidence in
asylum discourse, couched unimpeachably within a carefully articulated "proud
tradition" rhetoric (Richardson & Franklin, 2003, p. 187). William Hague's Conservative Party in 2000–1 placed asylum at the centre of their campaign as a key
issue facing the nation. In their manifesto, *Time for Common Sense* Hague maintained that:

> Over the centuries Britain has welcomed people who have been persecuted by oppres-
> sive regimes overseas. But now our ability to be a safe haven for the genuinely op-
> pressed is severely hampered by the virtual collapse of our asylum system. This chaos
> encourages unfounded asylum claims. Britain has gained a reputation as a soft touch for
> bogus asylum seekers (Hague, 2001, p. 31).

In a speech to the Social Market foundation the previous year, Hague repeatedly emphasised Britain's, "long tradition of providing hospitality to men, women and children fleeing persecution", and argued that that tradition was now "under threat":

> Not because our people have lost their sense of hospitality; not because we are unwilling to honour our obligations to genuine refugees; least of all because the British people are racist or xenophobic. The problem confronting us is that a system to identify and protect refugees, which was designed half a century ago is near collapse in today's utterly different world (Hague, 2000).

This calling into question of the right to asylum of the post–World War Two ideological consensus, and of international laws and principles on human rights then, was in no part to be attributed to changes in the British state's identity as a willing protector, a welcoming and "tolerant" nation, Hague contends, but rather to the "collapse of the asylum system" and its exploitation by asylum seekers. Meanwhile, the New Labour government's growing anxiety to show their "toughness" on asylum seekers was being demonstrated through new immigration and asylum legislation and policy announcements to "crack down" on various aspects of the asylum process, such as the availability of state benefits for those seeking asylum and the purported prevalence of, "unscrupulous immigration advisors" (HMSO, 1998). "Toughness" was also signified through the sending home of Kosovar Albanian refugees following the NATO intervention in 1999, and tightening restrictions on the arrival of new asylum claimants—the urgency of which was apparently symbolised by the existence of the Red Cross camp in Sangatte, northern France and the policy objective of its closure which was under intense scrutiny in the national press (Buchanan, et al., 2003; Schuster, 2003; Thomson, 2003). In addition, the controversial asylum dispersal scheme, introduced under the Immigration and Asylum Act 1999 to relocate asylum seekers to regional locations away from the South East of England had attracted serious criticisms from refugee and human rights organisations, as well as the UN committee on the elimination of racial discrimination in its May 2001 report[2] (UNCERD, 2001). Indeed, the government's approach seemed to be pursuing the terms of the debate set by the right, and certainly not designed to challenge the vitriolic anti-asylum seeker coverage in some areas of the UK national press. In the months running up to the 2001 General Election, the then Home Secretary, Jack Straw's "crack down" to tighten borders, detain and deport refused asylum seekers who had "disappeared" once in the UK were widely reported (for example, BBC News, 2000a; Clarke, 2000; Grice, 2000; Taylorhome, 2000; Wooding, 2001) whilst the Conservatives and sections of the right wing press continued to amplify asylum as a problem, pushing for further and tougher action (e.g.: "YES, BRTAIN IS A SOFT TOUCH!" *Daily Mail,* 1st February 2001; "STRAW ASYLUM FAILURE; RECORD NUMBERS OF IMMIGRANTS FLOOD IN DESPITE TOUGH MEASURES", *Daily Mail,* 24th January 2001; "ASYLUM CASES RISE DESPITE THE STRAW CRACKDOWN", *Daily Mail,* 26th April, 2001).

Yet, there also seemed something of a contradiction in New Labour government policy on human rights at this time. Whilst an increasingly "tough line" was being taken on asylum, other measures, notably the incorporation of the European Convention on Human Rights into UK law through the Human Rights Act 1998 (HRA), seemed to promote them. According to Jack Straw, speaking on BBC Radio 4's *Today Programme* on 2nd October 2000, the HRA was "about bringing British rights home" (Straw, 2000). The need to domesticate the Human Rights Act and articulate it as essentially British reflects the concerns permeating debates at the time regarding sovereignty and control over UK law. If certain practices enshrined in other areas of UK law were to conflict with the HRA, which would prevail, commentators asked? (*Observer,* 21st February 1999) Didn't this threaten an undemocratic transfer of power over UK policy-making, emasculating Parliament before the law Courts? These tensions were dramatically played out in the case of the so called, "Afghan hijackers", who claimed asylum in Britain after fleeing the Taliban in 2000. During the ensuing and prolonged legal battle between the Home Office and the Afghan asylum seekers, their method of arrival (hijacking a plane) was represented, by government officials and some sections of the news media, to have obviously undermined the legitimacy of any claims upon the human rights obligations of the State—a piece of "common sense" which seemed all the more salient following the September 11th 2001 attacks in New York (Gross, et al., 2007; Moore, 2010). However, while this case connotatively linked asylum and human rights obligations with terrorism, and articulated a potentially antagonistic relation between human rights and the national security interests of Britain, it was certainly not unique in the news coverage of asylum in this respect, as I will explore in further detail below.

In the run-up to the General Election of 2005, both Prime Minister, Tony Blair and then leader of the Opposition Michael Howard again deployed the "proud tradition" rhetorical strategy whilst seeking to occupy "tough on asylum" political ground and voice reservations about human rights laws. In a speech to the Confederation of British Industry (CBI) in April 2004 for example, Tony Blair proclaimed, "We have a long heritage of welcoming those who are genuinely in need of our protection and this must continue" (Blair, 2004). The main purpose of Blair's speech to the CBI however, was to explain and justify new proposals for further controls upon immigration, including the proposal to introduce National Identity Cards as a necessary measure to "clamp down" on asylum seekers who "abuse" the system. Practices associated with controlling asylum were discursively linked in his speech to other paradigms: "illegal immigration", and securing the nation against the potential "extremism and intolerance" of those seeking to reside in Britain. Although successive pieces of legislation had introduced ever-more restrictive measures designed to control the arrival and manage the presence of asylum seekers, both Blair and Howard emphasised during the campaign that serious and pressing "concerns" about asylum were legitimate:

> People know that Britain's immigration and asylum system has broken down. They know that it is chaotic, unfair and out of control. They want politicians to be honest about the problem. And they want clear, fair and practical action to tackle it. For centuries Britain has welcomed people from around the world with open arms. We have a proud tradition of giving refuge to those fleeing persecution (Howard, 2004).

> Concern over asylum and immigration is not about racism. It is about fairness (Blair, 2005).

Further tough measures were necessary to ensure "fairness" the party leaders contended, which, as Blair adamantly argued, should be seen as a thing far removed from "racism". Both "toughness" and "fairness" remained, on different levels and perhaps for different reasons, important to the political strategies of both parties from this time. Yet, in order to occupy and maintain the ground of "fairness" it became increasingly important to disarticulate its meaning from that of particular concrete laws designed to protect the "human rights" of asylum seekers, whilst maintaining some allegiance or sense of attachment to a more general, or universal ideal of human rights. As such, Howard's pride in the tradition of giving refuge did not inhibit his suggestion in 2004 that the HRA should be scrapped—an idea that soon evolved and secured longevity within Conservative policy to replace the HRA with a "British Bill of Rights"[3] (BBC News, 2005b, 2006b, 2011; Cameron, 2006a, 2006b; Morris, 2004). Indeed, as a panacea for a range of "unfair" and/or threatening issues supposed to be facing Britain under New Labour and the HRA (including the habits of traveller communities, unfounded asylum claims and the exploitation of liberties by "extremists"), the British Bill of Rights policy was also positioned as a means to curb the power of judges whose rulings, it was argued, were becoming incompatible with the sovereign will of parliament and were threatening to compromise democratic governance. As I will explore in further detail below, this policy has featured importantly in stories concerned with direct political criticism of judicial power in this area and in the collocation of asylum with terrorism in political and news media discourse as security problems facing the British nation. The focus of political struggle here—to harness the universal content of "fairness" to each party's asylum policy, and to align those policies with the myths of British anti-racism and "proud tradition" on human rights can be seen as an indication of the establishment of a powerful equivalential frontier. This legitimatises the "common sense" exclusion of, and antagonism towards, contemporary human rights law and its implications in discourses surrounding asylum and other issues.

Rather than regarding the statement of Britain's "proud tradition" of humanitarian protection as an anomaly within discourses which overwhelmingly favour the restriction of asylum then, it can instead be seen to perform a necessary structural function. This applies not only to the "regimes of truth" surrounding asylum and the areas with which it may be linked, (such as national security) but also to the *episteme*, or what Laclau and Mouffe term the "social imaginary"—the mythical horizon in relation to which a sense of social order is constituted and "our" identities maintained. The next section will examine how mythical horizons have operated to secure new "common sense" associations with asylum and to legitimate the shifting meaning of human rights in the UK.

Social Myths and Political Conflicts:
Why Empty Signifiers Matter to Asylum Discourse

The concept of hegemony is central to Laclau and Mouffe's conception of the political and the operation of power through discourse. By emphasising the contingency of hegemonic formations and of all social identity we can "start conceiving of ways of developing social possibilities which could not exist if society were considered to be grounded in the will of God, in nature, or whatever there is" (Laclau, 2002, np). However, we still function *as if* our experiences of the world were somehow rationally grounded with reference to some kind of certainty or stable universal truth that is not potentially in flux and subject to re-articulation at any moment since, "the impossibility of a universal ground does not eliminate its need" (Laclau, 1996a, p.47). Discourse theory accounts for this by conceiving universality itself as contingent, the universal being "...both an impossible and necessary object" (Laclau, 2000b, p. 58). Instead of a "ground" guaranteeing social meaning (e.g., the economy in classical Marxism), Laclau and Mouffe refer to universality as a discursively constructed "horizon" in relation to which meaning is partially and temporarily secured. This horizon functions as a myth for the absent fullness of the social.[4] When a myth is particularly successful as such, Laclau and Mouffe refer to it as a "social imaginary"—a construction that "provides the ultimate horizon of meaning and action" in a particular historical and cultural moment (Torfing, 1999, p. 203). For example, the symbols, imagery or rhetoric of the so called, "war on terror", can be seen to have constructed myths, which have "stood in for" the absent fullness of national security. These myths have been constructed in powerful ways through the common narratives about asylum and asylum seekers in the mainstream news media, policy and the speeches of politicians. These will be explored further in the final section of this chapter. The myths through which asylum has been articulated during this period can be seen as elements in a wider discourse of security, and as evidence of the will to reconstruct a *social imaginary* in relation to which a more secure sense of British national identity can be promoted and the power and legitimacy of a vulnerable nation-state sustained.

Because any universalising-ordering system is conceived as a discursive construction that is always incomplete, the universal is always the object of hegemonic struggle around which particular interests compete to attach a certain meaning or sense of coherence. The universal is conceived as an empty place—

an empty signifier which, "can be partially filled in a variety of ways" and for Laclau, "the strategy of this filling is what politics is about" (Laclau, 1996a, p. 59). As the place of the universal, the concept of the empty signifier is "the very condition of politics and political change" and is key to the construction of any discourse as an ostensibly stable, delimited and meaningful structure. In Laclau and Mouffe's terms, "any discourse is constituted as an attempt to dominate the field of discursivity, to arrest the flow of differences, to construct a centre" (Laclau & Mouffe, 1985, p. 112). When empty signifiers are filled by particular contents, they become *nodal points*, "privileged signifiers that fix the meaning of a signifying chain" (Laclau & Mouffe, 1985, p. 112). The role of empty signifiers as nodal points in limiting the signifying chain is essential for the production of meaning, as this "establishes the positions that make predication possible" (Laclau & Mouffe, 1985, p. 112). So, because, for example, a term such as "security" is not in any essential or timeless way fixed to a particular content, in order to forge such a link, "a hegemonic struggle takes place to produce what will ultimately prove to be contingent or transient attachments" to that term, such that the particular social or political aims of conservatives, or of liberals, anti-racists or of feminists for example, could potentially fill or determine its contents (Laclau, 2000c, p. 185). The manner in which empty signifiers secure meaning is not through their attachment to any positive content, but rather because they

> ...name the positive reverse of an experience of historical limitation: "justice", as against a feeling of widespread unfairness; "order", when people are confronted with generalised social disorganisation; "solidarity" in a situation in which antisocial self-interest prevails, and so on (Laclau, 2000c, p. 185).

Any political struggle, according to Laclau, signifies two things in a "contradictory movement"—both its particular demand in relation to other particular demands, and its opposition to the system that it, in common with other demands (in a chain of equivalence), seeks to challenge:

> The function of representing the system as a totality depends, consequently, on the possibility of the equivalential function neatly prevailing over the differential one; but this possibility is simply the result of every single struggle always being already, originally, penetrated by this constitutive ambiguity (Laclau, 1996b, p. 41).

As such, the universal is always contaminated by the particular and vice versa because "the only possible universality is the one constructed through an equivalential chain" (Laclau, 2000a, p. 304). Each unit of signification is seen as "constitutively split" between its particular contents and a universality that exceeds it, each being "the undecidable locus in which both the logic of difference and the logic of equivalence operate" (Laclau, 1996b, p. 39). This means that a range of different political demands may not only signify their particular objectives but also a more universal equivalential objective—to exclude that which would challenge the system within which they are meaningful. This is useful for understanding how hostilities towards asylum seekers might be powerfully linked in their signification to other negative ideas, not due to any a priori rational relationship or natural tie, but contingently, through a universalising logic of equivalence. For example, "national security" functions as an empty signifier through which a universal function is articulated, linking demands to institute ever tighter controls on borders, asylum and immigration policy. But it is also an empty signifier in relation to which other political demands, such as combating crime and terrorism are articulated: each particular demand also signifies a more universal opposition to insecurity. It is thus that a chain of equivalence between demands that have no necessary link can be jointly articulated with asylum as threats to security and/or to the social order. Finally, a system of meaning organised in relation to such a universal principle always presupposes something beyond its limits—an exclusion. Yet the limits of the discourse cannot be represented directly (as there would be nothing to distinguish these as something other than another moment of the system). Instead, the limit is signified through an element that would threaten the system—a necessary but threatening element that Laclau and Mouffe, following Derrida, term "the constitutive outside" (Laclau, 1990, p.17). Because "the system cannot have a positive ground", it is only through this exclusionary function that the system itself can be signified. Exclusion is constitutive of the system, and makes the construction of differential identities possible, but at the same time it also subverts them—its conditions of possibility, but also of its impossibility (Laclau, 1996b). Elsewhere (Moore, 2010) I have examined how these logics have operated in the articulation of asylum in Britain, including the significance of what has been termed the "securitisation of migration" (Bigo, 2001; Bosworth & Guild, 2008; Buonfino, 2004; Clements, 2007; Huysmans, 2000, 2006; Huysmans & Buonfino, 2008; Lohrmann, 2000). In the final section of this chapter, I will trace in more depth how this securitising logic has operated through news media and political discourse to rearticulate the "asylum crisis" as a security threat, seen as a logical consequence of Britain's naïve openness to human rights principles and blind accommodation of what are perhaps now "outmoded" liberal ideals.

Human Rights vs. National Security

According to Buonfino, as "the border between security, terrorism, immigration and social fear has become very thin", securitisation has emerged as the dominant hegemonic discourse type on migration:

> ...motivated by the need for national governments to control influxes, placate media pressures and comfort public opinion against the fear of being swamped by foreigners (Buonfino, 2004, p. 23).

One way in which this "placating" and "comforting" has been manifested in the policy realm is through the development of new institutional arrangements and technologies of control within the immigration and asylum system—for example, the system of asylum seeker detention, electronic tagging and biometric data collection. These measures have themselves become important signifiers in the development and reproduction of a securitising discourse of asylum, contributing to the "commonsense" idea that pre-emptive measures are necessary to control asylum seeking through the restriction and tracking of the movement of asylum seekers, and default suspicion regarding the veracity of their identities and claims[5] (Moore, 2010). In this, there has been a clear emphasis upon physically controlling the arrival of asylum seekers as if they were an invasive force. In the Home Office's proposals for its 2007 Borders Bill, for example, Minister Liam Byrne and Parliamentary Under Secretary of State, Lord Triesman argue:

> Border control can no longer just be a fixed line on a map. Using new technology, particularly biometrics, and new approaches to managing risk and intelligence, we must create a new offshore line of defence, checking individuals as far from the UK as possible and through each stage of their journey. Our aim is to make legitimate travel easier yet prevent those who might cause us harm from travelling here (UKBA, 2007, p. 2)[6].

Through such militaristic metaphors, and armed with "new technology", Byrne and Triesman seek to offer "reassurance" that undesirable migrants will be kept "as far from the UK as possible". Whilst the 2007 Borders Bill did not deal with asylum exclusively, these aims are resonant with established measures and other policy proposals already conceived and instituted in the area of asylum. These include not just biometric surveillance technologies, but also the proposals (from 2003) for the "deterritorialisation" of border controls in the form of Regional Protection Zones (RPZ) and Transit Processing Centres (TPC)— measures designed to deal with asylum claims far beyond the borders of the European Union. Closer to British shores, extra-territorial border controls have involved the relocation of UK immigration personnel to ports across the channel through agreements with northern European countries (Betts, 2003).

As a result of such measures (and others included within the five major acts of Parliament on immigration and asylum passed into British law over the past decade), it is now virtually impossible to travel to British territory "legitimately" as an asylum seeker. As such, it seems almost inescapable that asylum seekers will be positioned within the "those who might cause us harm" category—in respect of which continuous vigilance and pre-emptive action is deemed necessary to protect national security. Although policy constructions such as these seem to present us, as Steve Cohen has argued, with a rather Orwellian paradox, it is nonetheless consistent with the equivalential logic through which asylum has been articulated as a threat, and through which the identity of the nation has been maintained (Cohen, 2006a).

In 2006, the right-of-centre think tank Demos published an essay by David Goodhart, editor of *Prospect* magazine, called *"Progressive Nationalism: Citizenship and the Left"*, in which he posited a "commonsense" equivalence between cultural diversity, asylum and immigration issues and potential social conflict. Despite acknowledging the "relatively calm" response to the 7th July 2005 London bombings, Goodhart's essay argues:

> [I]t is hard to believe that 7/7 will not keep security and identity themes at the forefront of political debate for years to come. The issue of Islamic extremism does unavoidably spill over into the wider debate about immigration and asylum (Goodhart, 2006, p. 11).

One of the ways in which this apparently "unavoidable" spillage was already being articulated, linking asylum with the threat of terrorism, was not through debate surrounding the circumstances of 7/7 itself (none of the perpetrators, of course, were asylum seekers), but through the frequent and sensationalised attention of politicians and the national news media to the activities, provocative rhetoric and backgrounds of controversial figures who first came to Britain as asylum seekers, such as the radical Muslim clerics, Abu Hamza, Omar Bakri

Mohammed and Abu Qatada. In a speech in August 2006, "Achieving lasting peace and security, at home and abroad", Conservative Party leader David Cameron asked, "Why has so little been done to minimise the impact of imams who come to Britain and preach, often with little knowledge or appreciation of British values?" (Cameron, 2006a) This question, ostensibly about the indirect, "societal threat" (Crelinsten, 1998) posed by the immigration of "cultural others" derives its real rhetorical power from an earlier passage in the speech, where Cameron asserts, "we must build the fabric of our own society so we can confront and defeat the twisted ideology that is perverting the minds of the potential terrorists" (Cameron, 2006a: np). Whilst Cameron echoed Goodhart's call that greater attention be paid to the protection and promotion of "British values" as a means to safeguard national security and national identity, Gordon Brown, as UK Prime Minister "in waiting" in 2006, expressed similar sentiments in his calls for a renewed sense of "Britishness" and civic pride in the Union flag. What Goodhart, Cameron and Brown were calling for was a less complicated, less heterogeneous organisation of social space—a clear division (the formation of an equivalential frontier) between "legitimate" social belonging and "dangerous identities" to be excluded as threatening. This consensus on "renewing Britishness" amongst mainstream political elites was not premised upon "British distinctiveness and difference" as a nation in the family of nations, but rather upon an antagonistic relation with those who, it was considered, threatened the existence of a collective British "we". In this, "security" is not positioned as a self-evident and "objective object", but rather seems to function as an, "absent presence", or an "empty signifier", in relation to which a chain of equivalence can be constructed. In respect of the dominant hegemonic, securitising discourse of asylum, this includes the contingent association and partial fixation of a range of discursive elements in a signifying chain, including the joint articulation of asylum with terrorism. My contention is that this securitising discourse, especially during the height of the "asylum crisis", firmly positioned asylum as representing a threat to the security of the law-abiding national majority and created conditions conducive to the politicisation and shifting articulation of human rights as a threat to national security.

As previous empirical research has identified, newspaper coverage of asylum and refugee issues in Britain escalated to unprecedented levels and degrees

Figure 1: Coverage of Asylum in UK Newspapers (reproduced from Moore, 2010, p.139)

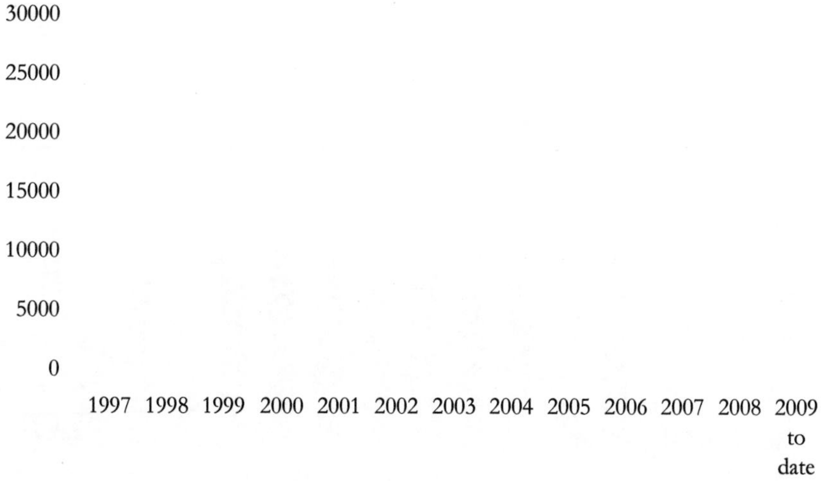

30000

25000

20000

15000

10000

5000

0

1997 1998 1999 2000 2001 2002 2003 2004 2005 2006 2007 2008 2009
to
date

of hostility between 1999 and 2003 (Buchanan, et al., 2003; Moore, 2010). As Figure 1 suggests, the volume of coverage reached its height in 1999, (largely surrounding the reporting of refugee issues in relation to the Kosovo war, the introduction of controversial proposals for the dispersal of asylum seekers away from London and the South East of Britain in the Asylum and Immigration Act 1999 and the reporting of asylum as a growing "problem" facing the UK). However, very high levels of coverage returned with the reporting of the closure of the Red Cross camp at Sangatte, northern France from the second half of 2001–2002 through which a supposed "asylum crisis" was constructed, and the General Election campaign of 2001, with coverage again reaching a peak in 2003 (Moore, 2010). Although a comprehensive quantitative analysis of newspaper coverage of asylum and refugee issues during this period is not my main purpose here, it is salient to highlight a particular correlation between this pattern of the general coverage and that of a small but significant subset of it. Figure 2 illustrates the volume and distribution of UK national newspaper coverage that in some way collocates asylum and refugee issues with terrorism. Whilst "terrorism" as an element of asylum and refugee coverage was particularly evident in the years of the terrorist attacks of 9/11 and 7/7, it also appears to reach a peak during 2003—the height of asylum coverage under New Labour.

Figure 2: Number of Articles Collocating Asylum Seekers or Refugees with Terrorism[7]

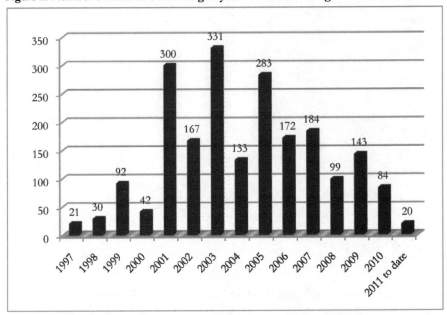

An extraordinary year in British politics, a number of asylum and national security related issues did in fact hit the headlines in 2003.

In February 2003, somewhat to the surprise of his Ministers, Prime Minister, Tony Blair promised to halve the number of asylum seekers arriving in Britain by September (a seemingly arbitrary target, later relegated to a "long-term goal") (Blair, 2003). This was also a year in which controlling the arrival and deportation of foreign nationals was highly politicised including proposals for substantive new asylum and anti-terrorism laws.[8] As highlights of the Queen's speech 2003, asylum and terrorism often featured jointly in newspaper headlines, as for example in, "WIDER POWERS ON TERRORISM AND ASYLUM." (*The Times*, 24th November 2003) Indeed, asylum and terrorism were linked in the reporting of a range of government and other political proposals, campaigns and diplomatic events. For example, a meeting of Ministers in Rome in September to discuss immigration and terrorism generated headlines such as: "TRAFFIC IN PEOPLE BANKROLLING AL QAEDA" (*Daily Mail*, 8th September 2003), while in the same month, the Association of Chief Police Officers' (ACPO) calls for a new border force to combat terrorism and illegal immigration linked "extremists" with "asylum seekers" in some reports, as for example:

> Plans have been drawn up to station thousands of officers at key airports and seaports to secure the country's "porous" frontiers from the growing threat of extremists and asylum seekers (*Daily Express*, 29th September 2003).

The articulation of such an equivalential frontier between "our security" and a range of threatening "others" including asylum seekers and terrorists, was also articulated in the shifting rationale for the introduction of National Identity Cards as, for example, reflected in one letter to *The Sun*: "their introduction will aid the fight against benefit cheats, villains, bogus asylum seekers and terrorists" (*The Sun*, 17th November 2003). Terrorism and asylum were linked more explicitly in some more specific stories as, for example, in the headline: "TERROR CHARGES DENIED BY ASYLUM-SEEKER" (*The Times*, 11th November 2003) reporting the charging of Algerian, Abbas Boutrab for offences under the Terrorism Act 2000 in Northern Ireland—a story in which the relevance of his status as an asylum seeker was neither justified nor explained. However, much speculation also featured in other coverage about the possibilities that asylum would provide a route into Britain for would-be terrorists. Ostensibly holding the government to account in suggesting that Britain's border security remained too lax in this area, the *Daily Mail* for example, conducted its own "under cover" investigation to draw attention to these supposedly new dimensions of "asylum crisis". "AN OPEN DOOR FOR CRIME AND TERROR" claims:

> TODAY, the Mail reveals in chilling detail the vulnerability of a nation that seems to have given up even trying to protect itself. Having already lost control of our own borders in an asylum crisis going from bad to worse, Britain is now exposed as wide open to any terrorist, gangster, health "tourist" or welfare fraudster (*Daily Mail*, 19th August, 2003).

Whilst the article claims to demonstrate the ease with which a false identity might be obtained, and speculates upon the range of threatening or criminal activities that might be associated with this, it does not provide any evidence to support the general link between asylum, crime and terror it suggests. However, such a general association is also repeated in the *Daily Mail*'s, sympathetic reporting of the Shadow Home Secretary, Oliver Letwin's speech to the 2003 Conservative Party conference, noting that:

In January Mr Letwin called for all asylum seekers to be kept on prison ships. The idea then was that they would be allowed to enter Britain once the security services had established that they were not terrorists (*Daily Mail,* 8th October 2003).

Elsewhere, such a "commonsense" association between asylum seeking and terrorist motives was linked with the idea that human rights concerns were responsible for a "failure" to tighten things up. For example, in "THE DEADLY SILENCE", Max Hastings provocatively asks:

So why does the Government continue to admit legal immigrants in increasing numbers and to make no serious effort to exclude illegal immigrants and asylum seekers? First, on the issue of asylum seekers, ministers perceive themselves bowing to the inevitable. The physical difficulties of keeping them out are enormous because Britain has abandoned effective frontier controls. The Government absolutely refuses to contemplate abrogating the half-century old human rights conventions as a preliminary to effective action. These are failures for which ministers should be harshly judged if or when a major terrorist atrocity takes place in Britain. Thanks to a reckless abdication of responsibility, the authorities no longer possess reliable knowledge of movements across our borders by terrorists, never mind immigrants (*Daily Mail,* 6th December 2003).

Throughout 2003, controversies surrounding the detention without charge of foreign national suspects under the 2001 Anti-Terrorism, Crime and Security Act (which had required Britain to opt out of article 5 of the ECHR), and Britain's inability to deport terrorism suspects to countries where they could face torture or persecution rumbled on (Amnesty International, 2003). Tony Blair, under intense pressure to secure credibility for his foreign policy decisions in the face of massive public protest against the UK/US invasion of Iraq and growing concerns about the reactionary direction of government policies, proclaimed to the Labour Party conference that he had "no reverse gear" (BBC News, 2003a). The right wing press implored the government to do more, railing against the strictures of the ECHR and calling its incorporation into UK law in the HRA a mistake. For example, campaigning comment pieces in the *Daily Mail* and *Daily Express* bemoaned, "a tidal wave of judicial activism" compromising the government's ability to implement, "commonsense" policies. Justice Collins was reported by the *Daily Mail* to be, "waging what amounts to a one-man battle against David Blunkett's attempts to tighten up our asylum rules":

Twice in seven years, he has used the law in an attempt to prevent the Government denying benefits to some asylum seekers. He also ruled that locking up asylum seekers breached their human rights, and that the Government couldn't detain foreigners suspected of belonging to Al Qaeda (*Daily Mail*, 2nd October 2003).

The increasing focus upon the HRA as an impediment to fighting terrorism was also often orientated around reporting the activities of "Muslim extremists", especially following the widely reported police and intelligence service raids on London's Finsbury Park mosque and a flat in Wood Green, North London. This was a location in the suspected "Ricin plot" to poison commuters on the London Underground where six Algerian men were arrested in January 2003. (BBC News, 2003b) Although it was later revealed that no Ricin as such had been recovered from the flat, and all but one of the suspects were eventually either not charged or acquitted of any involvement in terrorism, the Ricin story, as Fekete argues, "developed a life of its own", speculatively linked in reports of other suspected terror plots in Ireland, France and Spain in 2003-4 (Fekete, 2004). Whilst it is not my aim to establish the "truth" or otherwise of the Ricin plot, how the reporting of this story jointly articulated terrorism with asylum *as* truth, and the rhetorical force of this within contemporary debates about human rights is important. For example, in a front page splash, "POISON SUSPECTS WERE ASYLUM SEEKERS" the *Daily Mail* reported:

At least three of the ricin terror suspects were asylum-seekers living on benefits, it was revealed last night...The disclosures underlined fears that the country's overloaded asylum system is being exploited by terror groups (*Daily Mail*, 9th January 2003).

The Ricin story formed part of a wider discourse, which positioned the UK, and particularly London, as a "soft touch" and "safe haven" for terrorists—an idea which seemed both to borrow from the lexicon of dominant "asylum crisis" discourse and to more directly point a finger of suspicion at asylum seekers. This representation of the UK was also powerfully signified by the use of the term, "Londonistan", which linked the Ricin story to other news narratives warning of threats posed by radical clerics and other terrorist suspects, as in the following headlines:

THE MENACE IN OUR MIDST; WITH POISON SUSPECTS EXPOSED AS ASYLUM SEEKERS GIVEN HOUSING BENEFITS BY BRITAIN, NO WONDER THE FRENCH CALL OUR CAPITAL "LONDONISTAN" (*Daily Mail*, 9th January 2003)

FRENCH FURIOUS AT LONDON'S LAX SECURITY SAYS OUR MAN IN PARIS; SHOCK AS BLAIR'S FAVOURITE ENVOY LABEL'S BRITAIN "A SAFE HAVEN FOR TERRORISTS" (*Sunday Express*, 12th January 2003)

"REFUGE FOR TERROR" (*Daily Mail*, 22nd May 2003)

The purported arrival in Britain of terrorism suspects as asylum seekers was represented sardonically, positioning the element of asylum as an additional affront to British sensibilities, and/or as a predictable consequence of state failures to address the asylum problem. In "REFUGE FOR TERROR", for example, the *Daily Mail* comments:

> Well might exasperated foreign security services refer to London as "Londonistan". For the dossier David Blunkett has presented to a Special Immigration Appeals Commission amply confirms that this country is a haven for those who encourage, finance, plan and execute terrorist atrocities. It reveals that radical Moslems have played key roles in 11 major terrorist operations in the past eight years. And all too many have arrived as surprise, surprise asylum seekers. Individuals like the radical Islamic cleric Abu Qatada, who, as the Mail reported yesterday, is identified in the dossier as a leader of world terrorism (*Daily Mail*, 22nd May 2003).

Similarly, upon the arrest of those suspected of terrorism charges in the Ricin case, columnist Richard Littlejohn observes:

> So no surprises there, then. At least three of the terror suspects arrested in London this week turn out to be "asylum seekers" living on benefit. Most of the seven detained are believed to have entered the country on false papers…Two of them claim to be 17, although police are convinced they much older. This is a fairly common trick among "asylum seekers" since under-18s get in with no questions asked and immediately qualify for the top rate of handout…Is it any wonder our capital city is known internationally as Londonistan?…How can we be sure some of those pouring through the Chunnel aren't al-Qa'ida homicide bombers hell-bent on mass slaughter in Britain? Answer: We can't. The seven men arrested this week are only the tip of the poisoned umbrella. How long before an Algerian nail bomb goes off on the Tube? When it happens the Men in Wigs, the Government, the DSS, the Guardianistas, Islington Council and the rest of the legally-aided "human rights" lobby will all have blood on their hands (*The Sun*, 10th January 2003).[9]

Other articles introduced "Londonistan" in reporting the criticisms of Sir John Holmes, Ambassador to France, of the UK's anti-terrorism policies. Supposedly exposed as having been too careless or soft on Algerian terror suspects in light of the Ricin arrests, a *Sunday Express* article for example, claims this had been very damaging to UK-France relations—a neat circularity of argument positioning asylum as a cause and casualty of the Londonistan problem:

> ...the Government's failure to extradite a terrorist suspect to France has poisoned relations and made it impossible for him to do his job. He says the lack of trust has torpedoed cooperation to tackle asylum seekers or persuade French officials to support an attack on Iraq (*Sunday Express,* 12th January 2003).

It is perhaps testament to the sedimentation of the discourse at this time, that even when British nationals were reported as the terror suspects, as for example, in the Tel Aviv bombings reported in the *Daily Mail* in May 2003, asylum seekers were mentioned as if a linked element of the same problem. "EMPTY WORDS ON FIGHTING TERROR" argues:

> Is it any wonder that the Israelis have decided that they simply cannot rely on Britain to match its words about fighting international terrorism with tough and effective action? As over asylum seekers, the Government comes up with ideas for getting to grips with this danger. But how much faith can the public have in such moves, when the crucial political will to ensure that they produce results is so clearly lacking? (*Daily Mail,* 6th May 2003)

While each of these articles implied a clear link between asylum seeking and a terrorist threat, I am not, of course, arguing that any made direct claims that all asylum seekers *are* terrorists. However, I would argue that a phrase such as "the Home Secretary declares open house to so-called asylum seekers—including numerous potential terrorists" (*The Express,* 21st November 2003) does suggest a generalising assumption—that the possibility asylum seekers would be terrorists should not be unexpected—and that such an assumption is an important element of the discourse. Asylum seekers are plausibly positioned as potentially terrorists, but, moreover, as sharing something universal in their antagonistic relation to British interests. In the frontier discursively constructed between those who would safeguard the security of the UK, and those who would threaten it, a clear chain of equivalence is drawn in this coverage which links terrorism and asylum seeking and human rights as antagonistic to UK interests. These characteristics of asylum coverage would suggest that the "commonsense" collocation of asylum with a security threat served a powerful political purpose during this period, and may well have become sedimented within the dominant asylum discourse in the UK. This idea seems very plausible in view of more recent coverage featuring asylum alongside the idea of "Londonistan" in Wikileaked US diplomatic cables. In "WIKILEAKS: WHITEHALL IGNORED WARNINGS ABOUT "LONDONISTAN" DANGER", Christopher Hope reports:

> A leaked US diplomatic cable, sent five days after the July 7 bombings, said Britain ignored repeated warnings to stop granting asylum to Islamic extremists wanted in other countries for terrorism offences (*Daily Telegraph*, 26th April 2011).

The assumptions of the author of the cable, a military attaché to the Algerian Embassy, are not questioned in terms of their rationale or diplomatic context. Rather, they are reproduced unproblematically in the reporting of the leaked cable. Perhaps this lack of critical enquiry is in part influenced by something about Wikileaks journalism in general rather than asylum coverage in particular. However, what is clear is that "Londonistan" as a construct linking asylum and the threat of terrorism is reproduced uncritically in this article—a powerful condensation of complex assumptions and interwoven discourses serving to reinforce stigmatising ideas about asylum seekers.

Conclusion

The development of a perceived "asylum crisis" in the hostile coverage of some sections of the tabloid press under New Labour has not simply been a journalistic construction. The "asylum crisis" discourse has been fuelled by the development of ever more restrictive asylum and immigration policies and "tough" political rhetoric and practices surrounding asylum and refugee issues in Britain from the late 1990s. Especially post 9/11, asylum discourse has been conditioned by a social imaginary in which international terrorism and national security became pre-eminent concerns. In this context, the meaning of asylum for Britain and of human rights issues more generally was opened up to new discursive possibilities, as an equivalential frontier organised around the nodal point "security" was articulated through securitising political and news narratives. This provided, at least in part, the conditions in which asylum could be articulated, not just as a threat to the social order but through an equivalential relation to "terrorism" and "extremism", as a threat to national security. In this shift in meaning, the object of "human rights" has also played an important part. Human rights has not just been dislocated from its previously, fairly stable, universal content (the name of justice in the face of injustice) in mainstream political discourse. Rather, human rights has been re-politicised in its particular contents and rearticulated primarily as a "failed", or "naïve" liberal policy responsible for social and national vulnerabilities, insecurities and potential conflicts over sovereignty. This has not stopped mainstream politicians from continuing to claim a "proud history" of human rights for British national identity. Yet this contradiction has not attracted the critical scrutiny of the national press. Instead, it has been reproduced in news discourse as it has in the speeches of politicians, playing a necessary structural function within securitising discourses, and adding a melancholic rhetorical element to the articulation of asylum and human rights as antagonistic to the national interest.

Although the analysis above has highlighted the "Ricin terror plot" as one notable example, there have been a number of other stories during this period that also have jointly articulated asylum with terrorism and through which human rights have been called into question. Each suggest that securitising discourses on asylum have become very powerful, sedimented formations, which function *as if* they were natural and the commonsense or normative order of things in this area. But it is also important to note that securitising discourses are nonetheless unstable entities constituted through a relation between shifting logics of equivalence and difference contingently organised around the nodal point of security. The conditions of possibility for the formation or shift in such discourses clearly depend upon the wider forces determining this structure, but from a discourse theoretical perspective, there is at least the potential to begin to think how a more progressive set of ideas surrounding asylum might become possible.

Notes

1. A range of stigmatising synonyms, including: "Illegals", "asylum cheats", "clandestines", "undesirable migrants", and "would-be asylum seekers", also figured amongst the terms deployed to label asylum seekers and refugees during this period—imagined identities which always, of course stood in contrast to the mythical, unobtainable and always already deferred identity of those "desirable" asylum seekers who were "honest" or "genuine refugees", deserving of our protection.

2. The United Nations International Convention on the Elimination of All forms of Ra-

cial Discrimination requires signatory states to report every three years. In 2001, the response to the UK's submission noted the UK government's asylum dispersal system with concern as follows: 'The Committee expresses concern that the dispersal system may hamper the access of asylum-seekers to expert legal and other necessary services, i.e., health and education. It recommends that the State party implement a strategy ensuring that asylum-seekers have access to essential services and that their basic rights are protected.' (UNCERD, 2001)

3. Cameron asserted: "I believe it is wrong to undermine public safety—and indeed public confidence in the concept of human rights—by allowing highly dangerous criminals and terrorists to trump the rights of the people of Britain to live in security and peace". His case for the introduction of a British Bill of Rights to solve the perceived problems of the HRA was given a "B-" by his ex-Oxford University PPE professor. (Cameron, 2006a, p.11)

4. Following Derrida, any structure or system, including the structure of social order, is understood as necessarily unstable and incomplete. (Derrida, 1974)

5. Biometric identity management, for example, was first agreed EU level in 1991 and has been operational since 2000 in the form of "EURODAC", a database of fingerprints of all asylum seekers entering the EU which allows member states access to shared information about asylum claimants in order to cross check claims against records of asylum applications. Such developments, involving persons with no ordinary rights as citizens, have, it seems, served as a "testing ground" for new technologies and facilitated the institutionalisation of identity management systems. This, I contend, has served to render as "common sense" political rationales for the presence of such measures in the general armoury of state power, as evidenced in the proposals to introduce a National Identity Register in the UK.

6. So favoured is this phrase that it is reproduced in direct quotation in the 2008 white paper, "A Strong New Force at the Border" (UKBA, 2008, p. 6).

7. Data retrieved from the Nexis database, 15th May 2011 using the search terms: asylum seekers or refugees (major mentions) AND terroris! (major mentions) AND UK or Britain (major mentions). The following UK national newspapers included in the search: *Times, Sunday Times, Telegraph, Sunday Telegraph, Guardian, Observer, Independent, Independent on Sunday, Sun, News of the World, Mirror, Sunday Mirror, Daily Star, People, Daily Mail, Mail on Sunday, Express, Sunday Express.* Newswires were excluded. Duplicates were excluded on the basis of moderate similarity.

8. The Asylum and Immigration (treatment of Claimants etc.) Bill and Civil Contingencies Bill were proposed in the Queen's speech 2003, alongside draft proposals for an ID cards Bill.

9. Several articles, including this example, sought to contextualise and explain Ricin as a lethal chemical with reference to Georgi Markov—a Bulgarian political dissident assassinated in 1978 by his country's secret service with a Ricin pellet administered from an adapted umbrella.

Section Two—Crisis Reporting and the Representation of Migration

The chapters presented in section two explore the political significance and complexities of news media representations of contemporary global migration issues. Collectively dealing with migration reporting in a wide range of transnational, national and localised political and cultural contexts, the chapters each offer a distinctive critical analysis of journalistic representations of migration. They deal with a range of concerns including how news values, presuppositions and regular patterns of coverage regularly inform and shape migration news stories and the image or stereotypes surrounding certain categories of migrant. They also interrogate how framing, narrative or discursive strategies in migration reporting serve to condition and/or are conditioned by the social "truths", stereotypes or cultural norms that prevail within particular national, international or transnational publics and their social contexts.

Otto Santa Ana's chapter focuses upon the politics and news media representations of unauthorised immigrant workers in the United States. Santa Ana adopts a longitudinal approach in his analysis, reflecting upon the findings of a series of important empirical media content studies of migration in US broadcast and print news. The chapter explores how the images of irregular migrants and immigration have been shaped, especially at key moments of heightened political attention during protest events and proposals for legal reform, closely examining the conceptual metaphors through which immigrants and immigration have been depicted. Santa Ana's chapter strikingly demonstrates how the news media has rearticulated a racialised "animus" towards unauthorised immigrants since the 1970s, and offers a compelling argument that certain linguistic forms in migration reporting have enabled and restricted possibilities for political expression, legitimating a dominant view of immigrants and immigration as threatening and marginalising potentially opposing or divergent views.

The propensity of mainstream news media narratives to restrict the available possibilities of meaning in migration stories is also a central concern of Carol Farbotko's critical examination of "climate refugee" discourse. Taking as her focus reports surrounding rising sea levels in the Pacific islands region, Farbotko explores how self-referential assumptions about the "environmental crisis" inform the dominant narratives of "climate migration" in the journalism of wealthy industrial nations. The chapter demonstrates how such constructs and assumptions about "climate migrants" are radically challenged by the situated knowledges of Pacific island cultures, which offer very different understandings of migration and radically alternative stories about the relationship of journeying or voyaging Islanders to the sea. Climate migration, Farbotko argues, is a "contested discursive terrain", in which the idea of a "climate refugee crisis", as it is constructed by journalists in the West, may not necessarily represent the contemporary political concerns or interests of Islanders at all well or fairly, failing to consider the complexities of alternative cultural narratives and truths about human relationships to the environment, the sea and the meaning of migration.

Whilst Farbotko's argument draws attention to the political issues at stake when a subject of international geo-political significance such as the environment is linked with migration in the news, the relation between migration and global power relations is a central concern of Yan Wu, Xiangqin Zeng and Xiaoying Liu's chapter exploring the news framing of Chinese irregular migration to Europe. In their systematic content analysis of a decade of coverage in a Chinese-language national newspaper, the *Global Times*, Wu et al. explore how irregular migration is primarily reported in economic terms that emphasise the attractive opportunities encouraging migration to OECD countries and the positive qualities of entrepreneurialism and economic contribution of Chinese migrants. The globalisation of the world economy and economic liberalisation in China may mean that regular migration from a professional and more globally mobile Chinese population offers alternative news narratives focused upon the economic benefits of Chinese migration to and from Europe. Yet, Wu et al. contend, the highly restrictive migration policies of receiving countries also provide an important context—an important "ambivalence" surrounding issues of illegality in the reporting of economic migration in the *Global Times* (in stark contrast, of course, to the "major threat" discourses associated with smuggling and criminal gangs identified in the news media of European host countries). Ambivalence is also playing an important role in the coverage of migration and human rights issues, depending upon the political context.

Human rights are also a key concern in Jelena Bjelica's chapter, which critically explores the representation of human trafficking in the Serbian press. The chapter's feminist analysis critically scrutinises how the dramatic changes in the political context of Serbia and liberalisation of an authoritarian regime in recent years has wrought some important changes in the journalism industry. However, Bjelica's analysis of the representation of human trafficking demonstrates that certain norms and values, especially surrounding gender and security vis-à-vis Kosovo and Albanians, remain consistent with the politics of the old order, and continue to condition journalistic discursive practices in the Serbian press in highly problematic ways. In the reporting of human trafficking, Bjelica argues, victims "rarely have a voice" and moreover may even be stereotyped by misogynistic and stigmatising assumptions such that "trafficking as a crime or abuse of human rights is not positioned seriously as a humanitarian problem facing vulnerable people, and which needs to be addressed as such". This gendered discourse, the chapter contends, is deeply connected to wider prevailing issues of national political concern—organised crime and visa liberalisation—that are constructed as key threats to the security of the Serbian nation and primarily associated with Kosovo and ethnic Albanian populations in the region.

In the final chapter of the section, Xinji Jiang explores how Chinese migration to the UK has been represented in the British press, with a particular focus upon the tragic loss of life of 58 Fujianese migrants who were discovered having suffocated in the back of a container lorry en route to Dover, England, in June 2000. The chapter contrasts the intense coverage of this traumatic incident, together with that of a second tragedy, which was later to happen involving Fujianese migrant cockle pickers in Morecambe Bay in the north of England, with the historically low profile of Chinese migration in the British press. It is likely that these incidents contributed significantly to pressures for the introduction of new government policy in the area of asylum and immigration, most notably the Gangmasters (Licensing) Act 2004. Dover raised public awareness of Fujianese migration in the UK, however, Jiang contends, the press representation of "snakehead" migrant smuggler gangs from China both drew upon existing negative narratives and stereotypes surrounding asylum seekers in general in the UK, and, in the absence of alternative social knowledge about Chinese migration, linked with earlier threatening myths representing "dangerous Chinese Triad gangs" constituted in part through entertainment genres. Jiang's analysis illustrates that the economic threat of Chinese migrants as "a source of cheap and docile labour who might undermine the livelihood of their white contemporaries" combined with both contemporary political anxieties about migration, and a focus upon illegality in the coverage of the Dover incident reproduces long-standing myths about Chinese organised crime.

CHAPTER FIVE

U.S. Crisis Reporting on Mass Protests and the Depiction of Immigrants in the 40 Years after the Kerner Commission Report

Otto Santa Ana

US news rarely reports on mass demonstrations unless they are both sizeable and fall on a slow news day, but it does not fail to report on domestic demonstrations when blood is shed. In this country it is one kind of domestic crisis reporting. I will begin and end this chapter by discussing the news reporting about two such protests. The first is drawn from a well-known national study of the news reporting on a violent urban uprising that occurred in 1967 in Detroit, Michigan. I compare it to the television news reporting of a blood-spattered political rally in 2007 in Los Angeles. However, the greater part of this chapter is devoted to a review of the changes in U.S. news representation of immigrants and immigration policy issues over this forty-year period.

The 1968 Report on U.S. Crisis Reporting

During the summer months of the 1960s, the U.S. witnessed spontaneous outbreaks of mass violence in inner city neighbourhoods, as African Americans pushed back against the unjust police treatment that they had endured for generations. The summers of the sixties witnessed riots in the African American sections of major cities, including a 1965 Los Angeles uprising, one in Chicago in 1966, and several major disturbances in 1967, including one in Newark, New Jersey.

The 1967 riots in Detroit, Michigan, began on a hot summer night, after a police raid on an unlicensed drinking and gambling club, *the blind pig*.[1] Police arrested 82 people while 200 people voiced indignation. At 5 a.m. an empty bottle was thrown at a police car. Word spread that police were using excessive force, the crowd swelled and window smashing and looting began. The first radio reports, which in hindsight "left the impression that the scene was worse than it really was during the earlier hours," were broadcast around 8 a.m., and the first television report at 2 p.m.: "Violence broke out early this morning when police raided a West Side blind pig. A police lieutenant was hit with a rock, and one man was stabbed, as hundreds brawled for five hours." Another station falsely reported that an officer was killed (Singer, 1970, p. 240). The July 23rd police confrontation with African Americans on the city's Near West Side quickly escalated to a five-day urban conflagration. It was among the deadliest and most destructive riots in U.S. history. The state governor finally called in the National Guard and President Johnson sent in Army troops to restore order. Forty-three people died and over 2000 buildings were destroyed. News media extensively covered the events—also through the novelty of live television.

At the time Detroit was regarded as a positive exemplar of U.S. race relations. The city had a large and prosperous black middle class. These were the boom times of the auto industry, which provided high wages for its many black workers. Moreover Detroit had a new mayor who had recently restructured the police department. Additionally, African Americans had significant political representation: including two congressmen (half the then-total black representation in U.S. Congress); judges; representation on the city's board of education; on the housing commission; and several representatives in the state legislature. Still, these features of civic life did not change the daily interaction of ordinary inner-city people of colour with major American institutions.

President Johnson was upset by the riots and sought a deeper understanding of their causes. The president believed communist agitators had sparked the violence in the poorest African American urban neighbourhoods. He convened the National Advisory Commission on Civil Disorders, generally known as the Kerner Commission, giving it carte blanche and full authority to reveal the causes and to make recommendations.

With bracing honesty, the Commission reported in 1968 that the urban violence expressed the profound frustration of inner-city blacks with U.S. institutions, and its source was the deeply embedded structural racism of U.S. society. The report's most famous passage warned that the United States was "moving toward two societies, one black, one white—separate and unequal." The Commission marshalled evidence on an array of problems that plagued African Americans, including not only overt personal and institutional discrimination but also chronic poverty, high unemployment, poor schools, inadequate housing, lack of access to health care, and systematic police bias and brutality. The Commission recommended sweeping federal initiatives directed at improving educational and employment opportunities, public services, and housing in black urban neighbourhoods and called for a "national system of income sup-plementation." By 1968, however, Richard Nixon rode a conservative white backlash to the presidency, which insured that the Commission recommendations would be ignored.

The Commission focused its attention on the role of mass media news coverage of the violence. It pointedly asked, "What effect do the mass media have on the riots?" (p. 201), and concluded that "Despite instances of sensationalism, inaccuracy and distortion, newspapers, radio and television tried on the whole to give a balanced, factual account of the 1967 disturbances." The operative word was "try".

More specific and disheartening findings included: "Elements of the news media failed to portray accurately the scale and character of the violence that occurred. The overall effect was an exaggeration of both mood and event" and "Important segments of the media failed to report adequately on the causes and consequences of civil disorders and on the underlying problems of race relations. They have not communicated to the majority of their audience—which is White—a sense of the degradation, misery, and hopelessness of life in the ghetto" (p. 910). Forty years later we are now in a position to evaluate how U.S. news media have changed. We will return to the reporting on mass demonstrations in the final sections of this chapter, but now turn to the U.S. news media representations of immigrants over the past forty years.

U.S. Latino Immigration

Since 1967, we have witnessed the growth of an industrious population, un-authorised immigrant workers, and in my opinion the focus of greatest social animus in the nation has shifted from African Americans to unauthorised immigrant workers. Today U.S. nativists unfairly blame these immigrants as the cause (rather than an effect) of the nation's precarious domestic economy. Xenophobes are unmoved by explanations citing globalisation as the source of major demographic movement across the planet. Instead, they call for a quick solution to the nation's economic problems by getting rid of America's most vulnerable worker. I will review studies about the news media's reporting on immigrants since the time of the Kerner Commission, beginning with a content analysis of the print news of the 1970s, a study of one representative newspaper's coverage of an anti-immigrant period in the 1990s, and two studies about the news media's coverage of the current period. The first 21st-century study is a comparative study of national newspapers reporting on the day after the historic 2006 May Day marches, and the second is a study of network television news reporting by examining U.S. television news stories about a May Day 2007 immigration rights demonstration in Los Angeles.

U.S. textbooks extol the United States as a nation built by immigrants. However, while students are steeped in the pageantry of U.S. history, they seldom learn to appreciate the depth of its reprehensible acts and persistent inequities. A case in point is the history of Mexican-Americans. For most university students, it is news that in 1846, when President James Polk initiated the U.S./Mexican War, between 75,000 and 100,000 Mexicans were already living in the Southwest (Gutiérrez, 1995, p. 13), including my father's family.

The virulent racism with which 19th-century white Americans elevated themselves above all other people also infected relations with Mexicans, leading to the view that the Southwest was rightfully granted to white America, and that its Mexican residents comprised a contemptible mongrel breed that deserved little respect.[2] Today's Americans generally are not cognisant that the Mexican War led to the Treaty of Guadalupe Hidalgo, which guaranteed language, property, and citizenship rights to the Spanish-speaking residents of this territory (Griswold de Castillo, 1990). Moreover, from 1848 through the 20th century, the new border between Mexico and the United States was an arbitrary restriction on thousands of years of free movement of people north and south (Vélez-Ibánez, 1997). Thus it is painful to witness the continuing mistreatment of long-established residents of the historical lands of Mexico. In the 21st century Mexican and other Latin American immigrants have looked for work and settled across the United States, from California north to Alaska, and east to New York and Georgia.

In spite of its overwhelmingly immigrant origin and its self-satisfied adulation of the immigrants' contribution to its strength and wealth, the United States maintains a Janus-faced attitude of self-interest toward immigrants. When the country is in the growth part of the economic cycle, cheap labour is at a premium. During these times, U.S. commerce promotes the virtues of America, and its "American Dream" of the unbounded opportunity for the hardest worker. When the native-born Americans scorn essential labour, workers from other countries are recruited for the lowest-paid and least-desirable work. The immigrants come in great numbers, dream the Dream, do the work, and honour their end of the bargain. For example, from 1880 to 1920 with a population much less than 100 million the United States accepted 24 million immigrants (Brownstein & Simon, 1993).

However, as the economic cycle wanes, the second face is manifest toward the immigrants and their children. Then the immigrant is maligned as a menace. Evidence for this attitude abounds in U.S. history. For example, between 1921 and 1924 Congress set up a restrictive immigration quota system that disfavoured immigrants from Eastern and Southern Europe as well as Asia and Latin America (Higham, 1995). These attitudes have also turned punitive. Between 1929 and 1935, authorities mobilised the U.S. military to force the repatriation of 500,000 Mexican immigrants and their US-born children (Hoffman, 1974, p. 126), including my mother. The economic cycle and its concomitant binary attitude toward immigrants continue even in the present economic recession and its accompanying anti-Latino, anti-immigrant expression throughout the nation, and particularly in Arizona in 2010. We turn now to the major content analyses that reveal the nation's views of immigrants in the past forty years.

10 Years after Kerner

Celestino Fernández and Lawrence Pedroza (1982) comprehensively studied major corpora of both national and regional newspapers appearing over a seven-year period (1972–1978). They conducted a traditional journalistic content analysis, evaluating 949 articles dealing with unauthorized Mexican immigration published in four newspapers: *Los Angeles Times, New York Times, Washington Post,* and *Arizona Daily Star.* This was an immense amount of work in the days before computer-assisted scholarship, but it was not the first. Felix Gutiérrez (1987) based his earlier studies on a random sample of articles (n=114).[3]

Fernández and Pedroza (1982) studied many different kinds of journalistic content. For example they found that non-Latinos wrote 50% of these articles, 40% did not include a byline, and Spanish-surnamed individuals wrote a mere 10% of the articles. Of those with a byline, non-Latinos wrote 83% and Spanish-surnamed reporters wrote only 17% of the total. One author, Frank del Olmo of the *Los Angeles Times,* wrote most of the latter, which is a measure of the paucity of coverage.

Fernández and Pedroza noted that the number of articles about unauthorised Mexican immigrants increased during the 1970s, but underlined that the pieces were short, and while readers saw reference to immigrants more often, Fernández and Pedroza suggested that they "were not becoming more informed" (p. 13). Fernández and Pedroza also reported on other content-analytic measures, such as article heading and sources. They noted that the federal Immigration and Naturalization Service (INS) made up 50% of the sources. In contrast, scholars were the source of journalistic information only 3% of the time. Overall 8% of these sources tended to express positive opinions, while 75% registered negative opinions about unauthorised immigrants. Fernández and Pedroza noted an increase in the proportion of unsympathetic sources, and a decrease in the number of sympathetic informants through 1974. They concluded from their thorough study that Spanish-surnamed reporters drew from a "wider and more balanced range of sources" than non-Latino writers (p. 16).

The central issue in this chapter is the historical representation of politicised concepts such as IMMIGRANT.[4] Fernández and Pedroza stated that the term *wetback* had "widely been used as a derogatory label prior to 1970" (p. 13). In contrast, in the 1972–1978 period, they witnessed a steady decrease in the number of newspaper articles using this term. In 1972 it made up 15% of references, while in 1978, it was used only 4% of the time. Finally, Fernández and Pedroza noted that news writers rarely named the unauthorised immigrants whom they mentioned in their articles.

During the 1970s, Fernández and Pedroza noted that alternative, less derogatory terms such as *undocumented workers* and *undocumented immigrants* gained wide acceptance in the social science research literature. However, the newspapers used *undocumented* as an adjective only 12% of the time. The *Los Angeles Times*, which accounted for the largest number of articles and most Latino bylines, published 52% of all the articles that used the term *undocumented*. Again, this might be due to a single Latino news writer. By comparison, this term appeared in only 10% of references in the *Washington Post*. Fernández and Pedroza noted an increase in its use, from 2% of the articles published nationally in 1972, to 22% by 1978. However, Fernández and Pedroza state that almost 80% of newspaper references were to *illegal alien*, and the second most common term, at 56%, was *alien*. The use of the combination term, *illegal alien*, was fairly constant over the seven-year study, while the use of the single word, *alien*, decreased accordingly.

In their work Fernández and Pedroza made three evaluative terminological groupings for immigrant representation. The nouns *wetback, alien,* and the use of *illegal* as a noun were the most "distant" negative identifiers. They found negative terms in 83% of the articles, while the positive terms, such as the adjective *undocumented* appeared in 6% of their huge corpus. The third group appeared in 11% of the articles included *illegal immigrant* and *illegal migrant.* In 1982, Fernández and Pedroza called these terms "neutral". Today I would not accept this judgment, on the grounds of cognitive metaphor theory (Lakoff & Johnson, 1999).

Fernández and Pedroza found other use patterns for these evaluative references: non-bylined articles used derogatory terms approximately 90% of the time; and among bylined articles, Spanish-surnamed reporters were almost twice as likely to use positive identifiers (11%) as non-Latino writers (7%). Non-Latino writers used negative labels in 81% of their articles, whereas Spanish-surnamed reporters used negative references 75% of the time. Finally, in bylined and non-bylined articles the print media relied on the doubly derisive term *illegal aliens* almost to the total exclusion of positive language.

25 Years after Kerner: California's Proposition 187

Unauthorised immigration returned as a major concern to the U.S. public at the end of the Cold War in 1989. In California, its military-based economy took a severe blow; over 830,000 jobs were lost between 1990 and 1993. A ripple effect from the defence sector layoffs was felt throughout the state. The recession reduced state and local governmental incomes and created budgetary shortfalls. Meanwhile California had become more multi-ethnic. Seventy-five percent of foreign-born residents settle in seven states, with California at the top of the list. Nearly 25% of all authorised immigrants were settling in California during the 1980s. And overall, California's foreign-born population was about 22% of the population in the 1990s; in Los Angeles County it was 33%. Los Angeles Unified School District officially listed more than 75 mother tongues spoken in its kindergartens. While a plethora of cultures were represented, 85% of authorised immigration during the 1980s was from Asia and Latin America. Adding to an already large population of Mexican-origin citizens, the inevitable browning of California was apparent. Latinos made up over 30% of the population of the state. For Californians who presumed that U.S. society would always mean a preeminent Anglo-American culture, these demographic changes could be un-nerving.

The nativist reaction to the demographic change in the 1990s was a notorious state referendum, Proposition 187. The California electorate overwhelmingly passed the referendum even though its provisions were known to be unconstitutional. Proposition 187 was designed to supersede and radicalise federal law. Federal law already dictated sanctions against employers hiring unauthorised immigrant workers, and a federal policing body, the Border Patrol, to apprehend and deport such immigrants. Nonetheless, Proposition 187 would have denied a range of public benefits to unauthorised immigrants, including education and non-emergency health care. It would also have made school administrators, health care workers, social service personnel, police and other state employees responsible for determining the residence status of any "apparently illegal alien" (to use the controversial phrasing of the referendum) among their clients and for notifying the Immigration and Nationalization Service of suspected unauthorised immigrants for deportation. As expected, a federal court enjoined it the day after it passed.

Santa Ana and his student collaborators studied U.S. public discourse about immigrants of this time period (Santa Ana, Morán, & Sánchez, 1998; Santa Ana, 1999; 2002). Like Fernández and Pedroza, they studied 24 months of newspaper texts published before the 1994 vote on Proposition 187. Their content analysis was advanced in terms of its theoretical premises and empiricism. A total of 101 *Los Angeles Times* articles were scrutinised for a novel content analysis item, text metaphors. The study of metaphor for journalistic content analysis has been made possible because of the work on cognitive linguistic modelling by George Lakoff (1993) and his collaborators (e.g., Lakoff & Johnson, 1999). They theorise that metaphor, above other structures of language, establishes the basis of people's everyday comprehension of life. Metaphors provide a framework that people use to make sense of behaviour, relations, objects and people, even to the point that people forget that the semantic associations they created with metaphors are not natural, but merely conventional correspondences between one semantic domain and another. Thus, with an empirical analysis of the conceptual metaphors found in newspapers, the metaphors that journalists use to characterise immigrants can become a window onto the way they make sense of this group of people.

We will only talk about the one predominant metaphor for IMMIGRANT that Santa Ana's team found. The conceptual metaphor, IMMIGRANT AS ANIMAL was found in 87 separate instances in a 101-article corpus. There were so many individual instances of this metaphor that it could be subdivided, as presented below.[5] Immigrants were depicted, for example, as domesticated animals:

1. "They **herded** us together like goats," said one angry squatter.

As animals that are lured:

2. The **lure** is jobs, however ill paid, not welfare.
3. Wilson said he believed public benefits are a **lure** to immigrants.

As animals that can be attacked, and hunted:

4. Beaten-down agents, given only enough resources to catch a third of their **quarry**, sense the objective in this campaign is something less than total victory.
5. Beyond a store runs the I-5 [freeway], where the agents now must **quit the chase**.

As animals that are eaten:

6. The truth is, employers **hungering** for really cheap labour **hunt** out the foreign workers.
7. "187 backers **devour** the weak and helpless."

At times immigrants are seen as rats:

8. The rapid increase comes at a time when many state and federal officials are calling for beefed-up border patrols to **ferret** out illegal immigrants.

More often, immigrants are metaphorised as pack animals:

9. Mainland Chinese sovereignty has **spurred** an exodus.

10. Those who want to sharply **curb** illegal immigration include conservatives, liberals and most unions. [curb "metal mouthpiece used to control horses"]

Cognitive linguists theorise that conceptual metaphors, such as IMMIGRANT
AS ANIMAL, produce constitutive narratives that circulate in personal interaction
and the public sphere. Such discourses construct social structure and are types
of social practices within social orders that are expressed by individuals. People
function in terms of certain particular discourses/practices. As the discursive
practices are enacted, ideological practices are reaffirmed. Subject positions defined by these discursive practices confine both oppressor and oppressed people's lives in terms of knowledge and beliefs, social relationships and social
identity. By "subject positions," Michel Foucault (1980; Rabinow, 1984) refers
to the legitimated roles that society allots to individuals that provide identity and
standing. To use Lakoff's term, these discourse practices "embody" naturalised
ideological assumptions. As people live their lives, they enact the discourse
practices associated with their subject positions. By enacting the discourse practices, individuals tend to accept the ideology of the standing social order, namely
the institutional practices that sustain and legitimise repressive power relations.
When they go about their daily tasks and obligations, they take for granted a
good deal about the sources of oppression.

Thus the IMMIGRANT AS ANIMAL metaphor evokes a social structuring narrative. All conceptual metaphors of political discourses, in relation to other con-
gruent metaphors, set up a constitutive narrative that articulates a portion of the
standing social order. When juxtaposed to CITIZEN, the related concept that
was reserved for the white Anglo-Saxon or the Western European immigrant,
the narrative of IMMIGRANT AS ANIMAL reveals a remarkable worldview. In the
American view of society, the hierarchy of living things follows: *Citizens are humans, while immigrants are animals*. This hierarchy subordinates immigrants to citizens. Human beings are vested by birthright with privileges, such as human and
civil rights. It is a commonplace to presume that animals simply are not equal to
humans, and "by nature" cannot have such privileges.

This logical fallacy is called the fallacy of an Illicit Major Premise: A citizen
is human; Immigrants are not citizens; thus they are not human. This sophism
has been used in other circumstances and periods. For example, Lakoff and
Turner (1989) pointed out that degrading groups of humans has long been justi-

fied in Western European culture in terms of a purported natural hierarchy, the Great Chain of Being, which has been articulated since the time of Aquinas to justify social inequity. In its full extension, this hierarchy subordinates other living creatures to human beings, and ranks the inherent quality of humans from base to noble.

The IMMIGRANT AS ANIMAL metaphor and its associated narrative is racist discourse. Wetherell and Potter define racist discourse as one that

> establishes, sustains and reinforces oppressive power relations, …categorizes, allocates and discriminates between certain groups, …justifies, sustains and legitimates those practices which maintain the power and dominance. (1992, pp. 15–16)

Furthermore, this study indicated that journalists not only depicted immigrants as animals. In the corpus of 101 newspaper articles, news writers portrayed them as soldiers or invaders of the land, as weeds that infest the land, as burdens on society, and as diseases infecting the state. Indeed, all high frequency and less-frequent metaphors disparaged immigrants.

In addition to IMMIGRANT, Santa Ana and his student collaborators studied the metaphors for the demographic concept, IMMIGRATION. Again in the *Los Angeles Times* over a two-year period, 117 articles used metaphors to characterise IMMIGRATION. One such metaphor for immigrants is IMMIGRATION AS WAR:

11. Some believe that [Governor Pete] Wilson, by filing a lawsuit against the federal government and arguing that illegal immigration is tantamount to a **foreign invasion,** has made a whipping boy of migrants.
12. "People are saying, 'I don't like this **Third World takeover,**'" said Guy Weddington McCreary, a North Hollywood Chamber of Commerce member favouring the initiative. "It is literally an **invasion** and very upsetting."

Moving from depictions of individuals to depictions of the demographic movement of immigration, Santa Ana and his students found that water metaphors were commonly used. This might seem quite natural, even appropriate, but it must be emphasised that such verbal expressions are not exacting definitions, but mere conventions. Water metaphors are not the only possible conceptual construction of the demographic movement of people. The predominant metaphor for the process of the movement of large numbers of human beings to the U.S. in the 1990s turned out to be IMMIGRATION AS DANGEROUS WATERS:

13. **awash** under a **brown tide**
14. Like **waves on a beach,** these **human flows** are literally remaking the face of America
15. **a sea of brown faces** marching through Downtown would only antagonise many voters

Note in (12) and (14) the efforts of speakers, with the word *literal,* to make metaphorical references more real. Finally, IMMIGRATION AS INVASION was the least obscure anti-immigration metaphor in general use, because of its bold disregard of the evidence to the contrary. Consequently, it was frequently printed in scare quotes and was explicitly rejected at least once in the *Los Angeles Times* database by the advocates for immigrants:

16. "That is not an **armed invasion** coming across."

The most frequent conceptual metaphor for the demographic movement was IMMIGRATION AS DANGEROUS WATERS. Similarly to the metaphor, IMMIGRANT AS ANIMAL, the predominant demographic metaphor evoked an explanatory narrative in the 1990s that continues to be part of the U.S. standing social order:

> A flood of immigrants is flowing into America. It threatens to inundate white America. In small quantities the land can absorb an influx unchanged. In volume, however this flow threatens to change the contours of the land. The territory will not be able to absorb or control the flow. It will be eroded. The territory will be destroyed.

The corresponding ontology of IMMIGRATION AS DANGEROUS WATERS has four parts: Immigration corresponds to moving waters; the U.S. corresponds to a land subject to change from floods; increased immigration corresponds to an increase in the threat to the land; and the land's vulnerability to flooding corresponds to the U.S.'s vulnerability to change.

The study of conceptual metaphor in the texts of newspapers revealed another striking finding. In the 1990 data, both the opponents and proponents of Proposition 187 used the very same metaphors. The people who believed that immigration threatened U.S. sovereignty, and their opponents who believed that immigrants should not be blamed for economic downturns, employed exactly the same types of metaphors for immigrants and immigration, despite the fact that their political positions were diametrically opposed. While they did not utter the same words, the two groups employed similar metaphors to articulate divergent views. This implies that in California's public sphere of the 1990s, only one view about immigrants was articulated. There was no alternative set of metaphors. All parties used the IMMIGRANT AS ANIMAL, AS WEED, AS SOLDIER, AS BURDEN, and AS DISEASE metaphors. At best, spokespeople opposed to Proposition 187 repeated these metaphors in order to reject the claims of their conservative opponents. But the advocates for immigrant rights were unable to sustain an alternative set of conceptual images about immigrants, as evidenced in the *Los Angeles Times*. One might suppose that the *Times* knowingly sustained anti-immigrant language. However, in fact, the *Times* consistently rejected Proposition 187 in its editorials, and sought to inform the electorate with balanced news reports. Still, even the *Times* did not offer its readership a coherent alternative constellation of metaphors to contest the conservative, hegemonic worldview. Consequently, the advocates of immigrant rights tacitly accepted the worldview of their political rivals—in terms of conceptual metaphors. Of course, this put them at a decided disadvantage in the actual political debate. It offered the voting public no alternative option to the more coherent view, the anti-immigrant worldview. The electorate came to view immigrants in a bad light, and voted accordingly: there was no debate at the level of concept formation. However, this conceptual monopoly would disappear after 2004, to the chagrin of its promoters.

40 Years after Kerner

On January 7, 2004, at the beginning of his re-election campaign, President George W. Bush announced an immigration reform initiative in which he used astonishingly compassionate language when he spoke about immigrants. In a twenty-minute speech, Bush called immigrants, "Americans by choice," who are members of families of "talent, character, and patriotism," and who hold values such as "faith in God, love of family, hard work, and self-reliance." He further described the United States as a "welcoming society...by tradition and conviction," which is a "stronger and better nation because of the hard work and the faith and entrepreneurial spirit of immigrants." Bush unintentionally set off a powder keg of public expression of apprehension about the nation's unauthorised immigrants and immigration policy. It once again became a topic of the national public sphere, as it had been in the mid-1990s. Strikingly, members of his own political party ridiculed him for stating a truism: "Immigrants are hardworking, decent human beings." Bush had legitimised the language to refer to immigrants as people rather than as animals. His stature made its dissemination acceptable in the national sphere. However, like several other crucial elements of his presidential agenda, his "Americans by choice" speech (Bush, 2004) led to unintended consequences.

Although overshadowed in 2004 by the presidential re-election campaign and the Iraq war, the immigrant antagonists assiduously sought to repudiate the president. The Minutemen, a group of a couple hundred people who feared an army of brown-skinned invaders would cross the Mexican border, found a way. In an effective publicity stunt in March 2005, the Minutemen took up posts as symbolic sentinels along the US/Mexican border, claiming to defend the country against the immigration invasion. Latinos protested, and the president called them "vigilantes," but the Minutemen nevertheless captured the nation's attention. By December 2005, the U.S. House of Representatives had approved HR 4437, a bill that would make it a felony to be an unauthorised worker. Moreover, citizens who helped such workers in actions as benign as driving them to work could also be convicted of a felony. HR 4437 also would have imposed new penalties on employers who hire unauthorised workers, in addition to mandating the construction of fences along one-third of the US/Mexican border, and enacting a number of measures to further penalise immigrant workers. This U.S. House of Representative bill was then sent to the Senate for its consideration. The nation's response to the Minutemen's antics, as well as hundreds of editorials and letters to the editor across the country, signalled the start of another national anti-immigrant rampage.

In 2006 Latinos reacted to these events with marches. One Washington D.C. coalition held a rally in early March that shocked even the organisers. 5,000 people were expected and 30,000 gathered. Later that month, 100,000 protestors marched in downtown Chicago. Throughout the month thousands of people across the country assembled to protest against HR 4437 in Los Angeles, Phoenix, Atlanta, and other cities. On April 10 a nationwide call for marches displayed the movement's latent political power. Marchers showed up in unprecedented numbers in scores of cities and towns. The first crest of this new social movement came at the Great May Day March of 2006, when millions of people in hundreds of locales marched peacefully and proudly. The nation was divided. The massive support for HR 4437 and the Minutemen that had its principal impetus in national demographic changes was offset by millions of others who were calling for justice and respect.

Santa Ana and his student collaborators (2007) returned to study the conceptual metaphors about immigrants that were used in newspapers across the country in 2006, to gain some perspective on the constitutive imagery that was current in the discourse of the public sphere. They compared two samples of this discourse stream in mainstream national newspaper reports: at the height of national attention with the Great May Day marches of 2006, and; a second sample taken in October 2006, when President Bush signed the *Secure Fence Act* into law. The results were very different on these two dates. While research indicated for the past century that mass media constitutive metaphors for immigration included one or another form of dehumanising metaphors, this was not the case in May 2006. At this time the nation's newspapers articulated both human and non-human imagery at levels nearing parity (Bodossian & Santa Ana, 2007). However, 6 months later, mass media representations of the immigration issue returned in large measure to a single predominant image that once again demeaned unauthorised immigrants.

In a May 2 national sample of newspapers (the day following the marches) Santa Ana's researchers coded 969 immigrant or immigration metaphors. The patterning of these metaphors differed from the 1990 data in two significant ways. A new predominant conceptual metaphor, IMMIGRANT AS CRIMINAL, had displaced the predominant 1990 metaphor, IMMIGRANT AS ANIMAL. More importantly, the news media reported on the marches and the immigration debate using both affirming and negative language regarding immigrants. Fifty-seven percent of the metaphors were negative, but 43% of the May 2006 metaphors characterised the immigrant in terms such as worker, as individuals without documents, or someone who contributes to the nation. For the first time, U.S. journalists presented both sides of the debate on immigration reform with distinctive discourses.

While the media presented a rough balance of humane and traditional inhumane representations of immigration issues in May 2006, print news media representations about immigrants reverted as the marches receded from public memory. Over the summer an escalating sectarian war and rampant violence in Iraq, as well as Israel's invasion of Lebanon, directed public attention to foreign affairs. Mass media discussions about immigration nearly disappeared. More-over, early spring political manoeuvres to control the U.S. Congress after the midterm elections effectively ended any possibility of significant immigration legislation. Still, the U.S. Congress passed the *Secure Fence Act*, which President Bush signed on October 26, 2006. However, it was only a nod to the conserva-tive base of the Republican Party, since no money was apportioned to the bill.

The team sampled the print media in the days before and after President Bush signed the 2006 *Secure Fence Act*, coding 903 immigrant or immigration metaphors. These broke down into 67% nonhuman metaphors and 33% human ones. Of the five most prevalent metaphors, the negative IMMIGRANT AS CRIMINAL was dominant, at 38%. The other two negative metaphor were OBJECT (7%), and BURDEN (7%). The affirming metaphors counted with IMMIGRANT AS UNDOCUMENTED (11%), HUMAN (8%), and WORKER (7%). The overall decline in compassionate immigrant metaphors was clear, since WORKER and CONTRIBUTOR, each appear 50% less frequently in October 2006 than they did six months earlier. Moreover, there was no mention of the economic con-tribution of immigrants, or narratives of immigrants as hardworking individuals who benefit the nation. The print news no longer conveyed two rival constitu-tive metaphors that would frame the immigration debate in a balanced manner, as had been the case in May 2006, only six months earlier. Print news relapsed to its typical negative view of immigration.

However, print journalists occasionally used the term *undocumented* in Octo-ber 2006. Of course, the term *undocumented* conveys the human character of im-migrants, and had become a standard alternative to *illegal*, the negative term of preference. Journalists did not settle on a non-partisan term that neither de-meaned immigrants (e.g., *illegal*) nor understated the impact of movements of millions, e.g., *undocumented*. On occasion I have proposed the comparatively neu-tral term, *unauthorised*, which I use throughout this chapter (e.g., Santa Ana, 2006).

The October 2006 news articles on immigration ultimately were dominated by the CRIMINAL metaphor, which was found in 38% of all verbal imagery. Fur-ther, IMMIGRANT AS OBJECT, BURDEN, and WATER all increased in October 2006. Immigrants were portrayed as stubborn weeds or mounting heaps of trash that must be cleaned up, or as a costly illness that damaged the economic health and cultural dominance of the nation. Immigrants were described as forces that can wipe out entire communities and the traditional American lifestyle, or as potential terrorists and criminals seeking only to harm the nation. Given these descriptions, the only solution appears to be to build a fence, hire more border patrol agents, and build more detention centres. As the conservative narrative regained its traditional power to control anti-immigrant sentiments in the public sphere, the policy debate in the public sphere became increasingly one-sided.

Jacobson (2008) locates a sociological source for the shift of predominate constitutive metaphor for IMMIGRANT from the ANIMAL metaphor of the past decade to the CRIMINAL metaphor of the first decade of the 21st century. In one sense, it is an improvement, since immigrants are no longer characterised as lower forms of life. However, it is also a political shift of tactics, because when anti-immigration advocates excoriated the immigrant with racist terms, their language increasingly diminished their moral standing in the eyes of the general public. The terms of debate have now shifted away from the immigrant's family lineage to his or her legal standing. Advocates who favour the term *illegal* claim that unauthorised immigrants are criminals, who deliberately violate U.S. law by crossing its borders, and, once in the US, continue to abuse its social network of services. Therefore, they deserve punitive treatment. In contrast, their opponents favour the term *undocumented,* taking the position that immigrants are for the most part decent people who break minor laws in pursuit of a higher calling: to provide for their children. For this reason, Americans should treat immigrants with respect, protect them from exploitation, and welcome them into U.S. society.

Television News Imagery of a Bloodstained Demonstration

The extraordinary expression of pro-immigrant sentiment in 2006 led to considerable anticipation of the 2007 marches. National opinion was not settled and the news media had decidedly mixed ways to represent it. The 2007 marches were far smaller and did not command much media's attention. In Los Angeles, however, an immigration rights demonstration was marred by violence when a peaceful assembly of 7,000 who had gathered in MacArthur Park was assailed by 450 police officers firing munitions and using truncheons.[6] This time Santa Ana and his team (Santa Ana, López, & Munguía, 2010) did not study newspapers, but instead evaluated the television news media reporting of the marches and the violence perpetrated by the Los Angeles police, which will permit comparison to the television news reporting of the Detroit African American uprising of the summer of 1967.

In brief, the May Day 2007 news reporting was most accurate (and appropriately tentative) immediately following the police attack. However, on the following day, television news reports became increasingly inaccurate when the news reporters framed events in terms of violent marchers who incited a forceful police response. Television news teams thus blamed the victims for the violence they suffered, using linguistic and visual techniques that de-legitimated and misrepresented the protesters' actions.

This evaluation of 51 televised news reports (3 networks and 5 local stations) of the May Day 2007 rally and attack used three distinct methods. The team appraised the visual imagery and news story construction of the MacArthur Park events, the accuracy of televised news descriptions of the events, and the frequency of different spoken constituent metaphors that correspondents and anchors voiced to describe the human agents involved in these events. (1) To see how the networks visually represent violence and peace, the team analysed the visual elements of the news stories with social semiotic tools to reveal the visual symbolism with which the newsrooms projected social meaning and values (Jewitt & Oyama 2001; Rose 2001; and van Leeuwen 2001). (2) The team evaluated the factual accuracy of the televised news reports about the May Day incidents in MacArthur Park, by comparing them to the official LAPD report on the events, the *EMD*.[7] The team tracked the media's rendition of violence and peaceful actions during the event, attempting to answer the research question: Whom did the news media blame for the violence? (3) The team performed critical discourse analysis of the spoken language with which the television news correspondents and anchor reported the police attack on demonstrators. The team compared the spoken metaphors used to describe the agents in this event, namely the IMMIGRANT, the POLICE, the DEMONSTRATORS, and the MARCH itself.

In this first of three analyses, the team noted a clear bias against the immigration-rights advocates before the LAPD attack, and particularly on May 2. On that day, television news focused almost exclusively on the clash of LAPD with demonstrators who were deemed violent. In the second analysis, the team found a clear contrast in the framing narratives used by the LAPD and by the television news reporters to set up an arrangement of roles, characters, reader expectations and rules to evaluate the facts of the May Day events. In the *EMD*, the LAPD framed the events as a case of police misconduct, declaring that the police violated the marchers' First Amendment rights[8] when it forcibly cleared the peaceful assembly from MacArthur Park. The *EMD* blamed the police for inadequate event planning and command structure breakdowns. It described how police officers forcibly broke up the assembly by swinging batons and firing guns. The LAPD accepted responsibility for injuring 246 people with "more than 100 batons strikes" and at least 146 "less-than-lethal impact munitions," namely rubber bullets.

In contrast to the *EMD* police misconduct frame, television news used another conventional journalistic narrative. This riot suppression frame is entirely predictable, with stock villains, victims and heroes. In the U.S. television news narrative, the marchers were the violent agitators, and the police were lawful government agents who are charged with disciplining disorderly civilians. This narrative frame characterised the political rally as replete with aggressive demonstrators. The event became a face-off between two violent groups. In this frame, while the actions of some police officers may have been excessive, the marchers were ultimately responsible for the violence. In this news version of the events, the victims were not families with children in strollers or even the hapless street vendors, but news media personnel who were caught in the violence.

In the third analysis, the team performed a critical discourse analysis of the transcripts of 51 news stories, focusing on the metaphors that correspondents and anchors used when they spoke about the social agents involved in the day's events. Over the two days of reporting, reporters or anchors described the IMMIGRANT AS CRIMINAL, alien or otherwise inhumanely nearly two-thirds of the time, while they depicted the IMMIGRANTS AS WORKERS, as *undocumented*, or otherwise humanely the other third of occasions. Three spoken examples of the former:

17. Los Angeles County is home to more than a million **illegal aliens**, more than any other in the nation. It's no surprise the largest turnout among pro-amnesty marchers is right here. They draped themselves in the American flag, demanding amnesty for millions of **illegal aliens** who broke American law.[9]

18. Finally stepping up, the administration want to show they have done something. They have arrested 220,000 last year, deporting criminal aliens.[10]
19. Good evening, everybody. The **pro-illegal alien lobby** today...[11]

The media depicted the demonstration itself as peaceful only one-third of the time, and as violent nearly two-thirds of the time. Here are contrasting examples:

20. Here in Boyle Heights reaction was strong. They were very proud of the **peaceful demonstrations** of the march and they were angered and shocked at the police beatings.[12]
21. **Irate protesters clash** with authorities in Los Angeles on chaotic May Day.[13]
22. A large-scale immigration march spins **out of control**.[14]

The news characterised the marchers as peaceful or in otherwise humane terms less than 10% of the time, and violent, criminal, or in otherwise inhumane terms 83% of the time. The following quote was classified a depiction of the MARCHERS AS PEACEFUL PEOPLE:

23. It's unfortunate that the actions of a few individuals among the many thousands here throughout the day marching and demonstrating peacefully, and in a coordinated, organised way, the actions of a few who were clearly intending to cause disturbances and disruptions, that they, in fact, did do just that.[15]

Finally, the news media represent the POLICE in military terms (as keepers of social order) less than 10% of the time, including:

24. It will be a **maximum deployment** for them.[16]
25. No one is sure exactly how large the crowds here in Los Angeles are going to be. But Los Angeles police are on **tactical alert**.[17]

Otherwise the police were characterised as VIOLENT or otherwise using DISREPUTABLE terms, nearly 90% of the time.

In sum, the news media depicted both the marchers and the police as equally violent, in contrast to the police department's own version of events. Note that this generalisation mixes different television news reports (for example, local versus network, or FOX versus MSNBC) and combines the reports on May Day (before and after the attack) with reports aired on May 2. Splitting these data did not change the generalisation.

We noted distinct meaning-making trends. The news stories presented on the morning of May Day were framed in terms of two oppositions: the U.S. Immigration and Customs Enforcement agency (ICE) versus immigrants, and peaceful demonstrators versus anti-immigration advocates.[18] Moreover, television news editors skewed the representation of both immigrants and demonstrators visually on the morning of the march. They were depicted as generic masses with questionable legal status. No videographic and body conventions were employed to distinguish demonstrators from immigrants, and instead they tended to depict them all together as an inarticulate mass. Furthermore, the news teams used camera techniques to hold these individuals at a great distance from the television audience, by representing them as teeming masses. When immigrants or demonstrators were on camera, aerial coverage was used in seven out of the thirteen scenes, whereas only two scenes used the camera at ground level, representing demonstrators as individuals. In contrast, all other individuals depicted on screen were given full subjectivity and authority. For example, correspondents and anchors throughout the stories were always at a medium-close up scale and alone in the camera shot. Moreover, the only interviewee that any newsroom gave full subjectivity and authority was a well-known extremist who opposes immigrant rights.[19]

On the day after the police attack, network and local news shifted the story frame from descriptions of peaceful demonstrations and immigration reform to portrayals of violence. The newscasters posed two key questions: Who instigated the violence? And did the police use excessive force? These are the correct queries, but the newsroom riot suppression narrative pre-empted their answers. Whereas on May Day the visual sign structures generally set up an opposition between ICE and the immigrants, and between peaceful demonstrators and anti-immigration advocates, on May 2nd the opposition was the LAPD versus unruly demonstrators. Visually, this frame shift replaced images of peaceful marchers in white t-shirts waving U.S. flags with images of the LAPD in full riot gear swinging batons. The news stories showed some images of LAPD abusing marchers. However, they broadcast more images of officers beating journalists than beating protesters.

On May Day, the Los Angeles Chief of Police publicly accepted responsibility for his officers' actions. He also commissioned the *EMD* for a thorough review of the events of the day.[20] When the *EMD* was finally released to the public, it unequivocally condemned the police for the violence. Every local Los Angeles newsroom then reported the *EMD* findings. However, no newsroom disavowed its own reporting of the events in any way. There was no token "for the record" correction, in spite of the news media's self-appointed role as the U.S. democracy's fourth estate. To end, we are now in a position to evaluate the advances that television journalism has made since the 1968 Kerner Commission report by comparing the 2007 television news reporting of this demonstration.

Conclusion

Three generalisations can be made. (1) Since the 1970s, we can see a glacial softening of the predominate metaphor used to constitute the immigrant in the nation's eyes. Before the 1970s, local newspapers commonly used racial epithets. More professional reporting employed two predominant constitutive metaphors for immigrants: ALIEN or VERMIN. In the 1990s, it became ANIMAL. Today, the news media's preferred metaphor for immigrants, CRIMINAL, prejudges immigrants as malefactors. The news media continue to have a privileged role as a major source of the nation's discourse practices. However, they have not sought out or employed a neutral term of reference, such as *unauthorised*. Their sustained reference to *illegal* and comparatively desultory use of *undocumented* embodies the news media's naturalised ideological assumptions and relations of the subject spaces of IMMIGRANT and CITIZEN. The news media discourse practices are so insistent and casual that the semantic and cultural presuppositions of the metaphor become automatic and transparent in everyday public discourse for the nation.

(2) A good measure of journalistic balance on political issues is to judge whether or not the news media are articulating a single political narrative. In the past forty years, U.S. news media have, with one short period, used only one or another predominant cognitive metaphor, thus articulating a coherent and hence prejudiced narrative. With today's predominant CRIMINAL metaphor, the

media pronounces judgment on the moral character of unauthorised immigrants as a group. This news media language is not conducive to democratic debate.

(3) Our longitudinal review of television and newspaper news coverage of immigrants indicates that, *mutatis mutandis,* the failings noted in the Kerner Report still hold. Both television and print media to this day continue to demean communities of colour, in this case, unauthorised immigrants. When reporting on immigrant news events, U.S. news media tend to fall back on chauvinism, rather than its often-touted standards of truth and balance. The findings of television study of the police-instigated violence against immigrant-rights marchers are particularly disconcerting. The Kerner Commission's finding was that in spite of some inaccuracies, the news media "tried on the whole to give a balanced, factual account of the 1967 disturbances." This was not the case in 2007, when local and network television news misrepresented the events in MacArthur Park with its standard and in this case inaccurate riot suppression frame. The other Kerner Commission findings were that "news media failed to portray accurately the scale and character of the violence," and "media failed to report adequately on the causes and consequences of civil disorders," and they did "not communicate to the majority of their audience." These also apply to the 2007 reporting of the LAPD attack. Forty years after Kerner, little has changed when it comes to crisis reporting regarding domestic mass demonstrations.

Television news acted politically when it persisted in falsely depicting these marchers. The immigrant rights movement first impressed the nation with its great, dignified marches. While the television anchors expressed sympathy for the victims of 36-inch baton strikes and volleys of rubber bullets, their newsrooms characterised the peaceable marchers as violent. The nation's perception of moral rectitude has become increasingly important for the success of social movements in our ever more mediated world. Thus the news media effectively reduced the nation's support of the marchers by deprecating their moral authority (cf. McLeod & Detenber, 1999). However, if U.S. journalists believe that they have the fourth estate responsibility to defend the citizens' interests with balanced and accurate reporting, when these newsrooms falsely diminished the legitimacy of the immigrant-rights movement on May Day 2007, they also debased their own authority.

Notes

1. The bar's name referred in Prohibition era slang to police officers who had been bribed to take no notice of a speakeasy, namely an illegal drinking establishment.

2. Gutiérrez quotes such 19th-century viewpoints, such as that of South Carolina Senator John C. Calhoun, for whom Mexicans comprised "impure races, not as good as the Cherokees or Choctaws" (1995, p. 16).

3. Other scholars have undertaken analyses of earlier periods, but space considerations limit a pre-Kerner literature review. For example, Fernández and Pedroza noted: "Chavira found that in the 1930's and 1950's the Los Angeles Times tended to rely almost exclusively on official sources of information regarding the issue of Mexican immigration." Also see Flores (2003) for a study of the mediated representations of Mexican immigrants in the 1920s and 1930s.

4. Concepts and metaphors (which are abstractions) are indicated in the text in small caps, reference to words (lexical items) are presented in *italics*, and countable instances of text metaphors are marked with in **boldface**.

5. The excerpts taken from the *Los Angeles Times* and other news media have not been edited or modified. **Boldface** added to identify metaphors.

6. Consider, how network television depicted the assault by Alabama police and state troopers with truncheons and tear gas on 600 non-violent civil rights marchers in Selma, Alabama. Television news reporting of this 1965 event reversed national opinion and political opposition to the Voting Rights Act, which was signed five months later.

7. The EMD, *An Examination of May Day 2007 MacArthur Park* (Los Angeles Police Department, 2007), is a report written to allow LAPD to evaluate itself, to respond to adverse public opinion, as well as to present the LAPD's version of events for legal proceedings stemming from the attack. It was written in accordance with California state law, which mandates anonymity of individuals under police commission or legal investigation. It was also written with care to protect the legal rights of individuals as well as political interests of key constituencies.

8. The First Amendment to the U.S. Constitution guarantees the people's rights to the free exercise of religion, freedom of speech, a free press, the right to assemble peaceably, and to petition the government to redress grievances. These rights are afforded to all U.S. residents, not only citizens.

9. CNN *Lou Dobbs Tonight*. May 1st, at 3:00 p.m.

10. FOX-News On the Record with Greta Van Susteren. May 1st, at 7:00 p.m.

11. CNN *Lou Dobbs Tonight*. May 1st, at 3:00 p.m.

12. KCBS *CBS 2 News at 5*. May 2nd, at 5:00 p.m.

13. FOX-News *Hannity and Colmes*. May 2nd, at 6:00 p.m.

14. KCBS *CBS 2 News at 11*. May 2nd, at 11:00 a.m.

15. *CNN Newsroom*. May 2nd, at 10:00 a.m.

16. KTTV-FOX Morning News at 6 AM. May 1st.

17. *CNN Newsroom*. May 1st, at 10:00 a.m.

18. In 2003 ICE subsumed the roles of the INS. ICE refers to the U.S. Immigration and Customs Enforcement, a branch of the Department of Homeland Security, which is responsible for identifying and eliminating national border and infrastructure security vulnerabilities.

19. Rick Oltman, *Fox Online* at 9:00 a.m. on May 1st. Oltman has a long history of extremist affiliations. For example, in 1998 he participated at an Alabama protest against Mexican workers. The Council of Conservative Citizens (CCC), a white supremacist group that sponsored the event, advertised that Oltman was a member. The CCC "oppose[s] all efforts to mix the races of mankind." The CCC event featured an unrobed Klu Klux Klansman burning a Mexican flag (Southern Poverty Law Center, 2002). In 2009, Oltman was National Media Director for the Californians for Population Stabilization, which the Southern Poverty Law Center also lists as a hate group.

20. In September 2008, the LAPD announce that fifteen LAPD officers would face discipline for their role in the exercise of excessive force, for failing to rein in other officers, or lying to investigators during the inquiry. *Los Angeles Times* writer Joel Rubin stated, "The officers facing punishment represent a small fraction of the scores of police who were involved in the botched attempt to clear the park of marchers and journalists after a small group of agitators threw bottles and other projectiles at officers, police said. Many more officers, who otherwise would have faced possible discipline, could not be identified." Rubin noted that 315 people had pending lawsuits against the city over injuries, damaged property, and other claims due to the police assault (Rubin, 2008).

CHAPTER SIX

Skilful Seafarers, Oceanic Drifters or Climate Refugees? Pacific People, News Value and the Climate Refugee Crisis

Carol Farbotko

Introduction

Climate change is being defined and grappled with as a multidimensional global crisis. Once understood in public and political debates primarily as an environmental crisis, more recently it has also been approached as an economic crisis. Intersecting with economic and environmental crisis discourses—and reminding us of the "wicked" nature of the climate change issue (Hulme, 2009)—is the climate refugee crisis. The term "climate refugee" has been mobilised to describe the large numbers of people predicted to be permanently or temporarily displaced by rising sea levels, severe drought, cyclones and other effects of climate change (Edwards, 1999; Biermann & Boas, 2010). Low-lying islands in the Pacific are considered to be at the "frontline" of this displacement (Henry & Jeffery, 2008). The aim of this chapter is to explore how meaning is produced and contested in public debate over displacement of Pacific island peoples associated with sea-level rise, by juxtaposing the climate refugee discourse with alternative discourses of migration and journeying between and beyond Pacific islands.

I commence with an observation made by a number of climate social scientists: the term climate refugee has significant and sustained news value, particularly in the news media of the industrialised world. Low-lying Pacific islands, such as Funafuti in Tuvalu and the Carteret Islands in Papua New Guinea, have become highly visible in the news media since the late 1980s (Farbotko, 2005; Lazrus, 2009; McNamara & Gibson, 2009; Mortreux & Barnett 2009). Both places are consistently displayed as "disappearing islands" and their inhabitants are imagined as "climate refugees". Disappearing islands and climate refugees are also drawn on frequently in climate change campaigns of a diverse range of environmental groups, such as WWF[1], Greenpeace[2] and Friends of the Earth.[3] Scholars and policy makers, meanwhile, dispute the closely related concept "environmental refugee" and debate calculations of current and expected numbers of people around the world who might fit into such a category (Black, 1998, 2001; Myers, 2002; Warner et al., 2009; Biermann & Boas, 2010). Notwithstanding scholarly and policy disagreement over their existence and/or meaning, stories are regularly published in the news media claiming to identify the world's "first" climate refugees. While researchers have drawn attention to the significance of this discourse (e.g., Lazrus, 2009; McNamara & Gibson, 2009; Barnett & Mortreux, 2009; Farbotko, 2010b), little systematic media analysis of it has been undertaken.

Entering this contested discursive terrain, my intention is not to arrive at some truth about climate refugees. Rather, I explore how the climate refugee crisis has been produced and challenged. In particular, I pay attention to the role of the news media in locating the climate refugee crisis in very particular ways of being in, and journeying through, time and space. I juxtapose the climate refugee discourse with alternatives that speak to oceanic voyaging in the Pacific—specifically a "navigating" discourse and a "drifting" discourse. In this task, I draw on the insights of postcolonial scholars of the Pacific who have demonstrated that ocean, island, vessel and migration knowledges are always situated knowledges (Hau'ofa, 1993; Lilomaiava-Doktor, 2009). Hau'ofa (1993) points out that the lives of Pacific people, long characterised by movement and migration, are informed by notions of the largeness of Oceania as a connected "sea of islands" rather than by the smallness of discrete land masses. His essay is a prompt towards analysis and recovery of marginalised island meanings and experiences, a task I take up here in considering different discourses of journeys between islands and other places. This task is of use to critical media scholars seeking to understand how perspectives on mobility and space are made visible or invisible in the news media, in turn helping to constitute a climate refugee crisis.

Following this introduction, the chapter is divided into three sections. The first section presents key characteristics of three discourses of Pacific migration and journeying. One discourse produces the islander as climate refugee, a victim of rising sea levels. Another discourse, arising in the context of a cultural revival of ancient sailing technologies and practices, focuses on the islander as great seafarer. Still another discourse is found largely in Pacific cultural histories which record accidental and forced voyages, and the fate of those cast adrift from their islands in small canoes and fishing boats. The second section attempts a critical meditation on these migration and journeying discourses to explore how the crisis of Pacific climate refugees is constructed, and how it is contested and critiqued. The chapter concludes with a reiteration of the importance of multiple perspectives on narratives and practices of journeying among Pacific people, enabling a richer understanding of the ways in which inhabitants of small islands represent themselves as they face the prospect of sea-level-rise-related displacement.

Three Discourses of Migration:
Climate Refugees, Skilful Seafarers, and Oceanic Drifters

A Climate Refugee Discourse

Inhabitants of low-lying regions, particularly island nation-states comprised entirely of low-lying atolls, have been prominently identified as both "environmental refugees" and, more specifically, as "climate refugees". "Climate refugee" is a term that has gained currency in the media and civil society since the late 1980s to describe people who undergo forced migration linked to climate change effects, especially sea-level rise. McNamara and Gibson (2009) found an early use of the term by the Worldwatch Institute in 1988. The same year, Australians were informed in the *Sydney Morning Herald* that "Australia may need to take in a wave of environmental refugees from coral atolls in the Pacific and Indian oceans, according to two scientists".[4] The resonance of climate refugee stories continues to have currency. Guardian.co.uk, to take one of many possible examples, published a story in November 2009 titled "Global warming could create 150 million 'climate refugees' by 2050".[5] The article cited an underwater cabinet meeting held by the Government of Maldives to help personify the prediction made by non-government organisation Environmental Justice Foundation and included a quote from President Mohamed Nasheed of the Maldives stating people in his country did not want to "trade a paradise for a climate refugee camp".

The identification of Pacific people in particular as future refugees from climate change impacts has its origins in social science research[6]. The term climate refugee is frequently invoked to highlight the fact that populations at risk of displacement associated with climate change effects fall outside the ambit of protection provided to those legally designated as refugees by the United Nations Refugee Agency (UNHCR). No legal provisions providing redress for future migration events associated with the effects of climate change have been negotiated in international multilateral climate change fora, which focus on reducing greenhouse gas emissions and adaptation to climate change in place.[7] While McNamara (2006) has documented a lack of attention to formulating specific policy on environmental refugees at the United Nations, policy attention is turning towards "environmentally induced migrants". The term "climate refugee" has little favour at UNCHR because it is seen to be too easily answered by reactionary policies preventing movement without genuine concern for the welfare of populations involved (Warner et al., 2009). For some, it is a concept that tends to environmental determinism and does not offer a way of considering climate change and migration as part of a web of vectors which can operate in different directions depending on the circumstances of the people, place and power relations in question (Tacoli, 2009; Black, 2001). From this perspective, climate change adds complexity to an already complex story about the distribution of and access to resources as diverse as water, land, infrastructure, institutions, capital, the rule of law, kinship networks, education, aid and mobility among vulnerable populations (Black, 2001; Tacoli, 2009; Ribot 2009). Nevertheless, debate about the numbers of such environmental and climate refugees, how they might be protected under international law, and how such protection might be advanced, continues in some research and policy arenas (e.g., Biermann & Boas, 2010; Myers, 2002, Australian Greens, 2007).

"Disappearing islands" and "climate refugees" have been prominent in framing climate change as a crisis in the news media since the late 1980s. Only little attention has been given to this discourse by social scientists (cf. Farbotko, 2005; McNamara & Gibson, 2009). Media studies of climate change issues have largely been concerned with the ways in which climate change is framed as an environmental crisis, particularly focussing on how climate science is translated in the news media (e.g., Carvalho, 2007; Boykoff, 2007). The Pacific island nation-state of Tuvalu has been especially visible in news reporting on climate change migration (Connell, 2003; Chambers & Chambers, 2007; Mortreux & Barnett, 2009). Since the late 1980s:

> media publics have watched from a distance, partly in horror and partly with perverse impatience, for the first islands to disappear…the 10,000 inhabitants of the nine coral atolls and reef islands in the central Pacific Ocean that make up the archipelago of Tuvalu have become signifiers of the scale and urgency of the uneven impacts of climate change around the planet. Dramatic representations of rising sea levels in Tuvalu circu-

late; the cosmopolitan media is on hand to bear witness to flooding and destitution when seasonal king tides cause flooding on its islands. Many foreign journalists, researchers, environmentalists and documentary-makers who arrive during those king tides capture footage of flooding on the islands. Locals are photographed and interviewed. Islanders apparently witness their land dissolving into the ocean and attempt to find refuge on safe, dry, yet alien, expanses elsewhere. Dispatches of disappearing islands, apparently on the verge of evacuation, are sent to all corners of the cosmopolitan world. (Farbotko, 2010b, p. 48)

As the case of Tuvalu suggests, disappearing islands and climate refugees have sustained news value. It is important to explain this newsworthiness, and research into climate change representations can assist in this task. Brönnimann (2002), Doyle (2007) and Thornes (2008) provide a guide to understanding how apparently graspable concepts and visible entities are crucial for lay publics' engaging with climate change debate. News media translate complex climate change phenomena, often invisible to the naked eye or layperson's perspective, into event-based, visualisable news stories:

A prioritisation of the visible, at the expense of that which is hidden…reinforces the view that "seeing is believing", based, as this is, upon the empiricism of scientific knowledge. This belief in the visible has contributed to the difficulties encountered in the communication of climate change as a "real" and credible threat since the early 1990s. (Doyle, 2007, p. 145)

Reporting on climate refugees in the media serves the function to create an apparently visible embodiment of the effects of climate change. This need for embodiment is apparent in periodic reports of the "first" climate refugees on news websites, blogs and websites of various civil society organisations around the world. These range from regional Pacific media to specialist environmentalist press to blogs to large Western news corporations. Headlines of Carteret Islanders, Papua New Guinea include: "Rising Seas Create First Climate Refugees" (*The Star Online*, Toronto, 23 September 2009[8]); "First climate refugees start move to new island home" (*The Age*, Melbourne, Online 29 July 2009[9]) and "First 'climate refugees' look to relocate to PNG" (*Radio Australia News Online*, 13 February 2009[10]). For Tuvaluans, example headlines are: "Saving the First Climate Refugees" (*Good Online*, Los Angeles, 28 April 2009[11]) and, "What happens when your country drowns? Meet the people of Tuvalu, the world's first climate refugees" (*Mother Jones Online*, San Francisco, November/December 2009).[12] The people of Tegua, Vanuatu have been reported as "Pacific's first climate change refugees?" (*Islands Business Online*, Suva, 2007[13]), and, "Pacific Islanders become first official climate refugees" (Edie Legal Resource Centre Online, South Croydon, 7 December 2005[14]). Through such reporting, the climate refugee seems to appear in the news media and civil society narratives as a reality, albeit a contested one, the key proponents of which are foreign journalists, researchers, environmentalists and documentary-makers rather than island inhabitants. The news media attention paid to the climate refugee debate has also contributed to the substantial symbolic capital of small island nations, mobilised politically, for instance, at the Copenhagen Conference of Parties 15. There, the Tuvalu and Maldives delegations drew crowds of vocal supporters on-site and around the world as their ambitious interventions and strong demands for emissions reductions made their mark on the unfolding negotiations (Farbotko & McGregor, 2010). A very different effect of the news value of the climate refugee lies in attempts to harness sea-level-rise-affected places for profit. A climate change tourism narrative, framing disappearing islands as places to visit before they disappear, pays little attention to the ethical implications of such tourism (Farbotko, 2010a).

Interestingly, migration into New Zealand from Tuvalu has been widely reported in terms stating that the New Zealand government is accepting "environmental refugees". In the following extract from a news article, for example, it is assumed that the New Zealand government has a humanitarian refugee program specifically for Tuvaluan people:

> Unlike New Zealand, which in 2001 began accepting 75 Tuvaluans a year, Australia has so far not acknowledged the prospect of climate refugees.[15]

While the New Zealand government does accept up to 75 Tuvaluan migrants per year, the scheme operates as part of the Pacific Access Category, which is also open under various similar quotas to citizens of Kiribati, Tonga and Fiji. Kiribati is entirely comprised of atolls, and its population faces similar issues of sea-level rise to that of Tuvalu. Among the larger island nation states of Tonga and Fiji, however, populations are rarely represented as climate refugees. Moreover, the Pacific Access Category rules stipulate that migrants be aged between 18 and 45 and possess an offer of employment in New Zealand and English-language skills. Such requirements mean that migration to New Zealand via the Pacific Access Category is not accessible to older Tuvaluans, those who do not speak English well, or those who have no skills that are attractive to New Zealand employers. The migration scheme is largely economic, not humanitarian. However, labelling it an environmental refugee program clearly has greater news value, the effect of which perhaps suggests to the public that Tuvaluans and i-Kiribati have bilateral legal protection as climate refugees when they do not. It also leaves little room for alternative migration discourses, normalising understandings of displacement associated with sea-level rise in terms of the climate refugee. In a previous study of representations of Tuvalu and climate-related displacement in an Australian newspaper, I concluded that:

> appeals are made to stereotypes of island marginality, and Tuvaluan place identity is constructed in opposition to a centralized Australia that is physically more secure and safe in the event of sea-level rise. The Tuvaluan islands are thus identified as vulnerable to a future tragic submersion event. Australians become audience to this spectacle, both drawn to and shamed by the tragedy of a tropical paradise lost. (Farbotko, 2005, p. 288)

This study highlighted that it is the crossing of international borders that is frequently the scandal that constitutes the newsworthiness of climate refugee stories in the media, rather than the plight of displaced people in and of itself.

The journalist and the islander: In early 2006, king tides occurred on the island of Funafuti, capital of Tuvalu. These caused significant flooding and attracted many foreign journalists keen to capture evidence of sea-level rise. I interviewed and observed some of these journalists to gain insights into how journalistic practices mobilise a climate refugee discourse (see also Farbotko, 2008). Nick[16] was an employee of a broadcasting network based in an industrialised nation-state. By the second morning of his four-day stay he was pleased to have conducted several interviews and taken some footage of flooding. However, he still wanted to interview on camera an individual who was planning to emigrate from Tuvalu. He asked if I knew anyone with emigration plans. During many informal conversations and almost thirty semi-structured interviews several months earlier, I had only met two people who expressed a definite desire to build a future outside Tuvalu and explicitly linked this desire to fear about the impacts of climate change. When I returned, they had both left the country. On the previous day, I had met a girl, Mili, with whom I had become friendly during an earlier visit. While we were catching up, Mili had asked me if I knew anything about how a Tuvaluan might go about applying for permanent residency in Australia, as she wanted to move there with her husband and their children.

The family had spent time in an Australian city in the past for education purposes. On returning to Tuvalu, they had experienced tensions within their extended family group, and Mili believed that her nuclear family unit would be stronger if they lived abroad. I told Nick that I knew one person who was thinking about emigrating, although I specified that the reasons were not, as far as I knew, related to climate change. He was still interested in interviewing her. Mili was hesitant at first but then decided she would participate. When Nick started to set up his camera in her home, Mili changed her mind and opted out. She suggested that Fuli, another member of her household, might be willing to be interviewed. As it turned out, she agreed. I did not know Fuli, as she had been abroad during my earlier visit. Fuli seemed not to share Mili's embarrassment at the prospect of being filmed. Nick did not question Fuli about her thoughts on emigration before he agreed to the participant swap. Indeed, he started the camera rolling almost immediately, just pausing to explain who he was and why he was in Tuvalu. His first question to Fuli was "Why do you want to leave Tuvalu?" Immediately, Fuli's confidence vanished. She became flustered, giggling nervously and stammered "I don't know...because of the sea rising?" Nick tried to get her to relax, chattily asking her to describe her fears concerning climate change and to think about why she wanted to emigrate. Again she stumbled and spoke nervously about an uncertain future in Tuvalu. When the camera was turned off, Fuli's confident demeanour returned immediately. Clearly relieved that the interview was over, Fuli said emphatically, "Actually, I don't want to leave Tuvalu. I am just cautious about the future."

This event suggests that media representations of people in Tuvalu can reflect journalists' perceptions of the expectations of their media-consuming public. Such representations can fail to reflect complex engagements with the climate change issue (and with journalists) among Tuvaluans. For Nick, who keenly desired to capture either Mili or Fuli on camera uttering, in his words, three "short sharp sentences" about Tuvalu, migration and climate change, the motivations and even the intentions of the two women towards emigration were almost irrelevant. By employing a combination of leading questions and careful editing, Nick needed to dramatise and exaggerate the idea of a forced migration, which was not forthcoming from either woman. At the same time, he needed to downplay Fuli's complex thoughts and feelings about staying on-island and moving elsewhere. In subsequent conversations with her, I realised that Fuli, a well-educated and relatively affluent person, with political connections in her immediate family, is acutely aware of the significant role played by the international media in publicising Tuvalu's climate change risks, a role which has both support and opposition in Tuvaluan society. For example, in 2005, Honorable Elisala Pita stated in parliament, "we don't want these journalists to come and just make use of us, citizens of Tuvalu" (Tuvalu Parliament, 2005). Despite possessing this knowledge, Fuli did not articulate her concerns on camera to her own satisfaction. Nick subsequently told me that the Western audience for his programme would respond to things that they are fearful of—in this case, tides of desperate immigrants—so that is how he was advised by his editors to frame his story. Also, he informed me that his stories needed to be dramatic and newsworthy. His company had spent thousands of dollars sending him to Tuvalu so they wanted something gripping from him to show for it.

Nick's attempt to distil Fuli's complex feelings about climate change into a crisp story of environmental displacement is one way in which climate refugee subjectivities become sited, performed and reproduced in different places and by different groups of people. Contrastingly, islanders often argue for: firstly, reduced greenhouse gas emissions to prevent sea-level rise; secondly, adaptation on their islands to sea-level rise; and as a last resort, an orderly migration. They often reject the victimage they perceive to be attached to the term climate refugee (McNamara and Gibson 2009). Emeretta Cross, a climate activist who has Tuvaluan and i-Kiribati heritage, has written:

> What we want to demonstrate is that: we are not happy to be labelled victims and where is the glory in being titled "first Environmental refugees"? We know our rights. We want support in gaining better education and medical facilities for our people. Stop using us as points in global indicators of corporate misgoverning. Give us real solutions that will empower us to make sustainable choices as we adapt to our changing environment. (Emeretta Cross, 22 Sep 2009, email sent to Tuvalu Yahoo Groups mailing list)

McNamara's study of perceptions of environmental refugees among Small Island Developing State (SIDS) Ambassadors to the United Nations also points to an ambivalence towards the refugee category:

> SIDS ambassadors...resisted being constructed as "environmental refugees", and in turn opposed...being governed in the short term as "environmental refugees" through multilateral policy. Acceptance of the possibility of "environmental refugees" from climate change might be interpreted as appropriate because it responds to a potential fu-

ture problem, but it also leaves open the option that major industrial powers continue to engage in unsustainable practices, knowing that a "solution" would be forthcoming at the multilateral level to the issue of subsequent displacements. SIDS could find themselves in a situation where guarantees of protection for "environmental refugees"…means that their citizens do indeed become "environmental refugees", their populations become unstable and their sovereignty is challenged—because knowledge of such protection would lessen the demand on industrialised nations to curb CO2 emissions. (McNamara 2006, p. 248)

A *Vaka* Discourse

Gaining considerable momentum in the 1970s, a very different discourse of Pacific people leaving their island homes and journeying elsewhere has emerged—what I call the *vaka* discourse. It has roots in ancient history, but gained prominence in the context of a revival of ancient sailing technologies and practices, focusing on Pacific islanders as great seafarers. Sinavaiana and Kauanui (2007, p. 5) explain that *vaka* is a key metaphor for ongoing literal and figurative journeys among Pacific people. The *vaka* discourse centralises the achievements of the ancestors of Pacific island people, who navigated the Pacific Ocean, and settled its islands:

> *Vaka* were the world's first ocean-going craft. Not until thousands of years later would successful ocean-going vessels be developed in other parts of the world. *Vaka* were traversing the ocean highways of the Pacific long before the people of Europe had the ships or the skills to venture out of sight of land. For the people of the Pacific, *vaka* were more than just boats: they were the material and spiritual vessels that had carried a people—and their way of life—to new lands across the sea. (Howe 2006)

A research and cultural revival group in Hawaii named the Polynesian Voyaging Society (PVS) successfully re-enacted long ocean voyages. They built and sailed a replica of a double-hulled voyaging canoe called *Hokule'a*, capable of carrying dozens of people, without using modern navigational instruments. These voyages were significant in discrediting theories that the Polynesian islands were settled either from the Americas or by accident from Asia. The theories assumed that Polynesians had insufficient navigational and vessel-building skills to discover and settle uninhabited islands, and hence inferred such journeys could not have been completed by design (see Finney, 1994). The PVS was a hybrid project involving Polynesians and Micronesians, elders, academics, and workers—both indigenous and non-indigenous. The PVS's sometimes cooperative and sometimes conflict-ridden canoe-building and journeying projects also helped to shape, and were shaped by, contemporary national and regional solidarities, especially those of the Hawaiian (Finney, 1979). The voyages made by *Hokule'a* to places such as Tahiti, the Cook Islands and Satawal, became a way of articulating continuity in geo-cultural identities, blurring colonial distinctions made between "Polynesia", "Micronesia" and "Melanesia".

PVS activities have been a pivot around which the *vaka* discourse revolves; playing out in voyages, museums, school curricula, documentaries, books, arts festivals, and academic research. Much PVS discourse uses as key characters Pius (Mau) Piaulug and Nainoa Thompson. Piaulug was a master Pulawat navigator who was central to the PVS's relearning of ancient navigational techniques, Thompson was his Hawaiian student.[17]

The voyages of the PVS have a presence in the news media, but the *vaka* discourse only has significant news value among Pacific island audiences.[18] The discourse has a celebratory tone: cultural pride is attached to navigational and seafaring prowess that made *vaka* journeys possible. It was through their mastery of the double-hulled voyaging canoe, "an artefact of cultural genius" that Pacific people claimed the region as their own (Dening 2008, p. 151). Remastering the art of navigation became a strong source of cultural pride, especially in Hawaii where the effects of colonialism had seriously eroded it. This pride is articulated, for example, by political leaders:

> They have already proven beyond a doubt that their ancestors explored and occupied the Pacific with both purpose and precision. If that were all that their voyages meant, they might as well stop, for they have proven the point. But, no, they will not stop. What appeals to them, and certainly to me, is the image of the Pacific navigator, standing near the helmsman, never fully resting, sensing the world around him, the feel of the wind, its force and direction, the pattern of the waves and their multi-origin rhythms, the temperature and the direction of the ocean currents, the ever changing cosmos'. (Sir Geoffrey Henry, Prime Minister of Cook Islands, Sixth Festival of Pacific Arts, October 1992 cited in Finney 2003, p. 52).[19]

Central to the *vaka* discourse is the notion of taming the ocean. Pacific people's sense of history is invested with power derived from being "at home" on the ocean. Journeying is thus a way of being at home. Starting some 6,000 years ago they:

populated most of the habitable islands, not through chance and contingency, not by being blown or drifting as some foreign cynics earlier suggested, but by a highly skilled and motivated practice of sailing and settlement, in which "home" was as much the ocean as the land, and where the canoe was imagined as the still point and the world moving. (Jolly 2001, p. 420)

The theme of reclaiming and celebrating ocean spaces and times as "home" was central to an international travelling exhibition on Pacific voyaging, *Vaka Moana*, curated at the Auckland Museum:

For Pacific Islanders the ocean is not an alien element. It is not something to be feared, conquered or controlled. It is home...to the initiated, the ocean was a network of pathways connecting the living not only to each other, but to the voyages of their ancestors, and to the gods. It also offered a way into the future with the possibilities of sailing into new lands. (Howe, 2006)

In the *vaka* discourse, the voyaging canoe is the still point in a world of shifting horizons. This spatial positioning can be observed in the Pulawat system of navigation by stars, clouds, currents, swells, birds and winds that Mau Piaulug taught Nainoa Thompson, often referred to as wayfinding. According to Dening (2008, p. 147), "for a wayfinder, no knowledge, no image is stilled in either time or space." Wayfinding is the ability to orient a canoe in relation to islands, the stars, the climate, and the self on the ocean. It is the act of rooting oneself *en route*, via the medium of the canoe. The voyaging canoe is constantly reoriented, the centre of a universe in which islands and stars move past, but constantly define, the canoe's location (Finney, 1994; Kyselka, 1987).

When the Pacific islands were being navigated and settled for the first time, powerful journeying narratives became, and remain, embedded in the social identities of various groups of islanders. Maori people, for example, value accounts of voyages between Hawaiki (a homeland central to Polynesian cosmologies) and Aotearoa. The canoes that carried them, and the genealogies that trace descent back to those who came in those canoes, contribute strongly to Maori identities (Richards, 2008). Given its valued images of powerful island navigators embedded in social identities, it is perhaps not surprising that some of the islanders identified as imminent climate refugees are starting to mobilise components of the *vaka* discourse. A useful example narrative is from Carteret Islander environmental activist Ursula Rakova, who writes about the people of her island's response to the climate refugee discourse and the challenge of rising sea levels in terms of "sailing the waves on our own":

> For some time now, Carteret Islanders have made eye-catching headlines: "Going, going…Papua New Guinea atoll sinking fast". Academics have dubbed us amongst the world's first "environmental refugees" and journalists put us on the "frontline of climate change"…: "We do not need labels but action."…Tired of empty promises, the Carterets Council of Elders formed a non-profit association in late 2006 to organise the voluntary relocation of most of the Carterets' population of 3,300. The association was named *Tulele Peisa*, which means "sailing the waves on our own". This name choice reflects the elders' desire to see Carteret Islanders remain strong and self-reliant, not becoming dependent on food handouts for their survival.[20]

A Drifting Discourse

> A man [sic] who is not bound by the close ties of family and of property will sometimes take a canoe and a few coconuts and trust himself to the mercy of the ocean rather than endure the reproach of his fellows. In the uncertain currents of the atoll groups this is virtual suicide; and although it is tempered by an element of chance, the primary intention of the one who thus sets out is to sever himself from all past connections even by death. Often, one or more sympathetic companions will accompany him, and their intention in thus wilfully sacrificing themselves is to bring repentance upon the persons responsible for their friend's grievance. In many cases, the departure of young folks is deliberately undertaken in order to punish older relatives for some real or fancied misuse of their authority. Traditions show that this trait was not uncommon throughout Polynesia. (Kennedy, 1929, p. 1)

This passage contains a sombre account of some of the practices that are central to what I call the drifting discourse. Like the *vaka* discourse, it is concerned with past and present ocean journeys. But the vessels of this discourse are generally smaller boats—fishing vessels and runabouts—rather than the "monuments" that are the double-hulled voyaging canoes (Richards, 2008). Also different is the notion of ambivalent voyaging, rather than purposeful voyaging and navigating with a particular destination in mind. While the above account centralises suicide and death, this is only one aspect of the drifter discourse. It also incorporates ocean survival, knowledge of which is important for atoll dwellers and inhabitants of other very small islands in the Pacific. People on atolls remain highly dependent on the sea for food. Fishing is important to the cultural identity and diets of many atoll inhabitants. For people who spend long periods of time fishing in the ocean around their island, the prospect of becoming lost at sea is ever-present. Furthermore, for inhabitants of small islands who have suffered from social discord, sometimes leaving the island is perceived to be the only solution. Contemporary instances of such journeys are rare, but not unheard of (Taukiei Kitara, personal communication, 26 March 2009). In the past, exile from islands was a frequent form of punishment. These practices have given rise to a sense of the ever-present possibility of journeys with no specific destination, which is central to the drifting discourse. Although an idealised return home may be longed for, more likely is that the drifter will perish at sea, or wash up on another island.

In identifying the drifting discourse, I certainly do not resurrect theories that Polynesian settlement of the Pacific islands was accidental rather than purposeful. Rather, I consider drifting practices alongside and also interacting with those of seafaring prowess. *Vaka* journeys can be transformed into drifting journeys. Intentional journeys do not always go to plan: inclement weather, social discord and bad luck can lead to drifting; to losing one's way; and attempting to find it again. At the intersection of the *vaka* and drifter discourses is the poignant history of Tevake, a navigator from the Polynesian outliers of the Solomon Islands. He was known while alive as the last Polynesian navigator, and in 1970 embarked on a highly symbolic canoe "voyage of no return" at a time when he sensed his death was imminent. When this navigator chose death at sea, his wayfinding knowledge died with him there (see Lewis 1972, p. 309).

Crucial to the drifting discourse is the highly uncertain outcomes of drifting journeys. In the past, landing on another island could involve peaceful incorporation into another community or warfare. In cases of banishment, a small canoe may have been intended to function, quite literally, as a coffin but such intentions did not always come to fruition. Paalo (1981) explains the practice thus: "the most serious penalty that could be given was to exile someone from the island by putting him on a canoe and told never to return. This we called *fakafolau*."[21] One story is told about the punishment of a man named Kalihi on Nanumea (now part of Tuvalu) about 1874. His punishers took care to push him away from the island in a leaky canoe with no paddles.

On Nanumea, a man called Poepoe wanted to avenge the killing of his grandfather, an invader of Nanumea who was killed. When Popoe's father forbade him from undertaking revenge:

Poepoe set out in a canoe with his uncle Pikia to *folau,* or commit suicide at sea. No one heard about what happened to them until nearly 200 years later, in the 1960s, when some Tuvaluans living in the Solomon Islands heard a local tradition of Poepoe's canoe arriving safely at tiny Anuta island. (Isako, 1983)

Thus the vessel cast adrift by no means signifies a certain death. Contemporary instances of self-exile are sometimes intercepted and sometimes not (e.g., Lifuka, 1978; Taukiei Kitara, personal communication, 26 March 2009). Unexpected arrivals can also have profound effects on the recipient community, as in the case of Elekana. He was Tuvalu's "accidental missionary" who drifted from his native Cook Islands in 1861 and is heroized for his role in converting the island of Nukulaelae, where he landed in an almost-perished state, to Christianity (Goldsmith & Munro, 2002).

Attention pertaining to survival skills for *un*planned long-distance voyages is inscribed in cultural practices and legends. Another of Tuvalu's islands, Nukufetau, has a children's song that records the importance of survival skills at sea for fisherfolk:

The shout carried a long way above the village.

Sail the canoe to America, but take a lot of the edible pandanus nuts from the motu of Kavakava.

You must eat the eggs.

The big turtle walks up on the sand at Kaleanga.

It looks like a small canoe bringing food to the hungry.

It will lay a million eggs.

According to the anthropologist who recorded and translated this song,

men who go out to sea to fish in sailing canoes fear that the wind will change and they will be unable to get back to land. Nukufetau, where this game was collected, is exposed; and strong ocean currents pass by the atoll so the threat of being carried away is always present. (Lobban, 1984, p. 18-19)

In order for fisherfolk to successfully carry out their tasks, they need to face spending a great deal of time unexpectedly at sea, to know how to survive on the ocean, and to be able to attempt to make for land when driven off course. Arguably, this knowledge is as important to sea people as wayfinding is for navigating. Furthermore, wayfinding constitutes part of the knowledge necessary for survival at sea.

What the drifting discourse captures is a long history of the sea as a source of unexpected and unplanned connection to other lands. Survival at sea for fisherfolk today remains a matter of catching fish and rainwater, making vessel repairs, perhaps catching a shark and drinking its blood, and estimating one's position on the ocean. In these, the fisher's vessel is crucial. The small fishing vessel, like the larger *vaka*, is a "membrane positioned between human beings and the ocean upon which they sailed...an object of liminality, a built medium of transformation and success would always be in the balance" (Richards, 2008, p. 215). The importance of the small canoe for the atoll people of Kiribati has been described as follows:

> The imperative of survival demands the integration of people and place...The canoe is an expression of this complex interaction and is deeply rooted in social concerns, traditional values and practices, mirroring those enduring qualities of the traditional skills, ancient spirituality and survival that remain at the heart of what it is to be i-Kiribati. (Whincup 2007, p. 45)

The fishing canoe is a signifier of the meanings of climate change among the Tuvaluan community in Melbourne, Australia. A handmade model fishing canoe, made by one of its members, Tito Tapuango, was placed adjacent to a representation of a deserted islet as the centrepiece of the exhibition the community initiated and helped to develop at the Immigration Museum titled *Waters of Tuvalu: Nation at Risk*. Ambivalence seemed to characterise the issue of survival in this exhibition. The small fishing canoe and deserted islet together functioned as a reminder of a continuous, contemporary identity of, and practice by, Polynesian people as oceanic survivors as well as the significant threat of climate change to their islands. It was a means for people of Tuvaluan heritage to publicly confront the question of a difficult future, possibly one without habitable national territory and sovereignty.

Discussion

Pacific migration discourses are always vehicles for power. They are, for instance, a means for political constituencies in larger nation-states such as

Australia and New Zealand to relationally construct their own image as regional superpower, in the reflection of their small island neighbours (Fry, 1997; Farbotko, 2010b). In thinking of small islands as spaces fundamentally outside modernity, dependence on aid connections to the "industrialised world" seems preordained. At its most extreme, a litany of smallness in development discourses of the Pacific culminates in a doomsday scenario of population growth, environmental damage, poor governance and lack of economic performance, not to mention climate change impacts (Callick, 1993; cf Fry, 1997). Conventional—often Western—understandings of migration facilitate this imaginative geography, with emphases on uprootedness and rupture, and shiftings from periphery to core. Similarly, the climate refugee crisis discourse is one way in which an "industrialised world" reinforces its own interests as "centre" (Farbotko, 2008). Almost invariably, climate refugee debates are underpinned by a set of spatial assumptions that position people displaced by climate change in terms of very particular migration vectors: the flow of displaced people is deemed to inevitably originate in the developing world, and have as destination the industrialised world. This type of migration discourse tends to bypass certain types of questions: what does good governance mean in Pacific cultures? Whose interests are served in insisting that islanders will migrate to the developed world following displacement associated with sea-level rise? What policy mechanisms may enable islanders to migrate in ways that do not result in desperation and the necessity for refugee status? The climate refugee discourse, in sidestepping such questions, engages in a particular form of identity formation: those who become identified as climate refugees are used to reflect back a reiteration of industrialised world inhabitants, and their living practices, as "normal". Through the projection of their own fears of a warming world and desires to offer Western solutions to distant others, climate refugee advocates often imagine Pacific islanders as desperate and disempowered refugees. These imaginings enable Pacific migrants to be positioned as something to either fear or control by those in the industrialised world. The most prominent way in which this positioning occurs is via the highly contested issue of opening the borders of industrialised world nation-states to climate refugees. Even when the "core" is imagined as a space of salvation for those from "the periphery" in a climate change crisis, islanders are reduced to being necessary recipients of the compassion and protection of the industrialised world, as fearful climate refugees. Such accounts fail to take into account more complex journeyings by island people and their understandings of their voyages, in which climate change is just one of their challenges as they live in, and move about, a globalised world (Lilomaiava-Doktor, 2009; Hau'ofa, 1993).

It is in this context that representations of climate change as "crisis" are mobilised as persuasive mechanisms, aimed at changing behaviour and prompting action on climate change to reduce greenhouse gas emissions. Climate change fear is strongly associated with feelings of hopelessness and apathy (O'Neill & Nicholson-Cole, 2009) and fear often underscores the climate refugee subjectivities mobilised in the name of islanders in climate change news and campaigns in the industrialised world (see Farbotko, 2010a, 2010b). As increasing attempts to try and enrol particular groups of people to "tell" climate change stories are made among journalists and climate change activists, those who are designated as future climate refugees are often actively resisting the identity and building their climate change subjectivities in other ways. For instance, for Jane, a citizen of Tuvalu whom I interviewed, the prospect of forced migration coupled with the designation "environmental refugee" denies her the right to a fully equal identity as a member of the global community and her rights to be in her own space in the world:

> Jane: It is sad for me to think of that future. And we wouldn't like to eventually get forced out of our place and be classed as environmental refugees. That has a negative attachment to it. It's like considering ourselves like second-class citizens in the future. It devalues your feelings as a human being. It makes you feel small and negative about yourself. And it doesn't make you fully human. And the question is, who has the right to deny myself the joy of feeling human, of feeling fully human? Because we are born equal and we should be treated equally. (Interview participant—see Farbotko 2008, p. 245)

For other islanders, resistance to the climate refugee identity is avoided in favour of making space for ambivalent approaches to the question of displacement. Ursula Rakova (cited above) questions what journalists and academics are publicly announcing about the future of her community, and emphasises the foundation of an indigenous organisation to deal with resettlement issues.

Studies of political refugees in the media are important for understanding the climate refugee discourse, as political and climate refugees share a position of being implicated in a politics of fear. Gale (2004), for instance, has highlighted the highly contested migration trajectories of political refugees. The politics of fear deems refugees to be "calculating foreigners" from outside the "industrialised world" seeking to penetrate the borders of that world. At its most pronounced, they are perceived as free-riders deliberately exploiting the industrialised world for economic gain.

In the case of Hurricane Katrina, the media played a central role in shaping the language that came to characterise as refugees the people (many of them African Americans) displaced in New Orleans. Hurricane Katrina evacuations occurred inside the borders of the United States. Significantly, it was the image of the distressed and homeless human being that embodied the "climate refugee" in reporting on Katrina, location in relation to state borders notwithstanding. But the media also became the arena in which those labelled as refugees voiced their feelings on the label that had been attached to them in the process of making and selling news. One stated on CBS news, for example, "I can't stand people calling me a refugee. I am an American and I love America" (Masquelier, 2006, p. 737).

The resistance to the refugee label by Katrina evacuees and media audiences suggests that refugees are perceived as the antithesis of an idealised Western self-image:

> The discomfort that so many people in the United States reportedly felt at hearing (or reading about) fellow U.S. citizens being called "refugees" was revealing of their self-image. An image of power, prosperity, and self-sufficiency...all of this was now under threat, thanks to Katrina...The tendency to label Katrina victims as "refugees" was part of a racialized discourse that, through its emphasis on responsibility and accountability, surreptitiously excluded poor New Orleans residents from its public, thereby helping to naturalize social inequality. (Masquelier 2006, pp. 736–737)

Climate refugees have thus come to represent threats to treasured projects such as progress and industrialisation, as well as nationalist ideals that reinforce boundaries between "developed" and "developing worlds".

Political refugees are, in an embodied sense, different from climate refugees. For political refugees, statelessness often aligns with their location in spaces such as refugee camps, airports, detention centres, off-shore asylum processing centres, prisons, people-smuggling vehicles, boats in international waters, courts of law, refugee resettlement programs, language schools and so on. "Climate refugees" from the Pacific, however, are currently extraordinarily difficult, if not impossible, to locate in such spaces. Any present Pacific climate refugee reality is chiefly discursive. Despite images of islanders wading through flooded waters, and Al Gore falsely claiming in his documentary[22] that the citizens of Tuvalu have *all* had to evacuate to New Zealand, islanders are rarely, at least at present, found in detention centres or the court systems of industrialised countries. The distinction in the media between reporting on predictions of future displacement, and attempts to convey a present reality of Pacific climate refugees, is blurred as the media limits imaginings of displacement to the refugee discourse. Examples suggesting that there is a wider story than this discursive production include Fuli's discomfort answering Nick's questions in front of the camera and journalists forcing the question of migration to New Zealand into an imaginary climate refugee policy. These examples suggest that some of the questions being asked about "fleeing an inundated island" are being moulded to fit into a very particular climate refugee narrative. Problematically, this moulding of refugee subjectivities recalls a racialised hierarchical opposition between spaces of belonging in a globalised world that permits only rooted indigenous peoples but allows for mobile Westerners (Malkki 1992).

Understanding "climate refugees" in terms of islander victims and powerful industrialised world people tends to elide the "openness of the subject" (Pile 2008). It is arguable that Pacific discourses of journeying and being, on and across islands and ocean result in a type of subject formation that is inarticulable. Nevertheless Pile (2008) also argues that any attempt to understand identities through spatial practices involves the interrogation of the everyday: how do people ordinarily use and make spaces and places for themselves? Journeying is often a prosaic matter of earning income and studying in a globalised world. Even if such practices are more common among an educated elite, kinship relationships mean that less cosmopolitan islanders are likely to have well-travelled close family members. Furthermore, journeying is not limited to a leadership or tertiary-educated portion of society. A significant proportion of Tuvaluan and i-Kiribati men, for example, work as crew members for international commercial shipping companies. They spend up to eleven months of every year away from home, their remitted wages often of crucial importance for extended families.

The imagining of oceanic expanses, rather than small dry surfaces, as central to island ways of being, is also important. The sea cannot be neglected as a powerful marker of identity and practice for islanders. For Pacific people, "the ocean is our most powerful metaphor, the ocean is in us" (Hau'ofa, 1998). Land, although significant, does not delimit Pacific economic, social, and cultural values. It is in sea *and* land, "routes" *and* "roots"—a double dialectic through which Pacific people draw on their history as great navigators, travellers, seafarers, fisherfolk and survivors to identify as "Sea Peoples of the Sea of Islands" (Dening, 2008, 146; Clifford, 2001; Hau'ofa, 1993, 1998; Wood, 2003). Thus, it is important to challenge:

> the way in which Pacific peoples are often represented as simply rooted, as grounded in the land, partitioned by the borders of a village or an island, as static in place and time while foreigners—Europeans or Asians—are represented as mobile explorers, as invasive strangers. Such spatial language often transforms into a temporal language whereby Islanders are portrayed as stuck in times past, confined by the boundaries of tradition while foreigners are constructed as the agents of change and transformation—the voyagers, the planters, the labor traders, the missionaries, the colonial officials, the development agents. Even those theories hostile to colonial and capitalist penetration can portray the process as one of a rapacious mobile capital, engulfing Islanders who are imaged as hapless victims, trapped in the closed inertia of community, or lost in nostalgic recollections of times past. (Jolly, 2001, p. 419)

Thus, discussions of "migration" for people in the Pacific can be usefully informed by an understanding of Pacific ways of being and journeying, such as those of the *vaka* and drifting discourses, and how these operate with the discourse of the "climate refugee". All three discourses intersect and inform the ways in which Pacific people's identities are bound up in the journeys, disruptions and continuities that make up their comings and goings from islands.

Conclusion

Because voluminous narratives are emerging around a new subject, the climate refugee, public debate over it needs to be critically analysed in order to understand how climate change-related displacement and migration is perceived and acted upon by various participants in the discourse. I have attempted to draw attention to culturally situated productions of the climate refugee crisis, particularly in the news media. In focussing on the Pacific, I have not considered how other discourses of migration constitute and contest the climate refugee discourse around in and for other low-lying regions around the world. Seasonal migration around monsoons, for instance, may be very pertinent in South Asia. By juxtaposing three discourses on passages between and among islands and continents among indigenous people of the Pacific, I have elucidated how meaning is produced and contested in public debate over the climate refugee crisis, particularly in the news media. The first discourse produces the islander as climate refugee, a victim of rising sea levels. The second discourse, arising in the context of a cultural revival of ancient sailing technologies and practices, focuses on the islander as great seafarer. The third discourse is concerned with ambivalent journeys—survival when cast adrift from islands due to inclement weather, technical mishaps, or social exile, and with no definite destination. The role of news media actors in constructing particular configurations of journeying and being, on island and ocean among Pacific Islanders is significant: the Pacific navigator discourse constructs migration in terms of planning, navigation and seafaring prowess, and the ambivalent journeys discourse constructs migration in terms of chance, fluidity, adaptation and survival. Both are marginalised by media outside the Pacific, and contrast with the climate refugee discourse, which dominates the Western press, and emphasises disruption and disempowerment. Making room for alternative discourses in debate over the climate refugee crisis, I argue, is important for more productive conversations about sea-level rise and displacement that move beyond a perpetrator-victim binary. Multiple perspectives on narratives and practices of journeying among Pacific people enables a richer understanding of the ways in which inhabitants of small islands represent themselves as they face the prospect of sea-level-rise-related displacement.

Notes

1. For example: "The New Climate Deal: A Pocket Guide" http://assets.panda.org /downloads/wwf_climate_deal_1.pdf.
2. For example: "Greenpeace warns of 200 mln global warming refugees by 2040" http://rawstory.com/news/afp/Greenpeace_warns_of_200_mln_global__06192007.ht ml
3. For example: "Climate Justice" http://www.foe.org.au/climate-justice/overview-of-climate-justice
4. Peter Quiddington, "Scientists warn of islands' peril" *Sydney Morning Herald* 23 August 1988, page 7.
5. http://www.guardian.co.uk/environment/2009/nov/03/global-warming-climate-refugees
6. Studies such as Roy and Connell (1991) and Connell and Lea (1992) raised the issue of climate change and refugees in the Pacific. Geographer John Connell characterised Tuvaluans as inevitable future environmental refugees. The islanders were, in his opinion, on the verge of becoming economic refugees. Climate change would simply hasten the

process. This narrative was picked up in the Australian media (Farbotko 2010b).

7. Detailed consideration of migration questions is absent from the major international agreements on climate change: the United Nations Framework Convention on Climate Change (1992), the Kyoto Protocol (1997) and the Copenhagen Accord (2009).

8. http://www.thestar.com/news/world/article/699528

9. http://www.theage.com.au/national/first-climate-refugees-start-move-to-new-island-home-20090728-e06x.html

10. http://www.radioaustralianews.net.au/stories/200902/2491301.htm?desktop

11. http://www.good.is/post/saving-the-first-climate-refugees/

12. http://motherjones.com/environment/2009/11/tuvalu-climate-refugees

13. http://www.islandsbusiness.com/islands_business/index_dynamic/containerName ToReplace=MiddleMiddle/focusModuleID=5548/overideSkinName=issueArticle-full.tpl

14. http://www.edie.net/news/news_story.asp?id=10866

15. http://www.theage.com.au/news/national/pm-rejects-tuvalu-on-sea-level/2007/02/19/1171733684706.html 19 February 2007.

16. Pseudonyms used.

17. "Nearly every important navigational technique and concept encountered in Micronesia was matched by its Polynesian counterpart. Differences seemed to depend much more on local insular geographical features than on major cultural-linguistic variations. On the admittedly incomplete evidence available therefore, we would hardly seem justified in speaking of separate Polynesian and Micronesian navigational systems, though there may well have been some such distinction in the heyday of voyaging" (Lewis 1972, 11).

18. Voyages in 2010 by two canoes, *Jitdam Kapeel* from the Marshall Islands and *Simion Ho-kulea* from Yap were reported extensively in news and websites in English serving the Pacific region. For example, a Google search on these canoe names yielded sites such as: "Marshall Islanders revive ancient navigation skills", Pacific Islands News Association:

    http://www.pina.com.fj/?p=pacnews&m=read&o=14729267034bde2e926ec35920b05 a; "Marshall Islands Outrigger Canoe Makes Modern Voyage with Ancient Skills" Yokwe Online: "Everything Marshall Islands" http://www.yokwe.net/index.php?name =News&file=article&sid=2576; "Coast Guard Searching for missing canoe crew" Honolulu Star Bulletin http://www.starbulletin.com/news/20100520_coast_guard _searching_for_missing_canoe_crew.html). In contrast, no matches were returned us-ing these canoe names as search terms in the English language news publications cov-ered by the Factiva database.

19. Canoe voyaging is not exclusively a male domain: women have been involved in build-ing and crewing the Hoku'lea and other PVS vessels. There are mythologies of female sailors commanding vessels. Women were also typically responsible for the weaving of canoe sails from pandanus (Sinavaiana and Kauanui 2007).

20. http://ourworld.unu.edu/en/how-to-guide-for-environmental-refugees/

21. *Fakafolau*, along with other practices such as infanticide, did not survive the influence of the missionaries.
22. Al Gore, 2006. "An Inconvenient Truth." Documentary directed by L. David, L. Bender and S.Z. Burns, Paramount Classics and Participant Productions.

CHAPTER SEVEN

Chinese Irregular Migration into Europe: Economic Challenges and Opportunities in Media Representation

Yan Wu, Xiangqin Zeng & Xiaoying Liu

This chapter examines how public discourse of Chinese irregular migrants into Europe is represented in a Chinese-language national newspaper. Focussing on migration relations between Europe and China, we aim to analyse the links between irregular migration, economic models, control policies and public perceptions as represented in the *Global Times*. Based on a thematic analysis of *Global Times'* coverage of Chinese irregular migration in the past ten years (2000–2009), we examine the role mass media plays in representing irregular migration as a public discourse and its correlation to economic challenges and opportunities. We also look at how voices from various claims-makers, such as nation states, international governing bodies, professional communities and research bodies, pressure groups and non-governmental organisations (NGOs), as well as individuals, are represented in constructing such a discourse.

In representing global migration as a risk to regional economy and security, the news media plays a central role in generating public debate and impacting on migration policy-making. As Brewer and Gross point out, mass media provide not only "facts", but "frames that tell audience members how to understand particular policy controversies" (2010, p. 159). Since a frame is "a central organising idea or storyline that provides meaning to an unfolding strip of events, weaving a connection among them [and] suggests what the controversy is about, the essence of the issue" (Gamson & Modigliani, 1987, p. 143), the question of "whose framing of reality" (Ryan, 1991, p. 53), or whose interpretation of the issue, will be favoured by the media has a major effect on the public perception of migration as a risk.

Researchers in the interdisciplinary studies of migration and media have identified the key role mass media plays in intervening in the migration process. Firstly, global media function as important sources of information for potential migrants; secondly, the media construction of migrants in receiving countries largely determines the nature of public discourse and the general perception of migrants as either "desirable" or "undesirable"; thirdly, media from migration sending countries may connect with members from the diasporic community and reshape their cultural identity (King & Wood, 2001, pp. 1–2). Much research has been conducted in the area of how mass media may racialise, stereotype, and stigmatise unwanted migrants (van Dijk, 1988a; 1989; Campani, 2001; Kaye, 2001) and how the media can enforce migrants' social exclusion and marginalisation in the receiving society (Mai, 2005). However, most studies focus on the media representation of migrants in receiving countries. The sending country's perspective, especially the sending country's perspective of irregular migration in the context of economic development, is only marginally studied.

> 'Irregular migrants' (undocumented migrants or unauthorized migrants) describes people who enter a country without necessary documents and permits. There is no clear or unanimously agreed definition of this term. Some international organizations use it as an umbrella phrase for a variety of different phenomena involving people who enter or remain in a country of which they are not a citizen in breach of national laws. These include migrants who enter or remain in a country without authorization, those who are smuggled or trafficked across an international border, unsuccessful asylum seekers who fail to observe a deportation order and people who circumvent immigration controls through the arrangement of bogus marriages (The Global Commission on International Migration, 2005, p. 32)

A consensus approved by the Conference of Peripheral Maritime Regions of Europe General Assembly, on the other hand, holds that

> [t]wo different types of irregular immigration have been observed: firstly large numbers of immigrants who arrive at ports and airports, generally with tourist visas, and who then remain in European territory once their visa has expired, and secondly, a more dramatic form of immigration which sees immigrants arrive at the European coastline aboard unsafe craft which put at real risk the lives of those travelling and which, in many cases, have caused *fatalities*. (2007, p. 1 [empasis added])

Irregular migration occurs when migration policies limit regular migration but fail to enforce it perfectly, and therefore irregular migration can be interpreted as a gap between rules and their implementation. It is estimated by the Organization for Economic Cooperation and Development (OECD) that "between 10 and 15 per cent of Europe's 56 million migrants have irregular status and that each year around half a million undocumented migrants arrive in the

EU" (The Global Commission on International Migration, 2005, p. 32). In the European Union, the gap is currently mainly addressed by measures aimed at stricter border controls and deterring immigrants. Many of these measures appear to be a direct reaction to public *perceptions* of migration, especially irregular migration, as a threat to the labour market, the welfare state and national security.

Efforts in curbing irregular migration call for international collaboration between sending countries and receiving countries. Since the turn of the century, patterns of migration and the motivations of irregular migrants from China into Europe have demonstrated significant changes. Such changes are closely linked to economic opportunities in the receiving countries in Europe and the economic prominence of China as a rising world power. We propose that restrictive migration policies need to be reconsidered in the context of the globalisation of the world economy and of labour distribution, so that European countries may manage the opportunities and the challenges posed by Chinese irregular migration.

Irregular Migration from China:
Changing Patterns since the Turn of the Century

China is the world's most populated country with a population of 1.33 billion in 2007 and 1.43 billion in 2020 as projected by the United Nations Development Programme (UNDP, 2009, p. 192). China's international migration is primarily emigration and the total was 590,300 in 2005 and 685,800 by 2010 (UNDP, 2009, p. 144). Compared with most countries, China's international emigration rate (0.5%) and international movement rate (0.5%) are very low[1] (UNDP, 2009, p. 144). However, due to the sheer magnitude of its overall population, China is constantly viewed as a major country of migration and is perceived with fear. Moreover, Pieke (2004, p. 2) argues that such fear of migration from China is closely connected to the fear "of the coming Chinese age" in Western Europe.

Portrayed as a significant source of irregular migration into Europe, China has been depicted as a major threat and such a discourse is amplified in tabloid media. Media coverage of events such as Dover in 2000 and the Morecambe Bay Cockling Disaster in 2004 "drummed up the imagery of snakeheads, criminal gangs, exploitation and bogus asylum seeking" (Pieke, 2004, p. 2) among the

Chinese diasporic community. Even a quality paper such as the *Guardian* quoted Cabinet Minister Beverly Hughes as an official source in commenting on the deaths of Chinese cockle pickers in Morecambe Bay:

> It demonstrates yet again what can happen to people when the highly organized crimi-
> nal elements that are behind the trafficking in the first place—and here with Chinese
> people we are talking about the ruthless gangs, the snakeheads and so on who operate
> globally and transport people for labour exploitation—at what great risk people put
> themselves. (Lawrence et al., 2004, p. 3)

Such representations, however, "stand in contrast with the fact that an in-creasing number of migrants from China are arriving in Europe through regular channels" and in contrast with the relatively low number of Chinese migrants compared to other migrant groups (Laczko, 2003). Pieke (2004, p. 11) argues that "Chinese migration" in fact consists of "a kaleidoscope of flows, biogra-phies and ambitions [and Chinese migrants] simply have become much more mobile as part of their life in transnational social spaces" for a variety of rea-sons. Meanwhile, media representation of irregularity associated with Chinese migrants also undermines the positive contribution Chinese migrants make to the economy in Europe. Playing on the public fear of crime and cruelty associ-ated with human trafficking, the media, as Pieke (2004) contends, fails to ad-dress the government's responsibility for regulating seasonal agricultural work and the responsibility of employers.

Chinese immigrants in Europe have changed from geographically spe-cialised diasporic groups into "truly global transnational communities and pro-fessional migration networks" in the past decades (Pieke, 2004, p. 3). Since the economic reforms of China in 1978, new emigration from China has been inte-grated into existing communities of overseas Chinese worldwide and these communities have been experiencing multi-directional migration flows (International Organization for Migration, 2002). The established Chinese dias-pora has grown in both community size and in diversity in terms of ethnicity, source areas, socio-economic background, types of employment and entrepre-neurship (International Organization for Migration, 2002, p. 10).

Though the exact number is difficult to ascertain, irregular migrants from China were estimated at 500,000 in 2002 and the success rate of smuggling was 40% to 60% (Lin, 2002). Estimates of the number of Chinese irregular immi-grants in the UK ranged between 150,000 and 200,000 by 2009 (University of

Nottingham, 2009, p. 9). Though cases of human trafficking (based on the border apprehension data from the Chinese government) started to decline after 2005, Chinese trafficking victims remain the largest single nationality group, accounting for 17% of the known total of trafficking victims in the UK (University of Nottingham, 2009, p. 9).

Based on information received from the Ministry of Public Security in China, the main channels for Chinese to become irregular are: clandestine border-crossing over sea or inland borderline; human smuggling in cargo containers; getting through border ports with falsified documents; overstaying temporary residence permits after legal entry into destination countries for the purpose of tourism, study or labour contracts; transiting to a third country after legal entry into destination (Information Office, 2010).

Routes for clandestine border-crossing have expanded from the traditional sea routes to multiple routes via air and inland crossings as well. Gang Shi points out that there are two routes into Western Europe favoured by Chinese irregular migrants. The first is inland crossing, whereby Chinese migrants enter the Schengen Zone via Russia and the former Yugoslavia crossing into Italy. The second is a sea route starting at Shanghai, winding its way through the South China Sea into the Indian Ocean, reaching the Mediterranean, and entering Western Europe via Italy (Shi, 2004, p. 35). Zhou and Wang's (2004) study finds that the number of "overstaying" irregular Chinese in Europe has surpassed that of the traditionally predominant group who arrived via trafficking networks. "Overstaying" Chinese who enter their destination countries with authorised permits for study, tourism, business or temporary work but stay and seek employment after the legal residence permits expire have become the largest group of irregular Chinese overseas since the turn of the century (Zhou & Wang, 2004, pp. 16–17).

The International Organisation for Migration statistics (2003) reveal that over the last decade of the 20th century, the number of Chinese residents increased 260% to almost 50,000 in Italy and rose more than six-fold to 36,000 in Spain. Traditionally Chinese emigrants moved into the lower end of the labour market and engaged primarily in the sector of catering, trading, construction and manufacturing, mainly controlled by the established Chinese diasporic community. Chinese scholars believe that most of the emigrants from south-eastern coastal China are young unemployed males or peasants whose educational level is below the junior or senior secondary school level (Zhuang, 2001, p. 29).

However, Pieke points out that new migrants coming from diverse geographic regions in China demonstrate changed patterns in engaging in receiving countries' labour markets:

> mass migration not only provided cheap labour for the restaurants and shops owned by the established Chinese communities in western Europe, but also inserted a dynamism and appetite for expansion that led to the exploration of new economic niches (vending, import, garment manufacturing) and frontier areas in southern, eastern and northern Europe. (Pieke, 2004, pp. 3–4)

Changes in the occupational activities of new Chinese migrants in Europe to a degree reflect rising entrepreneurship in China and the prominence of China as a global economic power. A study shows that 40.5% of Chinese migrants engage in trade, with more than three thousand registered as businessmen in Paris. Chinese businessmen in Spain own over 3,000 shops in both wholesale and retail areas (Guo, Chen, Xie, Zhang, & Lin, 2009). Studies reveal that in Italy, Chinese migrants from Zhejiang Province account for the largest number of small business owners among non-European Union immigrants and have started expanding their entrepreneurial aptitude to the management of the entire productive process in the garment sector (Ceccagno, 2003). On the receiving end, China ranked second after India among top remittance-receiving countries and benefited from a remittance of US$33 billion in 2007 (World Bank, 2008, p. 76).

Media Representation of Irregular Migration from China

For this research, we conducted a thematic analysis of the coverage of irregular migration in the *Global Times* from 2000 to 2009. We sampled the *Global Times* articles from the *Apabi* database, an electronic newspaper archive in the Chinese language, by using a combination of key search terms such as "undocumented" (无证), "illegal" (非法) or "irregular" (非常规) combined with "migration/migrants" (移民). The list of search terms aims to be exhaustive and to include as much as possible combinations of relevant key words including: 假签证 (bogus visa); 非法签证 (illegal visa); 非法/未经授权滞留 (illegal/unauthorised overstay); 非法居留 (illegal residence); 非法入境 (illegal entry); 非法劳工 (illegal labour); 黑工 (illegal/undocumented labour); 无证劳工 (undocumented labour); 非法劳务 (illegal employment); 偷渡 (smuggling); 蛇头 ("snakehead", a figurative expression for "smugglers").

Table 1: The number of articles generated by search terms

	In the headline of the article	Anywhere in the article
1) Immigrants or migrants or migration or visa combined with:		
Undocumented	0	2
Irregular	0	0
Illegal	35	306
Bogus	1	4
2) Illegal combined with:		
Overstaying	2	56
Residence	2	35
Entry	7	81
3) Illegal or *Hei* (colloquial for illegal in Chinese language) or Undocumented combined with:		
Labours, work, or employment	13	85
4) Smuggling or smugglers	71	211
Total	**131**	**510**

The search generated a total of 131 news stories with key search terms in the headlines and 510 news items with key search terms anywhere in the article (Table 1).

The term "illegal" rather than "irregular" or "undocumented" is used much more frequently in *Global Times*' coverage. Although "illegal migration" and "irregular migration", to a large extent, are used interchangeably in public discourse (especially in media discourse) in China, these two terms have different sociological and legal connotations. "Irregular migrants", used to describe those who enter a country without the necessary legal documents and permits, is considered preferable by academics, international migration organisations, and NGOs. "Illegal migrants", on the other hand, has a strong connotation with criminality. Irregular migration should be defined as an "administrative", rather than a "criminal", offence in receiving countries, because irregular migrants could be the victim of uncontrollable situations in their home countries or the victims of crime including human trafficking and other forms of exploitation (Migrants' Rights Network & MigrationWork, 2009). Meanwhile, there is no universally accepted definition of unauthorised migration and the definition of illegal entry, stay or work may vary from country to country. The use of "illegal migration" may deny the humanity of irregular migrants (Koser, 2005, p. 7).

The choice of "illegal migrants" instead of "irregular migrants" in Chinese media coverage could be explained by the official affiliation of the *Global Times*. Founded in 1993, the *Global Times* is a comprehensive national newspaper featuring twenty-four pages, with a circulation of two million per issue distributed from Monday to Friday. Being a successful commercial paper on the one hand, the *Global Times* is at the same time affiliated with the Communist Party's organ *People's Daily* and shares with the *People's Daily* an international reporting network consisting of more than 500 correspondents worldwide. This official nature ensures that the *Global Times* represents China's perspectives toward domestic and international news events. The dramatic elements associated with irregular migration (especially fatalities associated with clandestine border-crossing) could be regarded as containing important news value for commercial papers and the media coverage of such incidents usually shows great compassion. However, public policies treat issues such as clandestine border crossing from a purely legal perspective and therefore the official standpoint usually characterises irregular migrants as "illegal". Representing the Chinese government's voice on news events, the *Global Times* unavoidably adopts the state response of emphasising the illegality associated with irregular migration.

Our search generated a total number of 510 articles relevant to irregular migration. Among them, 282 articles deal with Chinese citizens emigrating to North America and Europe via irregular channels; 14 stories are about the living conditions of irregular migrants from other countries (especially African countries) in China; and another 214 articles are on global irregular migration into mainly OECD countries.

For this research, we focused on the first category of news articles, i.e., how China is represented as a major irregular migrant-sending nation for OECD countries. The key research question focuses on the role national print media plays in reflecting the dominant official discourse and constructing public perception on irregular migration in China. A thematic analysis of 282 news stories

Figure 3: Themes of Chinese Irregular Migration into Other Countries as in *Global Times* (2000-2009)

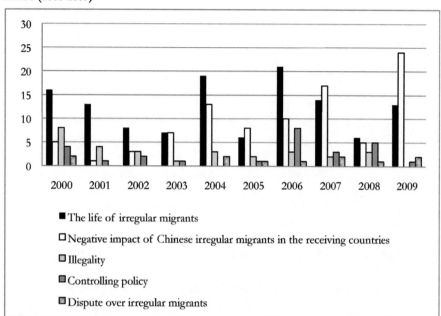

on irregular migration of Chinese citizens into other countries reveals five topical themes as observed in Figure 3.

Theme 1: The Life of Irregular Migrants

The hidden nature of irregular migration makes it unlikely to be observed and debated in the public sphere if not for news media coverage. The 24-hour news schedule is decided by news selection criteria such as timeliness, conflicts, and human interest, which could be found in reporting irregular migration. The revelation of secrecy, conflicts, and discrimination implicates strong emotion, which makes stories about irregular migration attractive topics for the news media. In the *Global Times'* coverage of irregular migration, breaking news events, especially migration tragedies involving casualties, illegality, and human emotions receive much media attention and are most likely to enter the news scheduling.

There are in total 123 news stories from the *Global Times* representing the danger and risks or hazardous living conditions of irregular Chinese overseas. The majority of these stories focus on the risks and dangers (106 articles) associated with the illegal migration process. Headlines, particularly constructing the officially endorsed perspective, orient readers' interpretation of the facts contained in the article.

In covering the notorious Dover tragedy in 2000, the *Global Times* article is entitled "Illegal immigrants found dead in container in the UK" (23/06/2000). Such a headline encapsulates the content (fifty-eight Chinese illegal migrants found dead in an unventilated lorry in Dover) as well as the orientation. Sourcing two survivors, the *Global Times* reveals a horrifying scene inside the container, which serves as a deterring factor to potential irregular migrants:

> [These migrants] were locked up in the container at the back of the lorry and they didn't know where they were heading. It was very dark inside and they couldn't see one another. It started when some of them fainted because of the lack of oxygen. Then more and more of them lost consciousness. Survivors began to shout and beat on the walls of the container, hoping the driver would notice. Some survivors climbed over dead bodies of their friends on the floor trying to reach the back door. (23/06/2000)

Meanwhile, this story refers to official sources such as the British Home Office and the Ministry of Foreign Affairs of China and structures the view that human smuggling organisations are responsible for the tragic loss of lives and must be contained. Such a standpoint is consistent with the Chinese government's controlling policy towards irregular emigration which could be exemplified in a document jointly issued by the Overseas Chinese Affairs Office under the State Council, Ministry of Foreign Affairs, Ministry of Public Security, Ministry of Foreign Trade and Economic Cooperation, and the Ministry of Labour on 1 April 1992:

> Currently, illegal Chinese migrants can be found almost everywhere in the world. Some are actually unable to make a decent living abroad, and some even joined the local mafia and are being forced to work illegally. The illegal migration mentioned above has not only to some extent affected the external image of our country as well as the development of friendly relations with some other countries, but also damaged the interest of local ethnic Chinese. In addition, the normal social order has been affected in some regions of our country where illegal emigration is rampant. The national interest will be seriously damaged and normal travelling of our citizens will also be affected if we leave this kind of situation as it is. Therefore, effective measures need to be adopted with the aim to comprehensively control and curb the illegal emigration wave. (cited in Chin, 2003, pp. 61-62)

Haberkorn observes that, "the informal information flow from target destinations to home country will focus rather disproportionately on positive aspects while minimizing or ignoring the more negative aspects" (1981, p. 273). It is believed that irregular migration decisions are made on a poorly-informed basis. By covering the risks, dangers and hazardous living conditions associated with irregular migration, the *Global Times* sets off the warning signal to potential irregular migrants. Similar messages can be found in its coverage of the tragedy of the Chinese cockle-pickers drowned in Morecambe Bay in 2004.

> Most of these Chinese labours were employed by British gang masters via Chinese "snakeheads". The snakeheads charged 20,000 pounds per head for smuggling illegal immigrants into the UK. Most stowaways could only pay part of the smuggling fee [before they left China] and pay the rest from their meagre wages [upon arrival]. Without authorised papers, these labours [...] often work at night and dare not raise voice against exploitation. (11/02/2004)

Coverage of the Morecambe Bay incident revealed the criminality of trafficking networks as well as the illegality associated with the exploitation of irregular migrants in the UK. In this article, government officials from both China and the UK and an English language newspaper from Hong Kong are used as sources. The readers' interpretation of the tragedy is oriented according to the perspectives in Table 2.

Table 2: Source-Perspective Relation

Source	Perspective
Deng: Chinese Consul general in Manchester	Chinese irregular migrants face hazardous working condition in the UK.
Smith: Labour MP	Those who employ and exploit migrants must be punished and the labour market must be regulated
Spokesperson: British Embassy in China	Collaboration between the UK and China will be strengthened in cracking down on criminal activities related to irregular migration
South China Morning Post	Triads control irregular migration in England and are responsible for the labour exploitation.

Theme 2: Negative Impacts of Chinese
Irregular Migrants in Foreign Countries

One major cause of irregular migration is the economic disparity between receiving and sending countries. Though China is the fastest-growing economy in the world, the development index of China is still low compared with most OECD countries. The potential high earning stimulates irregular migration and attracts young, able-bodied Chinese labour into Europe. As a consequence, the vast majority of Chinese stowaways appear to link themselves voluntarily to smuggling networks in order to achieve high earnings in Europe. However, against the background of the global economic downturn, conflicts between prosperous Chinese businesses and dwindling local businesses enter the media spotlight.

Articles categorised under this theme include stories about economic and policy conflicts between Chinese irregular immigrants and local communities in Europe. The "negative impact" of irregular migrants could be further categorised into the following four sub-topics: (1) conflicts between Chinese migrants and local community (41 articles); (2) unfair local policies towards Chinese migrants in general (25 articles); (3) criminality and disorder associated with irregular Chinese; (4) negative public perception of irregular Chinese (5 articles).

The hypothesis of the segmented labour-market theory can find support in stories such as "Migrants from Wenzhou Reshape the Italian Town" (28/01/2008) about Chinese migrants in Prato, Italy. The first wave of Chinese migrants to Prato was not checked by the local government because the Chinese were regarded as cheap foreign labour engaging in dirty, dangerous and demeaning jobs. However, with the arrival of more Chinese migrants engaging in business, one-tenth of local businesses were forced into closure and one tenth of local residents lost their jobs in the past two decades. In the meantime, according to the *Global Times*, Chinese business grew tenfold from 1992 to 2006, with 25% of the textile and garment companies in Prato run by ethnic Chinese. Sources used in such stories usually endorse European governments' efforts in curtailing irregular migration, especially organised human smuggling from China. For the Prato story, local Italian officials were quoted to condemn the illegality associated with irregular migrants from China. Problems associated with Chinese irregular migration such as the exploitation of the newly arrived migrants and the violation of health and safety rules in Chinese-run factories were also exposed.

In reporting controversies caused by Chinese irregular migrants in European countries, the *Global Times* features stories such as Chinese irregular migrants suffering from economic losses in Romania (23/01/2009); Chinese labour facing rising nationalist sentiment in Europe (16/04/2009); Chinese migrants facing more restrictive border control in Germany (08/10/2004); and Chinese labourers facing tightening controlling measures from the Russian authority (13/02/2009). Such an approach, as we observe, is consistent with the *Global Times'* long-held reporting strategy of endorsing the official discourse and discouraging or even curbing potential irregular migrants from China.

However, the *Global Times'* coverage of the "negative" impact of Chinese irregular migrants at the same time shows great sympathy towards overseas Chinese facing exploitation, racism, exclusion or controlling migration policies in Europe.

> Because of their illegal status, Chinese "black labourers" live a hard life. They have to work day and night to make both ends meet and have to endure bullying from the Arab and Black [migrants]. A young woman from Wenzhou was mugged twice, but she didn't dare to call police. (10/10/2002)

Chinese migrants are quoted in such stories to emphasise that it was the economic opportunities (such as vacancies in the labour market and potentially higher earnings) in Europe that attracts Chinese migration.

> Illegal immigrants could easily find a job in the "black-market" (underground economy) in Britain. Though the employment rate is high in the UK, more than 200,000 labours are still needed each year to fill in the labour void...British nationals are not willing to engage in dirty, degrading and dangerous jobs. As a consequence, 80% of the construction workers in the UK are foreigners as estimated by a British media. Most Chinese illegal immigrants cannot speak English and have no special training. They mainly work in catering, cleaning, cockle-picking, interior decoration, and other seasonal agricultural work. (10/03/2004)

The *Global Times* presents the argument and the counter-argument for the desirability of irregular migration into Europe and assesses irregular migration based on the segmented labour-market proposition, which sees Chinese emigration as a response of human mobility to the labour market demands in Europe.

Theme 3: Illegality Associated with Irregular Migration

Irregular migration can take place via various channels such as human trafficking and smuggling, illegal overstaying and bogus marriage. The *Global Times* devoted a substantial amount of coverage (29 articles) to the international controversies over illegality associated with irregular migration. The key issue in the media spotlight is human smuggling and how the international smuggling networks facilitate and boost the development of irregular migration.

Perspectives on organised crime in human smuggling or trafficking are usually constructed by presenting official sources in the news stories. *Global Times* journalists often quote official information-bearing institutions from receiving countries such as police, border agencies, crime investigation bureaus as well as official information bearing individuals such as spokespersons from government institutions, professionals, experts or scholars in the migration policy area.

> According to Italian police, three international criminal rings engaging in trafficking illegal Chinese into Europe were cracked. An ethnic Chinese was arrested while two Croatian nationals are still at large. These traffickers profited about 65 million USD from their criminal activities and they facilitated 5,000 illegal Chinese migrants into Italy in the past nine months. (04/08/2000)

In investigating Chinese irregular migrants working as cooks in Germany, the *Global Times* story "German Police Raid on 180 Chinese Restaurants" (19/08/2009) reveals the scale and gravity of the international smuggling operation. Information is sourced from a Hannover Criminal Investigation Bureau spokesman; German police officers; an official report from the German Federal Labour Agency, three Chinese illegal migrants, and a Chinese scholar. The German authority emphasises the illegality associated with human trafficking and the hazardous working and living conditions of Chinese migrants. To curb irregular migration from China, the German authority suggests that Germany should train its own chefs to replace cooks from other countries. Three Chinese irregular migrants provided testimonial statement of the exploitation in Chinese restaurants. A Chinese scholar, however, presents a totally different perspective. The Chinese scholar suggests that the police "raid" on Chinese restaurants was motivated by the sluggish employment market in Germany and that Chinese migrants as a whole (including Chinese businessman with legal status) were punished by Germany's reaction to the global economic downturn. Instead of condemning irregularity, the Chinese scholar is sourced to provide analysis of the contribution of Chinese irregular migrants to the underground economy in Europe.

This rather "defensive" standpoint is more obvious in the *Global Times'* story "An Investigation into Illegal Chinese Migrants Abroad" (08/09/2006). This piece of investigative journalism again sources heavily from official information-bearing bodies such as the Ministry of Foreign Affairs of China, the US Department of Homeland Security, the Immigration Bureau of Japan, and other similar organisations in other countries. Official sources are used to endorse the Chinese government's standpoint of calling for international collaboration in cracking down on irregular migration. However, approaches to handling irregular Chinese migrants differ. The Spanish official source reiterates its resolution to curb irregular migrants and points out that irregular migrants have no economic future in Spain. The UK official sources are concerned over the impact of irregular migrants on employment and call for regularisation of the domestic labour market. The Chinese official source firstly encourages its citizens to seek legal channels of overseas employment and investment. At the same time, the official source is quoted to defend the Chinese government's efforts in containing irregular emigration. The *Global Times* blames the US government for using illegal migration as an excuse to criticise China's domestic politics, especially in its response to the pressure from international public opinion to curb irregular emigration. Defending its government for "the effective control over irregular emigration", the *Global Times* states:

> Mexicans constitute the largest illegal migrant group in the US and the largest group of Asian illegal migrants comes from India. An official from the Ministry of Foreign Affairs of China told the reporter that in the joint efforts in curbing illegal migrants, the Chinese authority has been collaborating with the US authorities in checking the identities of several hundred Chinese migrants each year. Therefore, the claimed number of "more than 200 thousand illegal Chinese migrants" [in the US] is based on flimsy evidence. The official also pointed out that the Chinese government has been consistently fighting against irregular emigration, taken tough measures in checking human smuggling organisations, and achieved effective results in cracking down on Chinese irregular emigration. (08/09/2006)

Theme 4: Controlling Migratory Measures

Though mainly regarded as an irregular-migration-sending country by Europe, China has been a receiving country of irregular migrants from countries such as Vietnam and North Korea and is becoming more popular as a destination country thanks to its booming economy in the past decade. We categorise 26 articles as stories reporting and evaluating controlling migratory policies with regards to irregular immigration into and irregular emigration out of China.

The news story "Illegal Entry, Illegal Residence and Illegal Employment is on the Rise in China" (11/05/2007) reports that 36,000 foreigners were found to have illegally entered, stayed and worked in China in 2006 alone and 9,560 of them were repatriated. The number of foreigners entering China rose at an average rate of 10% annually. The Beijing Municipal Bureau of Public Security reports that 237 criminal cases involving foreign citizens were filed and 200 cases (a rising rate of 49.2% comparing with the previous year) involving foreign citizens violating the public security regulations were investigated. Such stories expose a new phenomenon associated with China's globalisation. Thanks to its booming economy and opening up policy, China is becoming a reluctant host country of migration and faces pressure to contain irregularity both from within the country and from outside of the country. In dealing with this new phenomenon, the official discourse emphasis is on *controlling* measures as the only solution. Specialists such as legal professors were quoted in recommending tougher migration policies and a stricter legal framework in controlling the influx of immigrants into China.

Nonetheless, in reporting irregular emigration into other countries, the *Global Times* tends to probe into the effectiveness of controlling policy in containing irregular migration. Restrictive immigration policies combined with regularisation possibilities in receiving countries can be pull factors for irregular migration. Restrictive legal frameworks (e.g., difficulties in obtaining legal residence or work permits) may trigger irregularity when cheap foreign labourers are in fact needed by the economy (20/04/2001). Meanwhile, amnesty in Spain and Argentina; regularisation programmes in France (08/09/2006); and the recognition of asylum seekers in most European countries (17/09/2003) are regarded as having a pulling effect for Chinese irregular migrants.

In a story reporting 36 Chinese migrants found in two containers of a cargo mooring at the Vancouver port (20/04/2001), the *Global Times* questions that if restrictive legal frameworks, especially the limited quota for Chinese migrants into Canada, has effects on curbing irregularity.

> Huang Yi-wen, Executive Director of the Vancouver Association of Chinese Canadians said that the current immigration and visa application policies in Canada were too strict toward migrants from mainland China. These restrictive policies actually trigger irregularity. He suggest the Canadian government grant work permit visas to Chinese nationals and adopt a more relaxed migration policy encouraging Chinese migrants come to Canada via legal channels.

The dilemma in deterring irregular migration and ensuring human rights protection is also evident in the *Global Times'* coverage. Legal experts and civil society opinion leaders were quoted to provide a perspective on irregular migrants' basic human rights and dignity. The article also raised concerns over the inhumane treatment of stowaways by the Canadian immigration authorities and calls for special protection of women and children.

Theme 5: Disputes over Irregular Migration

A unique issue brought up by the Chinese national media is the emigration of corrupt Chinese officials into Western countries or controversial political dissidents applying for asylum in other countries. According to the official Xinhua News Agency website, it was estimated that up to May 2006, over 800 Chinese charged with corruption and bribery were living overseas seeking political asylum or other regularisation channels; 320 were found guilty and brought back to China for trials, and these corruption cases involve 70 billion Yuan (US$10.3 billion) of public funds (Xinhua Net, 2010). The *Global Times has* published 11 articles in the past decade reporting such an issue with 9 stories focusing on corrupt Chinese officials as irregular migrants and the consequent disputes aroused between China and receiving countries.

Chinese government officials claim that some of the corrupt officials fled to Western countries with falsified documents and sought asylum protection under the pretext of political persecution. Endorsing such a stance, *Global Times* reports from the following two perspectives. Firstly, the *Global Times* raised criticism of, and protested against Western countries for harbouring corrupt Chinese officials; secondly, the *Global Times* reported positively on the repatriation of Chinese corrupt officials from receiving Western countries.

A case in point is the long-disputed case of Chinese asylum seeker Changxing Lai in Canada. Lai, a Chinese businessman and entrepreneur from Fujian province who is regarded as "the most corrupt man in China" by the British newspaper, the *Sunday Times* (August, 2007), was prosecuted for smuggling and corruption in China. Lai fled to Canada in 1999 and was finally granted refuge, which had the potential to trigger a trade and human rights dispute between China and Canada (CBC News, 2009). In the following news story entitled "Corrupt Officials Fleeing out of China Must be Checked" (17/09/2003), the *Global Times* represents the official stance and quotes Chinese official sources blaming the lack of bilateral extradition treaties among sovereign states for providing shields to Chinese fugitives.

> Those Western developed countries that have not signed bilateral extradition treaties with China are seen as the best refuge by Chinese fugitives. Some Western countries offered the political asylum or residence permit to Chinese fugitives in the name of "protecting human rights and securing judicial independence", which enabled criminals to escape their due punishment. (17/09/2003)

In covering these stories, the *Global Times* firmly establishes the Chinese government as the key claim-maker and calls for international collaboration in curbing corruption according to the UN Convention Against Corruption.

Representation of the Connection
between Economic Models and Irregular Migration

The *Global Times'* coverage of irregular migration contains explicit evidence supporting the segmented labour-market proposition, which sees Chinese emigration as a response of human mobility to the changing labour market demands in Europe and North America. According to this theory, patterns of international migration are closely linked to economic structure in the countries of destination. Globalisation further facilitates the redistribution of labour worldwide by giving rise to a widening wealth gap, which is the principal reason for irregular migration (Shi, 2004). China has undergone sustained economic growth in the past decade and this rapid economic development is accompanied by an increasing army of surplus labour force in rural areas. The aspiration for economic improvement drives many out of the country with some resorting to irregular ways. The need for cheap labour forces in certain economic sectors in OECD countries (e.g., construction, farming and the catering industry), on the other hand, pulls labour forces from China (Li, 2007). Endorsing the segmented labour-market theory, *The Global Times* reports that irregular Chinese migrants largely complement the labour shortage of receiving countries. When receiving countries such as Italy cannot provide sufficient job opportunities, foreign migrants turn to other parts of Europe (*Global Times* 28/03/2005).

Irregular migration is closely connected to economic development and "[t]he in- and outflows fluctuate parallel to economic cycles" (Baganha et al., 2006, p. 20). The impact of the global economic crisis on irregular migration is explicitly discussed by the Chinese media. The year 2009 saw a sharp increase in labour disputes between Chinese migrants and local business worldwide, caused by the limited employment market and local protection policies. The *Global Times* accordingly covered a rising number of stories about the more restrictive migratory/economic policies aiming to "push" foreign migrants out of Europe under the pressure of the global economic crisis. Meanwhile, the *Global Times* also devoted an increasing number of news reports (thirteen articles in total in 2009) of return migration to China.

The segmented labour proposition does not imply that emigration is purely driven by poverty. The main origins of Chinese irregular migrants into Europe are coastal cities (such as Changle and Qingtian in Fujian Province) enjoying booming economic development in China. Skeldon (2000, p.17) therefore argues that "the principal reasons for the irregular migration are not to be found in absolute poverty but in the increased knowledge of opportunities available elsewhere—the very product of development." It could be argued that in the case of Chinese irregular migration, socio-cultural tradition can offer an explanation as to the motivation of irregular migration. Fujian Province, for example, was most intensively affected by the seaborne expansion of European colonies that "linked them to a wider global system" (Skeldon, 2004). Going out of China in coastal provinces such as Fujian, Zhejiang and Guangdong has therefore been a matter of tradition and culture (Pieke, 2004; Chin, 2003).

Conclusion

Irregular migration has received increasing media attention in China, especially in the past decade. Supported by an analysis of irregular migratory movement in and out of China and its social-economic context, this chapter studies the media discourse on Chinese irregular migration as represented in a national newspaper the *Global Times*. Five themes were outlined and the connection between irregular migration and economic models is explored based on an examination of the *Global Times'* coverage of irregular migration in the past ten years.

Our findings suggest that irregular migration is mainly reported as an external phenomenon with the media focusing on Chinese irregular emigrants into primarily OECD countries. The *Global Times* represents the Chinese government's voice and focuses on China's efforts in curbing irregular migration. One of the key themes is about how irregular migrants suffer from "abuse", "maltreatment", "labour mistreatment", "hardship", "arrest", "repatriation", "exploitation" or even "death" in other countries. With carefully chosen linguistic devices and news angles, *Global Times* clearly sends off a warning signal to potential irregular migrants. Through synchronic repetition (co-occurring headlines within one issue of a newspaper) and diachronic repetition (repetition over time), the *Global Times* delivers to its readers a conceptual understanding of irregular migration as associated with risk and danger.

Irregular migration from China into Europe which could be motivated by various reasons is primarily reported as closely linked to the segmented labour-market proposition. Emphasising economic opportunities as pull factors in OECD countries to Chinese irregular migrants, the *Global Times* at the same time heightens or even justifies the economic motivation of irregular migration. Entrepreneurship among Chinese migrants overseas and Chinese migrants' economic contribution to their host countries are usually reported positively while the socio-cultural motivation of irregular migration is hardly explored. An ambivalent attitude is therefore detected in the *Global Times'* coverage of irregular migration. It seems that the illegality associated with irregular migration is less of an issue as long as the migration experience fits into a pattern of economic development.

Similar ambivalent stances are also seen in the *Global Times'* coverage of human rights issues and its evaluation of controlling policies associated with irregular migration. The issue of human rights is brought up in stories about Chinese irregular migrants being mistreated by government officials in receiving countries, but the same issue is not applied in the *Global Times'* coverage of economic criminal suspects or controversial political dissidents seeking asylum overseas. The evaluation of controlling migratory policies also varies from story to story depending on whether irregular migration flows in or out of China.

With its rising economic power, China has become an increasingly import-ant business partner of Europe. To a degree, human mobility between China and Europe could potentially benefit the development of the economy on both sides of the Euro-Asian continent if a sustainable level of Chinese migration to Europe could be managed (Pieke, 2004). However, global capitalism encourages the free flow of goods and capital, but does not necessarily favour the free movement of people. Restrictive migration policies including curtailing social rights of irregular migrants are often adopted in receiving countries. From the sending country's perspective, however, irregularity poses a dilemma. On the one hand, China benefits from the remittance and other forms of financial gains from its emigrants; on the other hand, the complicated nature of irregularity poses challenges to national security, social order, jurisdiction and international relations. Since institutional sources are most frequently used by the news me-dia as key agents in information gathering and interpreting, the *Global Times* clearly reproduced the ambiguity in the dominant ideology in its coverage of Chinese irregular migration and illustrates how source availability shapes the representation of the interplay of different, and often incompatible, social and political establishments.

Note

1. For example, Guyana's international emigration rate is 33.5% and its international movement rate is 33.6%; Suriname has an international emigration rate of 37.2 and international movement rate of 39.4 (UNDP, 2009, p. 144)

CHAPTER EIGHT

Human Trafficking and National Security in Serbia

Jelena Bjelica

Introduction

A mixture of two discourses conditions the media representation of human trafficking in Serbia: the first concerns national security and the second cultural stereotypes about women that are deeply rooted in the patriarchal society of Serbia. Both discourses derive from the dominant, masculinised cultural identity of Serbia within which women are silent, voiceless, and passive social agents. These two socio-cultural discourses are reflected and constructed within the news media where primary definers of the news are mainly social and political (male) elites and where journalists, as immediate producers of media content, tend to reflect a "traditional world view" in media output (Muir 1987). This chapter discusses news media content and journalistic practices in Serbia with the aim of critically analysing the representation of human trafficking from a feminist position. As such, it examines how, under a transitional process towards democracy, certain stereotypes about women and Kosovo Albanians have been reproduced within a new normative system related to national security. The research explores the coverage of human trafficking in the Serbian press across seven Serbian national daily newspapers through two research methods: content analysis—a quantitative method, and critical discourse analysis (CDA)—a qualitative approach. Content analysis provides a systematic evaluation of the manifest content of the news during this period, applying explicit and consistent rules of sample selection and evaluation to examine the volume and broad patterns of reporting of human trafficking (Wimmer and Dominick, 2006). Ten units of measurement were applied to the sample (name of the newspaper, length, actors, speakers, sources, facts, themes, month of publication, labels and gender of speakers in the news). Whilst content analysis highlights certain discursive practices evident in the coverage, CDA explores the characteristics of the news discourse on trafficking in more depth, informed by Fairclough's argument that

...discourse, and any specific instance of discursive practice is simultaneously seen as language text (spoken or written), discursive practice (text production and text interpretation) and socio-cultural practice. (Fairclough 1995, p. 97)

Influenced by Fairclough's "three-dimensional model" of CDA, the research therefore assumes that discourse is "embedded with the socio-cultural structure on number of levels—in the immediate situation, in the wider institution or organisation and on societal level" (Fairclough 1995, p. 97). The analysis below therefore focuses on the rhetorical strategies through which trafficking news is constructed as meaningful (such as lexical choices, the use of metaphor and intertextual references, such as presupposition), but also the context of discursive production of journalistic discourse, as well as the wider social significance of the print news discourse on human trafficking in Serbia. In adopting a CDA approach, the study is intended as both feminist social research and a political intervention. As a feminist critique of news media representations of human trafficking, the study also assumes that to be "critical" is to take an explicit political stance and to reflect upon one's orientation as part of the research (Wodak, 2001). The sample of newspaper texts analysed was generated from the online print news archive in Serbia, *Ebart Documentation*[1] using the key words, "human trafficking", "smuggling" and "migrant*". Overall, 114 news items reporting human trafficking or events in relation to human trafficking published in the Serbian daily press in 2009 were included in the study, the majority of which (n100) were factual, or "hard news" articles (as opposed to comment pieces). The sample included seven newspapers, of which two were broadsheets (*Politika* and *Danas*), and five tabloids (*Vecernje Novosti, Blic, Glas Javnosti, Press* and *Kurir*). The context for journalism as a discursive practice in Serbia has shifted significantly in recent years, as changes in the political regime have had a significant bearing upon the newspaper industry. I explore this context further in the following section, illustrating the key characteristics of the publications included within this study. The main argument of this chapter is that the current media representation of human trafficking in Serbia illustrates the unfinished transition within Serbian society, being at the same time conditioned by that transition and conditioning the formation of the social and political discourses constituting the representation of women and security. By this I mean that the dominant official security discourse often inclines towards values and norms of the authoritarian regime, while the representation of women tends to reduce the female in Serbian society to an object and passive subject.

Legal Context and Overview of Human Trafficking in Serbia

The legislation on trafficking in human beings is relatively new in Serbia; the article on human trafficking was added to the Criminal Code only in 2003. During the Milosevic regime in the 1990s the problem of modern slavery was marginalised—almost non-existent in the public discourse and indirectly supported by the state through links between the governing structures and organised criminal networks. These connections became more apparent in the years that followed the fall of the Milosevic regime in October 2000. The transitional process following the fall of the authoritarian regime represented a unique moment in which new social and cultural values were encouraged through the socialisation of new criminal laws, including, for example, a series of legal measures which referred to the confiscation of property from persons involved in organised crime, as well as new legislation on human trafficking. As I will discuss in further detail below, the media played an important role in this process of "socialisation" through a "teaching of established norms and values by way of symbolic reward and punishment for different kinds of behaviour" (McQuail 1987). According to the US State Department Trafficking in Persons Report 2010, in Europe 14,650 victims of trafficking were identified in 2009.[2] In Serbia alone, police referred 112 out of 127 total trafficking victims identified by the government's Agency for Coordination of Protection of Trafficking Victims to service providers (Department of State, 2010). The majority of victims in Serbia, according to the same report, were Serbian nationals. After the fall of Milosevic's regime, the question of human trafficking was addressed by the newly elected democratic regime, although the new legislation and other state-driven measures were also fostered by numerous international organisations residing in Serbia, such as the Organisation for Security and Cooperation in Europe (OSCE), the International Organisation for Migration (IOM), the Council of Europe (CoE) and other UN agencies.[3] The role of international organisations in the transitional processes in Serbia is of particular importance in the process of socialisation of new social and political values. The entire democratic discourse and accompanying set of values in the political sphere of Serbia were introduced and validated in public by international organisations.[4] In 2000, Serbia with its newly democratic elected government was given a list of tasks to fulfil and achieve in order to become a member of European institutions including a potential candidate for membership of the European Union. Therefore, in the Serbian public sphere, EU integration discourse was appropriated and validated on a day-to-day basis such that it became an integral part of the national political discourse. To date, Serbia is still in the process of aligning its legislation and rule of law practices with the European value system (Council of Europe, 2010).

Stereotypes about Women in Serbian Society

Recent research on gender and media conducted by Media Centre Sarajevo demonstrates that the diversity of women's professions represented in the Croatian, Bosnian and Serbian press is narrower than that of men, concluding that, "as one could expect, professions dominated by women are homemaker/parent and sex-workers" (Jusic et al., 2006, p. 65). As a number of media studies have concluded, women are represented in traditionally reserved positions in society and rarely appear out of these predetermined casts (Kronja, 2004, 2006; Jusic et al., 2006; Van Zoonen, 1994). Such stereotypes about women, I would argue, are informed by what Barry calls a "sex-is-power ethic" (Barry, 1984), something which in the 1990s has been a dominant ethical norm in the Serbian public sphere. Barry identifies a sex-is-power ethic in the dominant social, political and economic order, manifested as institutionalised inequities and misogyny in job employment opportunities; exploitation in welfare systems; dehumanisation in pornography; and fundamental gender inequalities in one-to-one relationships. In the case of Serbia, I would argue further that inequalities in personal (one to one) relationships have been translated into the public discourse alongside a social, political and economic sphere still heavily dominated by males. These relations: personal and public are conditioned by each other and any transformation of power is dependent upon liberties acquired and validated in the both spheres. Van Zoonen (1994) observes that the media does not properly reflect many aspects of women's lives and experiences:

> Many more women work than media suggest, very few women resemble the *femmes fatales* of movies and TV series, and women's desires extend far beyond the hearth and home of traditional women's magazines. (1994, p. 30)

This is the case with media representation of women in Serbia, too. The American intellectual Walter Lipmann in his key writing *Public Opinion* from 1922, dealt at length with stereotypes. He associated the process of reproduction in printing with the reproduction of reality, and coined the term stereotype as a "referential mental image" (Lipmann, 1922). But, stereotypes are not mere mirrorings of reality. They are in fact "radicalised expressions of a common social practice of identifying and categorising events, experiences, objects and persons" (van Zoonen, 1994, p. 30). So, for example, although, since 1945 women have enjoyed the same civic-political rights as men in Serbia, Kronja considers how, with the advent of popular music television in Serbia during the 1990s, the aesthetics of popular turbo-folk and dance music developed into a mainstream musical genre. A unique mixture of a traditional folk music of Serbia and techno rhythm, this form of musical expression also introduced television audiences to images of female singers, dressed and stylistically constructed as highly desirable sexual objects (Kronja, 2004). Moreover, news reports, especially during 1990s, have tended to under-represent women professionals and to over-represent women either as victims or sexual objects (Kronja, 2004; Jusic et al., 2006). The latter is a particular characteristic of tabloid newspapers, which became numerous in Serbia during the Milosevic regime by comparison to the number of published broadsheets. Kronja argues, for example, that misogynist pornography, overwhelmingly present in the tabloids, reaffirms the ideological values and gendered identities of an authoritarian patriarchy (Kronja, 2006), whilst feminists have also identified that women with political tendencies are often reduced to sexual objects through media representations. For example, on the cover page of leading Serbian weekly *NIN*, a photograph representing the first woman to be Speaker to the Parliament of Serbia in 2002, Ms. Natasa Micic, did not depict her as a professional, but rather focused upon showing her legs. The caption under the photo said: *The Best for Serbia.*[5] This particular representation initiated a public discussion on the representation of women in Serbia (See for example, Milosavljevic, 2002)

In other words, during the Milosevic regime in the 1990s, not only were women underrepresented in the political life—making up only 2% of parliamentary representatives, they were also reduced, in some forms of media and popular cultural representation, to the status of sex objects (Bozinovic, 1996). With the fall of the Milosevic regime, however, these practices did not disappear, but on the contrary were appropriated into a new system of values introduced by transition.

Human Trafficking as a National Security Issue

Human trafficking and illegal migration following the United Nations Convention against Transnational Organised Crime and the two Protocols on Migrant Smuggling and Trafficking in Persons from December 2000, are more often seen as national and/or regional security issues, and a number of legal measures have been introduced within the European Union to address them in recent years[6] (Langberg, 2010). Although nation states often take draconian measures against illegal migration (migrant camps at the borders, expulsion of the migrants from the country, imposing high financial fines on migrants in Italy), the issues of illegal migration and human trafficking remain one of the key security concerns in 21st century.

In Serbia, the discourse on national security is not yet clearly defined. It is the site of conflict and contestation between two sets of values informed by civic-democratic and national-liberation models of thought. Ejdus (2008) on the issues of identity and security, inspired by Copenhagen School of Security Studies,[7] says that while civic-democratic security discourse represents the internal emancipation from threats (characterised by a human rights–centred approach), the national-liberation discourse defines security as external threats to the state and is often the version favoured by populist political discourses. Nonetheless, the genealogy of these two discourses on security can be traced in the history of the creation of the modern Serbian state. According to Ejdus, and as I will show later in the chapter, there were many more formative moments of national-liberation discourse in Serbia then than of civic-democratic security discourse:

> The formative moments in the creation and reproduction of the national-liberation cultural model are the rise of the Serbian state during Emperor Dusan and the Serbian Church during St. Sava; defeat in the Kosovo battle against Ottomans in 1389; demise of the medieval Serbian despotate in 1495; the first Serbian uprising in 1804...and finally the defiance and the military conflict with NATO in 1999. (Ejdus, 2008, p. 47)

The current security discourse in Serbia, reproduced by political elites in day-to-day politics, is a site of tension between these two models. This can be assigned to the fact that the current political elite in Serbia is situated between two sets of values: the national government is currently a coalition of power between the

Socialist party (formed by Slobodan Milosevic) and the Democratic Party, which fought against Milosevic's regime. The Kosovo myth,[8] and its centrality to the Serbian national identity narrative, additionally contributes to the complexity of the dominant discourse on security. The Serbian National Security Strategy (NSS) emphasises that

> ...terrorism, expansion of organised crime, corruption and illegal drug trafficking, as well as human trafficking that are most significant in Kosovo, are a burden to overall security in South Eastern Europe. (Republika Srbija, 2009, p. 5)

The NSS positions Kosovo as a key threat in relation to new wars, separatism, terrorism, organised crime and human trafficking. There is an unambiguous continuity from Milosevic's policies of 1990s to the Serbian NSS in making Kosovo Albanians the personification of everything threatening the Serbian national identity.[9] For Milosevic's regime, the representations of the Kosovo Albanians served what Ernesto Laclau's political theory designates as the "constitutive outside" (Laclau, 2000). For Laclau, informed by a post-structuralist school of thought, every identity is differential, and it has to refer to its other to fully constitute itself. This other is not something positively given, but only as an outside that threatens the existence of that identity and, at the same time, provides its relationality and meaning:

> [The "constitutive outside"] is an "outside" which blocks the identity of the "inside" (and is, nonetheless, the prerequisite for its constitution at the same time). (Laclau, 1990, p. 16)

Arguably, the over-representation of violent and sexual crimes of Kosovo Albanians in the Serbian news media has encouraged the development of more severe criminal justice measures. The significance of the construction of crime news in relation to ethnic or racial *others* in the media has been stressed by number of authors (for example, Hall et al., 1978). The material effects of media discourses have also been identified in the area of crime news. Mason (2007), for example, emphasises that media reporting magnifies violent and serious crime to the extent that prisons are constructed as the only viable solution. Similarly, in order to justify the draconian measures taken by governmentally controlled courts during the Communist regime, the news media amplified the crime rate in Kosovo, underlining the inter-ethnic dimension of it. News items dealing with the crime rate in Kosovo tended to include an ethnic prefix,[10] and the Serbian press overstated the violent and sexual crime of Kosovo Albanians. Distorted images appeared in nationwide media, which supported nationalist ideologies and justified a series of discriminatory measures undertaken by the Serbian government between 1989 and 1999. Currently, similar images continue to be used to justify the time and energy invested by Serbia's foreign policy into the "diplomatic battle for Kosovo." In the National Security Strategy of Serbia, gender equality is mentioned declaratively (Republika Srbija, 2009, p. 15), in the context that the Republic of Serbia is dedicated to the empowerment of women and enhancement of women to the decision-making positions, as well as to the strengthening of state mechanisms for gender equality.[11]

The Discursive Practice of Newspaper Journalism in Serbia

Tabloids and market-oriented media appeared only in the second half of the nineties in Serbia. This should be seen in the context of a general change in the society that came with the fall of Communism.[12] The acceptance of a liberal economy doctrine at the state level was manifested in journalistic terms with the appearance of privately owned media. The emergence of private media in Serbia in the 1990s represents a turning point in journalistic practice. Although it is an old-fashioned theory, it is important to note that after WWII, journalism in Yugoslavia and in Serbia fitted the Soviet Communist model of the press.[13] The journalist, according to the Code of Practice,[14] was described as a "socio-political worker" (Pesic, 1994, p. 12). On a daily basis the similarity between news items throughout different news outlets was regarded as evidence of "the strengths of the regime" (Siebert, Peterson & Schramm, 1956, p. 123).

However, in the course of the nineties journalistic practice in Serbia was changing. Media owners were aiming towards a free and democratic press and began to act as a counterweight to the authoritarian regime of Slobodan Milosevic. Journalism in Serbia fitted into, what Mancini (2005) calls a "polarized pluralist model."[15] After the fall of Milosevic's regime a new set of laws were adopted intended to serve as a sound basis for a free and independent press.[16] However, many of the first independent, private publications from the mid-nineties disappeared or passed into different ownership. At the same time, some of the state-owned media ceased to exist.[17] Despite these trends, most of tabloids and broadsheets founded in the second half of the nineties in Serbia are still publishing today, including, *Blic, Glas Javnosti, and Danas*. In addition, a new generation of tabloids appeared in Serbia in mid-2000 characterised by a lack of transparency in their structure of ownership, and a highly politicised and speculative genre of journalism. *Press* and *Kurir* are key examples of this new trend in thetabloid press, because the media content is based on political speculation, with limited numbers of sources and/or sourcing the stories to unnamed sources.

Politika (Politics) is the oldest daily in the Balkans, having been founded on 25 January 1904 by Vladislav Ribnikar. During Communism it was nationalised, while today it is a joint venture of Politika A.D. (an enterprise owned by the Government of Serbia) and Westdeutsche Allgemeine Zeitung (WAZ), where each party holds 50% of the capital. In the hands of the government during Communism and the Milosevic regime, it was known as the "governmental publication." Indeed, it seems that *Politika* established its brand by having been in governmental control. However, due to the government's continuing "controlling stake", it appears to have large influence upon *Politika's* editorial direction.

Danas (Today), was founded and is owned by a group of professional journalists. With its first issue in June 1997, *Danas* is one of the youngest newspapers in Serbia. The founders of *Danas* were the same professionals who led the independent newspaper *Borba* (before it was taken over by the regime in December 1994)[18] and who created and led *Nasa Borba (Our Struggle)* during the first and toughest months of its existence. Appearing in 1995, *Nasa Borba* was the first independent broadsheet, but it ceased to exist in 1998. *Nasa Borba* maintained editorial continuity with *Borba*, while *Danas* was established from ex-*Nasa Borba* staff.

Večernje novosti (Evening News) was founded as an evening paper in 1953. It is considered to be the newspaper with the highest circulation in Serbia, selling up to 230,000 copies per day. It was a publicly owned enterprise, later privatised, but still remains in local hands. The newspaper takes a stance to be fast, brief and clear. During Milosevic's regime, *Novosti* was considered to be one of the government's main mouthpieces. Loyal to the Milosevic regime, through party-installed editorial staff, the newspaper almost lost its professional credibility in that period. Today, the *Novosti* Company publishes several dozen different, mainly entertainment, newspaper and magazine publications.

Blic (Flash) was the first market-oriented tabloid in Serbia, appearing in 1996. The newspaper was founded by a group of Austrian-based businessmen, who simultaneously bought Bratislava's *Novy čas*. In 2004 Ringier AG, a Swiss private publishing enterprise, bought *Blic*. Ringier publishes more than 120 newspapers and magazines worldwide.[19]

Glas Javnosti (Voice of the Public) is a daily newspaper published in Belgrade. Although its first issue appeared on 20 April 1998, published by a group of journalists from *Blic*, *Glas javnosti* assumes continuity from another newspaper of the same name, which was published in central Serbia during 19th century.[20] Initially, *Glas Javnosti* was financially managed by Radisav Rodić who also owns *Kurir*.

Kurir[21] *(Courier)* is a high-circulation daily tabloid published in Belgrade. Its first issue appeared at the newsstands on 6 May 2003. The appearance of the newspaper is connected to the state of emergency declared following the assassination of Serbia's Prime Minister Zoran Djindjic, when another daily tabloid named *Nacional* was closed. Many of the former *Nacional* staffers found employment in the newly formed *Kurir*. The intellectual elite of Serbia sees the newspaper as defensive and supportive of the structures close to the former Milosevic regime. On 8 December 2005 it was announced that 90% of *Kurir's* staff and all but one member of its editorial board had left the paper and established a new daily newspaper, *Press*.

Press[22] *(Press)* is a daily tabloid newspaper published in Belgrade. Press Publishing Group also owns a daily newspaper aimed at businesspeople called *Biznis*, as well as a lifestyle weekly magazine, *Lola* and a glossy monthly magazine called *FAME*. Founded in late 2005, the company has quickly established itself as one of Serbia's leading media enterprises.

Media Representation of Human Trafficking in Serbia

The volume of coverage of human trafficking during 2009 varied in frequency across the seven daily national newspapers within the sample, as shown in Figure 4 (black bars indicates the broadsheets, grey the tabloids). Although threre was no clear pattern in the distribution of articles during the course of the year, most articles were published during the summer months, in June, July and August (see Figure 5 below). This can partly be attributed to an ongoing court process during this period,[23] partly because of the beginning of the summer season[24] and also partly because of the announcement of a liberalisation of the visa regime in Serbia.[25]

In the main, therefore, it would seem that the volume of reporting was event driven, or otherwise attributable to "natural" variations in news. Thus, it appears that human trafficking as a topic in the Serbian news shifted from being

Figure 4: Percentage Volume of Coverage (n114)

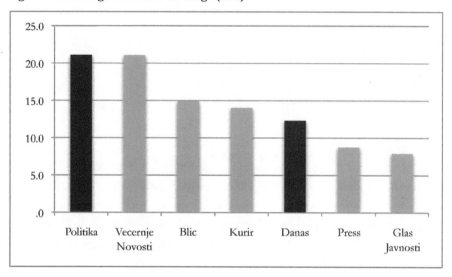

Figure 5: Variations in Volume of Trafficking Coverage during 2009 (n114)

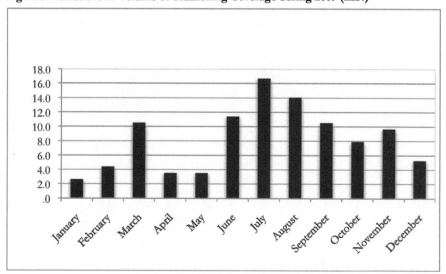

Figure 6: Themes of the Coverage (n114)

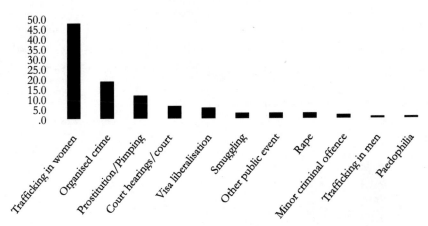

a new phenomenon in 2000, i.e., at the beginning of transition, to a "netural" phenomenon within the new social value system in 2009.

The themes through which the seven daily newspapers in Serbia dealt with human trafficking varied fairly significantly. Only half of the articles reported about human trafficking or related legislation, such as on the confiscation of property constituting the proceeds of crime.[26]

Most of the remaining articles focused upon reporting court hearings, or visa liberalisation. In 2009 several court cases for human trafficking against a number of individuals were in process in Serbia. The case against Mr. Bojan Gmijovic at the Special Court when Mr. Gmijovic proposed to the key witness Ms. Danijela Lazarevic, drew most of the attention. The headlines varied from informative, for example, *"Accused proposed in the court room"* (*Blic*, 27 June 2009) to labelling, *"Pimp proposed to the victim"* (*Kurir*, 27 June 2009), to metaphoric, *"From the sidewalk to the altar!"* (*Vecernje Novosti*, 27 June 2009). In the two later cases in which the labels and metaphor are used, the accent is given to the representation of the women. The crime as such is marginalised and a traditional representation of the women is reinforced, with the focus given to the marriage in the headline. The articles which dealt with visa liberalisation were more informative and human trafficking was framed as a political problem. For example the article, *"Visas for the countries from the black Schengen list"* (*Danas*, 3 August 2009) carries the commentary:

Most probably there will be formal and informal pressure from the EU on Serbia, as the
EU wants to reduce the possibility of Serbia being a transit country for illegal trafficking
of people and goods.

Other news items mentioned trafficking or the smuggling of migrants
within more general news items reporting arrests, or public events organised by
government or nongovernmental organisations. Some articles examined the
sentencing practices for trafficking in human beings. For example, the article
"Up to eight years for those who pay for sex services" (*Blic*, 17 August 2009) suggests
that legislators will review the law, and increase sentences. Typically however,
the extent of the "problem", or the number of victims of trafficking, were discussed. For example, the article *"The victim is also male"* (*Politika*, 5 January 2009)
explains at length other forms of human trafficking, besides trafficking for the
purpose of forced prostitution, introducing a genderless understanding of the
crime. In this article the findings of a study produced by a Serbian NGO, entitled, *Men as victims of trafficking*, are summarised. Interestingly, both the study and
the article emphasise that most of the male victims of trafficking in Serbia are
either Kosovo Albanians or Albanians and an NGO expert concludes in the article that most of the Albanians trafficked in or through Serbia are from rural
areas, with no basic education (Victimology Society of Serbia, 2004). The significance of the representational practices of the Serbian media of Kosovo Albanians will be explored in further depth in the following part of this chapter.

In some reports of arrests, however, a stigmatising discourse surrounding
the female victims is represented. *"Stripper—the special of the day"* (*Vecernje Novosti*,
13 November 2009), for example reports a story about three restaurant owners
in Novi Pazar,[27] who were arrested and charged for human trafficking whilst
using their business as a cover up for brothels. In the article not only is a rather
flippant metaphor used in the headline, but a number of presuppositions are
signified by the lexical choices of the article, e.g., "easy women" for prostitutes;
"slaves" for victims, "pleasure" or living the "high life" for frequenting prostitutes. The following quote from the article is maybe the best illustration:

The financial crisis had an impact on the prices for the services which "dancers" are
providing. An hour with girl is 50 EURO. In some unregistered places, prices are lower,
so the "pleasure" costs 20 to 30 EURO.

The lexical choices and presuppositions reaffirm a general misogynist discourse and stereotypes about women in Serbian society. Further, the article makes a case for prostitution, suggesting that not all of the girls are forced into prostitution and speculating that many of them make a lot of money which they use to buy houses or apartments. However, in other stories human trafficking was framed primarily as a crime, which goes against basic human rights. The news item entitled *"Stop Human Trafficking"* (*Kurir*, 9 March 2009), for example, quotes the Serbian Minister of Justice Ms. Snezana Malovic saying:

> No one may deprive another person of the right of liberty, objectify another person, or force the person to suffer crimes against human dignity or human rights.

Both the political elites cited and journalists reporting this case reproduce a human rights discourse, which has been acquired and validated in mainstream public policy with the fall of Milosevic's regime in 2000 and which has become an integral part of the new normative discourse of transition in Serbia.

It is also interesting to note the people or groups of people that are spoken about, or are the intiators of news events associated with trafficking. The frequency of certain actors in the news echos previously presented arguments. For example, most of the actors in the news are government officials, be it legislators or law enforcement agencies, or represenatatives of a governmental body which has a special mandate on human trafficking. This reconfirms the previously articulated notion that human trafficking is primarily a state security issue. However, the single largest category of actors is pimps or criminal offenders. By contrast the female vicitims of trafficking are almost voiceless and appear in media as passive subjects. A signifcant percentage of the actors in the news are Kosovo Albanians. In the following part of this chapter, I will explain the link between representational practicies of Kosovo Albanians in the Serbian press and human trafficking as an organised crime. It is important to note how Kosovo Albanians over a period of time have been constructed in the news as a key security threat, and how this threat has been approrited within the new value system.

Kosovo Albanians as a "National Peril"

In order to explain the genealogy of discourse on Kosovo Albanians in the Serbian public sphere, this section offers a brief historical account of the creation of the Serbian nation state. In particular, I focus upon the creation of a "Kosovo myth" as part of an exclusive Serbo-Slav narrative of the nation.

The Kosovo myth became a central element in the discourse of the nation amongst the Serbian intelligentsia only during the course of the 19th century (Popovic, 2007). In the early 19th century, national consciousness began to emerge in Serbia, on the wave of political modernity initiated by the French Revolution. Serbia's nation-building trajectory can be traced to a number of important local historical events, from the popular uprisings (the first in 1804–1813 and the second in 1815), to the establishment of a unified and standardised language (for example, the publication of a primer in the Serbian Language by Vuk Karadzic in 1814 followed by a dictionary in 1818; the translation of the New Testament in 1824).[28] Following the international recognition of Serbia's independence from the Ottoman Empire in 1878, the second half of the 19th century in Serbia was, in Anderson's words, "official nationalism" in practice.

> Such official nationalisms were conservative, not to say reactionary, policies, adapted from the model of the largely spontaneous popular nationalisms that preceded them. (Anderson, 2006, p. 110)

During the Serb-Turk war (1876–1877) the Kosovo myth became the political means of winning the hearts and minds of the people for the nation through state propaganda. The Kosovo myth has two main features both developed during the Renaissance: the heroic death of knight Miloš and the death over submission to Christianity of Prince Lazar. Additionally, the myth

> ...territorialises the opposition between the cross and the crescent, in which the Serb nation stands against the Islamic Orient and its "Albanian-Turk" version, on the side of Christianity. (Di Lellio, 2009).

Thus in the 19th century, nationalism appeared as a natural political principle of the nation (Gellner, 1983) and in Ejdus's terms constituted a key formative moment for national-liberation discourse. In particular, this meant that a revitalised Kosovo myth served the interests of the political elite of Serbia, as a recruitment narrative for engaging as many people as possible to fight the Ottomans still occupying the Balkan Peninsula. However, after gaining independence, Serbia continued fighting the war by other means. In 1899, the Government of the Serbian Kingdom, and more precisely the Ministry of Foreign

Affairs, published a collection of official memos from Serbian consuls based in Kosovo, then still part of the Ottoman Empire. Published in both Serbian and French, *Correspondence about Albanian Violence in the Old Serbia* (republished in 1989) contained documents describing widespread violence and criminal activities allegedly perpetrated by Albanians in Kosovo. The book listed numerous reports of murders, the pillaging of churches, rapes and abductions, attacks, plunders and robberies and, although unattributed to specific sources and only vaguely referenced: "as it was reported", official memos representing Albanian ferocity and impunity:

> The Albanians well armed and convinced they are free of liability, gave complete freedom to their ferocity, that nothing could stop their fanaticism and their hate. (Novakovitch, 1989, p. 16 [author's translation])

The publication served as an important element of the developing hegemonic discourse of the nation, which afforded no space in the newly created State for the non-Slav population in Kosovo, i.e., Kosovo Albanians. The practice of negatively representing Albanians continued throughout the 20th century, reaching its peak during the Milosevic regime. News media reporting on the one hand represented a public justification for contemporary atrocities committed in Kosovo, and on the other hand, a continuation and reaffirmation of a historically constituted imaginary border between ethnicities. With the fall of the Milosevic regime, the representation of the Kosovo Albanians remained still negative. Now, however, it was translated to a new security level, the Kosovo Albanians appearing in the news as a key figures in organised criminal networks, thus being seen as the key perpetrators, and later as victims of human trafficking.

As Kosovo Albanians have been represented as a threat to Serbian national security in this way, it is perhaps not surprising that each of the seven newspapers contained at least one item (as Figure 7 below shows), which linked human trafficking and organised crime to Kosovo Albanians. These news items were not necessarily directly about trafficking, but rather could be general news in which a paragraph or two about Kosovo as a criminal "nest" was inserted.

Figure 7: Kosovo Albanians Linked to Trafficking and Organised Crime (n16)

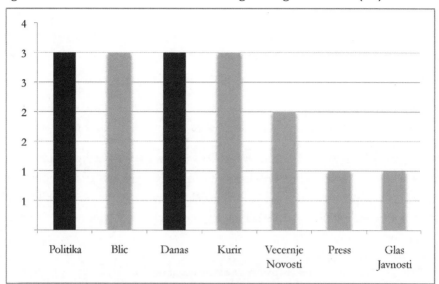

For example an article "Taci & Sachi" (*Kurir*, 25 January 2009), about the contract that the Kosovo Government has signed with marketing company Sachi & Sachi to improve the image of Kosovo as an independent state, included the following paragraph:

> However, this avant-garde move for Albanians can't change the existing image of Albanians—that is of a primitive people living in a country that is a nest of criminality, narco-mafia, war crimes and corruption.

Similarly, in an article entitled "They were Hiding Arms for the Entire Army Batch" (*Press*, 22 August 2009), again a paragraph was inserted into a general news story about the confiscation of weapons in southern Serbia, as follows:

> This is a great success for the police...South Serbia is the key route for organised crime, like human trafficking and trafficking in drugs and arms. Northern Macedonia, Kosovo and South Serbia is the key organised crime route. In this area on a yearly basis 500 to 600 victims of trafficking, drugs and arms are discovered. (General Ninoslav Krstic)

It is important to note that General Krstic is highlighting not only Kosovo, but also the regions in Serbia and Macedonia which are predominantly inhabitated by Albanians. In the article "Test for the State" (*Glas Javnosti*, 1

March 2009), about new legislation on the confiscation of the property that constitutes proceeds of crime, which in general terms reports on the implications of new legislation on the law enforcement agencies, again a paragraph is inserted that presents an unsubstantiated view of Kosovo constituting a human trafficking problem:

> One of the biggest problems in the Province is human trafficking and prostitution (Milorad Veljovic, Director of the Serbian Police)

Additionally, here Kosovo is not refered to by its name, but by its territorial status as Serbia sees it—the "Province".[29] Kosovo's supposed responsibility for trafficking is similarly emphasised in the article "Kosovo is the Greatest Threat" (*Press*, 7 October 2009), in which Dragan Sutanovac, the Minister of Defense warns:

> Terrorism and the expansion of organised crime, corruption, illegal drug and arms trafficking, human trafficking, are the most visible in Kosovo and Metohija, and represent the burden to the overall security situation in Southeast Europe.

On the other hand, the hard news items directly reporting on human trafficking —arrests, indictments, or court processes had nothing or very little to do with Kosovo Albanians. Therefore, it is important to note that Kosovo, which is a highly politicised issue in Serbia, (i.e., due to the unacceptance of Kosovan independence) is often characterised as a haven for criminality and as an international human trafficking problem through such labels and presuppositions. This is a particularly relevant point, I would argue, in the context of social and political transition in Serbia, in which such attributions can be used for political capital in the international arena.

Conclusion

In exploring the media representation of human trafficking in the Serbian press, this chapter has considered how trafficking has played an important role in the constructing of wider ideas and issues of political importance. When trafficking is itself the focus of a story, it is often reported in a summarised manner, listing the number of victims, police operations and cases within a court's jurisdiction. However, even in this kind of reporting, the victims of trafficking very rarely have a voice, and in some areas of the coverage, gender stereotypes and misogynistic assumptions appear to condition the kinds of stories that are told. In this, trafficking as a crime or abuse of human rights is not positioned seriously as a humanitarian problem facing vulnerable people, and which needs to be addressed as such. Moreover, at worst, trafficked women are themselves positioned as responsible or even as benefiting from their condition. In part, these stigmatising characterisations of trafficked women are linked to wider political issues, such as in reports concerning potential threats facing the citizens of Serbia, about visa liberalisation and organised crime. However, I have argued that these discourses linking human trafficking and organised crime are most powerful in stories articulating such problems with Kosovo and ethnic Albanian populations in the region. In this dominant discourse, the human trafficking issue continues to be primarily seen as a national security issue, which in patriarchal Serbian society remains an androcentric sphere of influence and power. Despite Serbia's transition to liberal democracy and international recognition, then, the discourses surrounding human trafficking in the press suggest the overall representation of women remains degrading, and it seems unlikely within such a system of values that the problem of human trafficking can be properly addressed.

Notes

1. The Ebart Documentation archive can be accessed through the web address: www.arhiv.rs

2. The International Organization for Migration (IOM) estimated that in 2000 over 120,000 persons were trafficked through the Balkans to Western Europe (Limanowska, 2005, p. 4).

3. For example, the OSCE Mission to Serbia supported the Serbian National Coordinator for Combating Human Trafficking in drafting the National Action Plan. In order to strengthen the National Referral Mechanism, the Mission has worked together with the Judges Association of Serbia to organise ten local multi-stakeholder workshops for police officers, prosecutors and judges on legal issues in investigating, prosecuting and trying human trafficking cases. The Mission, in co-operation with the Child Rights Centre, is providing specialist courses on combating child trafficking to local police officers and social workers. Finally, the Mission is running a joint project with ASTRA, a leading anti-trafficking NGO in Serbia, to prepare a manual for hotline organizations, which is expected to come out in early 2010 (OSCE, 2009).

4. In the cases where the legitimacy does not derive from a nation-state framework, it is rather "the exercise of authority which is supplanted by rational assent and conviction

to norms and principles, elicited by effective communication" (Steffek, 2003). For interesting studies on the legitimacy of international administration, in the case of Serbia these apply to the presence and lead of strong international organisations. See Zurn (2005), Steffek (2003), Hurrelmann (2007) and Kostovicova (2008).

5. See the *NIN* news archive for a reproduction of the offending front page: http://www.nin.co.rs/2002-12/12/index.html

6. The migration policy became more securitised following the 9/11 attack in United States. With the securitisation of the migration issue, human trafficking became a more salient security issue. For example, the European Conference on Preventing and Combating Trafficking in Human Beings—Global Challenge for the 21st Century brought together, on 18–20 September 2002, the EU Member States, Candidate Countries, neighbouring countries such as Russia, the Ukraine, the NIS as well as the US, Canada, China, international organisations (IOs), inter-governmental organisations (IGOs), non-governmental organisations (NGOs) and the institutions of the European Union. The overarching objective of the Conference was to provide an opportunity to take stock of trends in human trafficking and a European policy to respond to a challenge that risks undermining our fundamental values and the full realisation of an area of freedom, security and justice. For more information see http://www.belgium.iom.int/STOPConference/Conference%20Papers/brudeclaration.pdf

7. Informed by poststructuralist theory, the Copenhagen School of thought places the formation and construction of identity in the centre of security studies. The representatives of this school of thought argue for the importance of identity for understanding security issues (for example, see Buzan et al., 1998).

8. Although the current dispute about Kosovo territory between ethnic Serbs and ethnic Albanians is a long story for a footnote. In short—in June 1999, in the aftermath to the armed conflict between Serbian security forces and the Kosovo Liberation Army (KLA) on the ground and the 78-day-long NATO air intervention, Kosovo became an international protectorate according to UN Security Council Resolution 1244. Under the agreement that brought an end to the war, Kosovo came under UN administration, with a system of governance and security that in addition to the United Nations Interim Administration Mission in Kosovo (UNMIK) involved the NATO-led peacekeeping Kosovo Force (KFOR), the Organization for Security and Co-operation in Europe (OSCE), and the European Union. The talks over Kosovo's status were reopened in early 2007. Chaired by former Finnish president Marrti Ahtisaari, this set of talks led to the Comprehensive Proposal for Future Status of Kosovo. Although it was utterly rejected by Serbia this paper was a sound base for Kosovo's declaration of independence in February 2008.

9. During the Milosevic regime, it could be argued that beside Kosovo Albanians the Croats, Bosnians, Slovenians, and other nations of former Yugoslavia were also represented as the "constitutive outside."

10. Even when court statistics showed that inter-ethnic criminality was lower than intra-ethnical criminality, according to the Report of Independent Commission. (UJDI, 1990)

11. In fact the Strategy is referring to equality between sexes, not to the gender equality. I've translated "ravnopravnosti polova" as gender equality, since it fits better the legal context of the EU. The Serbian National Strategy for Enhancement of Women and on Gender Equality was adopted in early 2009. The Serbian Assembly passed the Law on Equality between Sexes in December 2009. The recommendations of the Council of Europe (1998, Rec. 14) to the member states refers to gender equality. The Serbian language distinguishes between these two words—gender and sex.

12. The tabloids were of a quite unusual format during the Communist period when state-owned media were the only newspapers available.

13. According to the *Four Theories of the Press*, there are four major theories behind the functioning of the world's presses. (1) the Authoritarian theory, which developed in the late Renaissance and was based on the idea that truth is the product of a few wise men; (2) the Libertarian theory, which arose from the works of men like Milton, Locke, Mill, and Jefferson and avowed that the search for truth is one of man's natural rights; (3) the Social Responsibility theory of the modern day: equal radio and television time for political candidates, the obligations of the newspaper in a one-paper town, etc.; (4) the Soviet Communist theory, is an expanded and more positive version of the old Authoritarian theory. The press contributes to the success of the state; only legal party members can publish; Government has "influence" over the press; no one can criticise the party (Siebert et al., 1956).

14. The Code of Practice is kind of Press Code (ethical guidelines) specific for the Communist regime.

15. According to Mancini (2005), on traces of Habermas's theory, the phenomenon of polarisation of society gives an identity to the media. Measuring the development of media market (1), political parallelism (2), the development of journalistic professionalism (3) and the degree and nature of state intervention in the media system (4), Mancini distinguished three models: the polarised pluralist (Mediterranean countries); the democratic corporatist (Northern Europe) and the liberal model (North Atlantic). Mancini offers a series of arguments why these three models differ from Siebert et al.'s "Four Theories of the Press", claiming that even if market-oriented, the journalism in Europe was often partisan. Articulating this new division of European and American journalism, Mancini insists that these models were defined by social-political historical development that is traceable in writings of many European scholars.

16. For example: Public Information Law; Broadcasting Act; Law on Amendments and Supplements to the Broadcasting Act; Law on Free Access to Information of Public Importance; The Constitution of the Republic of Serbia. The text of each can be found on the website of Media Centre Belgrade: www.mc.rs

17. *Politika Express* for example.

18. *Borba (Struggle)* was founded in 1922 and was originally published in Zagreb. After

WWII the office was moved to Belgrade. For a long time, *Borba* alternated pages in Cyrillic and Latin alphabet in the same edition. It became the voice of liberal leftist elites in Yugoslavia during the seventies and eighties.

19. http://www.ringier.com

20. www.glas-javnosti.rs

21. http://www.kurir-info.rs/

22. http://www.pressonline.rs

23. In June 2009 the Special Court for Organized Crime in Serbia was processing a case against Mr. Bojan Gmijovic accused of human trafficking. Mr. Gmijovic and his group smuggled Ms. Danijela Lazarevic via Hungary to Italy, where she was forced into prostitution. During the court hearings Mr. Gmijovic proposed to Ms. Lazarevic, which made the news in almost all newspapers in Serbia. In July the District Court in Belgrade was hearing the case against Mr. Safet Sajo Cucak, accused for human trafficking, who was defending himself by denying he was involved and by saying he was in love with one of the girls. The romantic spin in the Serbian newspapers on the trafficking court cases provides a further example of how the crime of trafficking has been trivialised in some sections of the press.

24. A number of articles dealt with the beginning of the summer season and in that regard increased travelling to neighbouring countries for work or summer holidays. The articles were warning readers, especially female readers of possible dangers in foreign countries: "Serbian citizens increasingly are the targets for human traffickers" (*Blic*, 28 June 2009), "How the search for a job ends in human trafficking" (*Danas*, 11 July 2009), "Human traffickers are targeting Serbs" (*Vecernje Novosti*, 19 July 2009).

25. The visa liberalisation of Serbia towards the Schengen countries was announced on 15 July 2009, to become effective on 19 December 2009. Before the Balkan wars of 1991 to 1999, a Yugoslav passport allowed visa-free travel to almost any country. Since 1991 almost all countries of the world were off limits for Serbian citizens. In the news, the decision of European Commission to lift visa requirements was heralded as historical. Thus, a number of articles of summer 2009 dealt with the visa liberalisation. Some of the articles were educative pointing the possible dangers while travelling free through Europe and, in that context, the human trafficking was elaborated.

26. In *Glas Javnosti* the article "Test for the State" (1 March 2009), looks at what kind of implications the new legislation on the confiscation of property will have on the law enforcement agencies.

27. Novi Pazar is a city and municipality located in the southwest Serbia, in the vicinity of the border with Bosnia, mainly populated by Muslim community.

28. The events listed were chosen for their importance in the creation of the nation state and national consciousness, therefore the list presents a specific combination of relevant political, as well as cultural events.

29. The Serbian Government did not recognise Kosovo independence declared on 17 February 2008.

CHAPTER NINE

Fujianese Migration and the British Press Coverage of the Dover Incident

Xinyi Jiang

Introduction: the Chinese Presence in the UK

People from China rarely occupy a significant position among the ever-present news headlines and the political agenda about migration and asylum seeking in wealthy receiving countries (Jiang, 2006). In the UK the presence of ethnic Chinese has had a long history (Holmes, 1988) and they were the third largest ethnic population according to the 2001 Census. However, they were "the least understood of all Britain's immigrant minorities" (Watson, 1977, p. 181), and "received very little attention" (Taylor, 1987). This situation has remained largely unchanged in recent years, despite some fundamental changes in Chinese migration over the last three decades (Jiang, 2006; Nyiri & Saveliev, 2002; Pieke et al., 2004). First hand knowledge of the British public about the Chinese probably still remains on the level of experiences gained from local Chinese restaurants or takeaways, and the British public continue to conceive of the Chinese as being "scattered", "isolated", "economically and socially self-sufficient and law-abiding" (Taylor, 1987, p. 1).

Whilst Cantonese-speaking catering workers from Hong Kong's New Territories used to represent the majority of the immigrant Chinese population in Britain, nowadays, the presence of Chinese from mainland China has become more prominent (Laczko, 2003; Nyiri & Saveliev, 2002; Pieke et al., 2004). Among them, those from Fujian province are a distinctive group. What is special about them was that many have deployed the illegal services of organised migration facilitators—so-called snakeheads. Little about this is however, recognised by the British public. Neither has this been of particular concern in mainstream public policy debates on issues of immigration, refugee and asylum seeking (Pieke et al., 2004). Compared to other major ethnically defined groups of refugees and asylum seekers, the Fujianese have had a comparatively low profile in terms of media representations, except for the incidents that happened at Dover in 2000 and Morecambe Bay in 2004 (Jiang, 2006). In terms of the academic research, the situation has not changed much either. It is still the case, as Watson (1977, p. 181) described it more than three decades ago, that: "only a handful of scholars have studied this group". Studies of recent Chinese immigrants, especially the Fujianese in the UK, are few (exceptions are, for instance, Jiang, 2006; Pieke et al., 2004).

As media scholars such as van Dijk (1988b, p. 150–151) point out, perceptions about issues that most citizens do not have direct experience of, such as those related to ethnic minorities, are often defined and communicated through news media by elite groups. The low profile of the Chinese population and the Fujianese migrants as well as the dearth of relevant academic studies in the UK makes it particularly important to investigate the reaction of the British media towards such incidents as Dover and Morecombe Bay. There are reasons to believe that incidents such as Dover and Morecambe Bay raised the public as well as the policy awareness of Fujianese migration and people smuggling. Since Dover, a number of rules and regulations about asylum and immigration have been amended[1] (Pieke et al., 2004). The Gangmasters (Licensing) Act 2004 was passed into law shortly after the Morecambe Bay tragedy, which, according to Jim Sheridan, the Renfrewshire West MP who introduced the gangmaster legislation, "threw a light on the exploitation of foreign workers" (BBC news, 2005a). Prior to this accident, however, Chinese irregular migrants, including the cockle pickers, "were a low priority" and treated with "a blind eye" by immigration service, as Labour MP for Morecambe and Lunesdale, Geraldine Smith, pointed out (BBC news, 2006a). The present study will focus on the Dover incident and investigate how it was covered by the British press. The results will also be put into a historical context of the representation of Chinese in British culture.

Sample Of the Press Coverage of the Dover Incident

In the morning of the 19th June 2000, the UK broadcast news reported on the attempted smuggling of sixty Chinese into the UK through the port of Dover (BBC news, 2000b). During a routine check conducted at Dover, Customs officers found 58 dead people and two survivors—all believed from China's Fujian Province—in the back of an airtight 18-metre-long white Mercedes lorry (2000b). Post-mortems confirmed that the cause of deaths was suffocation. Police quickly established that criminal "snakehead" gangs were involved in the incident. Arrests of the Dutch truck driver and a Mandarin interpreter were made and both were found guilty during a trial in April 2001 (BBC news, 2001).

For about a week from the 20th June 2000, this event occupied a significant position across the major UK national newspapers. In order to achieve a comprehensive view of this reporting across readership, political orientation, style and format of news coverage, six national daily newspapers including three broadsheets, the *Times, Guardian,* and *Daily Telegraph,* one middle-market newspaper, the *Daily Mail,* and two tabloids, the *Sun* and *Mirror,* were studied between 20th and 26th June 2000. During this period, these newspapers carried 106 articles about the incident. A further 13 articles were published in the Sunday press on 25th June, including reports in the *Sunday Times, Observer, Sunday Telegraph, Mail on Sunday, News of the World,* and *Sunday Mirror,* and these were also included in the sample. All types of articles that either took the Dover incident, issues related to smuggling, asylum seeking or immigration as their main themes were selected. Keywords including "Dover", "refugees", "asylum seekers/seeking", "Chinese", "Fujian", and "immigrants/immigration" were used in searching both individual newspapers' CD-ROM databases and the Nexis Executive electronic database, depending on the availability of the targeted data.

Analyses were based upon both the whole corpus of material and some comparisons drawn between differences in coverage in selected papers or articles. Drawing upon Hartmann and Husband's (1974) studies about ethnic news coverage in the British press in the 1960s, the analysis investigated a series of characteristics of the coverage in order to infer what kind of "public awareness" was created about the Dover incident, and the kinds of "subject-matter for discussion" provided by the coverage. Above all, Hartmann and Husband (1974, p. 133) concluded that the four different newspapers, *The Times, Guardian, Express* and *Mirror,* "were in close agreement about what the issues were, about what kind of things warranted most coverage and what least, about what aspects of the situation were newsworthy" in covering ethnic minorities. Their empirical studies suggested that "the coefficient of concordance across the four papers was .86" (Hartmann and Husband, 1974, p. 132). Similar results were drawn in van Dijk's (1991) studies of the British and Dutch press coverage of ethnic affairs in the 1980s, which revealed that in both countries, issues of race relations, immigration and crime are the most frequent subjects, whilst ordinary life of ethnic minorities was little covered. The reporting of the Dover incident in June

2000 reflected the general reporting characteristics in stories about ethnic minority groups identified by Hartmann and Husband and van Dijk, with a similar sequence of coverage across the sampled newspapers:

1. 20th June, the discovery, survivors' stories, government reaction
2. 21st June, start of the police investigation
3. 22nd June, arrest in connection with the incident
4. 23rd June, the charging of the Dutch lorry driver and two other suspects
5. 24th June, Coroner's inquest; 25 June (Sunday), feature articles from victims' home villages

Furthermore, van Dijk's (1991) many case studies of the British press, in particular that related to certain incidents (such as the urban unrest, or so-called "race riots" in Britain September and October 1985) also revealed a similarity among different newspapers in their chosen subjects, lexical properties in headlines, and style. This gives us a guideline in the analysis of the Dover coverage.

Data and Analysis

Case Studies of Headlines and Leads

Headlines and leads, "define the most important or most relevant information of the news item" because they are, "often the only information read or memorised" (van Dijk, 1988b, pp. 188–89). Headlines of the 39 articles on 20 June, i.e., the first day that the event was covered in the press, were chosen for an analysis of lexical details including topics/themes and labels attached to different agents. Three themes emerged across the press, including the death of victims, the smuggling organisation identified as responsible, and the torment of victims in the lorry. For the victims, labels were adopted which included "migrants", "Chinese illegal entrants", "refugees", "illegal immigrants", along with "human cargo", "stowaways", and "doomed cargo". The criminal aspect of the incident was suggested by expressions such as "smugglers", "snakeheads", "evil trade", "global racket", "ruthless gangs", "slaves of the Triads" featuring in different papers. Two positions towards immigration in general also emerged on the coverage of the 20th June, with headlines such as the *Guardian*'s, "OPEN THE DOOR: A MORE FLEXIBLE IMMIGRATION POLICY WOULD BOOST OUR ECONOMY", in contrast to the *Daily Mail*'s, "MR STRAW SLAMS

THE STABLE DOOR", and the *Mirror*'s, "SHUT DOOR TO TERRIBLE TRADE". An impression of such differences was also reflected in the "readers' letters section" from the *Guardian* (21st June) and *Times* (22nd June). Sympathy towards immigrants/asylum seekers and criticism about current policies were expressed in the *Guardian*, with statements such as:

> The White paper which preceded the Asylum and Immigration Act 1999 emphasised concern about illegal migration. Its analysis went wrong. It confused issues...

> A fitting memorial to 58 human beings would be to take our heads out of the sand and face up to the issue which will dominate the coming century.

In the *Times*, however, harsher and tougher measures towards arrivals were called for, whilst praise for the effectiveness of current policies was raised. It contained the following statements:

> The Immigration and Asylum Act 1999 is the most comprehensive reform of the relevant legislation for many years. It includes a range of practical measures to deal with asylum and to strengthen the system against abuse...

> This Government has also introduced tougher penalties against those convicted of facilitating illegal immigration and our law enforcement agencies are working closely with their counterparts abroad to help tackle this evil trade.

On the 24th June, all six newspapers published stories about the results of the post-mortem examinations. This provided an opportunity to compare the emphases and lexical properties of newspaper headlines and leads across different titles when they covered the same story, especially crucial information about "agents/actors/participants", "transitivity", "predicates", "state", "process", "result", and "modifier"—terms and analytic tools in critical linguistics that Fowler (1991, pp. 66–90) develops, based on Halliday's (1978, 1985) functional linguistics, for investigating the minute details of linguistic structure "to display to consciousness the patterns of belief and value which are encoded in language." (Fowler, 1991, p. 67) This is particularly useful in news discourse analysis when analysing the construction of representations, which signify "beliefs and values when writers are reporting or communicating on the world" (Fowler, 1991, p. 89). The headlines of these six stories are:

1.   "CHINESE BANGED ON THE WALL" AS AIR RAN OUT (*Times*)

2. MIGRANTS' DESPERATE LAST HOURS (*Guardian*)
3. HOW TWO IMMIGRANTS SURVIVED DEATH LORRY/CHINESE VICTIMS WERE GRASPING FOR BREATH, INQUEST TOLD (*Daily Telegraph*)
4. THE FRANTIC CRIES AS THE AIR RAN OUT (*Daily Mail*)
5. THEY HIT TRUCK WITH SHOES AS AIR RAN OUT (*Daily Mirror*)
6. DOOMED FIFTY-EIGHT BANGED ON LORRY FOR HELP (*Sun*)

Typically, a report starts in this way:

7. "The fifty-eight Chinese illegal immigrants who died being smuggled into Britain frantically hammered with their shoes on the side of the container in which they were trapped as their air ran out, it emerged yesterday" (*Daily Mail*, 24th June), or
8. "The fifty-eight Chinese illegal immigrants found dead in a sealed lorry banged on the sides with shoes to try to summon help, it was said yesterday" (*Daily Mirror*, 24th June), or
9. "The fifty-eight stowaways who suffocated in a lorry container banged on its sides with their shoes as they tried to raise alarm, an inquest heard yesterday" (*Sun*, 24th June)

The usage of intransitive verbs such as "died' (7), "suffocated" (9) and passive expressions such as "were trapped" and "found dead" for the actors/participants (the 58 Chinese) can be explained by several factors. Previous knowledge about the incident, especially the criminal involvement, had been in the press for several days. The focus of this reporting shifted to the death itself. The "action" of death did not seem to have an affect on another entity. Certain actions were, however, under control of agents and were deliberate activities, such as "banged" (1, 6, 8, 9), "hammered" (7), and "hit" (5) the lorry. Other deliberate activities included to "gasp" for breath (3), "summon" help (8) and "raise" alarm (9), and the predicate "try to" was used (8, 9), rather than expressions such as "failed to". Usage or tendency for "nominalisation" such as "desperate last hours" (2) and "frantic cries" (4), as well as modifiers such as "doomed" (6) also added to the vividness of the description. Another point to notice is the label of "illegal immigrants" was adopted in all six papers, which might have resulted from an official source naming the victims this way in a press release.

The coverage of this story also enables an examination of the journalistic practice of an inverted pyramid structure, which puts the most important or newsworthy information at the beginning. From the above examples, it is clear that across the press, death was deemed the highest news value in this story and the information that two people lost consciousness but actually survived was mostly excluded except in the *Telegraph*, indicating that a higher news value was accorded to death than to survival in this case.[2]

The above exercises gave an indication that different newspapers shared similar journalistic practices in terms of ascribing news value, establishing the major themes as well as adopting similar language styles when covering the Dover incident. Indeed, these practices determined that among the established criteria of newsworthiness, negativity (popularly interpreted as "Bad news is good news" [Hartley, 1982, p. 79]) was recognised as one of the top news values (Galtung and Ruge, 1973). Meanwhile, as further analysis will demonstrate, the negative news value of this incident was also demonstrated in its association with smuggling and illegal entry, alleged involvement of criminal Triads, violations of borders and conventions, and the presence of foreign bodies that were unwelcome and considered a threat to social order and security.

Negative Labels and Ambiguous Sympathy Towards the Victims

Negative and confusing labels have been acknowledged as a striking feature in the media coverage of refugees and asylum seekers. An ARTICLE 19 initiated research that included monitoring media coverage of the closure of Calais' Sangatte refugee camp found that 51 different labels were used to refer to the people in the camp, including inaccurate terms such as "illegal refugees" and negative terms such as "asylum cheat" (Buchanan et al., 2003, p. 9). A MORI (2002) survey also confirmed that negative terms from the media had a profound influence on the public. According to the poll, "85% of respondents associated negative words with media reporting" and among these negative words, "64% of the respondents said that the media use the term "illegal immigrant" when referring to refugees and asylum seekers...other words commonly associated with media coverage were "desperate", "foreign", "bogus" and "scroungers" (ibid).

Previous research has identified confusion among journalists for labelling the people they were writing about on issues of asylum and immigration. (Buchanan et al., 2003; Gross et al., 2007). Similar confusion existed among the labels for the Dover victims. The labels that appeared in my data seemed to fit into one of the three types: factual, political, and tabloid. The "factual labels" focused on the facts, such as "54 men and 4 women", "the fifty-eight Chinese people who died/were found dead", "fifty-eight human beings", "fifty-eight bodies/deaths/dead/corpses", "fifty-eight individuals", "survivors" and "victims". The "political labels" had an emphasis on asylum seeking/immigration and contained one of the three key terms, "refugees", "asylum seekers", and "immigrants". They were however, often supplemented by negative adjectives such as "bogus", "clandestine", "illegal", "economic", "abusive" or "cheat". Most of the "tabloid labels", as we can see here, had sympathetic or negative emotional connotations; examples include "human snakes", "stowaways", "human cargoes", "illegal cargo", "doomed victims", "the doomed fifty-eight", "nonpeople", and "human carnage". These three categories of labels were found in all of the sampled newspapers.

Perhaps some clarification of the legal status of the Fujianese in the UK would help to address the confusion in the popular terminology based on a small-scale qualitative study conducted by the author (Jiang, 2006). The definition by the Refugee Council (2005) of "illegal immigrant", one of the most popular labels, seemed to be applicable to those Fujianese who had "intentionally not made themselves known to the authorities and [had] no legal basis of being here." Meanwhile, the definition of an "economic migrant" as "someone who has moved to another country to work" (ibid) seems also applicable. Those who opted to enter the asylum application system should be labelled as "asylum seekers", even if they were given certain economic rights such as the right to work while their application was assessed (for those who had submitted an application for asylum over six months before 2001, see note 1). With only a very small number successfully granted "refugee" status, as statistics from the Home Office[3] (Home Office, 2007) suggest, the rest become "failed asylum seekers" as defined by the Refugee Council. Before 2004, the birth of babies in Northern Ireland provided a route through which Fujianese parents could obtain Irish passports and a more secure immigration status.[4] The complexity of immigration regulations and measures, as well as the constant tendency of government to change and further tighten up immigration controls, may have made defining the legal status of these Fujianese more difficult for journalists. In this light, it is perhaps not so surprising that in describing the migrants a profusion of terminology was generated.

Given the situation in which the Dover victims were found, the label of "illegal entrants" was probably more suitable than the popular "illegal migrants", although the former was hardly applied in the Dover coverage. The popularity of the term "illegal migrants" seemed to assume the victims' intention, i.e., staying in the UK illegally. Moreover, it is worthwhile looking at the negative perception towards them detected from the labels within the "sympathy for the dead" theme that is usually found in disaster/crime stories, and in the case of Dover, the claim that "Everybody across the political spectrum expressed sympathy for the victims" (*Guardian*, 20th June). Other than expressions of being "shocked", "saddened", or "appalled" (ibid), the usual condolences such as "our thoughts go to the families of those who died" that are usually directed at families of victims did not appear. Furthermore, those who might be related to the victims were treated with a level of suspicion. Kent Police, for instance, made an appeal to ask the Chinese community to help identify the bodies, but with the condition attached that those who came forward would have to provide information about their own immigration status (NCADC, 2000). This suggests that the crime investigation of Dover was also an immigration status investigation. As Vollmer (2008) points out, the UK government has made more breaches of immigration rules criminal offences. In other European countries, such as Austria, illegal entry and stay are only administrative offenses, "comparable to fast driving or illegal parking." (Kraler et al., 2008, p. 16)

The lexical description of the victims' circumstance was more sensationalising than sympathetic. The journey was defined as "shameful" (*The Times*, 21st June), "tortuous" (*The Times*, 21st June), and a "journey to death" (*The Times*, 20th June). The victims were a "fated band", "anonymous bodies", and a "foul-smelling cargo" (*The Times*, 21st June). Description of the death scene, according to the Customs officers quoted, was "absolutely sickening" with "piles and piles of bodies" (*Daily Mail*, 20th June). The search team were reported to be, "overcome by the most revolting smell", confronted with "the stuff of nightmares" and "a scene from Hell", had a "very traumatic experience", and needed "counselling" (ibid). In contrast to this "Hell" image, the two survivors are reported to have said that when they saw that the door finally opened, it was like "an angel had been sent from Heaven" (ibid).

Some reporters applied sympathetic descriptions about victims' personal details; but the emphasis was on economic destitution as the assumed driving force for migration. Victims' clothes were described as "cheap", including items such as "gaudily coloured boxer shorts, the odd filthy T-shirt and, for the luckier ones, shabby trainers" (*The Times*, 21st June). The fact that no luggage was found was emphasised: "They brought absolutely nothing with them. No bags, no money, no food, no water, no memento" (*The Times*, 21st June). To lump items of practical maintenance like food and water with a sentimental "memento" perhaps underlines the social gulf between the reporters and those they are writing about. However, for the reporters, it was their "wretched…existence in China's Fujian province" which "must have been to force them to make such a pitiful bid for freedom" (*The Times*, 21st June). Whilst the *Times* emphasised the push of a destitute situation at home as motivation for the Fujianese to leave their country, the *Daily Mail* emphasised the pull of the "easy economic pickings to be had in "honey pot" Britain" (*Daily Mail*, 20th June). Despite the different levels of sympathy expressed by the different newspapers, the frame of "economic migrants" was clearly applied to the victims. Moreover, some sources implied that the victims had themselves to blame. Jack Straw, the Home Secretary at the time, for instance was quoted as saying that "…this terrible tragedy must serve as a stark warning to others who might be tempted to place their fate in the hands of organised traffickers" (*Guardian*, 20th June). The economic immigrant dimension denied the Dover victims the status of unqualified innocence that victims of crime or disaster usually have.

Those to Be Blamed: Criminal Snakeheads and Other Governments

The dominant theme that criminal associations were responsible was supported by accusations of torture against the organisers that included beating, starving and forcing passengers to cross borders under death threats, kidnapping, slavery, sexual exploitation and even driving victims to suicide (e.g., *Daily Mail*, 20th June; *Daily Mirror*, 20th June), with occasional graphic description such as, "in one case a Chinese man had his ear cut off when he refused to rape a female captive" (*Mail on Sunday*, 25th June). Notably, the terms, "smuggling" and "trafficking" were used interchangeably (e.g., *Guardian*, 20th June), despite the distinction between them: trafficking often involves people being tricked or forced into arrival and then used for forced labour or prostitution and it is much more serious criminal activity than smuggling (Stalker, 2001, p. 52; Martin and Miller, 2000, p. 970). Based on the author's research (Jiang, 2006) and estimate,[5] it was likely that the victims of the Dover incident made an informed choice and were therefore involved in a smuggling rather than trafficking activity. However, the synonymous use of these terms would blur this distinction and therefore potentially highlight the aspect of criminality.

The newspapers also widely elaborated on the possible responsibility of the Belgium government based on a suspected connection between the victims and a group of Chinese of similar size that had been arrested previously by Belgian police but released and deported without escort. This suspicion was generally presented as fact (*Daily Telegraph* 22nd June; *Mirror* 21st June), or very likely to be true (*Daily Mirror,* 23rd June; *Daily Mail,* 22nd June; *Daily Mail,* 23rd June). But when the suspicion turned out later to be unfounded, the press largely ignored this development (except one mention at the end of a report in the *Daily Mirror,* 24th June). The Dover incident therefore provided support to the accusation that the UK government often made against some European "transit" countries about the latter's relaxed attitude towards people whose intended destination was the UK. (Kraler, 2009) The headline, "HOLLAND HOLDS THE KEY TO BACK DOOR INTO BRITAIN" (*Daily Telegraph,* 22nd June) is an example of this type of understanding of the situation.

It was not only the governments of these "transit" countries that came in for criticism. Blame was also laid on the Chinese government, whose alleged lack of cooperation was suggested to have made deportation difficult, and "without Chinese help", as one leading article declares, "…it is hard to see what more could have been done…here" (*Daily Telegraph,* 20th June; see also: *Guardian,* 26th June; *Sunday Telegraph,* 25th June). Through such references to the possible roles of other countries, the British government (and British immigration policies) were to a significant extent, absolved of responsibility by journalists.

Playing the Numbers Game

Statistics are one of the powerful and popular strategic devices used by the media to "enhance truthfulness, plausibility, correctness, precision, or credibility" (van Dijk, 1988c, p. 87). Nevertheless, it has also been noted that numbers matter not so much because of their precision, but because of the *impression* of achieving "precision and hence of truthfulness" (van Dijk, 1988c, p. 88). Numbers games have been particularly popular in media coverage of refugee and asylum issues.

The accuracy of migration statistics remains questionable in many countries (Hoffmann and Lawrence, 1996; Boyle et al., 1998; Castles and Loughna, 2005). The UK has a similar problem (Migrants' Right Network, 2009). Despite this, when covering issues related to migration statistics, the media often seem to attempt to leave the audience with the impression that figures are increasing and their countries are being "flooded" by migrants (Mollard, 2001; Speers, 2001; Buchanan et al., 2003). In Buchanan et al.'s study for example, it was found that numbers were sometimes given "without reference to their source or if obtained from unofficial sources, with little comment or explanation to properly inform the reader of their likely credibility" (Buchanan et al., 2003, p. 18).

Likewise, reliable data to calculate the actual numbers of the Fujianese did not actually exist at the time of the Dover incident. However, numbers were provided, sometimes with certain rhetoric, in the Dover coverage. Various speculations were made, such as: "Tens of thousands of Chinese are being illegally smuggled every year" (*Daily Mirror*, 20th June); "*More than* 900 asylum seekers from China arrived in Britain in March and April" (*Guardian*, 26th June); "*More than* 400 Chinese asylum seekers arrive in Britain each month" (ibid); "China's public security ministry says that *more than* 9,000 stowaways and more than 900 snakeheads were arrested last year by border police" (*Guardian*, 20th June, emphasis added). Articles represented a rapidly increasing tendency for Chinese to seek asylum in the UK, sometimes without any supporting statistical evidence except for generalised statements such as: "British immigration officials were alarmed at the rising number of Chinese asylum seekers this year" (*Guardian*, 20th June). In some cases, numbers were used, such as: "In the twelve months from March 1999 to March 2000 British officials detected 21,000 people trying to enter the UK clandestinely. In 1996 the figure was 61" (*Observer*, 25th June). Thus a massive increase was indicated without explaining contextualising factors such as improvements in detection techniques or the source or method of compilation of these statistics. In this way, an impression of an influx of Chinese asylum seekers/clandestine entrants was given.

Sources—Whose Voice Do We Hear?
Direct Description and Eyewitness Reports

Research on news sources has shown that journalists tend to rely on a limited number of authorities from particular bureaucratic organisations (Ericson et al., 1987, 1989; Manning, 2001). Van Dijk's (1988b, 1988c, 1991, 1993a) research on race issues in the British and Dutch press, for example, found that non-white groups are more likely to be spoken about instead of speaking for themselves. Journalists also tend to depend on white elites as sources, who, "are not only considered more newsworthy but also more reliable as observers and opinion formulators" (van Dijk, 1988c, p. 87). Buchanan et al.'s (2003) study of media coverage in the UK of the Sangatte camp, for example, supports van Dijk's findings in a British media context.

In the coverage of the Dover incident, authority figures representing political parties, the government, hospitals, the Refugee Council, police, business, media, and other "experts" who either officially represented, or whose statements showed parallels to, the interests of the UK government, were the most frequent sources. Among the 119 articles in my sample, 20, however, presented a perspective from the Fujianese migrants themselves, their solicitors as well as villagers, families and relatives from Fujian. Many of these stories were human-interest stories. Such stories can enable the reporter to play a more active role with more direct observation and help to authenticate coverage (see discussion in Hartley, 1982, p 90). These articles provided information about where these migrants came from, what their lives were like in China, why they came and how they managed their lives in the UK.

Human interest stories mostly appeared as features, providing the "soft" side of this event as a supplement to the "hard" news. However, because there was still no formal identification of the bodies at that stage, reporters had no certainty whether the families they wrote about were the actual families of those involved in the incident. The grief shown by the families which might have been involved was reported to express itself in anger towards local snakeheads (*Mail on Sunday*, 25th June). Family grief was an aspect of the coverage from Fujian. The focus of these stories was however largely directed towards the understanding that local, social and economic factors drive people to choose smuggling regardless of the risks. Casualties and accidents of being "poisoned, suffocated, frozen or baked to death by the vagaries of a route" (*Guardian*, 24th June; see also, *Sunday Telegraph*, 25th June) were therefore, according to these articles, fatalistically accepted in Fujian.

Reporters observed that peer pressure played an important role, too, since it was well known that "When one person goes abroad, the whole family makes money" (*Sunday Telegraph*, 25th June). The contrast between the families with and those without members abroad was reported to be sharp: the poor "lived in shabby terraces next to the walled patios and tiled balconies of the six-storey mansions owned by the rich—homes paid for by the families of illegal migrants to the West" (*Sunday Telegraph*, 25th June). Under such pressure, going abroad was described as the only way to prove one's value: "if you don't want to go, then you're not a real man. Being here and never having tried to leave, that amounts to a loss of face" (*The Times*, 22nd June). Observations that "… they can earn 30 times more in this country than back home" (*Daily Mail*, 22nd June) appeared repeatedly, reinforcing the "new life in the West" theme.

Investigative coverage on the side of the Fujianese already in the UK, however, seemed to suggest a contrasting reality—a possible "lifetime of poverty and debt" (*Sunday Telegraph*, 25th June), misery, a destitute and wasted life being the "non-people" "who do not speak the language" and who "were possibly indebted to the Snakeheads for ever" (*Daily Mail*, 24th June). The *Sunday Telegraph* (25th June) used the experience of a Chinese migrant from Fujian who was granted refugee status in the UK as an example. He is quoted in the article as describing his situation:

> I do nothing but work and sleep and I miss my family. I get bored on my day off. A lot of people in my position drift into gambling on the horses or at casino, or even crime…it is not easy living here.

Stories such as these also seemed to support Jack Straw's statement at the time that migrants were often given "all kinds of promises about the kind of life they would find when they got to Britain and even if they do get through alive they are often sorely disappointed when they arrive here" (*Guardian*, 20th June).

These feature stories revealed certain aspects of the social and cultural background of Fujian as well as offering some personal perspectives and experiences of the Fujianese. Whilst providing first hand evidence to support themes in the coverage that represented the victims as gullible, the smugglers' criminal activities as responsible for the deaths, and the casting of Fujianese as economic immigrants, such stories did not explain the apparent paradox between these disappointing experiences and the "30 times more earning ability" in the UK suggested by the reporters themselves, or why such disappointment failed to discourage others to follow suit, embarking on such potentially dangerous journeys with such unrewarding results.

Summary of Analysis

The textual properties in the Dover coverage suggest that the incident was mainly reported as a criminal case, with various references made to illegal organisations and activities. Confusion existed in naming and defining asylum seekers, refugees and immigrants with the tendency to derogate and stereotype them. The coverage relied predominately on official sources and played numbers games to exaggerate the problem of Fujianese being smuggled into the UK. Efforts were made to look at the reasons behind the smuggling and the experiences of Fujianese in the UK. Such investigative journalism however, remained limited and unable to answer further questions that arose.

To achieve a better understanding of the media representation of the Dover incident requires some contextual investigation, especially in relation to the under-representation of the Chinese in public life.

The Dover Incident in the Context of the
Under representation of the Chinese in the UK

To provide sufficient context for widening the focus of this chapter at this point, it is necessary to draw on a brief investigation of the historical discourses of public perceptions of the Chinese in Britain (Jiang, 2006). The long history of the Chinese presence in Britain has witnessed the formation of an attitude of tolerance towards and acceptance of this group and even acknowledgement of its self-reliance and diligence intermixed with other, more negative stereotypes and misconceptions, such as the potential threat Chinese pose to the labour market, and the perceived vices of gambling, drugs, and Triads associated with them (Jiang, 2006). Although compared to other ethnic minority groups in the UK, there were fewer major racist incidents that targeted the Chinese (May, 1978), anti-Chinese feelings and actions were however, often triggered in certain crises when they were considered to be a threat to British society. This was especially the case in earlier times when the Chinese directly competed in the mainstream labour market. One example was the anti-Chinese riots in Cardiff in

1911 which followed the accused blacklegging of Chinese seamen in the seamen strike (Cayford, 1991). Later on, with the majority of the Chinese turning to the catering business, they were no longer perceived to present a direct threat in the labour market (Baxter, 1988; Home Affairs Committee, 1985). However, mockery and suspicion towards the Chinese cuisine, catering workers and Chinese community as a whole continued (Chau and Yu, 2001). Still, more recent examples of anti-Chinese attitudes can be identified, including the 2001 foot-and-mouth epidemic in the UK and 2003 global SARS virus crisis when the Chinese community in the UK became a target of suspicion and Chinese restaurants in particular suffered from serious loss (Jiang, 2006, 2009; Jiang et al., 2009).

Based on an earlier association of the Chinese with drugs such as opium (Cayford, 1991), another more contemporary myth has developed since the 1970s, the stereotype of Chinese Triads (Watson, 1977). An association became established in news and entertainment media between the Chinese and drug smuggling and extortion rackets, despite little concrete evidence (Watson, 1977, p. 207). The theme of dangerous Chinese Triad gangs has reoccurred frequently (Parker, 1998a, 1998b) and the Dover incident presents another example. Statements such as "The trafficking is organised by Triad members known as Snakeheads" (*Times*, 20th June), or, "…the trade in human misery is a branch of international organised crime involving the Mafia and Chinese Triads" (*Sun*, 20th June) were common. A typical example can be found in the *Times*,

> …It involves evil, certainly; many clandestine migrants, whether they are refugees or people in search of economic betterment, end up as effective prisoners of the racketeers. Having promised to pay exorbitant "transit" fees out of future wages, they arrive deep in debt. Payment plus exorbitant "interest" is then taken out of often low wages, so that they can never be free of debt. Some Chinese illegal immigrants who try to escape this trap are kidnapped by British-based Triads who then force their families back in China to pay up. (*Times*, 20th June)

Overall, an enduring pattern of constructing the Chinese in the UK as "Other" is clearly visible throughout this history. This perception of otherness is also visible when analysing artistic or intellectual accounts of China from the past.[6] What is relevant here is that we should be aware that the importance of efforts to achieve some knowledge of a different culture is not necessarily about identifying the other, "but by the degree to which it enhances the self-esteem of the Westerner" (Sardar, 1999, p. 4). Rather than cross-examining the accuracy of the knowledge of China or the Chinese in the UK per se, to cite the historical and contextual review helps to remind us that such knowledge was and is constructed to reveal the "self" as the constructor of such "otherness". Whilst the media play a key role in communicating about issues with which the general public has little first-hand experience, media representations often tend to construct a dichotomy of inclusion and exclusion and,

> ...provide in-group members with information about out-groups or outcasts and the application of a consensus of social norms and values that helps define and confirm the own group. (van Dijk, 1988c, p. 123)

This is a process at work in the UK press construction of the public perceptions of the UK Chinese and China as much as in the othering of ethnic minority groups in other countries. Examples of studies into this phenomenon are ample. Hartley's (1992) study of news representation of Aboriginal communities in Australia pointed at a dichotomy of white Australians versus Aboriginal communities. Entman's (1997) research into television news production highlighted the dichotomy of white Americans versus African Americans. In a UK context, Allan (1999) identified a dichotomy of local "Christian whites" versus "local Asian Muslims". In a similar way, the press coverage of the Dover incident constructed a dichotomy between "us"—"us" being sensible, compassionate and responsible British people—and "them" as gullible and naive Chinese victims.

The news value discussion also provides another useful way of looking at why the Dover incident made newspaper headlines. The consonance as well as sudden and unexpected nature of the events represent important criterion among the list of news values by Galtung and Ruge (1973). That is to say, sudden events must conform to certain "presuppositions" and reflect assumptions based on some previously acquired knowledge to become news (van Dijk, 1988c, p. 121). In the Dover context, such "previous knowledge" included casualties happening to those who travelled without valid documents, especially those involving transportations including boats, lorries, Euro-tunnel trains and jumbo jets.[7] As such, the Dover incident could be readily represented as "a tragedy waiting to happen" (as suggested by the Conservative politician Ann Widdecombe reported in the *Daily Telegraph*, 20th June; and Jack Straw, *Sun*, 20th June; see also *Daily Mirror*, 20th June). Without reliable data about irregular migration, an assumption about its increasing tendency had formed. What happened at Dover was reported in this context. Most importantly, the media emphasis on the socio-economic motivation of the Fujianese, whilst supporting the argument that such low-skilled economic migrants would damage the British labour market (*Guardian*, 23rd June; *Daily Telegraph*, 20th June), also echoed the "threat" theme that has been consistently prevalent throughout the history of Chinese presence in the UK—a source of cheap and docile labour who might undermine the livelihood of their white contemporaries.

A general lack of knowledge of and studies about the Chinese in the UK, and in particular about smuggled Fujianese migrants, made comprehensive investigative reportage of a sudden incident such as occurred at Dover a difficult task for journalists. Answers to many of the questions, including who, how and most importantly, why, were either lacking or inadequate. Although a gloomy picture that emphasises the negative sides of Fujianese migration might seem a suitable response to such a tragic event, including its obvious criminal aspects, an in-depth investigation of the socio-cultural factors behind Fujianese migration and its impacts on UK society would have provided a very different understanding of the story and perhaps suggested an alternative approach for dealing with many issues related to this phenomenon. There have been historical and geographic factors in Fujian as a province where migration has been popular for centuries (Kwong, 1997; Chin, 1999; Pieke et al., 2004). The recent economical reforms in China and their impact on Fujian province also play a role (ibid). Migration from Fujian always adopts the form of chain migration (Young and Wilmott, 1957; Adams, 1968; Kwong, 1997). The establishment of close social and family networks in the UK has made Britain one of the popular destinations, in addition to the potential economic benefit (Jiang, 2006). Meanwhile, issues including smuggling organisations, trafficking, exploitation, poverty, social isolation and deprivation in their host country, to name a few, are also important areas to be looked at.

Reportage about the Fujianese in the UK in general remains fragmentary except on high-profile events including the incidents in Dover and Morecambe Bay. Lately, the problem of young Fujianese girls, many under aged, disappearing from care teams soon after arrival and being recruited into brothels across the UK started to emerge (*Guardian*, 11th October 2008). However, except a few social workers or organisations who dealt with these girls directly, public awareness remains low: "...in the UK, it appears, many in government, social services, immigration and the police are acting as if they have trouble believing at all" (ibid). One of the social workers said,

No one wanted to hear or was overly concerned about the kids going missing. The only calls I got from the Met police in London were saying they had fished the body of an Asian child out of the river and asking if it was one of mine. (ibid)

Are we waiting for another high-profile tragedy involving young Fujianese girls to happen before governments start to tackle this issue?

A case study of the press coverage of the Dover incident only scratches the tip of the iceberg of issues that concern Fujianese migration, including smuggling, trafficking, economic migration and asylum seeking. Whilst immigration laws and regulations are inadequate to offer answers and solutions, a lack of scholarship of this social phenomenon fails to provide useful perspectives— historical, cultural, socio-economic, to name a few—for a better understanding of this social phenomenon for the public and policy-makers. Likewise, a scarcity exists within the British society in terms of a discursive knowledge of the Chinese migration to the UK, historically and contemporarily, despite its importance. In such circumstances, news media have a hard job to keep abreast of this particular phenomenon and provide a comprehensive coverage of sudden incidents such as the Dover. Whilst the world's attention is turning to China's growing economic power, and the connection between China and the rest of the world is becoming closer, it is worthwhile to evaluate the role of clandestine immigration, in both sending and receiving societies. Ultimately, Fujianese migration is emblematic of the social impact of not only the migration-asylum nexus in British society but also the globalisation and its social transformation. Until such phenomena and their impact are addressed, tragedies that involve the smuggled Fujianese, or other irregular migrants, are bound to happen again.

Notes

1. Before 2001, for example, asylum applicants were granted a right to work six months after initial submission of their application. Since 2001, attempts have been made to complete the adjudication on applications within six months and detention centres for asylum seekers deemed likely to hide from authorities have been established (also see Glover et al., 2001).
2. The *Guardian* differed from the others in starting its lead on the latest developments in which two Chinese were charged. The article expanded on this point in its second paragraph, providing the pair's identities. Its third paragraph was similar to the leads of the other stories.

3.   According to the Asylum Statistics UK 2007 of Home Office (2007), 2,100 Chinese nationals applied for asylum seeking and 1,860 were refused.

4.   The right to a passport of a baby born to immigrant parents in the island of Ireland—including British-ruled Northern Ireland, was inserted in the 1998 Good Friday peace agreement. This was perceived as creating an unforeseen loophole to "passport tourists", and the citizenship right has been curtailed under new regulations following a constitutional referendum in June 2004. (Jiang, 2006, p. 196)

5.   During the fieldwork, the author met one Fujianese who claimed that he had had a narrow escape from being another victim of the Dover incident (Jiang, 2006)

6.   I have made this argument elsewhere, examining works including Coleridge's poem "Kublai Khan", writings of Karl Marx and Bertrand Russell on China, and the legacy of Puccini's operas Madame Butterfly and Turandot (see Jiang, 2006, pp. 63–83).

7.   For example, the Vietnamese boat people's experiences were made into several movies (such as "Turtle Beach", "Boat People", "Journey from the Fall"). Euro-tunnel trains have been jumped onto from bridges or ridden underneath. Even undercarriages of jumbo jets, with temperature of -40C or lower, have been targeted. Ten years since the Dover incident, smuggling in back of a lorry with risk of suffocation was still prevalent. As the *Daily Mail* (22nd July 2010) reported, three Vietnamese were found in the back of a lorry heading to cross the Channel at Dunkirk. Recent incidents also included the tragic death of 54 Myanmar migrants from suffocation in a seafood container in Thailand's Ranong province in April 2008.

Section Three—The Management of Migration in Journalistic Practice

The three chapters comprising the final section engage explicitly with journalistic practice in relation to migration. The rights and responsibilities of journalists in Western, liberal democracies are the focus of Blaagaard's chapter. By analysing the debates over the role of journalism following the publication of cartoons of the prophet Muhammed in a Danish newspaper in 2005, Blaagaard argues that journalists' self-perception as defenders of liberal values misses the fact that these democracies are neither homogeneous nor self-contained nor disconnected from global flows of information, people and values. Concepts such as multiculturalism and cosmopolitanism, tolerance *of* or obligation *towards* others, as well as conviviality have different consequences for journalism as an integrative force. Blaagaard also points towards new technologies and forms of citizen journalism that "develop new transnational ethics advanced through journalistic practice."

The concept of multiculturalism is also a concern though not the focus of Bayer's chapter on her experience of media diversity. Both Blaagaard and Bayer address issues that look at migration beyond the act of migrating itself. The discourse of migration—of recent arrival and non-belonging—continues to apply for years or even generations. Bayer's critical reflections on running a number of intercultural awareness training programmes offer interesting insights into the difficulties and opportunities of various approaches for intercultural dialogue and media diversity. Bayer puts these practice-oriented considerations in the context of debates over migration and integration in Germany. In relation to the latter the media has been officially identified as playing a key role. However, Bayer expresses concern that the institutional set up of the media in Germany may hamper these efforts and "none of these approaches will be truly fruitful until they start moving beyond the personal and tackle the structural level of media, especially news production."

While Blaagaard discusses journalistic practice in relation to migration in terms of ethics and Bayer engages with these issues on the level of training new generations of journalists, Harris' chapter zooms in on the experience of a working journalist's reporting on migration. Harris was the producer of a 2001 television documentary on the UK border—part of a BBC2 series on the UK

Immigration Service. By considering a number of critical studies on the coverage of migration, the nature of documentary filmmaking and the specific situations she encountered, Harris critically re-examines her own practice, points to systemic constraints and concludes that the programme may not have questioned the discourse of immigration policy sufficiently "asking not just how it was working (or clearly not)…but whether it was actually sufficient to deal with the issues of 2001, and global mass movement". At the same time Harris also provides an implicit but important challenge to the critiques of reporting of migration to address or at least take into consideration, everyday journalistic practice.

CHAPTER TEN

The (Multi)cultural Obligation of Journalism

Bolette Blaagaard

> Instead of being obsessed with laws and rights—approaching a tyrannical right to say anything—would it not be more prudent to call upon citizens to exercise their right to freedom of expression responsibly and to take into account the diverse sensitivities that compose our pluralistic contemporary societies?)[1]

The quote above by public intellectual and founder of what has been named Euro-Islam, Tariq Ramadan, raises three challenges to journalism today, in particular to what has become known as the Danish cartoon controversy and to the debates that followed. Firstly, Ramadan frames legal rights as being sustained by obligations (O'Neill, 2002), whereas much of the controversy centred on the issue of rights and freedoms. Secondly, Ramadan is questioning the normative claim to democracy as represented by Western societies frequently made during the controversy. He is suggesting that democracy takes many shapes and is supported by many cultures, and so we need to think of democracy alongside multiculturalism. So rather than imposing a strong Enlightenment narrative on the debates concerning Western democracy, we need to take into account the diversity of Western societies and indeed of democratic structures themselves. Finally, he is suggesting that cultures and cultural practices underpin legal rights and democratic politics. The latter two comments are particularly pertinent in relation to the case of Denmark and the Danish cartoon controversy on which Ramadan is focusing these comments. This is because of the specific Danish colonial history and because of Denmark's inability to deal sufficiently with this legacy and with its multicultural society, as this chapter will discuss.

Ramadan's position is in sharp contrast to the position defended by Flemming Rose, who was editor of the cultural section of the national Danish newspaper *Jyllands-Posten* in 2005 when the cartoons of the prophet Muhammed were published. Ramadan is questioning the currency of the liberal values of individualism, equality and freedom of expression on a global scale, which to Rose, were and are, tenets of Danish political stability and social welfare. Considering their diverging positions, it was unsurprising that when the Danish weekly newspaper, *Weekendavisen,* brought Ramadan and Rose together to discuss the cartoon controversy in January 2008[2] it resulted in a miscommunication of great proportions. Whereas Ramadan argued for respecting the other, Rose argued for tolerance of the other, which to Rose means that he neither needs to understand nor respect the other. Put simply, Ramadan approached the debate in terms of obligations or duty towards the other whereas Rose focused on the legal rights of the individual to speak, gather, and raise his or her opinions freely.

In this article I intend to introduce and analyse some of the events and debates that took place after the initial controversy and international crisis had blown over in the light of the concerns mentioned above. I rely on this linkage between the sequence of events to argue for a more serious acknowledgement of journalistic cultural power and importance, and in terms of global as well as politico-legal disputes. Using the Ramadan quote as guidance, I discuss journalism's complicity in sustaining implicit cultural assumptions and stereotypes, dressed up in narratives of legal frameworks and Western politics and values. I argue that journalistic practitioners as well as media theorists are called upon to rethink the foundations of journalistic practices in the face of multi-cultures and multi-media, and urge the reader to think of culture as a foundation of rights and freedoms, and journalism as a foundation of cultural expressions and understanding. Following this argument through, it calls upon journalists and citizens alike to reconsider the way journalism functions in a multicultural and transnational space. This article therefore also makes a theoretical bid for a development of transnational ethics advanced through journalistic practices. I explore the tension between the transnational cosmopolitan potential of generating a sense of proximity through wide-ranging media communications and nationally focused and nationally bound public expressions that are using this potential to initiate and engage in anti-migration and anti-Islamic debates, rather than empathetic hospitality or multiculturalism. I aim to show how Danish journalism is re-positioning and repossessing the journalistic role of constructing communities and national coherence (Anderson, 2006) in a time of ever-increasing transnational media potential.

The Cartoons and the Danish Political Context

This article does not attempt to explain the cartoon controversy, about which much has been said and written. During and shortly after the events took place the controversy was discussed by a number of scholars and it is now frequently featured in books and articles discussing issues of migration, "clash of civilisations" and of cultures, and European Islam. Recently a monograph book in English and solely on the topic of the cartoons has been published (Klausen, 2009). It explains the Danish context as well as analyses the events by means of interviews with implicated politicians etc. and it follows the many publications in Danish that came on the market in the years since the controversy. Although the controversy marked a political shift in Danish self-perception and international image[3] (Andersen, 2006), the controversy's aftermath—the return to the debate in the years that followed—allows us to see the underlying notions of nationhood, culture and democracy which were subdued during the immediate fighting between the camps, the dualist impulses (Klausen, 2009) in the battle of values (Andersen, 2006) or clash of civilisations (Huntington, 1996), for or against the reductionist ideas of "Islam" and/or "Western values".

To quickly recap the events that make up the controversy, it began in the context of a turn to the right in Danish politics. The early days of this millennium, the "noughties", have presented—not only Denmark—but continental Europe with a number of challenges and paradoxes concerning freedom of expression and issues of migration and integration. The response has often been a shift to the right. This upsurge in centre-right and right-wing party politics across Europe became evident on 4 June 2009 when European citizens voted in the EU parliamentary election. The election showed a significant rise in popularity of such parties in countries like the Netherlands, Denmark and the UK.[4] Sweden is the latest example of this turn. The parallel resurgence notwithstanding, the nationalist parties in the UK, the Netherlands and Denmark, among others, are not the same in each country and their popularity are not built on the same rhetoric or issues. The national specificities concerning colonialism, the Second World War and history of migration allow for differences between them. Denmark, for instance, similar to other Scandinavian countries such as Norway, has had a culture of complacency, a self-satisfaction linked to a national self-image of "rugged egalitarian individualism and innocence" (Gullestad, 2005, p. 44). Scandinavians pride themselves on being a "freedom loving, egalitarian and tolerant people" (Olwig, 2003, p. 215). These are all concepts that implicitly surface in the cartoon controversy and which will be discussed below.

It is important to my argument to stress that these dominant narratives of national identification patterns founded on innocence, humanism, tolerance and anti-racism are based partly on selective historical and cultural facts (Gullestad, 2005). They are also partly based, however, on disregarding other, less re-assuring and non-consensual historical facts, such as colonial oppression, the existence and the lasting legacy of the slave trade and the implicit assumptions and extrinsic manifestations of Protestant supremacy that underpinned these. Even more concealed is the extent to which these Euro-centric narratives have reached a hegemonic status among scholars, politicians, media and lay people alike, despite ample colonial evidence to the contrary (Olwig, 2003). Multiculturalism is tightly linked to formations of migration in Denmark—partly, because Denmark has avoided discussions about its colonial past and responsibilities, and partly, because of the lack of former colonial citizens in the country—unlike for instance in the Netherlands and in the UK. Public discussion in Denmark focuses on difference and diversity purely in connection to immigrants and in particular to Muslim immigrants and their descendants. This selective memory is less pronounced when it comes to the dramatic events of the Second World War, a topic which has received critical attention in Denmark. Gilroy (2006) calls this kind of selective attitude to national self-narration and collective self-perception, agno-politics or agnotology,[5] which is a form of structural blindness and which produces "new racism" based on cultural differences rather than overt biological or naturalised racism. The political context is far from immune to this debate. In Denmark for instance, issues of integration have surfaced in the national elections twice in a row, in 2001 and 2005, and raised Dansk Folkeparti (the Danish People's Party), a right-wing party that introduced the integration debate in particular in relation to Muslims to the mainstream political arena, to become the third largest party in parliament and the main support for the government coalition, which consists of Venstre and Det Konservative Folkeparti; both coalition parties are traditional and conservative parties. These political developments are in turn closely mirrored by the media and the sense of community belonging they represent through their coverage.

Danish media has time and again been proved to reproduce racial, ethnic and religious stereotypes (Hussain, 2002; Jensen, 2006; Andreassen, 2007). In the media, holding Danish citizenship for instance is not enough to be recognised as a Dane, rather Danish nationality is constructed as "closely connected to whiteness, to the white race" (Andreassen, 2005, p. 288). Cultural "naturalisation" of Danish nationality means that it persists as white and unmarked in the journalistic products and functions as the norm through which otherness is defined as un-Danish. Moreover, the Danish public and political debates often conflate the notion of "migrant" with the notion of "Muslim" (Andreassen, 2007; Jensen, 2006). In this political and mediated context, the cartoons were commissioned and published by the national newspaper, *Jyllands-Posten*. The cartoons were meant to critique a perceived self-imposed censorship in regards to poking fun at and questioning Islam that artists, journalists and other public performers practiced after 9/11. The publication sparked angry responses and violence across vast geographical and virtual spaces and threw Denmark—the nation and the state[6]—into a politically turbulent debate in a global context. The main events, the burning of embassies, flags and dolls dressed up to look like the Danish Prime Minister, and the deaths of more than 30 people in connection with massive demonstrations, took place in 2005–6. The debates that my argument focuses on took place a few years later, in 2008 and 2009.

Although, the cartoon controversy sparked interest from media worldwide, the subsequent events and debates returned to what could be termed the roots of the controversy: the Danish cultural and political context. The context is outlined above and is constructed and sustained as an "imagined community" (Anderson, 2006) by means of, for instance, the media and journalistic practices. In the cartoon controversy, I argue here, Danish journalism sought to reposition and repossess the journalistic role of constructing (imagined) communities and national coherence in a time of ever-increasing transnational media potential. Advanced technology makes cross-cultural communication possible via the Internet, mobile phones and other new media. These new developments have carried with them new genres of journalistic practices, such as blogging, social networking sites and other forms of viral communication flows. In this article, I use the term citizen journalism to refer to journalistic products from "ordinary", non-professional users, which is uploaded, shared, and commented upon in online but also in mainstream media. Citizen journalism is not purely an online phenomenon. Moreover it encompasses what is often called "meta journalism", or social news. That is, the practice of re-postings and virally distributed news. This is a very broad definition of citizen journalism, and a contested one at that. I use it here for clarity and in order to make a point about social and cultural developments rather than about technological advances (see also Allan & Thorsen (Eds.), 2009).

These new technologies are not culturally "neutral", but carry with them notions of particular values, such as transparency and accessibility (Ess, 2009). They are not inherently democratic either; rather they are based on a certain affluence and technological savvy. And finally, despite the transnational and viral character of new journalistic genres like citizen journalism, social networking sites, and blogging, journalism and news sharing, i.e., professional journalism, to a large extent, remains wedded to the idea of the nation and the national community as a cultural and mainly homogenous construction. Nevertheless, the new "journalists" present the potential of transnational and democratic change, which I seek to account for in this article. It is the imbrication of the digital technology and the social (Sassen, 2006) that introduces itself. The advanced media technologies and the national communities are interdependent although not hybrids, and it is within the structural framework of the national and multicultural community that farther-reaching communities may appear. Needless to say that the contrary is likewise true: narrower and closed communities may develop as easily as open, connecting and farther-reaching ones within the structural framework of the national (Downing & Husband, 2005). My hope is to build on Appadurai's (1996) observation that migration and new media are at an advanced stage of modernity:

> And few persons in the world today do not have a friend, relative, or coworker who is not on the road to somewhere else or already coming back home, bearing stories and possibilities. In this sense, both persons and images often meet unpredictably, outside the certainties of home and the cordon sanitaire of local and national media effects. This mobile and unforeseeable relationship between mass mediated events and migratory audiences defines the core of the link between globalization and the modern. (Appadurai, 1996, p. 4)

Today, of course, to the "friend, relative, or coworker" citizen journalist can be added and the mass media is moreover incorporated into that circuit of news. Through mass media and broadcasting corporations anyone's mobile phone footage, eye-witness report or pictures may become available to a large number of people as evidence of events happening in a different part of the world.

Transnational Technologies and Potential Cosmopolitanism

The transnational character of the aims of this article calls for an explanation as to how journalism relates to transnational ethics or cosmopolitanism. As introduced above, citizen journalism plays an important part in this relationship. Transnational ethics or cosmopolitanism is of relevance here when it is coupled with journalistic practice because of the integral connection between the nation and the journalistic profession. Journalism and the idea of the nation-state have a common history (Anderson, 2006). In support of the national community, journalism constantly and overtly builds on the idea that there is a common "we", a common frame of reference, to which a news item implicitly refers. Often that frame of reference follows the boundaries of the nation-state or a slightly wider (or at times narrower) ethnically or religiously defined community. This allows journalists to reproduce social imaginaries through repetition of cultural constructions and memories excluding minority groups and/or glossing over unrecognised multiculturalism within the national context. It follows that this relationship is questioned when we move increasingly from predominantly national community formations to transnational and globalised communities based on Internet and other new media communication. Both the reproduction of social imaginaries of homogenous societies and the move towards transnational community formations are confronted by new technological advances. The first confrontation relates to the impact of these advances on ethnic minority media, which is an under-researched area, and which is also beyond the scope of this article. However, the political and cultural complexities involved in regard to diversity of representation in transnational media and other technological possibilities are linked to the issues discussed in this article[7] because of the common focus on journalistic practices and their ethical implications. The second confrontation is between multiculturalism and the journalistic claim to objectivity when making the move beyond the borders of the nation state. Put succinctly, new media communication challenges both national and transnational journalism by making visible the many possible formations of cultural citizenship and their relationship to journalistic practice. Citizen journalism in particular brings light to this challenge, because of its potential to engender intimate connections and political and cultural solidarity across the globe through personal as well as political knowledge transfer and debate. It is because of citizen journalism's ability to bring light to the transnational diversity behind journalistic practices that it lends itself to a cosmopolitan theory. Cosmopolitan ideas assume what Appadurai calls imagination as a collective social and cultural practice (Appadurai, 1996, p. 5), i.e., we have to be able to imagine a common world, or several globally spanning connections and circuits, in order to create the global solidarity of which cosmopolitanism speaks.

Research on journalism and globalisation tends to focus on the technology part of these aspects. Technology is seen to enable (citizen) journalism to reach beyond national and cultural borders and to posit journalism either as the (universal) fourth estate or a direct political, democratic power (Anderson and Ward, 2007; Durham & Kellner, 2001; Berry, 2005) in a global village. A 15-second film made on a mobile phone showing Iranian people on the streets of Teheran during the election in 2009, for instance, may be posted online, cover unprecedented virtual grounds, and end up in loops in nationally and internationally broadcast media, urging presidents to comment upon or condemn the Iranian election. The technological developments also change the power positions within the journalistic practice. The editorial power held by journalists and editors—the gate-keeper role—is of late dispersed into a billion mobile phone users, bloggers and webmasters and has left the dual space of private and public realms merged and intermingled. (Couldry, 2009) Couldry (2009) argues that digital media is now integral to how selves appear. (Couldry, 2009, p. 438) There is no mediated centre to which we all need access in order to create the dialogue which constitutes the public sphere and a common society. It is inherent to who we are rather than an external centre. However, we still predominantly choose to receive our news from televised broadcast media rather than the Internet. As Hafez (2007) argues, the national "old" media still sit heavily on the administrations and flows of newsfeeds. In effect, "[m]edia production and use are proving conservative cultural forces in many parts of the world. They are generating a reality which the "globalization" approach struggles to cope with." (Hafez, 2007, p. 2) The two visions of the media: the integrated media of Couldry and the conservative "old" media of Hafez are not juxtaposed but are experienced simultaneously. "Old" media feeds into the way we imagine our worlds and ourselves in these worlds.

The cartoons were published in a national newspaper and the controversy was very locally based for the first six months after publication and, as I argue in this article, not only remained a national issue for many participants, but returned to these roots years after the dust had settled. Couldry argues that these conservative cultural media will not undergo radical change or decline. The point is rather that neither the Internet nor the traditional media is divorced from the social and material lives of people and economies behind the keyboards and computer screens, but is embedded in as well as an extension of them. This structure allows for a different kind of participatory mediation: citizen journalism. This new and flexible power structure likewise challenges the idea of a "mediated centre" hierarchy and allows the *citizen* in citizen journalism to hold a *potential* cosmopolitan or transnational citizenship and connect across borders and boundaries, although the practice of *journalism* remains nationally bound. Thus, citizen journalism has the potential to question the idea of national journalism and integration through media use and presents the potential of a cosmopolitan media and journalistic practice. However, the tension that resides within the national journalistic paradigm still persists. Journalism's claim to objectivity and its concomitant universalisation of a particular outlook and standpoint may well follow the profession across borders, if—that is—the technologically sustained cosmopolitan promise forgets the grounded fact of multiculturalism and the potential of diversity the personal connection within citizen journalism.

Multiculturalism and Journalism

The challenge of *multiplicity of media* is joined by a second challenge to the myth of the mediated centre, which is then the *multiplicity within societies*—migration and multiculturalism. Of late multiculturalism has been politically rejected in most countries of the EU and declared in crisis. (Modood, 2007; Phillips 2007) Much of the debates have been based on disagreements about the concept of *multiculturalism*. In this relation Parekh (2008) writes:

> For some [multiculturalism] means treating each cultural community as a world unto itself and involves cultural relativism. For others including myself, it means that no culture is perfect and that it benefits from a critical dialogue with others, and involves a rejection of relativism. (Parekh, 2008, p. fn7)

Paul Gilroy's (2004) concept of *conviviality* rather than *multiculturalism*, which amounts to a definition very close to Parekh's second statement in the quote above, is helpful. Gilroy's concept argues for interrelated respect and curiosity (i.e., an interest in knowing more) towards others. The crisis of multiculturalism has moreover been associated with a critique of cosmopolitanism. Modood (2007) develops an argument for a "multicultural citizenship" or "civic multiculturalism" (Modood, 2007, pp. 15–16) that finds inspiration in the example of Canadian multicultural policies as well as in Parekh's Report of the Commission for Multi-Ethnic Britain (CMEB). In his argument for a multicultural citizenship, Modood balances between an "emotional pull" of national identity and legislative adjustments towards inclusion of difference (2007, p. 19). Cosmopolitanism, Modood asserts, is too weak as a cultural concept and political structure to work. It lacks the emotional pull and will allow people to descend into the stronger nationalism when fear and terror present itself (Modood, 2007, p. 149). Phillips (2007) agrees with Modood's critique of cosmopolitanism. Cosmopolitanism is an attitude, she argues, multiculturalism is policy (Phillips, 2007, p. 70) and hence is politically more viable. The crux of Phillips' argument is that culture does not deny human agency and should be rescued from the discourses that position different cultures parallel but apart and with an overwhelming capacity to determine the range of agency of particularly its female members. Rather than cosmopolitanism, Phillips advocates multiculturalism without the limiting and disabling concept of culture. Both Modood and Phillips argue for political recognition of diversity within cultures. In Denmark however this policy-making multiculturalism in regard to the functioning of journalistic freedom is met with resistance. During the controversy, journalism was seen as the watch-dog and opposition in a democratic state and as such it was granted a kind of immunity from critique and discussion. Like freedom of expression, journalistic freedom is sacred. This was the line of argument the Danish politicians took in the cartoon controversy: Referring to the constitutional right to free speech and a free press, the Danish Prime Minister turned down an invitation from Danish imams to discuss the cartoons as a part of a larger multicultural problem in Denmark (Jerichow & Rode, 2006). It is the case however, as I argued above, that journalism holds a particular cultural power. This cultural power was overlooked and journalism was vehemently defended as an objective, political body; i.e., journalism was seen as the defender of democracy without an eye for what kind of democratic tradition and what political theories it employed and sustained. Journalism is increasingly challenged in multicultural and transnational relations, it seems therefore that a rethinking of journalistic power in political and cultural terms is required and a journalistic "leg" is needed in the arguments for a multicultural future—political policies are not enough.

There are then at least two reasons for adding a journalistic leg to the debates about multiculturalism: Firstly, the "emotional pull" is largely generated and sustained by media, including journalism. It would therefore seem necessary to Modood's civic multiculturalism. Secondly, the journalistic homogenous representation of the heterogeneous population has political consequences. It is thus important to rethink journalistic political and cultural representations in order to create multiculturalism without relativistic representations of cultures.

Nationalism can be seen as a cultural phenomenon rather than a political one. This is the starting assumption of Benedict Anderson's work when he writes that "...nation-ness, as well as nationalism, are cultural artefacts of a particular kind. To understand them properly we need to consider carefully how they came into historical being..." (Anderson, 2006, p. 4) It therefore makes sense to turn our attention to the role that journalism plays in multicultural societies. In his seminal work *Imagined Communities* (2006), Anderson talks about the printing press and capitalism and their impact on the construction of the nation-state. Anderson argues that the printing press revolutionalised the sense of community and helped construct the idea of the nation by publishing in the vernacular, which meant that it was accessible to a larger part of the population, cutting out the gate-keepers of the church and the aristocracy, and as such provided a coherent social imaginary based on sameness. Print capitalism was then the facilitator of the spreading of information and communication, not only in terms of linguistic translations (often) from Latin to the vernacular, but also in terms of cultural translations. That is, the vernacular also allowed translations to fit and market the texts in particular and homogenous cultures. But it also brought with it a different perception of *time*. *Simultaneity* enabled the ability to imagine other people doing other things at the same time without meeting or knowing each other. We can imagine a community. Most of all print-capitalism—the printing press—made it possible to print and distribute vast amounts of information that allowed the number of people who imagined themselves as part of a given community to grow rapidly. As such, the media is strongly connected to the idea of the nation. The repetition of "common sense" within the media continually sustains the idea of the nation as being "immemorial" and "glid[ing] into a limitless future" (Anderson, 2006, pp. 11–12). The media also tends to construct the nation as homogenous and unified, in order to serve as a nationally unifying narrative (Muhlmann, 2008).

As argued above in relation to Danish media, ethnic diversity that now makes up the European nations is often stereotyped or portrayed in deliberate "multiculturalist" ways. (Cottle, 2000, p. 11) Although, the structures are complex, today the nation is increasingly experienced as a multicultural space; however the voices that are heard and the faces that are seen in the media are strikingly homogeneous. (Cottle, 2000) The issue of the relationship between journalism and national belonging is then contested through the imbalance of representation within as well as outside the national boundaries. Identity and national belonging are constructions that have established themselves and sustained themselves through a number of discursive and material practices which also openly include the exclusions of others. The imagined community is bounded within the limits of "us". On the outside are "the others". Stevenson (2003) suggests breaking apart the notion of a unified identity by emphasising how we are all out of place, somehow. This parallels the work done by postcolonial thinkers and feminists. Gilroy (2004) for example likewise argues for *cosmopolitanism from below*—an estrangement, or a disloyalty to civilisation, as the feminist writer Adrienne Rich (1979) calls it. In the work by feminist and postcolonial critics, cosmopolitanism functions in terms of a transnational solidarity that assumes a critical detachment from universal claims. Rather than a politico-legal institution for cosmopolitan conduct, feminists and postcolonial thinkers have argued for ethical relations based on respect of difference. This kind of cosmopolitan attitude presents itself as a way in which journalism could develop in a multicultural society. It does not require policies, but ethics. Stevenson (2003) writes about cosmopolitanism that it needs to be coupled with ideas of multiculturalism. So, rather than choosing policies over attitudes (Phillips, 2007), Stevenson argues for a combination in light of the diverse and cross-national pulls that journalism as well as European nations are currently experiencing. It could be said that this cosmopolitan attitude constitutes all citizens' "right to be understood." (Husband, 2000, p. 210) Supporting a multicultural citizenship and the coexistence of differing cultural traditions and values, Husband notes that this needs to be followed up with equal access. This "right to be understood" would be a third generation human right, Husband argues (2000,

p. 209), and would provide a legal-political framework through which an egalitarian structural pluralism could be achieved (Husband, 2000, p. 213). Husband recognises the utopian quality of his theory, however the point in this theory—and in Stevenson's view—is that a multiplicity of voices within as well as outside the self needs to be represented and heard in the media in order to give a more inclusive and accurate picture of the society and nation. To Silverstone (2007) it is more than that, however; it is *hospitality* or an *obligation to listen*. In contrast to a right, an obligation opens up to communication and evaluation. It is thus not only about accessibility to the media centre, but also about assessability of what we are being told (O'Neill, 2002). New media structures give access but do not generate more trust in whether we are being told the truth, quite on the contrary, asserts O'Neill (2002). They do, however, potentially allow for more voices to be heard.

Tolerance and Respect

Returning, then, to the quote by Ramadan with which I began this article: In line with Parekh, who argues that Muslims "do not question the value of free speech but rather its scope and limits" (Parekh, 2008, p. 20), Ramadan argues that the cartoon controversy was less about freedom of expression and more about civic responsibilities.[8] Democracy is not simply about majority rule, but likewise about civil rights and liberties that allow multiple cultures to reside side by side. Recently Flemming Rose repeated in an interview that to him the lesson to be learnt from the cartoon controversy was about holding on to the liberal values of individualism, equality and freedom of expression on a global scale (Kastrup, 2008). Rose regards "the multicultural project" as a project forging relativism, a failed project that "has resulted in group rights which really pisses [Rose] off" (Kastrup, 2008). Relativism would represent liberal values of individualism, equality and freedom of expression parallel to any other values, such as freedom of religion and of religious values. It would mean to treat each cultural community separately and following the laws and traditions of each cultural community in its own right. To Rose multiculturalism therefore involves a reassessment and questioning of liberal values, which he is not prepared to engage in because it would be questioning democracy itself and subsequently the democratic function of journalism. To Rose democracy is less about civil liberties than about majority rule, which relative relations between multiple cultures

cannot sustain. Rather Rose argues for democracy's universal and global structure. He therefore advocates tolerance rather than respect, because tolerance is,
so to speak, a practice only available to the powerful or the majority. Tolerance
is a concept which involves "the marking of subjects of tolerance as inferior,
deviant, or marginal vis-à-vis those practicing tolerance." (Brown, 2006, p. 13)
It is a liberal democratic concept which often is seen as a universalisable concept. (Brown, 2006, p. 170) Its potential to become a universal value lies in its
perceived detachment from any cultural communitarian contexts, writes Brown
(2006). That is, in its assumptions of objectivity, which are likewise the assumptions of most traditional journalism:

> Non-liberal polities are depicted as "ruled" by culture or religion; liberalism is depicted
> as ruled by law, with culture dispensed to another domain—a depolitized and voluntary
> one…Culture is individual autonomy's antimony and hence what the liberal state pres-
> umes to subdue, depower, and privatize, as well as detach itself from. (Brown, 2006, p.
> 171)

It could then be added that a free press is often seen as a prerequisite for a
liberal democracy. When Rose is "pissed off" by the mushrooming rights of cultural and religious groups it is because these community-based demands are in
conflict with Rose's idea of liberal government. The "demand [for] special
treatment [and] insist[ence] that their religious feelings are considered…is incompatible with Western democracy and freedom of expression…" as Rose put
it in the accompanying text to the cartoons in 2005 (Jerichow & Rode, 2006, p.
14, my translation). However, what the cartoon controversy made apparent was
not the rights of minorities but rather the cultural basis of liberal law—that
which was supposed to be subdued, depowered and privatised. As Brown puts
it: "the conflict…exposes the nonuniversal character of liberal legalism and
public life: it exposes its cultural dimension" (Brown, 2006, p. 173). In other
words, the cartoon controversy disclosed Danish freedom of expression to be
based on an assumption of culturally homogeneous population disguised as
universal or objective standard. It exposed the Protestant Christian basis of
these cultural dimensions by presenting the Danish Muslims' rights as "special
treatment." There cannot be a global politics of tolerance except in a fully
"Westernised" liberal world or through complete colonisation.

This was further emphasised in 2008 when three men were arrested, suspected of planning to carry out a deadly attack on Kurt Westergaard, the car-

toonist who drew the infamous picture of Muhammed with a bomb in the turban. As a response to the arrest the major, national Danish newspapers reprinted the cartoon. Referring to freedom of expression the Danish newspapers covered the alleged murder plans, and as part of their coverage they unanimously decided to reprint the infamous cartoon. This political and cultural manifestation resulted in a lawsuit being filed against the papers collectively by a number of descendants of the prophet Muhammed. Recently one of these national Danish newspapers, *Politiken* settled a lawsuit out of court. Following this, the newspaper published a statement in which it apologised for the hurt caused by the reprinting. The settlement was met with stern reactions, not only from media experts, Islam critics and the like, but also from parliamentary politicians who all condemned the settlement. Thus, current Prime Minister Lars Løkke Rasmussen was disappointed that the newspapers did not "close ranks" on this issue.[9] The political leader of Dansk Folkeparti, Pia Kærsgaard, found it likewise "embarrassing that Tøger Seidenfaden [the editor in chief of *Politiken*] sold out Danish and Western values such as freedom of expression."[10] Broadly speaking the politicians' comments were denouncing the settlement agreement as producing a weak link in the struggle against non-Danish or non-Western culture. In these debates journalism was called back to the original purpose of journalism, which is not—as the tradition of the profession dictates —fourth estate'ism or a watch-dog function, but in defence of what is perceived as "our culture"—although in the service of the Danish politicians' views and political rhetoric. The national newspapers are called upon to stand shoulder to shoulder to defend the legal, and importantly the culturally justified, right to freedom of speech,[11] defined and cemented through the controversial debate following the publication of the cartoons. Politically as well as culturally and journalistically journalism was expected to defend a cultural citizenship based on the national context and within the national and ethno-religious boundaries. During the cartoon controversy the then-UN Secretary General, Kofi Annan was greeted with political protests and disbelief when he suggested in connection to the controversy that cultural integration is a two-way street (Jerichow & Rode, 2006). It would seem then that in the mediated nation of Denmark, rights are for the majority who hold the cultural citizenship and obligations are for the minority who may own the passport but not the cultural affiliation.

On the other side of the argument, Ramadan's call for respect is a call for conviviality (Gilroy, 2004). The civil liberties are manifested in legal rights and thus in fleshing out what falls within and what falls outside the rule of law. That is, civil liberties are also based in a form of tolerance. (Derrida, 2001) In his work on hospitality and cosmopolitanism, Derrida (2001) contrasts tolerance with the concept of hospitality, which he in turn sees as being unconditional. Unconditional hospitality is hospitality by virtue of its unconditionality. It is a practically impossible demand and our relation to the other must, then, always vacillate between the laws of rights and unconditional hospitality. Unconditional hospitality is the absolute surrender of possessions and as such an impossible ideal, hence constant negotiation—*differance*—is necessary to establish and maintain relations to others. This is not unrelated to Ramadan and Parekh's (2008) stance. Parekh argues:

> The aim [for secular liberal societies] should be *limited* in the sense of defending a particular society rather than prescribing a universal model, and *modest* in the sense of making a good case for it without claiming that no rational man can fail to be convinced by it. (Parekh, 2008, p. 26, emphasis in original)

That is, rather than stubbornly sticking to universal claims, both sides of the controversy need to let democracy do what it does best, allow space for negotiation and accommodation. We all have to meet the obligations put on us in order to ensure and sustain a society built on individual rights.

To sum up, the discussion could be identified as one of rights versus obligations from which an argument for hospitality emerges. These are terms on which Silverstone (2007) builds his theories of the cosmopolitan media. In his words:

> [t]he cosmopolitan individual embodies, in his or her person, a doubling of identity and identification; the cosmopolitan, as an ethic, embodies a commitment, indeed an obligation, to recognise not just the stranger as other, but the other in oneself. Cosmopolitanism implies and requires, therefore, both reflexivity and toleration. In political terms it demands liberty and justice. In social terms: hospitality. (Silverstone, 2007, p. 14)

Building on O'Neill (2002), Silverstone asserts that opposed to a right-based claim, for instance the right to free speech or free assembly, an obligation takes its starting point in responsibility, of what one ought to do, a conception of what is of the good. As such, obligations serve as a framework for rights. Obligations strive for communication, Silverstone argues. They presuppose a receiver or a communication partner, and they are not only a self-expression but must also sustain the conditions of communication. So when Silverstone talks about obligation to listen, he talks about hospitality in the sense of Kant's notion of man's right to presentation—to present him/herself. Silverstone translates this readily into the mediated space as the right to *representation*—to be listened to, and heard. Silverstone, thus, envisages media—and to Silverstone, media is *all* media—as the ideal ethical relation between others. That is, cosmopolitanism.

Silverstone's cosmopolitanism is then not merely an attitude as Phillips (2007) argues, but a journalistic practice and a possibility in an increasingly connected world. It requires both reflexivity and toleration, i.e., both a willingness to reassess one's own foundation as well as giving space for the voice of the other. However, it is important to recognise that firstly, it is a possibility and not a reality, and secondly, cosmopolitanism is founded in a culturally liberal conception of justice through its cultural connections and through the consequent technological advances. On the first point it is evident that racist and other discriminatory practices are present online and in media outlets of most kinds. Technology does not make the world more democratic, transparent or assessable. (O'Neill, 2002) Nor is journalism an objective practice or a neutral mouthpiece for a democratic world. On the second point, if the nation is partly constructed through and by the media, as Anderson argues (2006), citizenship is arguably formed by the media as a form of "cultural citizenship", as I argued in the previous discussion of Rose's and the Danish political and journalistic discourse. The media helps construct a nation-state that supports "an idea of a fundamental connectedness between members of the nation" (Husband, 2000). Charles Husband writes that "[t]his view of the world is usually constructed and sustained by a supportive "invention of tradition" (Hobsbawm, 1983) in which a selective amnesia toward the past allows for a consistent and positive account of the "national history" to be disseminated" (Husband, 2000, p. 202). This is of course very well in line with how the Danish media and Danish self-perception was laid out at the beginning of this article. Also, Rose's point of view is based in a conception of Denmark as a homogenous, unaltered, nation-state, i.e., a state valuing tolerance and individual freedom and equality. It is the imaginary, imaginative symbolic of common belonging, that is the basis of the conceptualisation of cultural citizenship. It is dependent on the emergence of an information society and communication (Stevenson, 2003). Silverstone's cosmopolitan citizen of the world is based in culturally constructed and sustained structures which once again confronts us with the *multiplicity of the media*. It is the interdependence of global cultural flows and technological media advances (Appadurai, 1996) that defines the cosmopolitan. The forced and voluntary mass migrations coupled with the transnational news flows via social network sites, Internet and mobile phones constructs a new set of connections, which in turn may make Silverstone's cosmopolitan feasible.

The Media and the Message

Despite the fact that the majority of us watch the news on television rather than on the Internet, the fact remains that the advanced media technology makes multiple voices available in the media that previously were silent or a selected few. The message of the offending cartoons travelled online as well as materially in suitcases of the delegation of Danish imams from Denmark to Syria and Saudi Arabia. In the case of the Danish cartoon controversy, the discussion could have been about minority groups' treatment by or integration in the Danish public sphere, but it was framed by the media as being about the pillar of democracy and of journalistic practice: freedom of the press. It was arguably never about either but rather about "Danes' prejudice against religion."[12] The Danish cartoon controversy was initiated by a newspaper and was therefore perhaps both about freedom of speech and about freedom of the press. The press, although an independent democratic organ, provides for debates of public importance and for the citizenry to make informed decisions. Therefore, freedom of speech in relation to the press moreover calls for a responsibility of the press (Silverstone, 2007)—or fairness (Ritter & Leibowitz, 2009)—all of which is based in a particular cultural context. In the case of citizen journalism the boundaries between freedom of the press and freedom of speech are blurred. Not only are *citizens* doing journalism, which questions the responsibility of the press to inform the citizenry in terms of democratic participation, but citizen journalism moreover may have roots in the national context and hold the potential of calling on a different, larger community—a transnational or cosmopolitan community. iReport, YouTube, Twitter etc., all facilitate these journalistic challenges and changes. The case of the cartoon controversy shows that the medium has become the message not only in the ways that McLuhan theorised it, but also quite literally: the uses and abuses of media and the material journalistic practice are the story, the message, of many of the news items following the debates, as is its democratic outreach potential. Citizen journalism is capable of reaching far beyond the nation-states and can do so in erratic patterns. However the technology as well as the politics supporting new media and citizen journalism is still underpinned by a particular cultural belonging.

One example of this, although by no means representative of all citizen journalism, is the Dutch politician Geert Wilders' short cut'n'mix[13] film, *Fitna*. *Fitna* was created to shed light on the perceived political and totalitarian ideology behind Islam, Wilders claims.[14] The film was ultimately a cut'n'mix'ed opinion on the cartoons broadened to encompass a general denouncement of Islam broadcast online (van Zoonen, Miheli, & Vis, 2010). The film is an example of how citizen engagements in the journalistic sphere may be (ab)used by all—right wing politicians as well as human rights activists. As such it is like any other YouTube video uploaded by private individuals, i.e., not journalists, although perhaps more expensive and politically potent due to the person behind the production—in effect a YouTube video with effective PR backing. That it is exactly that is emphasised by the use of Kurt Westergaard's cartoon depicting Muhammed wearing a turban shaped like an ignited bomb. *Fitna* thus tags itself onto the Danish cartoon controversy by opening the video with this image. It is a response video condoning the cartoons and the controversy it caused.

What this example sheds light on is a new kind of participation in news making, although a disparity still exists between majority and minority (Husband 2000). The participatory news making is earlier introduced as citizen journalism. Journalism, as well as new media and technology, therefore plays a particularly important role in this new phase of technological community construction. But not only that, the ways in which this new technology is an extension of the citizen as well as embedded in the national culture of the citizen calls on reflection and reflexivity. It needs to be coupled with a sense of obligation also towards difference in order to work as a democratic tool on a transnational basis. It is therefore important to see cosmopolitanism as a journalistic practice rather than an attitude or as a multicultural policy. That is, couple a sense of multiculturalism with willingness towards cosmopolitanism in journalistic practice. A journalistic "leg" in the multicultural debates and social developments therefore consists of a journalistic obligation to listen, curiosity and respect for the other in order to sustain a multicultural representation and education of national citizenries, and reflexivity on the cosmopolitan potential of as well as the cultural limits of new technology and traditional journalistic practices.

In the multicultural society of Denmark and in the international debates on the cartoon controversy as well as on similar cases, the cultural underpinnings of liberal democracy and journalism's role within it have been overlooked. Too often multiculturalism and migration as well as journalism are seen in political terms alone and moreover in terms of freedoms and rights. This discussion of the aftermath of the cartoon controversy and in relation to the concepts of tolerance, hospitality, rights and obligations and national and transnational belonging, has shown that not only do we need to theorise multiculturalism and migration in conjunction with a transnational connectivity or cosmopolitanism, but we also need to recognise that these future theories must encompass a critical assessment of the power of implicit and at times universalising cultural representation in journalistic practices.

Notes

1. Tariq Ramadan, "Cartoon Conflicts," *The Guardian* online: http://www.guardian.co.uk/media/2006/feb/06/homeaffairs.comment, accessed 20 July 20 2008

2. www.weekendavisen.dk accessed 4 January 2008.

3. Something that Denmark seems prone to of late; see *Armadillo*, a documentary about the Danish peace-keeping soldiers at Helmand province in Afghanistan that shocked Danes because of the soldiers' aggressiveness and violence etc.

4. Right wing parties in Denmark doubled their mandates; the UK's British National Party (BNP) won its first seats; Italy's Freedom Party kept its hold on the voters and so on (See http://www.spiegel.de/international/europe/0,1518,629142,00.html/; http://news.bbc.co.uk/2/shared/bsp/hi/elections/euro/09/flash/html/eu.stm).

5. See also Proctor and Schiebinger (2008).

6. I am using "nation" to mean the imagined community which I will return to shortly, and "state" to mean the political and legal community.

7. See Cottle (Ed.) (2000): "Introduction Media Research and Ethnic Minorities: Mapping the Field" pp. 1–30 for a mapping of the field and discussions on this topic.

8. http://watandost.blogspot.com/2006/02/tariq-ramadan-on-cartoon-controversy.html accessed 20 July 2008.

9. Jyllands-Posten 26.02.2010: *Statsministeren bekymret over forlig* http://jp.dk/indland/article 1993328.ece

10. Politiken 26.02.2010: *Politiken indgår forlig i Muhammed-sag* http://politiken.dk/indland/article910878.ece

11. Politiken 26.02.2010: *Politiken indgår forlig i Muhammed-sag* http://politiken.dk/indland/article910878.ece

12. Graham Holm, 2009, The Guardian Online: Comment is Free, Jan. 4 2010

13. Van Zoonen et al. define cut'n'mix as short films that take visuals, text, sound etc. from other films and mix it to make a new expression or opinion clear.

14. http://www.geertwilders.nl/

Beyond Culture—Awareness Training for Journalists and Their Potential for the Promotion of Media Diversity

Julia Bayer

In May 2008 eighteen young journalists were invited to take part in EMAJ, the Euro-Mediterranean Academy for Young Journalists, initiated by the Goethe Institute[1] in Amman, Jordan. The participants where selected according to their professional profile, motivation and work samples: nine from EU member states and nine from the Mediterranean countries taking part in the Barcelona Process[2] (Algeria, Egypt, Israel, Jordan, Lebanon, Morocco, Palestinian Authority, Syria, Tunisia, Turkey). The 12-day-workshop was designed to promote critical reporting in international contexts, to foster intercultural understanding and to enhance cultural sensitivity as a key qualification for journalists. The debates generated by the workshop were heated from the beginning, at some points close to escalation. At the same time, the participants spent an extremely intense and fruitful time together. Two weeks after the end of the workshop, one of them sent an email to the mailing list:[3]

Dear Everyone

Hope you have a nice Sunday… if you are in Europe I will say have a nice weekend..and if you are in the Arab world like me then have a nice start for your week.. and this is one cultural difference we didn't realize when we were in Amman.

I have story that I wanted to share with you coz it made me feel how I miss all of you.

Last Monday I was invited to an intercultural dialogue with students and professors from American universities in the Fulbright commission in Egypt (the commission is responsible for cultural exchange between Egypt and USA).

(…) Everyone including me was very enthusiastic and friendly and we kept talking about differences between Egypt and United states.. Misperceptions and similarities…we had a very friendly coffee break then we kept talking.. I discovered they were in Egypt since three weeks and they wanted to build long term relationships with us coz they are learning Arabic language.

At the end of the meeting the organizers in Fulbright told us that we are encouraged to exchange facebook accounts to continue communication with our American friends!!.

At this point exactly I felt that the whole meeting was totally crazy !! .. I looked around me in everyone's face.. I felt that those people were really friendly and they like my country .. but this is not enough to make them my friends.

And at this point too .. I remembered EMAJ and I remembered all of you ..i remembered our funny activities in the hotel [seminar] room with Bjorne and Julia and I felt that how different our relationship is ..and I said to myself "I like those American visitors but they are not my friends" .. "I didn't stay with them in the same room ..we didn't share a meal .. we didn't go out for shopping ..we didn't climb a mountain together ..we didn't swim in salty water or muddy shit ☺ ..we didn't work together ..... so why I am supposed to consider them friends.

…when I went out I looked at the building and I smiled .. there was a loud voice coming from inside my mind saying "EMAAAAAAAAJ .. EMAAAAAAAAJ."

In reaction to this email many rather emotional responses with the same tenor were shared over the network, later followed by requests for research support, exchanges of opinion on specific topics, mutual interviews for publications or blogs, first hand background information for an article or cooperation on reports in the countries of the network and information on further workshops or related international events. Even now, over two years later, and after the successful realisation of a follow-up workshop by some of the former participants, the network is still very active.

Workshops like these are run not only by the Goethe Institute but also by the Deutsche Welle Akademie[4] and by the WDR, one of the public broadcasting corporations in Germany. One project, launched by the WDR's commissioner for integration, was explicitly set in a framework with the aim to promote "the development of intercultural competence" and to foster "a journalism, that is sensitive and competent in terms of cultural diversity, migration and integration in times of globalisation" (Boundless project, 2009, http://www.wdr.de/unternehmen/programmprofil/integration/boundless.jsp, my translation). What could be labelled as "awareness training" can be seen as measures to counter what the media have neglected to address over the years and what they are reproached for: ethnocentrism, discriminatory biases and mis-representation of migrants.

Migration and the Media in the Federal Republic of Germany

Since the first officially recruited migrant workers, so-called "guest workers" (Gastarbeiter), came to Germany in the 1950s political and media discourses around migration have undergone several shifts and changes. The initial idea of these migrants returning to their home countries after a few years soon proved to be neither the intention of many of them nor wanted by the German economy. It became clear that they were going to stay and that migration processes were not to be reversed despite the recruitment ban of 1973. As a consequence, the discourse shifted to other measures of regulation, to the question of family unification, to education, to ghettoisation and to fears over foreign infiltration and crime. In the context of political refugees and asylum, further issues came up in the debate, including human trafficking, bogus asylum seeking and the exploitation of the welfare state. Later the humanist and at the same time exoticising and paternalistic idea of multiculturalism praised the colourfulness of the multicultural society (for an overview of the media discourse on migration in Germany see Jung, Niehr & Böke et al., 2000). Yet, a common trait in all these discourses that is powerful to this day is the labeling of immigrants as "foreign", as "non German", "non citizen", short as an opposition to "national Germans"—based on cultural differences. Migrants are not seen as a legitimate, integral, active and self-determined part of German society, but rather as an inevitable issue to be dealt with—with ever changing strategies (Terkessidis, 2006).

Parallel to these political developments the media have represented migrants with powerful and very persistent images that closely link migration to problems and threats to society (Gross, Moore & Threadgold, 2007; King & Wood, 2001; Müller, 2005; ter Wal, 2002; van Dijk, 2006). Since migrants themselves have limited access to public media production (as one important factor among others), it is the perspectives of the majority society about migrants that are being produced and continuously reproduced. In response to this situation calls for media diversity (in relation to diversity of content as well as employment) have increased in recent years.[5]

On the political agenda integration has become the new buzzword and strategy.[6] Over the last decade, Germany finally officially accepted that it could be considered an "immigration country", initiated changes in immigration law and in 2006 launched its first Integration Summit. A year later the German government enacted the so-called National Integration Plan.[7] While in her foreword Chancellor Angela Merkel acknowledges that most migrants in Germany have long found their place in society, she still sees deficits in integration. Thus she identifies integration as a key challenge of our time to which her government gives high priority. As part of the plan a special working group was set up to examine the potential role of the media in integration. In line with the chancellor's proposition, the approach of the working group is twofold: it sees integration as a social challenge as well as a duty, also for the majority society. At the same time the approach emphasizes economic aspects, i.e. migrants are also considered as users, readers, broadcasting fee payers and potential receivers of advertisement and sales messages. Based on these assumptions the working group identified different fields of intervention that should improve the media's role in integration: cultural diversity should become normal in programmes; more migrants should receive formal training as journalists; intercultural training should become a regular aspect within the media professions; media research should be intensified; media competence programmes for migrants should be implemented; and international exchange between broadcasting corporations should be established (Presse und Informationsamt der Bundesregierung, 2007, pp.159–160). Partly in reaction to this, partly beforehand, the two German public broadcasters (ARD with its 9 public broadcasting corporations and the centrally-structured ZDF) as well as the association of private broadcasters (Verband Privater Rundfunk- und Telemedien, VPRT) introduced guidelines and reached agreements concerning their role and their handling of migration and integration issues (WDR, 2004; VPRT, 2007; Zambonini, 2009; ZDF, 2007; ZDF, 2008). It is interesting to note that in their reaction the private broadcasters have described a status quo rather than worked out guidelines for future activities. They do not appear to see much need for change, because in their view they have already reached a sufficient level of employment and content diversity. However, despite some differences, the approaches generally address three different areas: Efforts should be made in terms of (1) content, (2) participation and (3) awareness:

1. On the level of content, cultural diversity should be treated as a normal aspect of society and be represented as a cross-cutting issue in all programmes. However, there are hardly any proposals as to *how* this could be achieved. The most frequent suggestions are to depict migrants as agents rather than as passive extras, as good rather than bad, as cop rather than as criminal. Yet there is no discussion about the dynamics of representation in general or about institutional racism. The discussion here seems to address far more quantitative than qualitative aspects.

2. On the level of participation, more migrants should be recruited as media producers, especially as presenters and actors but also as journalists. The migrants addressed here are mainly second or third generation, those who are high-skilled, speak perfect German and have been socialised in Germany—in short "very well integrated" people. Even though this is not stated explicitly, a look at the requirements for some of the initiatives to support migrants in the media, makes this clear. On top of having a "migration background" the participants are expected to speak German fluently, have a high level of intercultural competence, have started their studies of journalism at university or college or have completed one year of training on the job and have experience in journalism. One could argue that these people will make their way in any case—even without special support on account of their migration background. This leads to a wider debate about the necessity respectively of the paternalism of quota regulations and the like. Since this is not my focus here, I will rather stress those activities that operate on the level of awareness.

3. On this level, which I will address here in some detail, journalists and media producers should receive intercultural or diversity training. The potential and drawbacks of these will be discussed on a general level as well as in relation to the specific form of international exchange workshops.

"Systemic Bias" in the Media

While all these aspects are crucial prerequisites for long-term changes, none of them addresses fundamental systemic or structural conditions of the media that run counter to these initiatives.

Sociologist Augie Fleras speaks of the "conventional news paradigm as systemic bias" (Fleras, 2006, p. 179). While it is clear that news is only a part of all media programming, the general public perceives news as the media format that supplies hard facts about what is happening in the world and thus it has a strong impact on people's worldviews. Moreover, I would argue that most aspects of the "conventional news paradigm" also apply to many documentary formats and influence the design, choice and programming of entertainment shows, soap operas or feature films.

> ...the conventional news paradigm reflects a systemic bias—namely a bias that is institutional, not personal; consequential, not intentional; routine, not random; cultural, not conspiratorial; and structural, not attitudinal. (Fleras, 2006, p. 182)

Because of its systemic and structural nature, this bias is difficult to address. In my experience from talking to media producers in workshops and training programmes many media producers agree with the argument made by media theorists that news is actively created by news-makers and carries a certain bias. Yet, among media practitioners, even though this bias is acknowledged *theoretically* and there is consent that objectivity does not exist, many do advocate *striving* for objectivity as central to news production. This, they argue, could be obtained through a *fact-based, balanced* reporting that *shows both sides*. These conventions are strong, they stand for good journalism and are hardly questioned as to what they are: agreements—albeit widely accepted—that carry a certain media centrism, defined by Fleras as the "tendency of media to automatically interpret the world from their perspective as necessary and normal" (Fleras, 2006, p. 181). This tendency influences what passes as news in the first place but also what is considered as facts, as balanced or which sides of a complex story are heard, what part of it, from what perspective, and so on.

Fleras (p. 182) argues that the systemic bias is mainly due to the news medias' focus on negativity. "Only bad news is good news" or "if it bleeds it leads—if it scares it airs" are well known slogans in news making. With negativity as a news factor, migrants are highly overrepresented in the context of problem, crisis and threat, as various research projects into media content have shown (Gross et. al, 2007; King & Wood, 2001; Müller, 2005; ter Wal, 2002; van Dijk, 2006). Other news values such as relevance or impact, timeliness, prominence, proximity and bizarreness—especially in their combination—also promote this systemic bias that again supports the dominant discourse.

Negativity is of course a news factor that applies in general and not only to migrants. What is problematic, however, is the imbalance that develops, because migrants hardly make it into the news with anything other than what could be described as negative stories.

> In short, what is not said by the newsmedia may be just as important as what is said. The interplay of negative representations combines with the absence of complex characterization to foster a colour-coded news discourse whose "palemale" gaze is pro-white rather than anti-minority. (Fleras, 2006, p. 200)

The "palemale" gaze naturalises whiteness and with it existing journalistic conventions and power relations. Because this status quo is defined and continuously redefined as normal and universal it becomes invisible and is therefore hard to address at all (Dolan, 2006; van Dijk, 1993a).

When taking these correlations seriously, it seems that only a fundamental reform of the media system as such could bring about groundbreaking changes. As long as news reports are accepted and received as truths that are generally not questioned, they create certain worldviews that can strongly influence social realities. As long as a systemic bias exists that is closely linked to what is accepted as "good journalism" and permeates the global media system, it hardly seems relevant to make changes on the individual level of the participant of an awareness workshop. It is true that a single journalist stands little chance against such a strong system and its structures. On the other hand, no matter how strong the structures, the media system is not operating fully independently of individuals. Thus individual media workers do present a possible point of departure.

Awareness Training for Journalists

In the following I will focus on my experiences as a course leader in a special type of awareness training: workshops with a work-exchange component between Germany as well as other European countries and Arab countries. In the workshops I usually worked together with a colleague with journalistic background.

My Perspective as a Course Leader

Even though I draw on my fieldwork in a master-class of journalism, my background is not in journalism but in the social and cultural sciences with a focus on visual and media anthropology, in documentary filmmaking and in the teaching of theses areas to anthropology students. My perspective is informed by the postmodern reflexive and literary turn with its critical stance toward representation and by postcolonial theory. Subject position, power relations, political responsibility, reflexivity and questions of ethics and legitimation are crucial to critical anthropological theory and practice. Research as well as ethnographic writing are always embedded in historical and political contexts and are strongly influenced by the researcher's theoretical assumptions and subjective view. However, unlike in journalism, in anthropology the subjectivity of the researcher is not seen as an obstacle in the process of understanding but rather as its prerequisite, and is to be positively and reflexively integrated. The text itself should allow the reader to comprehend and reconstruct the development of knowledge. Accepting that ethnography always has strong aspects of literature and rhetoric and has a fictional touch to it, ethnographies can be seen as constructed or rather designed images of social realities that can be scientifically valid but do not lay claim to truth or objectivity (Clifford & Marcus, 1986; Fabian, 1983).

This view of anthropology can be seen in the context of a general postmodern and postcolonial critique of knowledge production and representation that also brought about a certain notion of "culture." Culture is here seen as a multitude of heterogeneous views and interpretations that in themselves create and recreate social realities. Truth cannot be seen as absolute, but only within social contexts where it is continuously negotiated and redefined. With such an understanding of culture, one needs to question the idea of cultural unities as they are often discussed in migration issues.

The merit of postmodern and postcolonial critique is certainly not a solution to some sort of a new form of anthropology, but rather a humble cautiousness and the awareness that anthropology (as any representation) can only be incomplete, fragmentary and subjective—posing, at the most, the right questions, even if no answers are in sight. Of course, academic anthropology is in most ways not comparable with media production (for a detailed comparison of the two fields see: Allen, 2005; Bruns, 2005). Yet, in the context of media and migration the intensive debate about the representation of culture that stems from anthropology is a central issue and can be helpful in conceptualising media diversity—because migration is often discussed and represented along the lines of culture and the alleged dichotomy of "self" and "other." This dichotomy has been questioned and scrutinised by postcolonial critics who see discourse as the basis of power inequality that is not only mirrored but at the same time consolidated by science, literature, art and media (Bhabha, 1990; 1994; Said, 1978; Spivak, 1988).

Approaching the situation from this background, I strongly advocate that further education in the field of media diversity is not and should not be related to a specific "culture." Especially in the context of migration, "culture" has often been used as an unchangeable marker of difference, as a fixed category that naturalises this alleged dichotomy of "us" and "them", "inside" and "outside." My focus is not on conveying sensitivity for specific cultural settings, as is often the case in intercultural training. Instead I try to work against an understanding of culture as a marker of difference and to sensitise the participants to their own perspectives, to the consequences of culturalisation and to the interplay of perception and representation in transnational contexts and globalised media worlds. To achieve this, I intentionally provoke intense debates on the role of journalism, on ethics of representation and on journalistic responsibility.

Yet, all the workshops had a cultural focus on the so-called Arab world. This special focus is certainly due to the overall political developments of recent years and especially the experiences of the controversy surrounding the publication of cartoons of the prophet Muhammad in a Danish newspaper in 2005. These developments and events generated substantial debate over journalistic ethics of representation and responsibility in cultural and religious contexts. At the very least the seemingly worldwide omnipresence of the topic made workshops like these possible in the first place.

While all of these workshops had the same basic concept behind them, they varied in terms of implementation that led to different challenges for the course leaders and different learning experiences for the participants.[8] Next, I will illustrate which of these differences inhibited or advanced the desired aims and objectives of the workshop and discuss the general challenges of such approaches. Instead of describing each workshop in detail, I will explore distinct factors that came together in different combinations and suggest best practice options—some of them already field-tested, some of them more orientated towards the future. This is not to be read as an exhaustive coverage but rather as a sharing of experiences that are to be continued.

Aims and Objectives

The basic idea of the workshops was to foster intercultural understanding as a general qualification for journalists, with a special focus on Arab countries. Twelve to eighteen young journalists from Germany as well as other European countries and from Arab countries were brought together to get to know each other, to work together, to establish strong networks and to eventually become journalists who are sensitive to the complexities of reporting difference and can make a real difference in reporting the world—in print, television, radio or on-line. In all workshops the main aim was to go beyond theory and discussion and to allow for genuine hands-on experience of working together journalistically with colleagues from different cultural backgrounds.

Participants and Group Makeup

Most of the workshops were aimed at young journalists from Germany and from Arab or Islamic countries. One of the projects focused on the Gulf States, but most took in the whole Middle East and the Maghreb states, sometimes also Islamic states outside these regions, such as Sudan or Indonesia. One project, EMAJ 2008, had participants from Euro-Mediterranean countries, including Israel. A wide mix of participants with different backgrounds is useful and the basis of the whole idea. While at first sight a cohort solely consisting of participants from Germany and Arab or Islamic countries seems easier because it is more focused, in my experience this also holds drawbacks. For one there appears to be a stronger dichotomy and culturalisation of "Germans" and "Arabs" in the group that is again reinforced by a language shared by each separate group, German and Arabic respectively. This was very different in the group of Euro-Mediterranean participants. Here the lingua franca English[9] was used much more and—maybe also due to the length of the workshop and the many social events—the group was less split into "Arabs" and "Europeans" but rather formed a common group identity of "we journalists who took part in the workshop". In a group where everyone has their own cultural background, individual personality becomes more important than national identity. One minor issue is that no matter where the workshop took place, almost all participants shared the experience of being in a foreign place that they did not know, experiencing the excitement of a new setting as well as the feeling of being an outsider, not knowing people, language or context.

Structure and Content—Workshop Only or Exchange

The workshops took two fundamentally different forms: in one case, the workshop itself was the core of the project and comprised enough time for the participants to work together on one journalistic piece in culturally mixed teams of two (or three) in the city where the workshop took place. In the other case, the participants came together for a kick-off workshop of usually one week and then continued in an exchange programme, working on joint projects for one week in each of the team's editorial departments.

In the "workshop only" version, working together on journalistic pieces during the workshop proved rather difficult due to time constraints. In the five-day workshop it was hardly possible, in the twelve-day workshop chances were a lot better. In general, print and radio were much easier to work with in such workshops than television, partly due to the technical requirements of television production. Teams usually depended on outside support from a camera team and video editor, who did not share the experience of the workshop and worked according to their usual routines. With print and radio the participants were able to produce their stories without outside assistance. A very positive aspect of the workshop-only programmes was that the teams had the chance to discuss their work together with the workshop leaders and the rest of their workshop group. This has proved to be extremely important and was not provided for in the exchange situation, where the teamwork took place outside the workshop situation in the respective countries. On the other hand, without exchange either the European or the Arab participants did not get a chance to visit their partners' home countries and make this genuine experience of working together in a different context.

In addition to the actual exchange experience, the "twinning", the process of putting together the teams, turned out to be a very relevant part of these types of workshops. Interestingly, on a superficial level, the participants (in this case the German side) acted open and tolerant. They appeared to be interested in new perspectives and culturally sensitive. But when it came to choosing a country for the exchange, a different picture emerged. In many cases, German participants were more than reluctant to go to certain countries such as Yemen, Sudan or Pakistan, while Egypt, Lebanon or Syria usually received a high personal ranking. Reasons for this were sometimes attributed to certain interests of their newsrooms back in Germany, sometimes concealed by putting forward an intense interest for one of the other countries. In some cases concerns over whether one would be able to work properly influenced the decisions on the German side: the strong belief that the different working style (an alleged laissez-faire attitude, unreliability of cameramen and informants etc.) in Arab countries would inhibit their own work, led participants to favour certain countries over others. Often, however, specific countries were openly rejected because of a concern for personal safety, for example fear of kidnapping in Yemen, terrorist attacks and the like. The warnings of the foreign office were at times cited, but frequently the participants just expressed a general concern that relied heavily on media representations. During the sometimes exhausting and time-consuming twinning process some deep-rooted prejudices came up and gave the group the chance to reflect on them. In this respect the workshops with an exchange programme gave more opportunity for discussions that offered a deeper insight into one's own ideas. On the side of the Arab participants the twinning was less conflict laden, because all were prepared to go to Germany. It was more a matter of which TV station than of which country. Expectations, though, were high in other respects: preferences for certain cities (either Berlin, because it is the most well-known of German cities or other cities where friends or relatives lived) or choices in line with certain hopes to advance one's career in a particular direction. Since Deutsche Welle was the only TV station Arab colleagues knew first-hand, many opted for an exchange with DW, in some cases also because of the expressed hope to establish contacts that might someday lead to a job offer.

One of the major drawbacks of the exchange setup was that the workshop leaders could not catch up with the participants during or after the exchange. While during the workshop everyone seemed open, interested and tolerant, sometimes, just as had happened in the twinning process, the problems came up during the exchange, when the participants were more or less on their own without the backup of the workshop and the chance to share their experiences. While an exchange is a great chance, if it is not supplemented and supported by another plenary meeting, its positive effects can backfire.

Team-Research or Team-Production

The hands-on experience was an important aspect of all workshops. The specifics of the tasks, however, led to very different experiences. In some workshops the participants were asked to do the research in pairs, but produce a piece each. These pieces were then discussed in plenary. I will call them the team-researchers. In other workshops they were asked to produce one final piece that they both had to agree on. I will call them the team-producers.

For the team-researchers, the experience of working together was limited to the phase of research. In contrast to the team-producers, they did not go through the intense learning experience that comes with the process of discussion and negotiation over a final joint piece of work. However, their work—two pieces on the basis of the same research—made the differences in perspective very transparent for the whole group and led to interesting discussions, sometimes even harsh criticism from their peers. Team-research was much less time- and energy-consuming than team-production, yet, when working on individual pieces the participants were less challenged in their working routines and only had to actively defend their positions in the final discussion. When working together on one piece, those assumptions that appeared to be internalised, unquestioned parts of working routines could all of a sudden be heavily challenged. While this has high potential to bring about a good learning experience, it can also backfire and be very disturbing for some participants—especially when they are left alone with their experience, as was the case in workshops with an exchange element.

In a future workshop-only scenario but with more time, it would be fruitful to have a two-step assignment: first, a short individual piece based on team-research and second a team production on a new topic that is then discussed by all. This would combine the potential of both assignment types while reducing the negative aspects. Since hands-on working experience is the assignment most asked for by participants (as opposed to theoretical input) it would be worth allocating more time for it.

Experiment or Publication

One of the big questions that always turns up is whether or not the pieces produced within the workshop should be published. The big challenge is to come up with new creative forms, topics or perspectives that counter stereotypes, go beyond established views or question the taken for granted—and yet to meet the requirements of professional journalism. For the participants the aim or the assignment to publish can generate positive pressure to take up this challenge. For the newsroom it is an incentive to take part in such a workshop, because it guarantees a product and thus compensates for the absence of their journalist and—in cases of exchange—the "hassle" of hosting a foreign journalist for a week. On the other hand, for the participants it can also lead to negative pressure that inhibits creativity and courage. Especially for freelancers, it is imperative to produce something that is not only designed for publication but will definitely be accepted by an editor. Otherwise they will loose money, which can, in retrospect, discredit the whole workshop. Thus, the pressure to produce an acceptable and publishable piece can run counter to the aims of the workshop. If on the other hand the team-work is defined from the beginning as an experiment that should offer a maximum of freedom, creativity and courageous innovation, this can lead to a minimum of motivation. An assignment like this is soon criticised as far-fetched, not in line with the actual working conditions, unrealistic and not worth pursuing, and thus also lacks support from the participating newsrooms. In my experience, to strike the right balance, it is absolutely necessary for the participants to have clear assignments that give precise and output-orientated guidelines in order to be productive in such a short time. While there will always be participants who ask for more freedom and feel restricted by too much presetting, I found that too much freedom can lead to disorientation and even log-jam. Simply because anything is possible in theory, nothing seems possible in practice anymore.

However, it is important to have these relatively strict guidelines from the very beginning, as part of the project description in the first call for participants. Knowing, for example, that experimental pieces on the overarching topic of "human rights" or "migration" or "water" will be assigned to teams makes it clear for participants and newsrooms under which conditions they take part in the workshop and allows for ideas to develop in a certain direction. An early setting of a framework that leaves enough flexibility if the group develops different ideas is in my experience the most fruitful way forward. The most important point is that the discussion of the specific topics of the working groups is given enough space in plenary discussions and that enough time for initial research is given early enough in the process. The better prepared and thought-out a topic is, the more likely it is that the teams have a positive working experience.

It is difficult to find the ultimate solution for the question of publication or experiment. Both aims have their potential and their drawbacks. A satisfying mode would again be more time, so the workshop could start with a more open form of experiment, before building on these experiences to continue with a piece that is to be published. Irrespective of the form that is finally chosen, it is important to have a clear-cut deal with the participants as well as with the newsrooms beforehand, to prevent the participants from being torn between different expectations.

Workshop Content—Focussing on Skills or Critical Reflection?

Even though in my exposés I explicitly advocate training that focuses strongly on the role of journalists, on the relationship between perception and representation, and on journalistic ethics of representation and responsibility, in all cases there was a strong demand for a focus on "culture" in the sense of intercultural communication (Hall, 1969; Hofstede, 2001; Hofstede & Hofstede, 2009) from the funders. At the same time, in most workshops the funders requested professional journalistic skills as part of the curriculum. However, in my opinion, these workshops are not the place to focus on established journalistic skills such as research, different journalistic forms, composition and the like. In most cases the German or European journalists felt that they lost time with journalistic basics that had been strong in their education and are part of their daily routine. For Arab participants, I had the impression that some of the journalistic input, like the clear distinction between different genres such as hard news, report, comment, reportage, feature, etc. was not relevant to them because the journalistic skills came from a very European, if not German, point of view—at least the way they were presented in the workshops. They only related to the working structures and routines of the Arab participants in a limited sense. I would rather see the participants of such workshops as fully fledged professional journalists who know how to do their job in their respective working environments very well. Rather than giving input on established journalistic skills, I would put an even stronger focus on critical sensitivity to one's own perspectives, on structural biases and power relations, and on the consequences of culturalisation of social problems as *additional* journalistic skills that are not yet part of the standard curriculum.

"Culture" is, of course, a big issue in such workshops. They are designed and announced as an intercultural training of some sort, in that they bring together journalists from different cultural backgrounds in order to gain understanding for cultural differences. Thus culture, stereotype and prejudice are almost "must-have" topics. In the workshops I held, culture was an issue, partly because it was asked for by the funders, partly because I included it in my workshop proposals. With the experience I have now, I would try to do things differently. Great things are expected of culture, as if everything could be solved once there was an understanding of cultural differences. The workshops have shown that most participants are already very aware of these differences; they reflect on them, they are open to differences and tolerant. Because of this knowledge base, input on culture during the workshop was often not very well accepted, sometimes even resented. Yet, my experience is that this knowledge is only on a superficial level. Only after some time, beyond the specific workshop situation, over lunch or during a city tour, often in the subtext, and especially when it came to working together, sometimes very persistent and strong value-based prejudices broke through—but usually when it happened, the participants were left alone with these experiences, especially while on an exchange. In combination with the pressure of producing a publishable piece this could lead to frustration. It did not seem possible for the participants to transfer what they learned in theory during the workshop to the actual situation outside of it.

In my view "culture" as a topic is not irrelevant; on the contrary, but it needs to be addressed on a different level and in a different form. I would reduce the input on culture during the workshop and support some sort of supervision for the participants during or after their working phase. There they would have the chance to share their experiences with the other participants and/or with the workshop team and gain some helpful insight for their future work. On top of that, it is crucial to include racism as a topic in the workshops. This, however, is particularly difficult, because people get defensive very quickly when talking about some, often subtle forms of racism, such as discrimination in language, that may implicate them. As van Dijk suggests (1993a, p. 180) members of elite groups consider themselves to be free of racist behaviour, which they associate with "overt right-wing racism" only. Yet, in the workshops I have delivered so far this kind of training has not been asked for and I have not actively fought for including it. However, whenever I made a small hint in the direction of institutional or structural racism in the media, there was little to no response. If not directly denied, at most there was a reaction like "yes, this might exist, but..."—it either cannot be changed or it is not on us to do something about it. Similar reactions came from many of the participants. In a discussion on perspective and the problematic issue of ever-repeated images and stereotypes in the media, one of the participants just handed over responsibility to the reader, saying that there is a broad variety of media offerings, that it was the readers' fault if they did not gather the information they needed and that he could not see structural racism in the media at all. The participants' resistance against the topic is in my opinion an indicator for its necessity. A stronger focus on racism in the training would promote the dimensions of structural and systemic discrimination and power relations (Bildungszentrum Bürgermedien, 2006).

Young Journalists or Established Editors

Usually one aspect of the workshops was the analysis of existing media coverage with respect to its underlying assumptions, its stereotypes or discriminatory tone.[10] My experience with it is the following: While open or extreme examples were easily detected, the more subtle aspects were often either not realised or not accepted as problematic. A common rejection was the assertion "this is just bad journalism". This is of course a knock-out argument that limits further discussion. Yes, simplifications and generalisations as the following (from an article in *Stern* magazine) are *bad* journalism:

> The Islamic world is leaning back in its belief in conspiracy. Neither the governments nor the common people have much to oppose the agenda of Al Qaida. They actually share their ideology of the new crusaders who want to destroy Islam and to subjugate the Muslims. (Reuter, 2007, p. 44, my translation)

But they are also very *common* in journalism, and that is why we talked about them. Also, the working routines were sometimes so internalised that even the idea of challenging them seems unthinkable. One example that came up was the use of archive material and/or symbolic footage to illustrate certain—certain what? Facts? Ideas? Assumptions? The presumption that no image is "innocent" of meaning was not too difficult to convey—but that does not necessarily rock working routines. Even young journalists who were not yet well established had already internalised the "rules of journalism." The critical analysis of journalistic pieces—even of articles that had nothing to do with the participants—was quickly taken personally as criticism of journalism in general and therefore strongly rejected. That, I would argue, was partly due to the participants' journalistic education, but also to the everyday expectations of their editors and to working routines. However, in some of the cases where participants worked together in research and then each wrote their own article, the discussion of the articles proved to be very fruitful. Feedback from the other participants seemed to be more readily accepted.

Taking this into account one could question whether training for young journalists can be fruitful if the established colleagues higher up in the hierarchy inhibit their endeavours. Yet, on the level of established journalists it is even more difficult to make an impact. In my experience, journalists say of themselves that they are not very open to criticism of their work—especially not from outside the journalistic criteria such as objectivity, balance, the clear distinction of fact and opinion, etc. While open discrimination is an issue and is seen as not acceptable among media practitioners, there is little awareness for the subtleties of structural and systemic discrimination. Reaching the editors high in the hierarchy would need to be institutionalised through, for instance, continuing professional development programmes in order to tackle the structural biases and barriers that inhibit more sensitive and non-discriminatory reporting.

The hierarchical structure of journalism makes it crucial to address two distinct groups: people aspiring to be journalists who are—in an ideal case scenario—not yet too deep in the routines, and open to the topic, and senior editors who are in decision-making positions. While for the young journalists awareness training combined with an exchange programme and the establishing of strong networks is a good starting point, for the senior editors racism and structural bias could be the topics of choice, because they are the ones who make changes possible. In order to be successful, a workshop needs the full backup and support of the newsrooms taking part in such programmes. This has often not been the case.

In general it can thus be said that a stronger focus on racism and structural bias is necessary not only for the young journalist but also and maybe especially on the higher levels of decision-making. Yet, putting this forward too strongly might not only keep away participants but could also lead to difficulties with the funders. Hierarchical structures and power relations are strong obstacles to a mainstreaming of such an approach. To put racism on the agenda and make it clear that today's racism comes in different forms but with the same mind-set and consequences as before, will be one of the challenges of such workshops.

The Workshop Leaders

I have so far only worked in German teams, together with a journalist. For one, this was due to the fact that the workshops were held by German institutions; but it had also practical reasons. In one case the funders wanted to engage a second trainer from the host country, but could not find anyone appropriate for the job. I am sure that this was more a question of time constraints than a general problem. However, preparing a workshop over the phone and via email with a colleague I had never seen before was difficult enough; a language barrier to also contend with would not have made it any easier. A meeting beforehand was rejected as too expensive. I do not believe these practical concerns should prevail. If the team is not able to fruitfully work together, how can they expect that from the participants? I am sure that a diverse trainer team would bring in different dynamics than two workshop leaders with very similar ideas of conducting a workshop and concepts of journalism.

Institutionalisation and Sustainability

As with any useful initiative, stand-alone workshops can be seen as a positive contribution to promoting the topic. Every participant has the potential to influence his or her work environment. Yet, without being institutionalised in any way, these stand-alone workshops are not sustainable. Regular reruns that build on former experiences and networks could offer a much more sustainable impact. Institutional, financial support from a newsroom is also important, as a commercial professional development seminar that an individual journalist pays for out of his or her own pocket will probably not be booked, because of the high cost and the rather long duration. The experience of the ARD ZDF Medienakademie (the official institution for professional development of the public broadcasters in Germany) shows that journalists take a maximum of one or two training seminars a year and often opt for topics that allegedly relate more directly to their work, such as interview or research training. In 2009 they offered their first workshop that explicitly tackled issues of diversity, entitled *Gender— Diversity Aspects in Everyday Media Work* (*Gender—Diversity Aspekte im Medien-*

Alltag). It addressed the topic of diversity in terms of gender, age and cultural and religious socialisation. Its aim, as announced in the project description, was to engage critically with the images we carry in our minds, to question them and come to more differentiated views that can see diversity as a chance for shared experiences and media output. The workshop attracted so few participants that the new strategy of the academy is to include diversity as a cross-cutting topic in all of their workshops. One way to achieve this, is to include this topic in their "train the trainer" workshops.[11] When even a two- or three-day seminar does not get booked very well, it becomes clear that awareness-raising workshops like the ones I discussed here, have a much better chance of being successful, if they are supported not only institutionally, as is the case with Deutsche Welle Akademie or the Goethe Institute, but if they also receive the full support of the participating newsrooms.

In this context the EMAJ 2008 workshop of the Goethe Institute in Amman presents a very interesting case of self-sustainability. The workshop itself was a follow-up project and initiated by participants of the Euro-Mediterranean Youth Parliament 2007 in Berlin. Former participants of EMAJ 2008 again organised the follow-up project EMAJ 2009 in Amsterdam. This model only works with strong institutional support and with very motivated journalists. However, in terms of effect and sustainability this project has been extremely successful. EMAJ was not only a fruitful experience; it became the "baby" of some of the participants. They worked for about one and a half years to set up the follow-up seminar. With their experiences the second workshop changed in format and content, but according to the website,[12] the spirit of EMAJ 2008 continued. An ambitious project like this is probably in many ways too much to ask for. It cannot be taken for granted or expected from participants to get involved with so much enthusiasm in a follow-up project. Also, if such an expectation for involvement had been clear from the beginning, it might have been too overwhelming a task to even begin and could have put off institutions that might otherwise have cooperated, because it would have meant too much responsibility. Yet, the offer of the Goethe Institute to support another instalment was prerequisite for the participants to even think about it and start taking the project into their hands. Involving the participants in the next project is useful, not only for the content, because they can draw on first-hand experiences and it is very motivating to pass on one's own experiences, but also in terms of sustainability. From the email conversation of the EMAJ network that I have followed loosely for about one and a half years now, I am positive that at least for some participants the EMAJ spirit—transnational working relationships at peer-level that enable critical exchange instead of painting the ever-recurring images of the presumed "other"—has deeply influenced their work life as journalists.

Conclusion

In this chapter I set out to explore the potential of awareness training for journalists to promote media diversity and, ultimately—for the German context—the media integration of migrants. The potential of such workshops certainly lies in the intensity of personal contacts. Young journalists that establish friendships and share working experiences with colleagues from different parts of the world, with different cultural and personal backgrounds, can later build on these experiences and contacts in their daily work. In an optimistic view they can be seen as future decision makers and influencers who will pursue the concept of cultural diversity in their specific media environment. Thus awareness training such as the ones sketched above can be seen as one useful approach, as a first step complementary to the other tasks the German broadcasting corporations have set themselves, i.e., adjustments in content and encouragement and facilitation of diversity in employment.

Yet, in my opinion, none of these approaches will be truly fruitful until they start moving beyond the personal and tackle the structural level of media, especially news production. Power relations, systemic bias, racism and the nature of representation need to be addressed with priority—not only on the level of awareness workshops, but also in terms of guidelines of media integration and efforts to improve content and employment politics. As long as a "palemale" gaze is seen and continuously reproduced as "the normal" media perspective, there is hardly a chance for emancipatory aspects of media diversity and a real change in media representation—be it of migrants or of any other marginalised group of people.

Notes

1. The Goethe Institute is commissioned by the German government to represent and promote German language and culture worldwide and to foster cultural exchange.

2. The Barcelona process is a partnership forum for dialogue and cooperation in the Mediterranean region.

3. Colloquial English, spelling and punctuation mistakes in the original. My ellipses are marked by brackets: (…).

4. Deutsche Welle Akademie is the training centre of Deutsche Welle, Germany's state-funded international broadcaster.

5. See for example: Media Diversity Institute: http://www.media-diversity.org (28/12/2009). Another research project entitled *Media Integration of Ethnic Minorities* started in 2002 (German Research Foundation) as cooperation between the Institute of Journalism of the Technical University Dortmund and the sociology department of the University Siegen: http://www.integration-und-medien.de

6. When diversity comes up in the debates in Germany, it is usually used more as an empirical description of a status quo, mostly in the context of "cultural diversity", but not as normative political concept as in the USA or Canada (see also: Linder, 2007).

7. Presse- und Informationsamt der Bundesregierung (ed.) 2007: Nationaler Integrationsplan. Neue Wege, neue Chancen. Berlin. http://www.bundesregierung.de /Content/DE/Publikation/IB/Anlagen/nationaler-integrationsplan,property=publicationFile.pdf

8. Since I have not yet conducted follow-up research on long-term effects of these workshops I speak only of the direct experiences in the workshops.

9. The working language English in the workshops is problematic. The fact that none of the participants is speaking in their mother tongue, which is so important as the main means of communication in journalism, is often inhibiting fast and direct communication. However, I don't see an alternative, since simultaneous translation would be even more exhausting and more open to misunderstandings.

10. This approach is also promoted in the Diversity Toolkit of the European Union Agency for Fundamental Rights, FRA. The free hardcopy version offers examples of news clips of different European broadcasting corporations on DVD: http://fra.europa.eu/fraWebsite/press/materials_trainings/diversity_toolkit_en.htm

11. Personal communication with Margrit Benecke, head of "Programm" department (09.12.2009). For an overview of the academies activities see: http://www.ard-zdf-medienakademie.de

12. EMAJ 2009: http://www.goethe.de/ins/nl/ams/prj/ema/enindex.htm

CHAPTER TWELVE

Reporting Migration—a Journalist's Reflection on Personal Experience and Academic Critique

Janet Harris

I approached the writing of this chapter primarily as a practitioner, having worked in television documentaries for 16 years and having made a documentary for a series on the Immigration Service, *Welcome to Britain*, which was nominated for a BAFTA in 2002. I read Gross, Moore and Threadgold's (2007) study on the coverage of asylum on British television news, and it was with their criticisms and points in mind that I constructed this piece, in the hopes of examining how faults arose, but also reflecting on the constraints faced by a practitioner, and on the strengths of such a documentary. Philo (2007) makes the point that discourse analysis of content alone cannot reveal all that happens in a scene, and I hope this chapter perhaps illustrates the worth of incorporating the practitioner's side in any study and understanding of the media. To this end I will first examine the history of the series, and the situation in 2001. I will then examine the constraints when making such a programme and the responsibilities faced by programme makers which all impact on the film. I will relate my film, to academic criticism levelled by authors such as Gross et al. (2007) and Buchanan, Grillo and Threadgold (2003), and end with some reflection on the positive contribution, which I believe the documentary made to the media coverage of migration.

The Situation in 2001 and the History of the Programme.

In February 2001 as a staff Producer/Director in the BBC Documentary Department in London, I was asked if I would like to make the first in a series of four one-hour films for BBC2 on the Immigration Service. I had worked on the highly acclaimed BBC series *The System* on the Department of Social Security and had just finished making two films for a BBC1 series with the police in

Brighton, so it was felt that my experience of working with governmental institutions would be an asset.

The documentary department of the BBC had previously also made series on the Foreign Office, and the Ministry of Defence, although the idea of making a series about the Immigration Service had been in discussion for about ten years, and negotiations with the service and central government in Whitehall had been going on for almost as long. During that time the subject of migration was increasingly discussed in the media, and Roger Courtiour, the department's "Mr Fix-it" who had been the key negotiator in access to all other government departments was pressing for the series to be made.

A report by the International Organisation for Migration (IOM) claimed that the number of migrants in the world had doubled between 1965 and 2000, from 75 million to 150 million (IOM, 2000). Migration had also become a highly political issue, especially when it occurred in the form of asylum. Castles and Miller write that the early '90s were a "period of panic about asylum" (2003, p. 106). They add that the construction of a "Fortress Europe" impacted on legislation and treatment of refugees and asylum seekers. This legislation restricted access to refugee status. Citizens of certain states were required to obtain visas before departure; diversion policies were enacted where asylum seekers could be returned to certain countries if they used them as transit routes; and the 1951 UN Refugee convention excluded persecution through 'non-state actors' such as the Taliban (p. 106). The Schengen Agreement of 1995 which had 10 signatories by 2000 (excluding the UK and Ireland) and the Dublin Convention of 1990 also had an impact on the treatment of asylum seekers and the work of the Immigration Service.

By 2001 the issue was part of William Hague's election manifesto, and Lynn and Lea (2003, p. 430) state that reporting on the issue of asylum increased in volume and hype during May 2001, to portray the immigration situation as being in a state of crisis.

In this context the documentary series was considered highly topical. The brief of the series was not a study of the global refugee situation, but to look at how the UK Immigration Service was dealing with the perceived current problem on the British border, to show the work of the Immigration Service in its day-to-day dealings with travellers and its relation to asylum and irregular migration. This meant both filming with the department, and with the people with whom they dealt. I was asked to make the first of the four films in the series, to be based at Dover, where many of the asylum seekers, refugees and regular travellers and holiday-makers first came into contact with the Immigration Service. The series was then to cover the consequent stages in the process, at other Immigration Service centres, including Croydon where the screening or detailed interviews took place; the enforcement section, that is at the section of the Immigration Service responsible for the enforcement of immigration laws and the detention centres, where those in breach of the immigration laws were held. These programmes were made by two other directors who also filmed with Barbara Roche, the Minister for Immigration at the time. My episode was to be the first in the series, entitled *Border Control.*

I was given a set number of filming days with a crew, determined by the budget, and the rest of the time was spent in the office in London, researching or filming. The film was shot between February and June 2001, with 7 days filming in the Red Cross–run migrant camp at Sangatte, near Calais on the French side of the English Channel; 2 days filming with the Immigration Service and French police on the Channel Tunnel which connects Britain and France. I also spent 17 days and nights at Dover filming with the Immigration Service and the Facilitation Service Unit (FSU). The FSU was the only such unit in the country set up to investigate human trafficking, composed of four Immigration Officers, a Detective Inspector, Detective Sergeant and eight Detective Constables from Kent Police. We also had a press officer from the Immigration Service, who had been an Immigration Inspector in Dover, assigned to us to help us with access and obviously to keep an eye on what we were doing when we filmed on any Immigration Office (IO) property. However, he did not accompany us at all times, for example when filming in Sangatte, with Migrant Helpline, with asylum seekers not on IO property or on night filming.

The first hurdle was to develop an understanding of the process of immigration, that is, the laws pertaining to immigration, as I felt the audience had to understand what and why the immigration officers were doing what they did. Understanding the law also helped us to identify which people might be good to film in that they would illustrate various anomalies or stresses experienced by the service. We then had to decide how best to convey these aspects, then find people who were not only willing but also best in terms of television to be filmed. The criteria of who and how one chooses 'the best people' is too extensive to investigate fully here, but in this context, was illustrative of a particular type of the migrants we reported on, or as mentioned, could illustrate a particular stress within the service. They would also have to be engaging to an audience, have the confidence to speak on camera, and be able to describe the job in a way that would be understood by the audience.

I had very little time to do this initially, as filming on the other programmes had already started when I joined the series, so there was no time to fully research the larger issues surrounding immigration. This was not unusual at that time, as a documentary producer was usually a generalist, who was expected to be able to film any subject. Budget restrictions also hampered the time available for in-depth research, or to pay others with specialist knowledge to assist. With the destruction of the documentary department since, and the increasing use of freelance staff, producers now tend to be pigeon-holed by subject.

I will examine how the style of the documentary impacted on its content later, but mention here that it also affects the research stage. *Border Control* was primarily an observational documentary, following the tradition of *cinema verite* where one films actuality, with the intention of observing real events unfolding. We did not set up events or reconstruct them, but had to respond to events and could only film what was happening. It was of vital importance therefore, to know when certain events might be likely to occur so we could be there with a camera. Thus having the right contacts to get information to know what was or what might happen, and to build up trust to follow that through those events, were of major importance. One of the most depressing but most frequent sentences one hears when making an observational film is "you should have been here yesterday!"

Also, filming in such a large institution can initially seem quite a mountain to climb, as the choices to be made are very wide. For example, there were a large number of people available to film in Dover, and it is from this that one had to select a few people who would hopefully represent a fair portrayal of the Immigration service at Dover: 1 AD (Assistant Director); 200 IOs (Immigration Officer), 20 CIOs (Chief Immigration Officer), 6 Inspectors; at SEPST (South East Ports Surveillance Team—the freight control at Dover): 50 IOs, 9 CIOs, dogs and dog handlers; at the FSU: 8 Detective Constables, 4 IOs.

Filming a documentary involves a substantial amount of paperwork because of the ramifications of insurance, copyright and legal issues. A contract had been signed with the Immigration Service by the BBC to allow filming, which I will discuss below. In addition to the contract we had to get permission to film on any site we accessed, and obtain permission and release forms from all the people we filmed, both Immigration Officers and members of the public. We also had to negotiate access to any other institutions, agencies, organisations and businesses.

To film with the FSU we had to sign a separate contract with Kent Police. This was not easy at the time, as two recent BBC programmes had upset the police and they initially refused to see us. Permissions also had to be granted from other police constabularies and British Transport Police who were also present at the border controls. Permissions and access also had to be sought from HM Customs, the Port of Dover Harbour Authority, the Dover Asylum Screening Unit (DASC), the freight train company EWS, P&O ferries and from Special Branch, which we were not allowed to film.

Permissions to film were also obtained from Migrant Helpline and the translators who were employed on an ad hoc basis by the Immigration Service at Dover, and the Red Cross, which ran Sangatte. To film in the tunnel area we had to get permission from Eurotunnel, the vice consul in Lille, the prefet, the head of the Police Aux Frontieres (PAF) which had 70 police officers on the site of the camp, and 35 Brigade Mobile de Recherche (BMR), and the Eurotunnel private security company SPGO. With the institutional arrangements in place, one then still has to persuade each person being filmed to sign a general release form. These release forms are unaffectionately known as "blood chits'" in the BBC, as it is felt the signatory signs over everything including their blood to the BBC. There were problems in signing these for the residents at Sangatte, which I will discuss later.

We were also very careful about the terminology used to describe the asylum seekers and refugees, although we had to use the terms "asylum seekers and refugees". In the documentary itself we questioned the dubious label "illegals", by including the statement of an Iraqi man living in Sangatte. He explained that the only way many European countries accepted someone as a refugee was if they had the appropriate papers, but that the very fact of having to be a refugee meant that they had no papers. Not having papers, however, is often the reason why they are labelled as "illegals."

In the introduction to the finished film we cut together statements from Immigration Officers and from asylum seekers saying how they saw the situation. We then followed various cases of people applying for entry at the Port of Dover with interviews from both the Immigration Officer, and where we could, from the person applying for entry. We also followed a couple of investigations by the FSU into on-going human trafficking cases. Interwoven with these narratives were individual tales of refugees in Sangatte, interviews with the Red Cross representative, interviews with the authorities in France and with officials from the transporters who were being fined for carrying so-called "illegals" into the United Kingdom. The Immigration and Asylum Act 1999 introduced fines of £2000 for each illegal passenger found. This caused much anger amongst the hauliers, especially the small companies. We filmed one Irish owner/driver who was subsequently fined £50,000. EWS were not allowed by the French authorities to search their freight trains in France and in just over a year had been fined half a million pounds which they were refusing to pay. I wanted all sides to have their voice, that is, the hauliers, British and French immigration officers and those seeking asylum, to try and portray the situation *and* its impact on those involved with the Immigration Service in Dover.

Constraints

One of the main problems as a programme maker, especially when trying to justify programmes to academics, is that they often forget that a television programme has to be entertaining. If no-one watches it, it is wasted, however worthy it may be. It therefore has to adhere to certain news values and narratives, and these narratives can drive or shape a programme of limited duration, even where the intention was to address certain issues rather than just portray the drama of events. Hopefully the right balance is struck – where the issues are raised and explored *through* the events portrayed.

One of those events in relation to migration happened in Dover in June 2000, when 58 people from China died while being illegally transported into the United Kingdom. This dramatic event had a huge impact on the work at Dover, and on the subsequent coverage of that work. The actions of the FSU both in its investigation and in the unfolding narrative of pursuing certain smuggling teams made good entertainment, and highlighted what was an important issue within the Immigration Service, that is that increasingly merciless criminals were taking advantage of those wanting to enter the country, and were finding new ways to break the law. However, this narrative focus might have had some unintended ramifications. By concentrating on the work of the FSU in the programme, the complexity of the issue as a whole was reduced to a series of combative measures designed to weed out those "who abuse the asylum system and prevent "illegal immigrants" from entering the country in the first place" (Buchanan et al., 2003, p. 12). This was re-enforced by the grammar of documentary itself.

Using Nichols' (1991) categories of documentary, *Welcome to Britain* was primarily an observational documentary, but it was also expository. As the latter, it was an informative work to attempt to show and explain the situation in which the Immigration Service in Dover operated. This genre uses actuality, or scenes shot in an observational style to illustrate the arguments. As mentioned, this style arose from the *cinema verite* tradition where the camera is an observer. As director I directed the camera, not the people involved in the scene. There was no reporter on screen, but using interviews, voice-over commentary and through the footage itself, I tried to explain both the work of the Immigration Service, the thoughts of those who worked for it and the experience of those people with whom it dealt. The observational style drove the dramatic narrative of the cases and people involved. I wrote the commentary to explain factual aspects to the audience, for example, in relation to the Schengen Agreement, but the commentary was not meant to provide any judgement or opinions on the matters presented. I wanted the audience to hear the different points of view and as far as possible to make up their own minds. Of course, I did choose the arguments put forward, but included statements I did not necessarily agree with, but which did reflect the opinion of the person filmed, or the view of an organisation the person presented.

In his study on French and US immigration news coverage, Benson states that narrative-driven formats focusing on "persons" and "personal attributes" ultimately "restrict the room for deliberative exchange of ideas including explicit critical evaluations that hold the major parties and their elected officials accountable" (Wessler, cited in Benson 2010, p. 8). Lewis, Brookes, Mosdell and Threadgold (2006) and Karim (2004) both point out that the focus on incidents rather than on broader causes facilitates their adoption into the ideological framework and the exclusion of facts which lie outside of its construction. For example, the frequent incidents of finding so-called "illegals" in the back of lorries and on the trains and their dramatic impact was presented in a framework of a failure of containment, as it appeared to those who found the "illegals." Other frameworks were not considered. Later in the series where the incidents filmed were of migrant workers employed illegally and often abusively on fruit-picking farms, the framework changed to that of an immigration system which actually *made* asylum seekers work illegally because they were not allowed to work. The framing both was constitutive of and contributed to the inclusion of incidents which excluded other readings.

The argument was one that arose from the perceived reality of those who worked in the immigration system, and of a perception in the media at the time, which was that immigration was out of control. The Immigration Officers in Dover only described what they saw. They did not talk of the bigger picture or an alternative analysis of the immigration situation. The drama, the reality, of what the Immigration Service saw was of people crossing the channel "illegally" every night and the reaction of those who dealt with this. For example, a Chief Immigration Officer estimated that there had been 30,000 illegal entrants in the past year. As it was this service I was filming, their views could not but be included. To satisfy the "entertainment" requirement of the documentary, I filmed the drama, thus enforcing the perception that it was a situation out of control.

However, it was also through the drama that I hoped to convey the humanity of the personal stories of those caught up in the system. The FSU was shown trying to track down gangs of people traffickers. At the time, the main one was based in Germany. This gang was smuggling lorries packed with Indians, who arrived in boxes in the back of trucks, sitting on 3-legged stools with pot plants to try and confuse the carbon monoxide detectors. Drama was also conveyed in the individual stories of the people in Sangatte who for many reasons were trying to get to the UK. The main argument became one of humanity and inhumanity, of trying to make an audience understand and empathise with the plight of those who had to leave their homes, and of the difficulties of those who had to deal with a complicated and sometimes baffling legal system.

However, the concentration on drama, on events and on the "human" side of the story perhaps cost the programme depth in another direction, something Gross et al. (2007, p. 27) pick up on in their study of the coverage of refugee and asylum seeker issues in the context of television news: the failure to "deconstruct the (immigration) policy discourse, leaving it unquestioned…thus the Government appears to have lost control, not because of 'bad policy' but because asylum seekers 'are out of control'." In other words, many assumptions of those immigration officers and the baffling legal system itself remained relatively unquestioned.

To some extent I hoped that questions about the policy would arise from seeing evidence that the policy was not working. However, when making an observational series, in this case, about the Immigration Service and its work, it is difficult to crowbar in fundamental challenges to perceived reality. Such a challenge would have had to come from within. If no one within that system questions policy, that is, the *why* instead of the *how*, or brings up alternative discourses, the nature of observational documentary does not allow for such a challenge to be introduced from outside. In filming IOs interviewing migrants and in my interviews with them, the dominant discourse is emphasised. On this point Gross et al. (2007, p. 25) put forward the argument made by Douzinas (2000) and Lui (2002) that the "very legal definitions of the asylum seeker or the refugee are de-humanising". Similar to what Buchanan et al. (2003) suggest, our use of statistics provided by the Immigration Service, did not challenge the accepted discourse. By providing the "facts" about these apparently "overwhelming" numbers and the control of borders we became partially complicit with the "problematic immigration" discourse.

On reflection I could perhaps have challenged the dominant discourse mentioned above by including the argument surrounding the existence of the camp at Sangatte, and thus opened a debate about immigration policy itself. Buchanan et al.'s (2003) study highlights the coverage of the closure of Sangatte after we had finished filming. At the time of our series, Home Secretary Jack Straw was having discussions about its closure, and the media covered it heavily, but I felt at the time that the focus of our programme was on the British side of the Channel, with the Immigration Service in Dover, so we focused on the people in Sangatte who wanted to get to Britain, not on the discussion about the existence or otherwise of the camp.

Likewise, the visuals tended to re-enforce this picture of a system being overwhelmed, with rows of mainly young men queuing up at Sangatte, or waiting to be interviewed in Dover. Visual action influences the pacing and arrangement of television, and visuals encourage an event-led format; "the narrative is tied to visual so that more thorough information about the relevance of an event to a broader topic or issue may actually be inhibited by the use of more visuals" (Altheide, 1987, p.165). For example of the 10 days and nights we filmed in the freight lanes or at Dollans Moor where the EWS trains stopped, we filmed 25 Kosovars and 6 Afghans arriving illegally on the 10th April, 24 Indians arriving on the 12th April; on 26th April a Polish lorry driver brought in 3 Ukrainians; on the 25th April we filmed 4 Chechens and 1 Azerbaijani who hid on the train at Dollans Moor, whilst 20 people were found in the freight lanes at Dover. These visuals helped add up to a picture of a system being overwhelmed.

Previously I have mentioned the contract signed with the Immigration Service without which no filming could have taken place. In academic analysis of embedded journalism it is the signing of a contract with the military, which excised many critics (Brandenburg, 2007; Lewis et al., 2006; Miller 2003). The main criticism is that by signing a contract one submits to a form of blanket censorship. I was an embedded documentary maker with the British Army in the invasion of Iraq in 2003, and from my experience would argue that there are other less obvious factors, some mentioned above, which play a greater role in determining what is and is not filmed. In the documentary department we had to sign contracts with institutions being filmed for many years. They have to be drawn up for purposes of insurance, for copyright and transmission repeats but the BBC never gives up editorial control. In all the documentaries I have made with contracts being written, the institution concerned has had the right to correct a fact that is wrong, but not change an opinion, or an editorial line. The contract lays down the bones of the agreement. As in most areas of journalism, issues such as access, subject matter and opinions are all subject to negotiation, and can be argued as one films.

Another criticism of embedding, which could be applied to observational film making, which of necessity spends days and nights with those being filmed, is of journalists becoming too close to those filmed. As with the embedding debate, I would argue that experience develops what Graham Greene described as "a cold splinter of ice in the heart" (1971), that is the observing eye which always watches what is happening, and judges whether it would make good television, whether it be sympathetic or detrimental to those beside you. This journalistic practice perhaps protects one from overt partisanship. However, what is possibly more invidious is that by existing in the world of the Immigration Officer it is difficult to question that discourse. As stated above, if the programme observes that world view, it is difficult to stand outside and question that view.

Another problem of being "embedded" is that when one is seen to be filming with the side that one is accompanying, that is with the Immigration Service, the police or the Army, it can be difficult to negotiate access to film with the "other side." When filming people at Sangatte we had to tell them we were making a film about the Immigration Service, but many thought we were from Special Branch and many were too frightened to talk to us. We had to blob out the faces of those who did agree to be filmed, which in my opinion immediately associated them with criminal behaviour, as television blobs the faces of *sub-judice* cases and those in trouble with the law. We had to do this because of the migrants' fears of the policies enshrined in the Dublin Convention. The Convention states that if you can be proved to have come from one of the signatory countries, you will be returned to it, as they assume responsibility for the case; thus their fears that being filmed in Sangatte would mean being returned to France when the programme was transmitted. It is also hard to empathise with a person whose face and eyes you cannot see, so my desire to tell the stories of those seeking asylum before they were accepted, and to elicit an empathetic connection with them, was much constrained.[1]

Some NGOs concerned with refugees or asylum were also highly suspicious of what we were doing, and our seeming to be "with" the Immigration Service. I have had experience of some NGOs dislike of journalists on other series, and evidence of what Gross et al. (2007, p. 15) highlight as their simplistic promotion of "positive" stories, which make cooperation difficult. It was often the NGOs who insisted on editorial control, which we could not and would not grant, so they would not help us, nor give us permission to film with them or their clients. The Red Cross and Migrant Helpline, however, were extremely helpful, and I think we showed the invaluable work they did.

Beside access, another major constraint in the making the documentary was the time factor. Although for many news journalists, an hour-long programme may seem a very generous amount, there were many issues that I could not explore, and many issues which could just be touched upon briefly. I would have liked to explore immigration policy itself in more detail, but did not, for one, because of time, and for another because of the four-part structure of the series. I knew that one of the subsequent programmes would be filming with Barbara Roche, the Home Office Minister for Immigration, which seemed a far more appropriate conduit for asking political questions than in my programme. Time also played a role in terms of how long and which part of the migration experience we could cover in the documentary. For instance I would have liked to explore the fate of some of the asylum seekers we filmed at Dover, but did not have the time window in production to wait to see what happened. Again, I knew that further programmes were following the stories of those caught up in the process, though not necessarily the story of the people I interviewed. Also as Gross et al. (2007, p. 8) point out coverage is never only the responsibility of an individual journalist. This is not to say that I did not voice my concerns to the series producer, and hoped the subsequent films would deal with these matters, but my influence was limited on this matter by the hierarchical structure of the industry.

Thus issues such as the format and style of the programme affected the content of the documentary. The fact that the film had to entertain influenced narrative imperatives such as empathy for contributor, the concentration on drama, and practical issues such as the bureaucracy involved and the embedding with the Immigration Service were all issues which have to be considered when making a documentary and which act as constraints on the film itself.

Responsibilities

I would identify two sets of responsibilities for a producer on this type of documentary. The first and most obvious is to the people one films. The BBC Editorial Guidelines are very specific in our responsibility to protect vulnerable people (section 8). I had a great deal of experience filming with children, and victims of crime when making documentaries on the police, in prisons, and with victims of rape. Their stories, rights to privacy, fears and hopes have to be tempered with the journalist's desire to use these to illustrate an issue or to move along the narrative in a programme. There are times when one has to make a decision not to film, or not let the whole story be told in order to protect the contributor. Additionally, an individual's story should be put into context.

For example, many of the refugees I spoke to in Sangatte had left their home because they could not find work. Many of the Poles and Lithuanians filmed at Dover also had the same complaint. However, as pointed out by Castles and Miller (2003, p. 32) it was never as simple as not being able to find work. There were often both push and pull factors behind their decision to leave their homes, and their choice of the UK as a destination. Underdevelopment, conflict and human rights abuses were motivations for leaving, and a desire to find a better life, to join friends or family in the UK, the pull to come. To include the statement "I want to find work in the UK", I felt would have fed straight into what is described as the *Daily Mail* discourse of sponging economic migrants (Buchanan et al., 2003). Yet I didn't have the space in the programme to explain the background to the histories' of various countries or the present situation there, so I often left the statement about coming to the UK to find work out, or chose to include much more simple stories of persecution leading to the seeking of asylum, which viewers could understand without time-consuming explanation. Most of the asylum seekers I filmed had come mainly from countries hit by war, violence and chaos, such as Iraq, Afghanistan, and Chechenya, so I did not feel I was misrepresenting them. At the time of filming, the chief of the Tunnel Police in France, Dr Lajarrige, stated that 70% of the "clandestines" at the Tunnel site were Afghans and Iraqis. However, this simplistic contrivance of focussing on people from highly visible conflict backgrounds justified Chouliaraki's criticism that television's

> cinematic emphasis on immediacy offers no horizon of historicity in which the massive displacement of refugees today can be understood as a political and humanitarian issue. (2008, p. 842)

The brief of the series was not a study of the global refugee situation, but as stated above to look at how the UK Immigration Service was dealing with the perceived current problem on the British border. To examine the wider context was beyond the scope of the immediate brief. I did include a story of an Iraqi refugee who had lost his job because of the political situation, and hoped that this would challenge the dominant media discourse that equates asylum seekers with "economic migrant." With reference to the issue of economic migration and away from that of asylum seeking, I also included a statement by an Immigration Officer who had refused entry to a Polish carpenter saying that he felt great sympathy for the carpenter who was just trying to get a better life for himself and his family, and he would probably do the same in a similar situation.

Through these inclusions, I hoped to convey the complexity of the issue and the fact that there was not an easy right or wrong answer, but there was some humanity on both sides of the immigration desk. Nina Berstein, the chief metropolitan immigration reporter of the *New York Times* argues that for a complex issue such as immigration, "showing the human-ness [sic] becomes very important...this human narrative becomes the way to connect with the reader" (cited in Benson. 2010, p. 8). Again, although there is an inherent problem in its simplicity, it is the drama of the narratives which can draw the viewer in and make them empathise with the asylum seeker, but it is these stories which also emphasise the dominant discourse of a system out of control because of the influx of such people.

Faults

Many issues arose from constraints that I have mentioned, but the main one I perceived was accepting the framework of immigration/asylum as perceived by the Immigration Service in which the policy was presented as a series of combative measures designed to weed out those "who abuse the asylum system" and prevent "illegal immigrants" from entering the country. Another criticism of the media coverage on asylum raised by Gross et al. (2007) is the acceptance of the belief that human rights have a price; the conceptualisation that the human rights of one individual or group is considered "necessarily to compromise those of others" (p. 82). Although this mercantile view was never stated in my film, it was implicit in some of the statements made by the Immigration Officers, and not challenged by myself. I think this was evidenced in the alarm expressed by the numbers of asylum seekers "getting into" the country. The Immigration Officers did not say why they were alarmed, but this alarm could be translated as their fear of a compromising effect on those "legally" in the country.

There was no explicit criticism of policy such as the Dublin Convention or explanation of shortcomings in its application for humanitarian protection. There was also no explicit criticism of some specific effects of policy, such as the debate that restrictive measures in the European Union might actually be creating a greater demand for trafficker services. For instance, it has been argued that the deaths of the 58 Chinese transported to Dover in 2000 might actually be the consequence of these restrictive laws (Gross et al., 2007).

Strengths/Opportunities

Wolfsfeld (2004) states that the media never initiate a political event or process, they only react. I would argue that the access we obtained to the Immigration Service allowed us to film events which had not been seen by the public before, and in fact did initiated debate about immigration in general and the treatment of asylum seekers in particular. Later episodes showed deportations, and told individual stories of those imprisoned and deported which again had not been seen, and which contributed to the debate in the media, and a further series about the Immigration Service.

I would argue that we gave a voice to those who often do not have one. At a time when much of the media was trying to get access to the Sangatte camp we were the only media company to be allowed to film inside and interview the residents. This I would argue gave their voices more context than that of many other sources many of which were looking to exploit the panic discourse established by such papers as the *Daily Mail*. At the time the debate on whether to close the camp was growing, and Jack Straw was discussing the possibility of moving the camp further south into France. By showing the human story behind the individuals interviewed we tried to counter the fear of the faceless mass of the Other poised to "invade" the United Kingdom.

By giving a voice to such people and following their stories, I would argue that we showed the chaos of the system, so recognising the disempowerment and vulnerability of the asylum seekers. We also showed both the Immigration Officers and asylum seekers being constrained by an inadequate system. Benson (2010, p. 4) states that critical statements made by journalists or their sources perform a "signalling" function of their own "by calling attention to incoherent policy planning, ideological mystification, ineffective administration or misleading information, thus raising questions and concerns that may prompt further private or public inquiries." Lynn and Lea (2003, p. 448) point out that "dissenting voices" set up a counter discourse, where it is the government and those acting on their behalf that are seen as untrustworthy. In their study, the voices were letter writers, but I would argue in the case of the documentary, those who spoke out about their situation and desire to come to the UK can be included in this category.

Conclusion

It has been extremely interesting to critically re-examine the film I made and appraise it in the light of various academic criticisms. In retrospect, I think the later films in the series probably addressed some of the failures I have mentioned, but some of the issues remained: the observational style of the series, driven by dramatic narrative, events and visuals determined what issues were covered and how they were presented. In filming the world of the Immigration Service, which included those asylum seekers, refugees and immigrants who came into contact with them, I feel we did not question the discourse of immigration policy, asking not just how it was working (or clearly not), or the issues in its implementation, but whether it was actually sufficient to deal with the issues of 2001, and global mass movement.

However, I think the programme did give a voice to those who are not often heard, and did place the subject of immigration, asylum and refugee issues into a public arena where it was debated. One of my favourite reviews was from Peter Preston in the *Daily Mail* who with great satisfaction stated that the whole series was "ill-timed", as it concentrated on a "system that is on its last legs" (Preston, 2001 p. 51), which in my view showed that we had been entirely successful in raising doubts about a questionable system at a time when questions should be raised.

Note

1.   We also had problems with the signing of the release form, a condition for filming which the BBC and other broadcasters insist on. Again, because of the fears of the Dublin Convention, people in the Sangatte camp were unwilling to sign. They also feared possible retribution for their families at home, if they were to be identified. In the end, and with consultation with the BBC's editorial policy department, we merely asked them to write their nationality and mark their signature with a cross.

Conclusion

Terry Threadgold

Berkeley et al. (2006) in their literature review on new immigrants for Joseph Rowntree as part of the latter's migration and social cohesion research initiative, found the media portrayal of these issues from 1975 to 2005 to be central to the question of social cohesion, believing that it affected not only public opinion but also the construction of immigration policy (ICAR, 2004, p. 11; Berkeley, Khan, & Ambikaipaker, 2006, p. 23). For them "daily news coverage" and "moral panics in the media" which "maintain a public perception of *perpetual crisis* about immigration policies and social problems" was the fourth most important characteristic of "the receiving context [for new immigrants] in Britain" (square brackets are mine: 2006, p. 21, 25). The other important elements of that context were the general absence of any accurate knowledge of different kinds of immigration, or of changes in immigration patterns, either in relation to statistics or to conditions of exit in sending countries or about the characteristics of entrants themselves. By 2004, there was already a good deal of evidence about the limited nature of public understanding of these issues and its relationship to media representation. MORI polls (commissioned by a variety of different organisations, 2000 Reader's Digest; 2003 MigrationWatch UK; 2004, Amnesty International UK, Refugee Action, Refugee Council) give evidence more than anything else (1) of widespread ignorance of the histories, contexts and reasons which produce migration including asylum seekers and refugees, (2) of the complexities involved in historical and global flows of migration, and (3) of the facts and realities of being an asylum seeker or a refugee in the UK. What people seemed to believe tied in quite closely with then already well-evidenced and researched patterns of media coverage over a long period (Speers 2001; Buchanan, Grillo, & Threadgold, 2003; www.ramproject.org.uk). One of the key elements of that media coverage is the narrow range of migration which is actually seen to have "news value", so narrow in fact that by 2006 research in the UK showed that asylum had become almost synonymous with migration in both coverage and perception (Gross, Moore, & Threadgold, 2007). The symbiotic link between this and "problems" with policy (Berkeley et al. 2006 above) has also been a remarkably stable element of this discourse for a very long time. Kyambi (2005) lists all the restrictive immigration policies constructed in the

UK from the 1905 Aliens Act to the 2002 Nationality, Immigration and Asylum Act, specifying the nature of their restrictiveness in each case and commenting on the tendency to focus on non-white immigration in relation to race relations in all of them (2005, pp. 8–9). The aim of this book then has been to explore the absences in the discourse on migration as well as the presences and to provide a fuller and more nuanced account of the issues in a wider context than the UK alone.

Section 1: Migration Reporting and the Discursive Construction of Crisis

The work in this first section is theoretically diverse and I want to argue here that theory matters in this kind of research. The issues are complex and have for too long been insufficiently theorised, often relying on relatively decontextualised content analysis of media texts alone (Threadgold, 2009). The theories used here range from the use of Marx and Hegel (Bauder) where crises are seen as indicative of contradictions which are potentially transformative and may initiate dialectical change, to the related idea of migration as a "permanent and existential crisis for the nation state" which certainly produces change, but perhaps not the change we would want (Gross). Moore uses post-Marxist discourse theory (Laclau & Mouffe, 1985) to focus on the "commonsense" association of asylum with national security issues, exploring the way in which this particular "crisis" was constructed through the contingent collocation in the media she analyses of elements of otherwise quite disparate discourses. It is this contingency which allows "liberal democratic values" in the form of "human rights" to be re-constituted in the media stories in her sample as a threat to the stability and security of the British nation. Her work makes extensive use of the concepts of hegemony, hegemonic struggle and the contingency of discursive structures, seeing the possibilities of both change and contradiction in the latter and showing how these almost accidental processes of change drive in turn both "tough" political rhetoric on the part of governments and migration policy change.

Bauder's chapter raises interesting issues in relation to the different responses of settler (Canada) and ethnic (German) nations to migration but in other ways parallels Moore's post-Marxist understanding of the potential, in contingency, for change, seeing material crises as the triggers for both media coverage and legal and policy change. Again contextualisation is critical in order to understand the genesis of the media narratives and the political and policy responses.

The first section of the book also explores new aspects of the counter-discourse on migration which attempts to challenge the terms of the media discourse (Threadgold, 2006; Moore; Chouliaraki). Solidarity is here redefined as *private choice* and *self-fulfilment*, substituting de-politicised sentimental self-expression for the politics of population displacement. Chouliaraki's is an important chapter which focusses on real global crises and theorises and deconstructs what amount to new kinds of approaches to changing public opinion on the migration issue and these crises at national and international levels. These are seen here to be at least as problematic as the earlier myth-busting, positive/negative accounts of media representation of these issues (Threadgold, 2006, 2009). Chouliaraki concludes with suggestions about the alternative possibilities for more plural, dialogic encounters through new media, looking at actual examples of good practice (e.g., the BBC website), arguing for "an alternative vision of reflexive solidarity" which will recognise "human vulnerability as a political question."

This conclusion connects this first chapter nicely with the first chapter in the final section of the book, which does similar work and will be discussed below. Chouliaraki also directly situates the work of Bauder, Moore and Gross, all of whom suggest and indeed theorise the potential for changing the discourse on migration and show contingent change in action. What they, and the majority of the work in this field have not yet been able to do in fact is to actually radically change the media discourse. They are able to record contingent and systemic change but they cannot make it happen in particular directions. Thus reflexive solidarity is a theoretical construction not a media reality and the link between terror and asylum happens contingently, not because it is useful or intended. These issues are some of the most challenging in this whole field and there have been many critiques of the work (the counter-discourse) which has set out to challenge the media discourse or to engage audiences with the serious political and human issues around migration or difference in new ways. I have argued elsewhere (Threadgold, 2009) that the myth-busting discourse around the media representation of migration is actually driven by the content analysis on which it depends, and thus forced to engage with the media narrative on its own terms instead of starting from somewhere else as Chouliaraki's examples do. And while the textual and visual analysis of UN appeals and celebrity advocacy clearly shows many of the same flaws, we also need to be asking how audiences react to these new genres. It could be that "voice" for refugees would be more about the way someone in the street recognises them than their absence from a self-interested moment of advocacy which might in fact in all its neoliberal self-interest nonetheless change the manner of that recognition. I do not believe that we have yet asked enough of these questions.

Machin and Mayr's 2007 work on the *Leicester Mercury* is an interesting case study here. It is worth quoting Machin and Mayr's conclusions, based on detailed discourse analysis of the newspaper, in full:

> We no longer find [in the *Mercury*] the association of ethnic minorities with crime or with negative immigration issues. As such this model is difficult to criticise. Yet our analysis shows that the multicultural society found in the government's model newspaper still finds it difficult to articulate real differences. Further it is clear that, while the newspaper does include a broader range of voices these are carefully selected. This means that certain issues are excluded. Those who suffer poverty and social exclusion are invisible as are those who may simply have very good reasons for wishing only to enjoy their own difference. (p. 28)

There are parallels here with Chouliaraki's and Gross's findings in this book. Like Chouliaraki, they see the model of difference which is produced as a neoliberal one, a model failing to see or understand that there is anything more than neoliberal choice involved in making integration or social cohesion happen. It is arguable that we need to do much more work on these kinds of alternative discourses, and on the contingent possibilities for change, precisely because the effort to engage in conversation about the issues, while only a "talking cure" as Machin and Mayr (2007) have argued, nonetheless "plays a performative part in the politics of recognition" at a number of levels which even those involved have perhaps not yet fully understood or questioned. That performativity seems to me to be in real need of careful analysis along with the "archive" which generates all of these narratives. Media stories do indeed always contain the traces of what Sara Ahmed (2004, p. 14) has designated an "archive":

> An archive is an effect of multiple forms of contact, including institutional forms of contact (with libraries, books, websites), as well as everyday forms of contact (with friends, families, others). Some forms of contact are presented and authorised through

writing (and listed in the references), whilst other forms of contact will be missing, will be erased, even though they may leave their trace.

As Ahmed has also pointed out so cogently in relation to asylum stories, some emotions (e.g., hate) get "stuck" to some bodies, some words and language, and indeed some narrative structures, "stick" to asylum bodies. They do not have however, "any fixed referent", they could, and indeed do, "stick" performatively, to *any* bodies, whether there is any evidence that the bodies are dangerous or not (p. 47): "Such a discourse of "waiting for the bogus" is what justifies the repetition of violence against the bodies of others in the name of protecting the nation." The examples in Moore and Bauder of the contingent collocation of asylum/migration with terrorism are cases in point. Thus intertextuality, power and the sheer complexity of the "archive" in which emotions and beliefs about asylum are embedded, are a partial explanation about why the counter-narratives of asylum fail consistently to change the hegemonically mediated ones. The problem as Ahmed points out is that you cannot change emotional attachment to narrative regularities or the way those regularities stick to asylum-seeking bodies simply with facts, and assuming that you know that and can do that is often a form of white privilege.

Mapping the sources of the "archive" which inform and maintain the media narrative is complex. Van Dijk (1996) provides a good place to start, looking at media, political, corporate, academic and educational discourses. Blommaert and Vershueren (1998) in a similar study reinforce Ahmed's points above in a very different theoretical mode, showing how: "mainstream pro-migrant rhetoric shares ideological work with anti-migration rhetoric" (p. 21) by participating in the "management of diversity" and becoming complicit in its construction of diversity and migration as "worries" (pp. 11–15) in need of management by the powerful in which "minority members are not even allowed to participate" (p. 15).

What has to be addressed is the intertextual burden of all of these narratives and their embodied textual histories in a range of other institutions and discursively constructed realities. Media, political, legal, policy, advocacy and corporate representations are produced through the discursive constructions circulating in, and embodied by, those who inhabit a number of powerful institutions including from time to time ourselves. These inhabitants talk to journalists, who also read the complex languages and discourses of these same institutions. These languages and discourses are about whiteness, about national identity, and about the nation state. They are the imaginings of a powerful elite (a powerful and under-researched archive) and the lives of both the working classes and new migrants, including asylum seekers, are caught up in the narratives which perpetuate these realities, mediated by rituals of journalistic practice and struggles between powerful and incompatible interests.

Section Two: Crisis Reporting and the Representation of Migration

These issues are taken up again in different ways in the second and third sections of the book. The second section of this book considerably broadens the debate about the media representation of migration but also contributes to an understanding of the huge stabilities of the global media and policy discourses around these issues.

Some time back Stephen Castles (2004), looked at the assumptions that seem to drive migration policy in order to understand *why migration policies fail*. He argued that two beliefs continue to influence policy formation: a belief in market behaviour, based on neo-classical cost benefit calculations as an explanation of why people move; and a bureaucratic belief that regulations designed to categorise migrants and to differentially regulate their admission and residence will effectively shape their aggregate behaviour (2004, pp. 205–227). He also argued, like Berkeley et al. (2006) and Kyambi (2005), that both migration policy and the media stories which feed from it and drive it and its embodied and performative consequences ignore a number of basic issues about migration: the agency of the migrant, the structural, and economic dependence of both sending and receiving countries on emigration and immigrant labour, the nature of the migration industry (including people smuggling, trafficking and so on), the importance of chain migration networks and of the demographics of these (e.g., family reunions), and the way policies become "opportunity structures" for forms of resistance at local levels (Castles, 2004, pp. 208–10).There is a failure to address root causes which is the result, according to Castles, of "fundamental interest conflicts" and this produces a huge gap between policy rhetoric and action. For Castles, policy as currently conceived is "really about regulating North-South relationships and maintaining inequality" (p. 223). If then policy refuses to address this issue, its aim to contain/"stem the tide" of asylum seekers is "doomed to failure" (p. 223).

What Castles said of policy still holds and could also be said of the media, which both follows and engenders policy in its interaction with elite sources and the archive, and also, as a result, fails to address root causes or any of the other elided and neglected complexities in Castles' account. Castles' work therefore provides an excellent way in to understanding the importance of the work done by the chapters in the second section of this book. These chapters look across a range of sending and receiving migration contexts at a wide variety of kinds of migration and contextualising factors, raising many of the issues which Castles, and Ahmed above, argue are usually elided or forgotten in policy and media discourses.

Santa Ana's chapter which introduces the section, reviews changes in the US representation of immigration in the forty year period between 1967 and 2007, these two "framing" years marked by domestic demonstrations "where blood is shed" in Detroit and Los Angeles respectively. The Detroit case is interesting and could be paralleled with the later riots in northern England which produced the Cantle Report (Cantle, Kaur, Athar, Dallison, Wiggans, & Joshua, 2006). President Johnson set up the Kerner Commission to investigate the causes of the riots. When it reported in 1968, it identified the source of the riots as the deeply embedded structural racism of US society, arguing that the US was in fact "two societies" (cp. Cantle Report), and listing all of the areas where this entrenched racism operated. The list includes all major institutions (education, health, social welfare, housing etc.) and parallels again the later findings of Cantle and others (Threadgold, Clifford, Arwo, Powell, Harb, Jiang et al, 2008) in the UK. The complaint about the media in Detroit is that it exaggerated the violence and made no effort to report on its causes. Demonstrations with bloodshed, Santa Ana argues, make for good news stories.

Santa Ana then moves on to review studies of media coverage of contingently different immigrant groups between 1967 and 2007. The analysis of the 1990s media coverage of Proposition 187 moves beyond content analysis to the use of narrative and discourse analysis framed by Lakoff's work on metaphor, identifying a racist discourse which is very familiar from the UK and other contexts, in which the *alien* as *animal* is contrasted to the citizen, identified with *invasion, weeds, burdens, disease*, and described through metaphors of war and water (*floods, flows, awash with*) (Threadgold, 2009). Even more remarkable than these similarities in the global journalistic representations, is the evidence that both pro- and anti-proposition 187 groups used the same metaphors. That is there was no alternative discourse here, and even the LA Times, which was anti-Proposition 187, still used them. This is of course the point made by Blommaert and Vershueren (1998) of the Belgian situation they describe and by Ahmed in the UK (see above) about the discourses of tolerance which project racism onto less powerful others but do not see it in themselves. Forty years after Kerner, Santa Ana describes one of those moments of contingent change theorised above in section 1. He describes a moment of hope when George Bush made his "welcoming society" speech in 2004, talking of immigrants as being "Americans by choice". He then records the unpredictable consequences of this moment in December 2005 when the law changed (HR4437) to make it a felony to be an unauthorised worker producing an anti-immigration campaign. The final study in this chapter of the television, not print media, coverage of the Los Angeles marches in 2007, focuses on the important aspect of visual bias in tele-visual reporting, and notes again the use of non-factual narrative and meta-phorical framing of the events, as well as the elision of significant information. Santa Ana's conclusion then is that the US media, despite contingent and occasional minor changes, has only used one or two narratives over a period of forty years and that the recommendations of the Kerner report are still relevant, still in need of implementation. This of course takes us back to the much wider institutional context with which I began, to the "archive" and its sources in and across all of the institutions with which immigrants have to deal, not just the media.

The chapters by Bjelica and Farbotko take these issues into other institutional contexts to do with war and climate change and explore migration in the very different contexts of post-Milosevic Serbia and the Pacific Islands. They also challenge a number of our taken-for-granted notions about the media, taking us back to other theories of the press and to very different ways of narrativising identity and movements of people. Bjelica's detailed account of the development in the nineties of the media in Serbia from a Soviet Communist model where to tell the same story across news outlets was a mark of the strength of the regime, to a "polarized pluralist model" and the desire for a free and democratic press, reminds us that there are in fact very different ways of doing journalism, and that what she calls the social responsibility theory of balance and impartiality, which has proved to be problematic in the representation of migration in the UK, is only one of many versions of the media as institution.

Farbotko on the other hand shows precisely and at first-hand how a Western discourse of displacement is imposed on Pacific peoples by Western journalists who can neither access nor understand the alternative discourses and narratives in which these people position themselves. Her chapter also raises the question of the categorisation of migrants and the way this connects to attempts to regulate or imagine their movements, for the "climate change" or "environmental" migrants she discusses, despite the vulnerability of their low-lying island homes, and the global corporate responsibility for that vulnerability, have at present no legal protection as asylum seekers or refugees, and like the victims of Hurricane Katrina in the United States, resist the refugee label and the image of the "distressed and homeless individual" it embodies (see also Gross et al, 2007). Farbotko demonstrates with remarkable simplicity and incisiveness the way one islander's refusal or inability to articulate to a journalist her anxieties about being constructed by the media as victim and spectacle, is nonetheless, under editorial constraint, "moulded into a very particular climate refugee narrative" about "tides of desperate immigrants" which effectively silences other ways of storying and being. The exploration of the archive and the histories which sustain these different and usually untold narratives and identities, of the waka and drifting discourses, show just how limited and unimaginative the Western discourses into which these peoples' lives and identities are co-opted actually are. Farbotko's argument is that these self-representations of empowered seafaring and adaptation and survival are marginalised by media outside the Pacific.

The postcolonial theorisation in this chapter is a potentially very useful adjunct to the toolbox of theory this book as a whole articulates, reinforcing Castles' arguments above about the differences which structure migration debate, media coverage and policy directions. Climate change and migration events associated with it, as Farbotko points out, add complexity to an already very complex story about differential access to resources and power, enabling, in this case Pacific migrants, to be positioned as "something to fear or to control". The discourse of core and periphery, and the Western spatial assumptions that displaced people always originate in the developing world and are heading for the industrialised world, parallels arguments in earlier chapters in this book about the construction of self in relation to the refugee as other. Thus, as Farbotko puts it: the construction of climate change refugees is "used to reflect back a reiteration of industrialised world inhabitants, and their living practices, as 'normal.'" Postcolonial theory and indeed social and political geography have much more to offer the migration debates with which this book engages.

Bjelica's chapter is an explicitly feminist account of transitional democracy in Serbia, focusing on the media's socialisation role, in terms of embedding a "new normative system", new laws and policies strongly influenced by the many international organisations and governments involved in this post-war process of democratisation, and on the media representation of the human trafficking of women of and by Kosovo Albanians. The latter reveals the unfinished nature of the transition. Her analysis of the role of international organisations is of critical importance. It is important to observe that the democratic discourse and values these organisations introduced to Serbia appear to make the under-representation of women in public life and their over-representation as stereotyped sex objects visible, at the same time as it brings into discursive conflict what Bjelica identifies as a "civic democratic security discourse" which is human rights based, and an older national-liberation discourse in which the "Kosovo myth" is central to the Serbian national identity narrative. The emergent democratic media's role in all of this, as well as the role of apparently pro–human rights international organisations, is it seems to me highly problematic.

Her content and discourse analysis of newspaper representation unpacks an extraordinary complexity of discursive construction, demonstrating the misogynistic construction of women in trafficking trials and other contexts, and showing how, in the transitional context, this takes priority over the newly introduced normative discourse on human rights or crime. There are some interesting comparisons to be made here with Moore's discussion of the mobilisation of human rights discourse in the UK and anti-immigration opposition to it. Above all however, what becomes clear as she works her way through her detailed media analysis is that, as in other contexts (Threadgold, 2009), the huge stability of narrowly framed media narrative, here the over-representation of the violent and sexual crime of Kosovo Albanians, has impacted significantly on public policy and the criminal justice system, pulling the complexities of the entire intertextual archive, and of many institutions, into this very complex story.

Moreover, it is the very "democratisation" of the media, and the influence of Western discourses and narratives, which appear to make these representations possible. What Bjelica shows is how the "Kosovo myth" is appropriated into the new news value system where it can now be framed by the same kind of narrative of the dangerous other, criminalised and responsible for their own fate, that has been typical of these representations in other national contexts around very different issues. We should recall here the work discussed above of Blommaert and Vershueren on the discourse of tolerance, the way it shares work with anti-immigration discourse, and Ahmed's work on the neoliberal discourses which have the same effect and use the same languages as anti-immigration discourses. Santa Ana's work also alludes to this, and so does Farbotko's when she discusses the way climate change activists as well as journalists, attempt to "enrol particular groups of people to 'tell' climate change stories", positioning themselves as compassionate protectors, and the "core" of the industrialised world as the "salvation" for fearful, powerless and silenced climate refugees. All of this takes us back to Chouliaraki's analysis in chapter 1 of this book and compels some very self-reflective analysis of the contingent change produced by crises of various kinds and of our own potential, and often unpredictable, complicity in the very narratives, discourses, representations and processes we seek to change.

The chapters by Wu et al. and Jiang take us into another space, the space of Chinese migrations and again of people trafficking, but they also force us again to compare the work of different media systems, moving us back and forth between Chinese and English language newspapers and between the UK and China. They also point, in ways that are unusual in studies of the media and migration, to the functions of the media in sending countries where the media provides information for potential migrants, but also connects with members of the Chinese diaspora in receiving countries to impact on the construction of their cultural identity. Indeed studies of the media coverage of these issues in sending countries, especially studies looking at the sending country's perspective in the context of economic development, are, as they point out, "only marginally studied." They argue, in the same vein as Castles above, that restrictive migration policies in receiving countries (here Europe) are (a) driven by public perceptions of risk produced by media constructed crises and (b) unfit to deal with either the opportunities or the challenges posed by Chinese irregular migration in the "context of the globalisation of the world economy and of labour distribution."

Wu et al.'s content analysis of the media coverage of these issues in the *Global Times* is an important adjunct to the work we have seen in other chapters, particularly that which has shown pro- and anti-migration discourses to share significant elements. Here we find sending and receiving discourses to do the same although there are important differences. The *Global Times* is affiliated with the Communist Party, represents the Chinese government's voice on news events but is also a successful commercial paper. This compares in interesting ways with Bjelica's account of the development and transitional nature of the Serbian media. The Chinese paper typically refers to "irregular" migration as "illegal", a consequence, according to the authors, of its official affiliation where clandestine border crossing is seen from a purely legal perspective Wu et al. observe that the accounts of exploitation, racism, exclusion and controlling migration policies facing Chinese irregulars in Europe are treated in the *Global Times* with considerable sympathy, appearing to understand and to want to present the case for and against irregular migration in terms of the economic disparity between sending and receiving contexts. It is seen here, much as Castles outlines above, as the response in human mobility to labour market demands in Europe.

The paper is also ambivalent about illegal migration, "often seeing it as less of an issue if it fits a pattern of economic development." Thus the language of coverage, its discourse and narrative, is remarkably similar to parallel coverage in Western and European newspapers, but the interpretation and the function of the stories is nonetheless often very culturally specific and has a different political focus, framing the events differently for different audiences and purposes.

Of interest in both Wu et al. and Jiang is the account of trafficking associated with Fujian province in China and the alternative narrative and discourse on trafficking which emanates from that quarter. As Wu et al. argue, and Jiang confirms, "the vast majority of Chinese stowaways link themselves voluntarily to smuggling networks in order to achieve high earnings in Europe." Fujian province was "most intensively affected by the seaborne expansion of European colonies", so that leaving China from coastal provinces such as Fujian, was and is a matter of tradition and culture, but one which is completely elided from the dominant trafficking and snakehead narrative. Farbotko's account of climate refugees in the Pacific tells a similar story.

It is also important to record here some of the other observations made by Wu et al. on irregular migration, which they see as caused not by absolute poverty, but rather as the very product of development and increased knowledge of opportunities available elsewhere as well as in long-standing socio-cultural traditions as in Fujian. This whole phenomenon could be seen as a postcolonial case of "the empire striking back."

Jiang's chapter returns us to coverage in the UK, providing a very detailed and useful analysis of the coverage of the Dover and Morecombe Bay incidents, alongside, as discussed above, a reading of the history and the facts of Chinese irregular and other migration into the UK. Her chapter is particularly useful as well in taking us back to the stereotypical representations and the narrow range of narratives and subject positions which this media discourse allows, pointing to the replication in her media sample of many of the stereotypical characteristics identified in other work. She also points, as does Farbotko, to the imposition of the Western narrative on others, exemplified in the typical media assumption in the UK, that economic destitution is the reason people subject themselves to trafficking, a version of events radically challenged here in her work and by Wu et al. There are many parallels between the representation of these tragedies about death, illegality, crime and snakeheads, improper border crossings and security issues and their news value, and media behaviours in Serbia around trafficked Albanian Kosovars, in China about illegal migrants there, and in Santa Ana's account of Latino migration into the US. The twenty stories Jiang finds which actually explore the Fujian question and compare the "new life in the West" theme with the reality of the "lifetime of poverty and debt in the UK" do a much better job and parallel the coverage in the *Global Times* discussed above. The other issue Jiang's work raises is again the issue of the use of sources and the "archive" of institutional quotations and discursive complexities which is intertextually woven through all of these media stories in whichever context, in whichever country, in relation to whichever kind of migration. As Jiang argues, in the absence of scholarship and research into the details and complexities of migration issues of the kind she is addressing, and I would add, in the context of the kind of work done in media institutions and specifically in relation to the definition and performativity of the genre of news, it is difficult for the media to "keep abreast of this particular phenomenon and provide a comprehensive coverage." Contextual and contingent change does happen, is visible, in the archive and its texts, in response to various kinds of crises and localisations. To make that change happen in any directed and politically motivated way is much harder. That is the subject matter or focus of the work in the third section of this book, and takes us back to issues raised initially in section 1.

Section 3: The Management of Migration in Journalistic Practice

This section of the book moves from theory and theoretical practice to the practice of journalism and the theoretical practitioner. Blaagaard's chapter uses events around the Danish cartoons incident in 2005 and later in 2008, to engage in a radical deconstruction of Danish (and therefore Western) journalism and the principles which underpin it. At the same time, she shows how new technologies and new forms of global and international communication, including the citizen journalist, challenge those principles in fact, producing change which may (again contingently and unpredictably) be more or less democratic, more or less cosmopolitan, but which does allow more voices to be heard. And yet, the "old" media continues to shape our imaginings of our worlds and our selves, and remains, despite the potential of cosmopolitan and transnational citizenship to connect across borders, doggedly fixed in place and nation bound. Blaagaard focuses on the "whiteness" of Danish journalism, the limits of the nation allowing journalists to reproduce dominant social imaginaries which exclude minority groups and the multicultural spaces they inhabit, at the same time as new media communication challenges this kind of national journalism and makes visible the many different kinds of cultural citizenship and their relations to kinds of journalism that we have seen in section 2 above.

As she argues in relation to the Danish cartoons incident in 2005 and debates that followed in 2008, journalism was seen as the "defender of democracy" without any attempt to question the kind of democratic tradition or the "political theories it employed" to maintain its cultural power. The debate centres around a "tolerance" which entails neither respect nor understanding of the other, and the rights of the individual to freedom of speech and opinion. As we have seen in section 2 above, and as Blaagaard argues, a free press is often seen as the prerequisite for a liberal democracy, but what the cartoon controversy showed was the very cultural specificity of "liberal legalism and public life", demonstrating that Danish "freedom of expression" was "based on an assumption of a culturally homogeneous population" and "disguised as a universal or objective standard." Perhaps even more stunning in its implications is Blaagaard's argument that there "cannot be a global politics of tolerance except in a fully "Westernised world" or through complete colonisation."

Her alternative deconstructive position is to do with Gilroy's conviviality and Derrida's hospitality and cosmopolitanism. This is also the basis for Silverstone's theory of a cosmopolitan media: an ethic, an obligation to recognise the stranger as other, and the other in oneself, the obligation to be responsible, and the right in mediated space to be listened to and heard. Blaagaard is clear that this is a possibility not a reality, but believes that the very multiplicity of the media now, along with the diversity of forced and voluntary mass migrations and transnational news flows, may construct a new set of connections, which will make Silverstone's theoretical cosmopolitanism a reality.

Bayer's work in the second chapter in this section describes a reflexive process of trying to make these connections happen through cultural awareness training with multicultural groups (German and Arab/Islamic) of young journalists. Theoretically this chapter is informed by reflexive anthropology and the work of Clifford and Marcus on writing culture, an approach which emphasises the constructed nature of all cultures, the positioned nature of all discourse, and encourages a focus on one's own position, and on the same kind of self-reflexivity emphasised in Blaagaard's work above. The cultural power of Western journalism is again in evidence here in the tensions in the workshops between working with the conventions of that journalism—balance, impartiality, news values—and the need to focus on critical theory in order to deconstruct and critique those very conventions, to address the whiteness and exclusive nature of that journalism and explicit issues of racism both within the group and within the media.

The media context here is German and again the representation of migration is shown to be very similar to the stereotypes and normative narratives we have seen in other contexts throughout this book. The sheer difficulty of finding new ways of telling migration stories in the context of the workshops when the journalistic conventions exert a systemic bias through participants' belief in this as "good journalism" makes for interesting and challenging reading and is reminiscent of the ways in which in both China and Serbia, in the chapters by Wu et al. and Bjelica above, the adoption of Western media conventions, genres and narratives seems to have given rise to a repetition of the same in terms of migration stories. There are reminders here too of Chouliaraki's critique of the limits of UN and celebrity advocacy narratives as alternative discourse.

What does seem to work are the personal contacts made in the workshops, in which Bayer believes there is great potential, and indeed evidence, that transnational working relations do subsequently influence the lives and work of these young journalists. However, the denial of racism, and the complexity of the power relations in the workshops which made critique difficult (it is often taken personally) are also reminiscent of the account in Blaagaard's work of the condemnation of the out of court settlement and apology offered by one Danish newspaper in 2008 when the cartoons were reprinted in relation to the Kurt Westergaard incident. Bayer is concerned that changing individuals will never change the system, ultimately concluding that individuals are a possible place to start, but understanding that much more work on the "palemale" gaze which is "continuously reproduced as the "normal" media perspective" and on employment practices to produce a more diverse workforce, will all be necessary before there is any significant change in the media representation of migrants or any other marginalised group.

The third paper in this section takes us from theory and group practice to an individual self-reflective journalist exploring her own practice and presenting her own perspective on academic critique of her own and others' practice. Harris gives a detailed account of her experience of making a television documentary, the first programme in the series *Border Control*, the brief being to look at the way the UK immigration system was dealing with the "problem" on the British border. For the various reasons that Harris develops, the documentary reinforced the perception in the immigration system and in the media at the time that immigration was out of control, and this remained unquestioned as a premise throughout the making of the documentary. It was not in other words ever considered, as Castles considers it above, or as happens in the coverage in the Chinese language *Global Times*, that the policy of containment itself might be the problem, and not the asylum seekers. Harris nonetheless believes, and argues, that the documentary did give a voice to those who are seldom heard, did show the chaos of the system and the vulnerability and disempowerment of asylum seekers, and did initiate debate about immigration in general and asylum seekers in particular.

As one of the academics whose work and criticisms she reads closely in going back to critically re-examine the film she made, I find her self-reflection impressive and her positioning between academic theory and analysis a difficult place to be and to negotiate. Significantly, as I have argued elsewhere (2009), the academic critique to which she is responding is also limited and constrained by the media discourse and by content analysis as a methodology. But her conclusion is about what she intended as a documentary maker, not necessarily about what audiences, other than the *Daily Mail* journalist quoted in her conclusion, actually took away from the documentary. And this is where the archive, the hate that sticks to some bodies, and the intertextuality of repeated and cumulative representations return to haunt us. Far too often audiences read vulnerability and disempowerment as criminal, find the voice of the voiceless simply unbelievable (that story cannot be true), remain firmly embedded in the narrative they believed when the documentary started rather than engaging in debate, and fail altogether to achieve that cosmopolitanism which would be hospitable, in Derrida's sense, to the other. Harris's assumptions here are important and professionally based, but they are very like those of the makers of another BBC programme, *You The Judge*, broadcast on Asylum Day 2003 (http://news.bbc.co.uk/1/hi/programmes/asylum_day/3055809.stm), an interactive programme where the audience was asked to act as immigration official and to judge dramatised versions of asylum seeker stories as being worthy or not of asylum. In this case it was possible to witness and quantify audience reactions and they were certainly, in all their diversity and negativity, not what the journalists expected.

In a sense it is the lack of diversity in the media as institution, and journalism's continuing belief, as argued in Blaagaard and others above, in a homogeneous "we" and in the unified and universal values of "the nation" and its "tolerance", that lie behind the belief that media events will produce impartial and reasoned debate of a kind that is nowhere consistently evident in the actual multiplicity of the social worlds/contexts, identities and realities to which the media now speaks. And yet there is debate, and the talking cure does matter as we have seen in the arguments in Bauder and Moore about crisis and dialectical change, in Chouliaraki and Blaagaard in relation to good and bad new media activities, new voices, and good BBC websites and coverage. There is also the debate analysed by Gross, which not unlike Harris's work, explores in great detail the actual highly orchestrated and largely invisible professional journalistic practices which construct and mediate public understandings of migration in an election context.

Hargreaves and Thomas (2002, p. 7), recommended that: "the news media should redouble their efforts to engage with Britain's ethnic minorities." In 2011, we still seem a long way from that laudable aim. There are still very few studies which have really investigated the importance of such mediated engagements in relation to, and as, processes of integration and social cohesion (although the studies do not use these terms). Cunningham and Sinclair in

Australia (2000), Cottle (2000), Morley (2000) and Gillespie's (1995) research are cases in point. Gillespie presents the issues as being about "cultural change" and "cultural translation" but actually shows us a cosmopolitan media at work in Southall:

> In Southall, the redefinition of ethnicity is enacted in young people's collective reception and appropriation of TV. Transnational and diasporic media representing several cultures are available in Southall homes, offering a range of choices of symbolic identification. This range is sometimes felt to be too wide, as when, in situations of international conflict such as the Gulf War, young people find themselves facing difficult or even painful dilemmas. On the other hand, in key respects the range is not wide enough: young people complain for example, that too few images of "Asian" style and beauty are available which they feel able to take as role models. Yet the very coexistence of culturally diverse media is a cultural resource. It engenders a developed consciousness of difference and a cosmopolitan stance. It encourages young people to compare, contrast and criticise the cultural and social forms represented to them by their parents, by significant others present in their daily lives and by significant others on screen. This is the kind of context in which the construction of new ethnic identities becomes both an inevitable consequence and a necessary task. (pp. 205–206)

The forms of "social exclusion" from the media, here suggested in "the absence of role models", remains a serious issue for the UK media, and for most of the countries and national media dealt with in this book. Cottle (2000) explored the full extent of this exclusion, ranging from employment and recruitment strategies, to "deep-seated news values" and forms of representation themselves (see also Hargreaves & Thomas, 2002). These issues are an important part of the context which has produced the media reporting of migration in the UK, and as we have seen in a range of other countries including Germany, Canada, Serbia, Denmark and China.

In work on media coverage of migration, there has only been one UK study which has actually looked comparatively at minority ethnic/faith newspapers (published by Ethnic Media Group) and mainstream papers (published by Trinity Mirror) in the London boroughs and compared their coverage of asylum (Smart et al, 2007). This research found significant difference in coverage. The ethnic press is less likely to represent asylum seekers and refugees in relation to crime, more likely to represent asylum seekers and refugees as skilled contributors to the economy and more likely to use asylum seekers, refugees or ethnic minorities as sources. Santa Ana in this book records similar differences in coverage under Latino bylines in the United States.

The whiteness that is at stake here is not just a mediated whiteness, not just a problem with the media or with journalists. It is an issue with every major institution in our Western societies and the journalistic rituals of sourcing and balance ensure that it circulates, and finds its way into the media coverage of the issues through a variety of textual and embodied encounters characteristic of the entire circuit of mass communication (Miller, Kitzinger, Williams, & Beharrell, 1998). There is much more work to be done on the complexity of media narratives, their often serial nature, on the intertextuality, which due to the specific poetics of media news stories as ritualistic professional practices, actually forms so crucial a part of their construction. There is more too to be done on cosmopolitanism and embodiment.

And if we thought any of this would be easily solved or had changed, we need only to look and listen. Over the past two weeks as this conclusion has been coming to an end, we have been confronted in the UK with the scandal of the phone-hacking demise of the Murdoch empire's *News of the World*, the daily mediated representation of drought, famine and the hopelessness of refugees in Somalia and neighbouring countries, the repatriation to China from Canada of a well-known Chinese dissident, and the horror of the Norwegian killing of ninety-three innocent people by an apparently lone gunman seeking to save the world from migrants and cosmopolitanism. The latter event has unleashed again the whole complexity of the migration debate and its associated crises, both real and constructed, on a global scale. Moreover, in a remarkable acknowledgement of the power of the media, and with a concomitant denial of one individual's right to freedom of speech, indeed a public declaration of *intolerance* of what that individual stands for, the charges against him and any pleas he may have made, have been heard in a closed Norwegian court. This leaves us with these questions: Is silencing the answer, or is debate and dialogism, which at least engages in the dialectic of contingent change set in motion by crises? These remain the important questions with which the chapters in this book engage and with which we must all continue to engage if we are ever to find a way to a cosmopolitan media and a Derridean hospitality. In the meantime effecting small changes in local places may be the best we can do and the most we are obliged to do.

References

Adams, B. (1968). *Kinship in an urban setting*. Chicago, IL: Markham.

Agamben, G. (1998). *Homo Sacer. Sovereign power and bare life*. Stanford, CA: Stanford University Press.

———(2005). *State of exception*. Chicago, IL & London, UK: University of Chicago Press.

Agnew, J. (1994). The territorial trap: The geographical assumptions of international relations theory. *Review of International Political Economy*, *1*, 53–80.

Agnew, J., & Corbridge, S. (1995). *Mastering space: Hegemony, territory and international political economy*. London, UK: Routledge.

Ahmed, S. (2004). *The cultural politics of emotion*. Edinburgh, UK: Edinburgh University Press.

All Parties (2010, March). *Prime Ministerial debates—programme format*. Retrieved from http://www.bbc.co.uk/blogs/theeditors/pm_debates_programme_format.pdf

Allan, S. (1999). *News culture*. Buckingham, UK: Open University Press.

Allan, S., & Thorsen, E. (Eds.) (2009). *Citizen journalism: Global perspectives*. New York, NY: Peter Lang.

Allen, P. (2011, 3rd June). Crisis talks in fight to stem migrant hordes, *Daily Express*.

Allen, S. L. (2005). Activist media anthropology. Antidote to extremist worldviews. In E. W. Rothenbuhler & M. Coman (Eds.), *Media anthropology* (pp. 285–294). Thousand Oaks, CA: Sage Publications.

Altheide, D. L. (2002). *Creating fear: News and the construction of crisis*. New York, NY: Aldine de Gruyter.

———(1987). Format & symbols in TV coverage of terrorism in the US & Great Britain. *International Studies Quarterly*, *31*, 161–176.

Amnesty International. (2003). *United Kingdom: Justice perverted under the Anti-terrorism, crime and security Act 2001*. London, UK: Amnesty International.

———(2010). *Libya of tomorrow: What hope for human rights*. London, UK: Amnesty International.

Andersen, L. E. (2006). *Den tabte uskyld*. Odense, Denmark: Syddansk Universitetsforlag.

Anderson, B. (2006). *Imagined communities: Reflections on the origin and spread of nationalism*. London, UK: Verso. (Original work published 1991)

Anderson, P. J., & Ward, G. (Eds.) (2007). *The future of journalism in the advanced democracies*. Aldershot, Hampshire, UK: Ashgate.

Andreas, P. (2000). Introduction: The wall after the wall. In P. Andreas & T. Snyder (Eds.), *The wall around the West: State borders and immigration controls in North America and Europe* (pp.1–11). Lanham, MD: Rowman and Littlefield Publishers.

Andreassen, R. (2005). *The mass media's construction of gender, race, sexuality and nationality. An analysis of the Danish news media's communication about visible minorities from 1971 to 2004.* (Doctoral dissertation). University of Toronto, Toronto, Canada. Retrieved from http://www.rikkeandreassen.dk/

Andreassen, R. (2007). *Der er et yndigt land.* Copenhagen, Denmark: Tiderne Skifter.

Appadurai, A. (1996). *Modernity at large. Cultural dimensions of globalization.* Minneapolis, University of Minnesota Press.

Archibold, R. (2010, April 23). Arizona enacts stringent law on immigration, *New York Times.* Retrieved from http://www.nytimes.com/2010/04/24/us/politics/24immig.html

Aughey, A. (2010). National identity, allegiance and constitutional change in the United Kingdom. *Nations and Nationalism, 16,* 335–353.

August, O. (2007, July 1). The most corrupt man in China. *Sunday Times.* Retrieved July 8, 2010, from http://www.timesonline.co.uk/tol/news/world/asia/article2009598.ece

Australian Green Party (2007) Migration Amendment (Climate Refugees) Bill 2007.

Back, L. (2009). Beaches and graveyards: Europe's haunted borders. *Postcolonial Studies, 12,* 329–340.

Baer, F. E. (1982). "Give me...your huddled masses": Anti-Vietnamese refugee lore and the "image of limited good". *Western Folklore, 41,* 257–281.

Baganha, M. I., Doomernik, J., Fassmann, H., Gsir, S., Hofmann, M., Jandl, M., Kohlbacher, J., & Reeger, U. (2006). International migration and its regulation. In R. Penninx, M. Berger, & K. Kraal, *The dynamics of international migration and settlement in Europe: A state of the art* (pp. 19–40). Amsterdam, Netherlands: Amsterdam University Press.

Bailey, O. G., & Harindranath, R. (2005). Racialized "othering": The representation of asylum seekers in news media. In S. Allen (Ed.), *Journalism: Critical issues* (pp. 274–286). Berkshire: Open University Press.

Balibar, E. (2006). *Strangers as enemies: Further reflections on the aporias of transnational citizenship.* Paper presented at the Institute on globalisation and the human condition, 16 March. McMaster University, California, USA.

Barry, K. (1984). *Female sexual slavery.* (2nd ed.). New York, NY: New York University Press.

Barth, F. (Ed.). (1998). *Ethnic groups and boundaries: The social organization of cultural difference.* Long Grove, IL: Waveland Press. (Original work published 1969)

Bauder, H. (2008a). Dialectics of humanitarian immigration and national identity in Canadian public discourse. *Refuge, 25*(1), 84–93.

————(2008b). Immigration debate in Canada: How newspapers reported, 1996–2004. *Journal of International Migration and Integration, 9*, 289–310.

————(2008c). Media discourse and the new German immigration law. *Journal of Ethnic and Migration Studies, 34*, 95–112.

————(2008d). Neoliberalism and the utility of immigration: Media perspectives of Germany's immigration law. *Antipode, 40*, 55–78.

————(2008e). The economic case for immigration: Neoliberal and regulatory paradigms in Canada's press. *Studies in Political Economy, 82*, 131–152.

————(2009). Humanitarian immigration and German national identity in the media. *National Identities, 11*, 263–280.

————(2011). *Immigration dialectic: Imagining community, economy and nation.* Toronto: University of Toronto Press.

Bauder, H. & Semmelroggen, J. (2009). Immigration and imagination of nationhood in German parliament. *Nationalism & Ethnic Politics, 15*, 1–26.

Bauman, Z. (2004). *Wasted lives: Modernity and its outcasts.* Cambridge: Polity Press.

————(2007). *Liquid times: Living in an age of uncertainty.* Cambridge, UK: Polity.

Baxter, S. (1988). *A political economy of the ethnic Chinese catering industry.* (Unpublished doctoral dissertation). The University of Aston, Birmingham, UK.

BBC News. (2000a, November 21). Straw pledges asylum crackdown. *BBC News Online.* Retrieved from http://news.bbc.co.uk/1/hi/uk_politics/1033545.stm

————(2000b, June 19). 58 dead in port lorry. *BBC News Online.* Retrieved from http://news.bbc.co.uk/1/hi/uk/796791.stm

————(2001, April 5). Driver jailed for immigrant deaths. *BBC News Online.* Retrieved from http://news.bbc.co.uk/onthisday/hi/dates/stories/april/5/newsid_2467000/2467923.stm

————(2003a, September 30). Blair vows no reverse on reform. *BBC News Online.* Retrieved from http://news.bbc.co.uk/1/hi/uk_politics/3149164.stm

————(2003b, January 7). Terror police find deadly poison. *BBC News.* Retrieved from http://news.bbc.co.uk/1/hi/uk/2636099.stm

————(2005a, February 5). Morecambe Bay: 1 year on. *BBC News Online.* Retrieved from http://news.bbc.co.uk/1/hi/uk/4238209.stm

————(2005b, March 21). Tory traveller plans "not racist". *BBC News Online.* Retrieved from http://news.bbc.co.uk/1/hi/uk_politics/4365287.stm

————(2006a, March 24). Man guilty of 21 cockling deaths. *BBC News Online.* Retrieved from http://news.bbc.co.uk/1/hi/england/lancashire/4832454.stm

————(2006b, June 26). Tory bill of rights slammed. *BBC News Online*. Retrieved from http://news.bbc.co.uk/1/hi/5115912.stm

————(2011, February 16). David Cameron: UK human rights law review "imminent". *BBC News Online*. Retrieved from http://www.bbc.co.uk/news/uk-politics-12482442

Bechhofer, F., & McCrone, D. (2007). Being British: A crisis of identity? *Political Quarterly*, *78*, 251–260.

————(2008). Talking the talk: national identity in England and Scotland. In A. Park, J. Curtice, K. Thompson, M. Phillips, M. C. Johnson & E. Clery (Eds.), *British social attitudes: The 24 report* (pp. 81–104). London, UK: Sage.

Beck-Gernsheim, E. (2007). *Wir und die anderen: Kopftuch, zwangsheirat und andere mißverständnisse* (Erweiterete Ausgabe). Frankfurt am Main, Germany: Surkamp Veralg.

Beck, U. (2005). *Power in the global age: A new global political economy* (K. Cross, Trans.). Cambridge, UK: Polity.

Beise, M. (2004, May 25). Wirtschaft macht druck bei der zuwanderung. *Süddeutsche Zeitung*, p. 19.

Bell, S. (2001, July 18). No way to fight terrorism. *National Post*, p. A15.

Bendel, P. (2004). Totgesagte leben länger: Das Deutsche zuwanderungsgesetz. *Gesellschaft–Wirtschaft–Politik*, *53*(2), 205–212.

Benhabib, S. (2007). Democratic exclusions and democratic iterations. Dilemmas of "just membership" and prospects of cosmopolitan federalism. *European Journal of Political Theory*, *6*(4), 445–462.

Benson, R. (2010). What makes for a critical press? A case study of French and US immigration news coverage. *The International Journal of Press/Politics*, *15*, 3–24.

Berkeley, R., Khan, O., & Ambikaipaker, M. (2006). *What's new about new immigrants in twenty-first century Britain?* York, UK: Joseph Rowntree Foundation.

Berry, D. (2005). Trust in media practices: Towards cultural development. In D. Berry (Ed.) *Ethics and media culture. Practices and representations*. Oxford, UK, & Burlington, MA: Focal Press.

Betts, A. (2003). The international relations of the "new" extra-territorial approaches to refugee protection: explaining the policy initiatives of the UK government and UNHCR *Refuge*, *22*, 58–70.

Bhabha, H. K. (1990). The third space. Interview with Homi Bhabha. In J. Rutherford (Ed.), *Identity, community, culture, difference* (pp. 207–221). London, UK: Lawrence and Wishart.

————(1994). *The location of culture*. London, UK: Routledge.

Biermann, F., & Boas, I. (2010). Preparing for a warmer world: Towards a global governance system to protect climate refugees. *Global Environmental Politics*, *10*(1), 60–88.

Bigo, D. (2001). Migration and security. In C. Joppke & V. Guiraudon (Eds.), *Controlling a new migration world* (pp.121–145). London, UK: Routledge.

Bildungszentrum Bürgermedien (Ed.). (2006). *Intercultural media training in Europe. Handbuch für trainInnen, mitarbeiterInnen und redakteurInnen.* München, Germany: Kopaed.

Bishop, M., & Green, M. F. (2008). *Philanthrocapitalism: How the rich can save the world.* New York, NY: Bloomsbury Press.

Black, R. (1998) *Refugees, environment and development.* Harlow, UK: Addison Wesley Longman.

Black, R. (2001). Environmental refugees: Myth or reality? *UNHCR Working Papers, 34*, 1–19.

Blair, T. (2003, February 7). Interview with Jeremy Paxman. *Newsnight.* Retrieved from http://news.bbc.co.uk/1/hi/programmes/newsnight/2738771.stm

————(2004, April 27). PM Speech on migration to the CBI. Retrieved from http://www.number10.gov.uk/Page5708

————(2005, April 22). Full text: Tony Blair's speech on asylum and immigration. *Guardian.* Retrieved from www.guardian.co.uk/politics/2005/apr/22/election2005.immigrationandpublicservices

Bleasdale, L. (2008). Under attack: The metaphoric threat of asylum seekers in public-political discourses. *Web Journal of Current Legal Issues, 1,* Retrieved from http://webjcli.ncl.ac.uk/2008/issue1/pdf/bleasdale1.pdf.

Bloch, A., & Schuster, L. (2005). At the extremes of exclusion: Deportation, detention and dispersal. *Ethnic and Racial Studies, 28*, 491–512.

Blommaert, J., & Verschueren, J. (1998). *Debating diversity: Analysing the discourse of tolerance.* London, UK: Routledge.

Bodossian, K., & Santa Ana, O. (2007). A fleeting moment of balanced U.S. journalistic coverage during today's immigration policy debate. *NACLA: Report on Americas, 40*(6).

Boltanski, L. (1999). *Distance suffering: Politics, morality and the media.* Cambridge, UK: Cambridge University Press.

Bosworth, M., & Guild, M. (2008). Governing through migration control: Security and citizenship in Britain. *British Journal of Criminology, 48*, 703–719.

Boykoff, M. T. (2007). From convergence to contention: United States mass media representations of anthropogenic climate change science. *Transactions of the Institute of British Geographers, 32*, 477–489.

Boyle, P., Halfacree, K., & Robinson, V. (1998). *Exploring contemporary migration.* Harlow, UK: Longman.

Bozinovic, N. (1996). *Women question in Serbia in XIX and XX century.* Belgrade, Serbia: Feministicka 94 & Women in Black.

Brandenburg, B. (2007). Security at the source: Embedding journalists as a superior strategy to military censorship. *Journalism Studies, 8,* 953–963.

Brewer, P. R., & Gross, K. (2010). Studying the effects of framing on public opinion about policy issues. In P. D'Angelo, & J. A. Kuypers, *Doing news framing analysis: Empirical and theoretical perspectives* (pp. 159–186). New York, NY: Routledge.

Bröll, C. (2001, July 5). Mittelständler wirbt für "green card auf Indonesisch", *Frankfurter Allgemeine Zeitung,* p. 19.

Brönnimann, S. (2002). Picturing climate change. *Climate Research, 22,* 87–95.

Brown, W. (2006). *Regulating aversion.* Princeton, NJ. & Oxford, UK: Princeton University Press.

Brownstein, R., & Simon, R. (1993, November 14). Hospitality turns to hostility. California has a long history of welcoming newcomers for their cheap labour—until times turn rough. *Los Angeles Times,* p. A1.

Bruns, M. (2005). Speaking with the sources. Science writers and anthropologists. In E. W. Rothenbuhler & M. Coman (Eds.), *Media anthropology* (pp. 295–300). Thousand Oaks, CA: Sage Publications.

Buchanan, S., Grillo, B., & Threagold, T. (2003). *What's the story? Results from research into media coverage of refugees and asylum seekers in the UK.* London: Article 19 (The Global Campaign for Free Expression).

Buonfino, A. (2004). Between unity and plurality: The politicization and securitization of the discourse of immigration in Europe. *New Political Science, 26,* 23–49.

Bush, G. W. (7 January 2004). *President Bush proposes new temporary worker program.* Remarks by the president on immigration policy, Washington, D.C. Retrieved March 19, 2007 from www.whitehouse.gov/news/releases/2004/01/20040107-3.html

Buzan, B., Wæver, O., & de Wilde, J. (1998). *Security: A new framework for analysis.* Boulder, CO: Lynne Rienner.

Calhoun, C. (2007). *Nations matter: Culture, history, and the cosmopolitan dream.* Abingdon, UK: Routledge.

Calhoun, C. (2008). Cosmopolitanism and nationalism. *Nations and Nationalism, 14,* 427–448.

Calhoun, C. (2010). The idea of emergency: Humanitarian action and global disorder. In D. Fassin, & M. Pandolfi (Eds.), *Contemporary states of emergency.* Cambridge, MA: Zone Books.

Callick, R. (1993). Pacific 2010: A doomsday scenario? In R. V. Cole (Ed.), *Pacific 2010: Challenging the future, Pacific Policy Paper 9* (pp. 1–11). Canberra, Australia: National Centre for Development Studies, Australian National University.

Cameron, D. (2006a). Achieving lasting peace and security, at home and abroad: Speech August 15, 2006. Retrieved January 4 2007, from http://www.conservatives.com/popups/print.cfm?obj_id=131435&type=print

————(2006b, June 26). Balancing freedom and security—A modern British bill of rights. *Conservative Party*. Retrieved from http://www.conservatives.com/News/Speeches/2006/06/Cameron_Balancing_freedom_and_security__A_modern_British_Bill_of_Rights.aspx

Campani, G. (2001). Migrants and media: The Italian case. In R. King, & N. Wood, *Media and migration: Construction of mobility and difference* (pp. 38–52). London, UK: Routledge.

Cantle, T., Kaur, D., Athar, M., Dallison, C., Wiggans, A., & Joshua, H. (2006). *Review of community cohesion in Oldham*. Coventry, UK: Institute of Community Cohesion, Coventry University.

Carvalho, A. (2007). Ideological cultures and media discourses on scientific knowledge: Rereading news on climate change. *Public Understanding of Science, 16*, 223–243.

Castles, S. (2004). Why migration policies fail. *Ethnic and Racial Studies, 27*, 205–227.

Castles, S. & Loughna, S. (2005) Trends in asylum migration to industrialized countries, 1990–2001. In G. L. Borjas & J. Crisp (Eds.), *Poverty, international migration and asylum* (pp. 39–69). Basingstoke, UK: MacMillan Press.

Castles, S., & Miller M. J. (2003) *Age of migration: International population movements in the modern world* (3rd ed). Basingstoke, UK, & New York: Palgrave Macmillan.

Cayford, J. M. (1991) In search of "John Chinaman": Press representation of the Chinese in Cardiff, 1906–1911. *Llafur: Journal of the Society for the Study of Welsh Labour History 5*(4), 37–50.

CBC News. (2009, December 2). *Vancouver fugitive thorny issue in Canada-China relations*. Retrieved July 9, 2010, from http://www.cbc.ca/canada/british-columbia/story/2009/12/02/bc-china-canada-fugitive.html

Ceccagno, A. (2003). New Chinese migrants in Italy. *International Migration, 41*(3), 187–213.

Chambers, A., & Chambers K. S. (2007). Five takes on climate and cultural change in Tuvalu. *The Contemporary Pacific, 19*(1), 294–306.

Chau, R. C. M., & Yu, S. W. K. (2001). Social exclusion of Chinese people in Britain. *Critical Social Policy, 21*, 103–125.

Chebil, M. (2011, April 19). Migrant spat puts strain on EU open borders, *France 24*. Retrieved from http://www.france24.com/en/20110419-tunisia-migrant-train-blockade-comes-under-legal-attack-ventimiglia-french-police-italy

Chin, J. K. (2003). Reducing irregular migration from China. *International Migration, 41*(3), 49–72.

Chin, K. (1999). *Smuggled Chinese: Clandestine immigration to the United States*. Philadelphia, PA: Temple University Press.

Chouliaraki, L. (2004) Watching September 11th: A politics of pity. *Discourse & Society, 15*, 185–198.

————(2010). Post-humanitarianism: Humanitarian communication beyond a politics of pity. *International Journal of Cultural Studies, 13*, 107–126.

————(2011). The theatricality of humanitarianism: A critique of celebrity advocacy. *Communication and Critical/Cultural Studies, 8*, 363–381.

Citizenship and Immigration Canada. (2009). *Facts and figures 2008.* Retrieved November 11, 2009 from http://www.cic.gc.ca/english/resources/statistics/facts2008/permanent/01.asp

Clarke, C. (1998). Counting backwards: The Roma "numbers game" in central and eastern Europe. *Radical Statistics, 69*, 35–46.

Clarke, J. (2008). Still policing the crisis? *Crime, Media, Culture, 4*, 123–129.

Clarke, M. (2000, November 20). With detention centres overflowing, Straw orders jails to find room for asylum seekers. *Daily Mail.*

Clements, L. M. (2007). Asylum in crisis. An assessment of UK Asylum law and policy since 2002: Fear of terrorism or economic efficiency? *Web Journal of Current Legal Issues, 3.* Retrieved from http://webjcli.ncl.ac.uk/2007/issue3/clements3.html

Clifford, J. (2001). Indigenous articulations. *The Contemporary Pacific, 13*(2), 468–490.

Clifford, J., & Marcus, G. E. (Eds.). (1986). *Writing culture: The poetics and politics of ethnography.* Berkeley: University of California Press.

Cohen, R. (2000). The incredible vagueness of being British/English. *International Affairs, 76*(3), 575–582.

————(2006). *Migration and its enemies: Global capital, migrant labour and the nation-state.* Aldershot, Hampshire, UK: Ashgate.

Cohen, S. (2001). *States of denial.* Cambridge, UK: Polity.

Cohen, S. (2003). *No one is illegal: Asylum and immigration control past and present.* London, UK: Trentham Books.

————(2006a). *Deportation is freedom! The Orwellian world of immigration controls.* London, UK, & Philadelphia, PA: Jessica Kingsley Publishers.

————(2006b). *Standing on the shoulders of fascism: From immigration control to the strong state.* Stoke on Trent, UK: Trentham Books.

Cohen, S., Humphries, B., & Mynott, E. (Eds.). (2002). *From immigration controls to welfare controls.* London, UK, & New York, NY: Routledge.

Colley, L. (1992). *Britons: forging the nation 1707–1837.* New Haven, CT: Yale University Press.

Conference of Peripheral Maritime Regons of Europe. (2007, October 18). *Opinion from the CPMR: Managing irregular immigration in the peripheral regions in the European Union.* Retrieved Feburary 24, 2010, from http://www.crpm.org/pub/docs/139_crpmppp070001-en.pdf

Connell, J. (2003). Losing ground? Tuvalu, the greenhouse effect and the garbage can. *Asia Pacific Viewpoint, 44*, 89–107.

Connell, J., & Lea, J. P. (1992). My country will not be there: Global warming, development and the planning response in small island states. *Cities, 9*, 295–309.

Coole, C. (2002). A warm welcome? Scottish and UK media reporting of an asylum-seeker murder. *Media Culture and Society, 24*, 839–852.

Cooper, D. (2007). *Celebrity diplomacy and the G8: Bono and Geldof as legitimate international actors.* Centre for International Governance Innovation, Working Paper No. 29. University of Waterloo, Canada.

Cottle, S. (2009). *Global crisis reporting.* Milton Keynes, UK: Open University Press.

Cottle, S. (2000). Introduction media research and ethnic minorities: Mapping the Field. In S. Cottle (Ed.) *Ethnic minorities in the media: Changing cultural boundaries.* Buckingham, UK, & Philadelphia, PA: Open University Press.

Cottle, S. (Ed.). (2000). *Ethic Minorities and the Media: Changing cultural boundaries.* Buckingham, UK & Philadelphia, PA: Open University Press.

Cottle, S., & Nolan, D. (2007). Global humanitarianism and the changing aid-media field: "Everyone was dying for footage." *Journalism Studies, 8*, 862–878.

Couldry, N. (2009). Does "the media" have a future? *European Journal of Communication, 21*, 437–449.

Council of Europe (2010, December 7). *Committee on the honouring of obligations and commitments by member states of the council of Europe (monitoring committee): Honouring of obligations and commitments by Serbia.* AS/Mon(2010)34rev. Retrieved from http://www.assembly.coe.int/CommitteeDocs/2010/20101217_amondoc34rev_2010.pdf

Crelinsten, R. D. (1998). The discourse and practice of counter-terrorism in liberal democracies. *Australian Journal of Politics & History, 44*, 389–413.

Cunningham, S., & Sinclair, J. (Eds.). (2000). *Floating lives: The media of Asian diasporas.* St Lucia, Australia: Queensland University Press.

Danso, R., & McDonald, D. A. (2001). Writing xenophobia: Immigration and the print media in post-apartheid South Africa. *Africa Today, 48*(3), 115–137.

Dauvergne, C. (2005). *Humanitarianism, identity, and nation: Migration laws in Canada and Australia.* Vancouver, Canada: UBC Press.

———(2007). Security and migration law in the less brave new world. *Social and Legal Studies, 16*, 533–549.

Day, M. (2011, May 14). Flood of north African refugees to Italy ends EU passport-free travel, *The Independent.*

de Waal, A. (2008). The humanitarian carnival: A celebrity vogue. *World Affairs Journal, Fall.* Retrieved from http://www.worldaffairsjournal.org/articles/2008-Fall/full-DeWaal.html

Dening, G. (2008). Respectfulness as a performance art: Way-finding. *Postcolonial Studies, 11*, 145–155.

Department of State (2010). *Trafficking in persons report* (10th ed.). Washington, D.C: Government Printing Office. Retrieved from http://www.state.gov/g/tip/rls/tiprpt/2010/

Derrida, J. (1974). *Of grammatology*. Baltimore, MD, & London, UK: The Johns Hopkins University Press.

Derrida, J. (2001). *On cosmopolitanism and forgiveness*. New York, NY, & London, UK: Routledge.

Di Lellio, A. (2009). The missing revolution in Serbia: 1989–2008. *International Journal of Politics, Culture and Society, 22*, 373–384.

Dieter, H., & Kumar, R. (2008). The downside of celebrity diplomacy: The neglected complexity of development. *Global Governance, 14*, 259–264.

Dietrich, S. (2004, May 25). Unüberbrückbare gegensätze. *Frankfurter Allgemeine Zeitung*, p.1.

Dolan, K. (2006). *Whiteness and news. An ethical inquiry into the construction of "realities"*. Paper presented at the annual meeting of the International Communication Association, Dresden International Congress Centre, Dresden, Germany. Retrieved November 9, 2010 from http://www.allacademic.com/meta/p93194_index.html

Douzinas, C. (2000). *The end of human rights*. Oxford, UK: Hart Publishing.

Downing, J., & Husband, C. (2005). *Representing "race". Racisms, ethnicities and media*. London, UK: Sage.

Doyle, J. (2007). Picturing the clima(c)tic: Greenpeace and the representational politics of climate change communication. *Science as Culture, 16*, 129–150.

Durham, M. G., & Kellner, D. M. (Eds.) (2001). *Media and cultural studies: Key works*. Malden, MA, & London, UK: Blackwell Publishing.

Economist (2011, April 11). The next European crisis: Boat people, *Economist*. Retrieved from http://www.economist.com/blogs/charlemagne/2011/04/north_african_migration

Edwards, M. J. (1999). Security implications of a worst-case scenario of climate change in the south-west Pacific. *Australian Geographer, 30*, 311–330.

Ejdus F. (2007). Security, strategic culture and identity in Serbia. *Western Balkans Security Observer 7*, 38–64.

EMAJ (2009). *Euro-Mediterranean academy for young journalists*. Retrieved from http://www.goethe.de/ins/nl/ams/prj/ema/enindex.htm

Entman, R. M. (1997). African Americans according to TV news. In E. E. Dennis & E. C. Pease (Eds.), *The media in black and white* (pp. 29–36). London, UK: Transaction.

Ericson, R. V., Baranek, P. M., & Chan, J. B. (1987). *Visualizing deviance: A study of news organisations*. Milton Keynes, UK: Open University Press.

————(1989). *Negotiating control: A study of news sources*. Milton Keynes, UK: Open University Press.

Ess, C. (2009). *Digital media ethics*. Cambridge, UK, and Malden, MA: Polity.

Euler, R., & Schwan, H. (2002, January 27). Zuwanderung besser steuern. Interview mit Minister Bouffier zur Ausländerpolitik. *Frankfurter Allgemeine Zeitung*, Rhein-Main Titelseite, p. R1.

Fabian, J. (1983). *Time and the other. How anthropology makes its object*. New York, NY: Columbia University Press.

Fairclough, N., & Wodak, R. (1997). Critical discourse analysis. In T. A. van Dijk (Ed.) *Discourse as social interaction–discourse studies: A multidisciplinary introduction, Volume 2* (pp. 258–284). London, UK: Sage.

Farbotko, C. (2005). Tuvalu and climate change: Constructions of environmental displacement in the *Sydney Morning Herald*. *Geografiska Annaler Series B-Human Geography, 87B*, 279–293.

————(2008). *Representing climate change space: Islographs of Tuvalu* (PhD thesis). University of Tasmania, Hobart, Australia.

————(2010a). "The global warming clock is ticking so see these places while you can": Voyeuristic tourism and model environmental citizens on Tuvalu's disappearing islands. *Singapore Journal of Tropical Geography, 31*, 224–238.

————(2010b). Wishful sinking: Disappearing islands, climate refugees and cosmopolitan experimentation. *Asia Pacific Viewpoint, 51*, 47–60.

Farbotko, C., & McGregor, H. V. (2010). Copenhagen, climate science and the emotional geographies of climate change. *Australian Geographer, 41*, 159–166.

Fariclough N. (1995). *Critical discourse analysis*. Harlow, UK: Longman Group.

Fekete, L. (2004). Anti-Muslim racism and the European security state. *Race & Class, 46*(1), 3–29.

————(2005). The deportation machine: Europe, asylum and human rights. *Race & Class, 47*(1), 64–78.

Fernández, C., & Pedroza, L. R. (1982). The border patrol and news media coverage of undocumented Mexican immigration during the 70s: A content analysis in the sociology of knowledge. *California Sociologist, 5*(2), 1–26.

Fife, R. (1999a, April 7). Airlift of refugees causing a rift in NATO alliance: Relocation is politically sensitive in much of Europe. *National Post*, p. A12.

————(1999b, July 3). Yugoslav, Serb officials barred from Canada: CSIS, Immigration asked to watch for attempted entries. *National Post*, p. A4.

Finney, B. (1994). The other one-third of the globe. *Journal of World History, 5*, 273–297.

————(2003). *Sailing in the wake of the ancestors: Reviving Polynesian voyaging*. Honolulu, HI: Bishop Museum Press.

————(1979). *Hokule'a: the way to Tahiti*. New York, NY: Dodd, Mead and Company.

Fleras, A. (2006). The conventional news paradigm as systemic bias. In R. Geißler & H. Pöttker (Eds.) *Integration durch massenmedien. Medien und migration im internationalen Vergleich* (pp.179–222). Bielefeld, Germany: transcript.

Flores, L. A. (2003). Constructing rhetorical borders: Peons, illegal aliens, and competing narratives of immigration. *Critical Studies in Media Communication, 20*, 362–387.

Fortier, A-M. (2005). Pride politics and multiculturalist citizenship. *Ethnic and Racial Studies, 28*, 559–578.

Foucault, M. (1980). *Power/Knowledge: Selected interviews and other writings 1972–1977* (C. Gordon, Ed. and Trans.). New York, NY: Pantheon Books.

Fowler, R. (1991). *Language in the news: Discourses and ideology in the press*. London, UK: Routledge.

Fry, G. (1997). Framing the islands: Knowledge and power in changing Australian images of "the South Pacific". *The Contemporary Pacific, 9*, 305–344.

Gale, P. (2004). The refugee crisis and fear—populist politics and media discourse. *Journal of Sociology, 40*, 321–340.

Galtung, J., & Ruge, M. (1973). Structuring and selecting news. In S. Cohen & J. Young (Eds.), *The manufacture of news: Deviances, social problems and the mass media* (pp. 52–63). London, UK: Constable.

Gamson, W., & Modigliani, A. (1987). The changing culture of affirmative action. In R. Braungart, *Research in political sociology vol.3* (pp. 137–177). Greenwich, CT: JAI Press.

Gardiner, A. (Programme Editor). (2010, April 15). *The first prime ministerial debate* [Television broadcast]. London, UK: ITV. Transcript retrieved from http://news.bbc.co.uk/1/shared/bsp/hi/pdfs/16_04_10_firstdebate.pdf

Gellner, E. (1983). *Nations and nationalism*. Ithaca, NY: Cornell University Press.

German Research Foundation. (2002). Media Integration of Ethnic Minorities Research Project. Retrieved from http://www.integration-und-medien.de

Giddens, A. (1987). *The nation and violence: Volume 1 of a contemporary critique of historical materialism*. Berkeley: University of California Press.

Gillespie, M. (1995). *Television, ethnicity and cultural change*. London, UK: Routledge.

Gilroy, P. (2004). *After empire. Melancholia or convivial culture?* London, UK: Routledge.

————(2006). Colonial crimes and convivial cultures. In K. Aktion (Ed.) *Rethinking Nordic colonialism: A postcolonial project in five acts*. Nordic Institute for Contemporary Art. Retrieved November 1, 2008 from www.rethinking-nordic-colonialism.org

Global Commission on International Migration. (2005, October). *Migration in an interconnected world: New directions for action.* Retrieved July 15, 2010, from http://www.gcim.org/attachements/gcim-complete-report-2005.pdf

Glover, S., Gott, C., Loizillon, A., Portes, J., Price, R., Spencer, S., Srinivasan, V., & Willis, C. (2001). *Migration: An economic and social analysis.* RDS Occasional Paper No. 67. London, UK: Home Office.

Goffman, E. (1981). *Forms of talk.* Philadelphia: University of Pennsylvania Press.

Goldsmith, M., & Munro D. (2002). *The accidental missionary: Tales of Elekana.* Christchurch, New Zealand: Macmillan Brown Centre for Pacific Studies University of Canterbury.

Goodhart, D. (2006). *Progressive nationalism.* London, UK: Demos.

Greene, G. (1971). *A sort of life.* London, UK: Penguin Books.

Grice, A. (2000, April 18). Straw ready to force Kosovars back home. *The Independent.*

Griswold de Castillo, R. (1990). *The treaty of Guadalupe Hidalgo: A legacy of conflict.* Norman, OK: University of Oklahoma Press.

Gross, B., Moore, K., & Threadgold, T. (2007). Broadcast news coverage of asylum April to October 2006: Caught between human rights and public safety. Cardiff: Cardiff School of Journalism, Media and Cultural Studies. Retrieved from http://www.cardiff.ac.uk/jomec/resources/BroadcastNewsCoverageofAsylum.pdf

Gullestad, M. (2005). Normalising racial boundaries. The Norwegian dispute about the term *Neger. Social Anthropology, 13,* 27–46.

Guo, Z.-J., Chen, J., Xie, P., Zhang, D.-D., & Lin, A-W. (2009). *2008 World Chinese entrepreneurs development report.* Beijing, China: China News Service.

Gutiérrez, D. G. (1995). *Walls & mirrors: Mexican Americans, Mexican immigrants, and the politics of ethnicity.* Berkeley: University of California Press.

Gutiérrez, F. (1987, June 15). California newspaper coverage of undocumented workers. Paper presented to the California State Advisory Committee to the U.S. Commission on Civil Rights in Los Angeles, CA.

Haberkorn, G. (1981). The migration decision-making process: some social-psychological considerations. In G. F. De Jong & R. W. Gardner (Eds.), *Migration decision making process: Multidisciplinary approaches to microlevel studies in developed and developing countries* (pp. 252–280). New York, NY: Pergamon Press.

Hafez, K. (2007). *The myth of media globalization.* Cambridge, UK: Polity Press.

Hage, G. (2003). *Against paranoid nationalism: Searching for hope in a shrinking society.* London, UK: The Merlin Press.

Hague, W. (2000). Common sense on asylum seekers. London, UK: Conservative Party.

————(2001). Conservative party election manifesto 2002: Time for common sense. London, UK: Conservative Party.

Hall, E. T. (1969). *The hidden dimension.* Garden City, NY: Doubleday.

Hall, S. (1990). Cultural identity and diaspora. In J. Rutherford (Ed.), *Identity: Community, culture, difference.* London, UK: Lawrence & Wishart.

————(1997). *Representation: Cultural representations and signifying practices.* London, UK: Sage in association with the Open University.

Hall, S., Critcher, C., Jefferson, T., Clarke, J., & Roberts, B. (1978). *Policing the crisis. Mugging, the state, law and order.* New York, NY: Palgrave Macmillan.

Halliday, M. A. K. (1978). *Language as social semiotic.* London, UK: Edward Arnold.

————(1985). *Introduction to functional grammar.* London, UK: Edward Arnold.

Hamood, S. (2008). EU-Libya cooperation on migration: A raw deal for refugees and migrants? *Journal of Refugee Studies, 21,* 19–42.

Harding, A. (2011). Condition of Somali refugees in Kenya worsening, *BBC News.* Retrieved from http://www.bbc.co.uk/news/world-africa-14356198

Hargreaves, I., & Thomas, J. (2002). *New news, old news: An ITC and BSC research publication.* London, UK: Independent Television Commission.

Harris, P. (2011, July 10). Jose Vargas joins fight for immigration reform after he admits: I am an illegal alien, *Guardian.* Retrieved from http://www.guardian.co.uk/world/2011/jul/10/illegal-us-journalist-jose-vargas

Hartley, J. (1982). *Understanding news.* London, UK: Routledge.

Hartmann, P., & Husband, C. (1974). *Racism and the mass media: A study of the role of mass media in the formation of white beliefs and attitudes in Britain.* London, UK: Davis-Poynter.

Hau'ofa, E. (1993). Our sea of islands. In E. Waddell, V. Naidu, & E. Hau'ofa (Eds.), *A new Oceania: Rediscovering our sea of islands* (pp. 2–18). Suva, Fiji: School of Social and Economic Development, University of the South Pacific in association with Beake House.

————(1998). The ocean in us. *The Contemporary Pacific, 10*(2), 391–410.

Hay, C. (1996). Narrating crisis: The discursive construction of the winter of discontent. *Sociology, 30*(2), 253–77.

————(2007). *Why we hate politics.* Cambridge, UK: Polity

Hegel, G.W.F. (2005). *Phänomenologie des geistes,* Paderborn, Germany: Voltmedia. (Original work published 1807)

Henry, R., & Jeffery, W. (2008). Waterworld: The heritage dimensions of "climate change" in the Pacific. *Historic Environment, 21,* 12–18.

Hier, S. P., & Greenberg, J. L. (2002). Constructing a discursive crisis: Risk problematization and illegal Chinese in Canada. *Ethnic and Racial Studies, 25*, 490–513.

Higham, J. (1955). *Strangers in the land: Patterns of American nativism, 1860–1925*. New Brunswick, NJ: Rutgers University Press.

HMSO. (1998). *Faster, fairer, firmer: A modern approach to immigration and asylum*. London, UK: HMSO. Retrieved from http://www.archive.official-documents.co.uk/document/cm40/4018/4018.htm

Hobsbawm, E. (1983). Introduction: Inventing traditions. In E. Hobsbawm & T. Ranger (Eds.) *The invention of tradition* (pp.1–15). Cambridge, UK: Cambridge University Press.

————(1990). *Nations and nationalism since 1780: Programme, myth, reality* (2nd ed.). Cambridge, UK: Cambridge University Press.

Hoffman, A. (1974). *Unwanted Mexican Americans in the Great Depression: Repatriation pressures, 1929–1939*. Tucson: University of Arizona Press.

Hoffmann, E., & Lawrence, S. (1996). *Statistics on international labour migration: A review of sources and methodological issues*. Geneva, Switzerland: International Labour Office.

Hofstede, G. (2001). *Culture's consequences. Comparing values, behaviors, institutions, and organizations across nations* (2nd ed.). Thousand Oaks, CA: Sage Publications.

Hofstede, G., & Hofstede, G. J. (2009). *Lokales denken, globales handeln. Interkulturelle zusammenarbeit und globales management*. München, Germany: Beck Verlag.

Holmes, C. (1988). *John Bull's island: Immigration and British society, 1871–1971*. Basingstoke, UK: MacMillan Press.

Home Affairs Committee. (1985). *Chinese community in Britain: Second report from the Home Affairs Committee, session 1984–5, volume 1*. London: HMSO.

Home Office. (2007). *Enforcing the rules: A strategy to ensure and enforce compliance with our immigration laws*. Retrieved from http://www.ukba.homeoffice.gov.uk/sitecontent/documents/managingourborders/enforcementstrategy.pdf?view=Binary

Honig, B. (2001). *Democracy and the foreigner*. Princeton, NJ: Princeton University Press.

Hopgood S. (2008). Saying "no" to Wal-Mart? Money and morality in professional humanitarianism? In N. M. Barnett & T. G. Weiss (Eds.), *Humanitarianism in question: Politics, power, ethics* (pp. 98–123). Ithaca, NY: Cornell University Press.

Howard, M. (2004, September 22). Full text: Howard's speech. *BBC News*. Retrieved from http://news.bbc.co.uk/1/hi/uk_politics/3679618.stm

Howe, K. R. (Ed.). (2006). *Vaka moana: Voyages of the ancestors*. Auckland, New Zealand: David Bateman Ltd.

Hulme, M. (2009). *Why we disagree about climate change: Understanding controversy, inaction and opportunity*. Cambridge, UK: Cambridge University Press.

Huntington, S. (1996). *The clash of civilizations and the remaking of the world order.* New York, NY: Simon and Schuster.

Hurrelmann, A. (2007). Multilevel legitimacy: Conceptualizing legitimacy relationships between the EU and national democracies. In J. DeBardeleben & A. Hurrelmann (Eds.), *Democratic dilemmas of multilevel governance.* Basingstoke, UK: Palgrave Macmillan.

Hurrelmann A., Schneider, S., & Steffek, J. (Eds.) (2007). *Legitimacy in an age of global politics.* Basingstoke, UK: Palgrave Macmillan.

Hurrelmann, A., Leibfried, S., Martens, K., & Mayer, P. (2007). Transforming the golden-age nation: A framework for analysis. In A. Hurrelmann, S. Leibfried, K. Martens, & P. Mayer (Eds.), *Transforming the golden-age nation* (pp. 1–23). Basingstoke, UK: Palgrave Macmillan.

Husband, C. (2000). Media and the public sphere in multi-ethnic societies. In S. Cottle (Ed.) *Ethnic minorities in the media.* Buckingham, UK, & Philadelphia, PA: Open University Press.

Hussain, M. (2002). 4.2 Denmark. In J. ter Wal (Ed.) *Racism and cultural diversity in the mass media. An overview of research and examples of good practice in the EU Member States, 1995–2000.* Vienna, Austria: European Monitoring Centre on Racism and Xenophobia.

Huysmans, J. (2000). The European Union and the securitization of migration. *Journal of Common Market Studies, 38,* 751–777.

————(2006). *The politics of insecurity: Fear, migration and asylum in the EU.* London, UK, & New York, NY: Routledge.

Huysmans, J., & Buonfino, A. (2008). Politics of exception and unease: Immigration, asylum and terrorism in parliamentary debates in the UK. *Political Studies, 56,* 766–788.

Hyndman, J. (2000). *Managing displacement: Refugees and the politics of humanitarianism.* University of Minnesota Press.

ICAR (2004). *Media image, community impact: Assessing the impact of media and political images of refugees and asylum seekers on community relations in London.* London: Information Centre about Asylum and Refugees in the UK.

ICAR (2008). FAQs—the politics. Retrieved July 26, 2009, from http://www.icar.webbler.co.uk/11543/faqs/frequently-asked-questions.html

Illouz, E. (2003). *Oprah Winfrey and the glamour of misery: An essay on popular culture.* New York, NY: Columbia University Press.

Immigration Legislative Review Advisory Group. (1997). *Not just numbers: A Canadian framework for future immigration.* Ottawa: Ministry of Public Works & Government Services Canada.

Information Office (2010, February 23). Chinese Emigration Since 2000. [Interview by X. Zeng].

International Organization for Migration. (2000) *World migration report 2000.* Geneva, Switzerland: International Organization for Migration.

————(2002). *Recent trends in Chinese migration to Europe: Fujianese migration in perspective.* Geneva, Switzerland: International Organization for Migration.

Irish Times. (2011, April 20). Migrants "suffered badly" on boat from Tripoli, *Irish Times.*

Isako, T. (1983). Nanumea. In H. Laracy (Ed.), *Tuvalu: A history* (pp. 48–57). Suva, Fiji: Institute of Pacific Studies.

Jacobi, R. (2003, July 7). Grün ist die hoffnung. *Süddeutsche Zeitung.* Nachrichten, p. 1.

Jacobson, R. D. (2008). *The new nativism: Proposition 187 and the debate over immigration.* Minneapolis: University of Minnesota Press.

Jamieson, A. (2011). Wave of "Arab spring" refugees heading for Britain, *Daily Telegraph.* Retrieved from http://www.telegraph.co.uk/news/uknews/immigration/8528121/Wave-of-Arab-spring-refugees-heading-for-Britain.html

Jensen, T. (2006). Religion in the newsrooms. In J. Sumiala-Seppánen, K. Lundby & R. Salokangas (Eds.) *Implications of the sacred in (post)modern media.* Gothenberg, Sweden: Nordicom.

Jerichow, A., & Rode, M. (Eds.) (2006). *Profet-affæren—om 12 Muhammed-tegninger og hvad siden hændte. Dokumenter og argumenter.* Copenhagen, Denmark: Dansk PEN.

Jewitt, C., & Oyama, R. (2001). Social semiotics of visual meaning. In T. van Leeuwen & C. Jewitt (Eds.), *Handbook of visual analysis* (pp. 134–156). London, UK, and New Delhi, India: Sage Publications.

Jiang, X. (2006). *Fujianese migration on the margin: A study of migration culture through history, media representation and ethnography.* (Unpublished doctoral dissertation). Cardiff, UK: Cardiff University.

————(2009). The virtual SARS epidemic in Europe 2002–2003 and its effects on European Chinese. *Health, Risk and Society, 11*, 241–256.

Jiang, X., Elam, G., Yuen, C., Voeten, H., de Zwart, O., Veldhuijzen, I., & Brug, B. (2009). The perceived threat of SARS and its impact on precautionary actions and adverse consequences: A qualitative study among Chinese communities in the United Kingdom and the Netherlands. *International Journal of Behavioral Medicine, 16*, 58–67.

Jolly, M. (2001). On the edge? Deserts, oceans, islands. *The Contemporary Pacific, 13*, 417–466.

Jordan, B., & Brown, P. (2006). The Sangatte work-visa holders: A "natural experiment" in immigration policy. *Parliamentary Affairs, 59*, 509–521.

Jung, M., Niehr, T., & Böke, K. (2000). *Ausländer und migranten im spiegel der presse. Ein diskurshistorisches wörterbuch zur einwanderung seit 1945.* Wiesbaden, Germany: Westdeutscher Verlag.

Jusic, T., Moranjak-Bamburac, N., & Isanovic, A. (Eds.) (2006). *Stereotyping: Representation of women in print media in South East Europe.* Sarajevo, Bosnia and Herzegovina: Mediacentar.

Karim, K. H. (2004). Making sense of the "Islamic peril": Journalism as cultural practice. In B. Zelizer & S. Allan (Eds.), *Journalism after September 11* (pp. 101–116). London, UK: Routledge.

Kastrup, M. (2008, July 14). Det er langt fra o verstate. *Fyns Amts Avis*, p. 9.

Kaye, R. (1998). UK media portrayal of asylum seekers. In K. Koser & H. Lutz (Eds.), *The new migration in Europe: Social constructions and social realities*. Basingstoke, UK: Macmillan.

———(2001). Blaming the victim: An analysis of press representations of refugees and asylum seekers. In R. King & N. Wood (Eds.), *Media and migration: Constructions of mobility and difference* (pp.53–70). London, UK: Routledge.

Kennedy, D. G. (1929). Field notes on the culture of Vaitupu, Ellice Islands. *The Journal of the Polynesian Society, 38*, 1–99.

King, B. (2006). Articulating stardom. In P. D. Marshall (Ed). *The celebrity culture reader* (pp. 229–251). London, UK: Sage. (Original work published 1985)

King, R., & Wood, N. (2001). Media and migration: An overview. In R. King & N. Wood (Eds.), *Media and migration: Constructions of mobility and difference* (pp. 1–22). London, UK: Routledge.

Klausen, J. (2009). *The cartoons that shook the world*. New Haven, CT: Yale University Press.

Klepp, S. (2010). A Contested asylum aystem: The European Union between refugee protection and border control in the Mediterranean Sea. *European Journal of Migration and Law 12*, 1–21.

Koser, K. (2005, September). *Irregular migration, state security and human security*. Retrieved July 15, 2010, from http://www.gcim.org/attachements/TP5.pdf

Kostovicova D. (2008). Legitimacy and international administration: The Ahtisaari settlement for Kosovo from a human security perspective. *International Peacekeeping 15*, 631–647.

Kraler, A. (2009). *Regularisation: A misguided option for or part and parcel of a comprehensive policy response to irregular migration*. IMISCOE Working Paper No. 24. Austria: IMISCOE.

Kraler, A., Reichel, D., & Hollomey, D. (2008). *Counting the uncountable. Data and trends across Europe —Austria report*. Clandestino project. Retrieved from http://research.icmpd.org/fileadmin/Research-Website/Startseite/Clandestino/clandestino_report_austria_final_2_1_.pdf

Kronja I. (2004). Turbo folk and dance music in 1990s Serbia: Media, ideology and the production of spectacle. *The Anthropology of East Europe Review, 22*(1), 103–114.

———(2006). Politics as porn: The pornographic representation of women in Serbian tabloids and its role in politics. In T. Jusic, N. Moranjak-Bamburac & A. Isanovic (Eds.), *Stereotyping: Representation of women in print media in South East Europe* (pp. 187–216). Sarajevo, Bosnia and Herzegovina: Mediacentar.

Kumar, K. (2010). Negotiating English identity: Englishness, Britishness and the future of the United Kingdom. *Nations and Nationalism, 16*, 469–487.

Kwong, P. (1997). *Forbidden workers: Illegal Chinese immigrants and American labour*. New York, NY: The New Press.

Kyambi, S. (2005). *Beyond black and white: Mapping new immigrant communities*. London: IPPR.

Kyselka, W. (1987). *An ocean in mind.* Honolulu: University of Hawaii Press.

Laclau E. (1990). *New reflections on the revolution of our time.* London, UK, & New York, NY: Verso.

————(2000). Foreword. In D. Howarth, A.J. Norval & J. Starvakakis (Eds.), *Discourse theory and political analysis* (p. xi). New York, NY: Manchester University Press.

————(1996a). Subject of politics, politics of the subject. In E. Laclau (Ed.), *Emancipation(s)* (pp. 47–65). London, UK, & New York, NY: Verso.

————(1996b). Why do empty signifiers matter to politics? In E. Laclau (Ed.), *Emancipation(s)* (pp. 36–46). London, UK, & New York, NY: Verso.

————(2000a). Constructing universality. In J. Butler, E. Laclau & S. Žižek (Eds.), *Contingency, hegemony, universality: Contemporary dialogues on the left* (pp. 281–307). London, UK, & New York, NY: Verso.

————(2000b). Identity and hegemony: The role of universality in the constitution of political logics. In J. Butler, E. Laclau & S. Žižek (Eds.), *Contingency, hegemony, universality: Contemporary dialogues on the left* (pp. 44–89). London, UK, & New York, NY: Verso.

————(2000c). Structure, history and the political. In J. Butler, E. Laclau & S. Žižek (Eds.), *Contingency, hegemony, universality: Contemporary dialogues on the left* (pp. 182–212). London, UK, & New York, NY: Verso.

————(2002). Ethics, politics and radical democracy: A response to Simon Critchley. *Culture Machine, 4.*

Laclau, E., & Mouffe, C. (1985). *Hegemony and socialist strategy: Towards a radical democratic politics.* London, UK, & New York, NY: Verso.

Laczko, F. (2003, July). *Europe attracts more migrants from China.* Retrieved July 2, 2010, from http://www.migrationinformation.org/feature/display.cfm?ID=144

————(Ed.) (2003). Understanding migration between China and Europe. *International Migration. 41*(3), Special Issue.

Lakoff, G. (1993). The contemporary theory of metaphor. In A. Ortony (Ed.), *Metaphor and thought* (2nd ed.) (pp. 202–251). Cambridge, UK: Cambridge University Press.

Lakoff, G., & Johnson, M. (1999). *Philosophy in the flesh: The embodied mind and its challenge to Western thought.* New York, NY: Basic Books

Lakoff, G., & Turner, M. (1989). *More than cool reason: A field guide to poetic metaphor.* Chicago, IL: Chicago University Press.

Landy, K. M. (2001, July 12). Scale up the war against terrorism. *National Post,* p. A19.

Langberg, D. R. (2010). *Human trafficking in the 21st Century.* Washington DC: Project for National Security Reform. Retrieved from http://www.pnsr.org/web/page/662/sectionid/579/pagelevel/3/interior.asp

Lawrence, F., Pai, H.-H., Dodd, V., Carter, H., Ward, D., & Watts, J. (2004, February 7). Victims of the sands and the snakeheads. *The Guardian*, p. 3.

Lazrus, H. (2009). Perspectives on vulnerability to climate change and migration in Tuvalu. Source: Studies of the University: Research, Counsel, Education. Bonn, UNU Institute for Environment and Human Security (UNU-EHS).

Lefebvre, H. (1991). *The production of space* (D. Nicholson-Smith, Trans.). Oxford, UK: Blackwell. (Original work published 1974)

————(2003 [1978]). Space and the state. In N. Brenner, B. Jessop, M. Jones & G. MacLeod (Eds.), *State/space: A reader* (pp. 84–100). Malden, MA: Blackwell.

Lemke, T. (2001). The birth of bio-politics: Michael Foucault's lectures at the College de France on neo-liberal governmentality. *Economy and Society, 30*, 190–207.

Lewis, D. (1972). *We, the navigators: The ancient art of landfinding in the Pacific*. Canberra, Australia: Australian National University Press.

Lewis, J., Brookes, R., Mosdell, N., & Threadgold, T. (2006). *Shoot first and ask questions later: Media coverage of the 2003 Iraq War*. New York, NY: Peter Lang.

Li, X. (2007). An overview of overseas Chinese. In Z. Li & Y. Wang, *Annual report on international politics and security* (pp. 195–213). Beijing, China: Social Sciences Academy Press.

Lifuka, N., & Koch, K-F. (1978). *Logs in the current of the sea: Neli Lifuka's story of Kioa and the Vaitupu colonists*. Canberra, Australia: Australian National University Press.

Lilomaiava-Doktor, S. (2009). Beyond "migration": Samoan population movement (Malaga) and the geography of social space (Va). *Contemporary Pacific, 21*, 1–32.

Limanowska, B. (2005). *Trafficking in human beings in South Eastern Europe*. Sarajevo, Bosnia and Herzegovina & Warsaw, Poland: UNDP. Retrieved from http://www.unicef.org/ceecis/Trafficking.Report.2005.pdf

Lin, S. (2002). A study on generation mechanism for irregular migration: A case study of Fujian migrants. *Youth Studies, 10*, 8–18.

Linder, A. (2007). *Diversity mainstreaming in der westlichen medienlandschaft*. Retrieved December 28, 2009 from http://www.andreaslinder.de/index.html?/wissenschaft.html

Lipmann, W. (1922). *Public opinion*. San Diego, CA: Harcourt Brace & Company.

Littler, J. (2008). "I feel your pain": Cosmopolitan charity and the public fashioning of celebrity soul. *Social Semiotics, 18*, 237–251.

Lobban, W. D. (1984). *Tafaoga usuusu a tamaliki Tuvalu: A collection of children's singing games from Tuvalu*. Tuvalu: USP Centre.

Lohrmann, R. (2000). Migrants, refugees and insecurity. Current threats to peace? *International Migration, 38*(4), 3–22.

Los Angeles Police Department (9 October 2007). *An examination of May Day 2007 MacArthur Park*. Report to the Board of Commissioners. Los Angeles: Los Angeles Police Department.

Lui, R. (2002). Governing refugees 1919–1945. *Borderlands e-journal*, *1*, Retrieved from http://www.borderlands.net.au/vol1no1_2002/lui_governing.html

Lynn, N., & Lea, S. (2003). "A phantom menace and the new apartheid": The social construction of asylum-seekers in the United Kingdom. *Discourse and Society, 14*, 425–452.

Machin, D. & Mayr, A. (2007). Antiracism in the British government's model regional newspaper: the "talking cure". *Discourse and Society, 8*, 453–478.

Mahtani, M. (2001). Representing minorities: Canadian media and minority identities. *Canadian Ethnic Studies, 33*(3), 99–133.

Mai, N. (2005). The Albanian diaspora-in-the-making: Media, migration and social exclusion. *Journal of Ethnic and Migration Studies, 31*, 543–561.

Malkki, L. (1992). National geographic: The rooting of peoples and the territorialization of national identity among scholars and refugees. *Cultural Anthropology, 7*, 24–44.

———(1995). Refugees and exile: From "refugee studies" to the national order of things. *Annual Review of Anthropology, 24*, 495–523.

———(1996). Speechless emissaries: Refugees, humanitarianism, and dehistoricization. *Cultural Anthropology, 11*, 377–404.

Mancini, P. (2005). Is there a European model of journalism? In H. de Burgh (Ed.). *Making journalists* (pp. 77–93). London, UK: Routledge.

Manning, P. (2001). *News and news sources: A critical introduction*. London, UK: Sage.

Marcuse, H. (1964). *One-dimensional man: Studies in the ideology of advanced industrial society*. Boston, MA: Beacon Press.

Marks, M. P., & Fischer Z. M. (2002). The king's new bodies: Simulating consent in the age of celebrity. *New Political Science, 24*, 371–394.

Martin, L., & Veness, P. (2011, July 31). Govt to send first boat-load to Malaysia, *Sydney Morning Herald*. Retrieved from http://news.smh.com.au/breaking-news-national/govt-to-send-first-boatload-to-malaysia-20110731-1i60x.html

Martin, P., & Miller, M. (2000). Smuggling and trafficking: A conference report. *International Migration Review, 34*, 969–975.

Marx, K. (2001). Das Kapital: Kritik der politischen ökonomie. Erstes buch, der produktionsprozeß des kapitals. In K. Marx & F. Engles (Eds.), *Werke No. 23* (20th ed.). Berlin, Germany: Karl Dietz Verlag. (Original work published 1867)

Marx, K., & Friedrich E. (1953). *Die Deutsche ideologie*, Berlin, Germany: Dietz Verlag.

Mason, P. (2007). Misinformation, myth and distortion: How the press construct imprisonment in Britain. *Journalism Studies*, *8*, 481–496.

Masquelier, A. (2006). Why Katrina's victims aren't refugees: Musings on a "dirty" word. *American Anthropologist*, *108*, 735–743.

May, J. P. (1978). The Chinese in Britain 1960–1914. In C. Holmes (Ed.), *Immigrants and minorities in British society* (pp. 111–124). London, UK: Allen & Unwin.

McAndrew, J. (Executive producer). (2010, April 22). *The second prime ministerial debate* [Television broadcast]. Bristol, UK: British Sky Broadcasting. Transcript retrieved from http://news.bbc.co.uk/1/shared/bsp/hi/pdfs/23_04_10_seconddebate.pdf

McCarthy, T. (1990). Private irony and public decency: Richard Rorty's new pragmatism. *Critical Inquiry*, *16*, 355–370.

McDougall, D. (2006, November 26). Now charity staff hit at cult of celebrity. *Observer*, p. 38.

McIntyre, A. (2006). *After virtue*. London, UK: Duckworth. (Original work published 1981)

McKay, F. H., Thomas, S. L., & Warwick Blood, R. (2011). "Any one of these boat people could be a terrorist for all we know!" Media representations and public perceptions of "boat people" arrivals in Australia. *Journalism*, *12*(5), 607–626.

McLeod, D., & Detenber, B. H. (1999). Framing effects of television news coverage of social protest. *Journal of Communication*, *49*, 3–23.

McNamara, K. E. (2006). The politics of "environmental refugee" protection at the United Nations (Unpublished doctoral dissertation). University of New South Wales, Australia.

McNamara, K. E., & C. Gibson. (2009). "We do not want to leave our land": Pacific ambassadors at the United Nations resist the category of "climate refugees". *Geoforum*, 40, 475–483.

McNevin, A. (2006). Political belonging in a neoliberal era: The struggle of the Sans-papiers. *Citizenship Studies*, *10*, 135–151.

McQuail, D. (1987). *Introduction to mass communication theory* (2nd ed.). London, UK: Sage.

Meier-Braun, K.-H. (2002). *Deutschland, einwanderungsland*. Frankfurt am Main, Germany: Surkamp.

Merrill, J. C. (1989). *The dialectic in journalism: Towards a responsible use of press freedom*. Baton Rouge: Louisiana State University Press.

Migrants' Rights Network & MigrationWork. (2009). *Irregular migrants: The urgent need for a new approach*. London, UK: City Parochial Foundation. Retrieved July 15, 2010, from http://www.migrantsrights.org.uk/downloads/policy_reports/irregularmigrants_fullbooklet.pdf

Miller, D., Kitzinger, J., Williams, K., & Beharrell, P. (1998). *The Circuit of Mass Communication: Media Strategies, Representation and Audience Reception in the AIDS Crisis. Glasgow Media Group*. London, UK: Sage.

Miller, D. (2001). Nationalities in divided societies. In J. Tully & A.-G. Gagnon (Eds.), *Multinational democracies* (pp. 299–318). Cambridge, UK: Cambridge University Press.

Miller, D. (2003). *Tell me lies: Propaganda and media distortion in the attack on Iraq.* London, UK: Pluto Press.

Milosavljevic, M. (2002, December 19) *Reformists against sexists.* Belgrade, Serbia: *NIN.* Retrieved from http://www.nin.co.rs/2002-12/19/26462.html

Ministere Des Affaires Etrangeres. (1989). *Documents diplomatique. Correspondance concernant les actes de violences et de brigandages des Albanais dans la Vieille Serbie (Vilayet du Kossovo) 1898–1899.* Belgrade, Serbia: Državna štamparija.

Mirkinson, J. (2011, June 22). Jose Antonio Vargas: I am an undocumented immigrant [Video file], *The Huffington Post.* Retrieved from http://www.huffingtonpost.com/2011/06/22/jose-antonio-vargas-undocumented-immigrant_n_882012.html

Modood, T. (2007). *Multiculturalism.* Cambridge, UK: Polity Press.

Mollard, C. (2001). *Asylum: The truth behind the headlines.* Oxford, UK: Oxfam.

Moore, K. (2010). *A cultural study of asylum under New Labour.* (Unpublished doctoral dissertation). Cardiff University School of Journalism, Media and Cultural Studies, Cardiff.

Morley, D. (2000). *Home territories: Media, mobility and identity.* London, UK: Routledge.

Market and Opinion Research International (MORI). (2002). *Attitudes towards asylum seekers for "refugee week".* Retrieved from http://www.mori.com/polls/2002/refugees.html

Morris, N. (2004, August 24). Tories push to scrap Human Rights Act. *Independent.* Retrieved from http://www.independent.co.uk/news/uk/politics/tories-push-to-scrap-human-rights-act-557638.html

Mortreux, C., & Barnett, J. (2009). Climate change, migration and adaptation in Funafuti, Tuvalu. *Global Environmental Change-Human and Policy Dimensions, 19,* 105–112.

Moses, J. W. (2006). *International migration: Globalisation's last frontier.* London, UK, & New York, NY: Zed Books.

Muhlmann, G. (2008). *A political history of journalism.* Cambridge, UK: Polity Press.

Muir, A. R. (1987). *A women's guide to jobs in film and television.* London, UK: Pandora Books.

Muir, D. (2011, July 30). Somali refugees: Waiting for food and hope, *ABC News International.* Retrieved from http://abcnews.go.com/International/somali-refugees-waiting-food-hope/story?id=14190857

Müller, D. (2005). Die darstellung ethnischer minderheiten in Deutschen massenmedien. In R. Geißler & H. Pöttker (Eds.), *Integration durch massenmedien. Medien und migration im internationalen vergleich* (pp. 83–126). Bielefeld, Germany: transcript Verlag.

Myers, N. (2002). Environmental refugees: A growing phenomenon of the 21st century. *Philosophical Transactions of the Royal Society of London Series B: Biological Sciences, 357*, 609–613.

Nairn, T. (1981). *The break-up of Britain.* London, UK: Verso.

National Coalition of Anti-Deportation Campaigns (NCADC). (2000). *We are economic migrants and asylum seekers too.* Retrieved from http://www.ncadc.org.uk/archives/filed%20newszines/news20/58.html

Nevins, J. (2007). Dying for a cup of coffee? Migrant deaths in the US-Mexico border region in a neoliberal age. *Geopolitics, 12*, 228–247.

Nichols, B. (1991). *Representing reality: Issues and concepts in documentary.* Bloomington: Indiana University Press.

Novakovitch, S. (1989). *Correspondence about Albanian violence in the old Serbia.* Belgrade, Serbia: Plato Press. (Original work published 1889).

Nyers, P. (1999). Emergency or emerging identities? Refugees and transformations in world order. *Millennium: Journal of International Studies, 28*, 1–26.

Nyiri, P., & Saveliev, I. (Eds.) (2002). *Globalizing Chinese migration: Trends in Europe and Asia.* Aldershot, UK: Ashgate.

O'Doherty, K., & Augoustinos, M. (2008). Protecting the nation: Nationalist rhetoric on asylum seekers and the Tampa. *Journal of Community & Applied Social Psychology, 18*, 576–592.

O'Neill, O. (2002). *A Question of trust. BBC Reith Lectures.* Cambridge, UK: Cambridge University Press.

O'Neill, S., & Nicholson-Cole, S. (2009). "Fear won't do it." Promoting positive engagement with climate change through visual and iconic representations. *Science Communication, 30*, 355–379.

Office of the Special Representative and Co-ordinator for Combating Trafficking in Human Beings. (2009). *An agenda for change: Implementing the platform for action against human trafficking.* Vienna, Austria: Organisation for Security and Cooperation in Europe (OSCE). Retrieved from http://www.osce.org/files/documents/e/a/40765.pdf

Olwig, K. F. (2003). Narrating deglobalization: Danish perceptions of a lost empire. *Global Networks, 3*, 207–222.

Orgad, S. (2011). Proper distance from ourselves: The potential for estrangement in the mediapolis. *International Journal of Cultural Studies, 14*, 401–421.

Paalo, P. F. (1981). "Tuvalu mo te atua": An attempt at interpretation (Unpublished Bachelor of Divinity dissertation). Pacific Theological College, Suva, Fiji.

Paasi, A. (2001). Europe as a social process and discourse—Considerations of place, boundaries and identity. *European Urban and Regional Studies, 8*, 7–28.

Parekh, B. (2008). European Liberalism and "the Muslim question." *ISIM Papers, 9*. Amsterdam, Netherlands: Amsterdam University Press.

Parker, D. (1998a). Chinese people in Britain: Histories, futures and identities. In G. Benton & F. N. Pieke (Eds.), *The Chinese in Europe* (pp. 67–95). London, UK: MacMillan Press.

————(1998b). Rethinking British Chinese identities. In T. Skelton & G. Valentine (Eds.), *Cool places: Geographies of youth cultures* (pp. 66–82). London, UK: Routledge.

Pearl, Daniel (Programme Editor). (2010, April 29). *The final prime ministerial debate* [Television broadcast]. Birmingham, UK: BBC. Transcript retrieved from http://news.bbc.co.uk/1/shared/bsp/hi/pdfs/30_04_10_finaldebate.pdf/

Pesic, M. (1994). *Manipulations on television Belgrade.* (Unpublised masters dissertation). Department of Journalism, City University, London.

Pecora, V. P. (2001). Introduction. In V. P. Pecora (Ed.), *Nations and identities: Classic readings* (pp. 1–42). Malden, MA: Blackwell.

Phillips, A. (2007). *Multiculturalism without culture.* Princeton, NJ, & Oxford, UK: Princeton University Press.

Philo, G. (2007). Can discourse analysis successfully explain the content of media and journalistic practice? *Journalism Studies, 8,* 175–196.

Pieke, F. N. (2004, March). *Working paper 94 Chinese globalization and migration to Europe.* Retrieved July 1, 2010, from http://www.ccis-ucsd.org/PUBLICATIONS/wrkg94.pdf

Pieke, F. N., Nyiri. P., Thuno. M., & Ceccagno, A. (2004). *Transnational Chinese: Fujianese migrants in Europe.* Stanford, CA: Stanford University Press.

Pile, S. (2008). Where is the subject? Geographical imaginations and spatializing subjectivity. *Subjectivity, 23,* 206–218.

Pitcher, B. (2009). *The politics of multiculturalism: Race and racism in contemporary Britain.* Basingstoke, UK: Palgrave Macmillan.

Popović, M. (2007) *Vidovdan i časni krst.* Belgrade, Serbia: Library of the Twentieth Century.

Prantl, H. (2004, May 5). Otto Potemkins gesetz. *Süddeutsche Zeitung,* p. 4.

Presse & Informationsamt der Bundesregierung (Ed.). (2007). *Nationaler integrationsplan. Neue wege, neue chancen.* Berlin, Germany. Retrieved December 28, 2009 from http://www.bundesregierung.de/Content/DE/Publikation/IB/Anlagen/nationaler-integrationsplan,property=publicationFile.pdf

Preston, P. (2001, Sept 18) Bordering on madness: Television. *Daily Mail,* p. 5.

Proctor, R. N., & Schiebinger, L. (Eds.). (2008) *Agnotology. The making and unmaking of ignorance.* Palo Alto, CA: Stanford University Press.

Pugh, M. (2004). Drowning not waving: Boat people and humanitarianism at sea. *Journal of Refugee Studies, 17,* 50–69.

Rabinow, P. (Ed.). (1984). *The Foucault reader* (Trans. C. Porter). New York, NY: Pantheon.

Rajaram, P. K. (2002). Humanitarianism and representations of the refugee. *Journal of Refugee Studies, 15,* 247–264.

Refugee Council. (2005). Tell it like it is: The truth about asylum: A pocket guide for the general election. Info centre: UK asylum law and process. London, UK: Refugee Council. Retrieved from http://www.refugeecouncil.org.uk

Renan, E. (2001 [1882]). What is a nation? In V. P. Pecora (Ed.), *Nations and identities: Classic readings* (pp. 162–176). Malden, MA: Blackwell.

Republika Srbija. (2009). Strategija nacionalne bezbednosti Republike Srbije. Belgrade, Serbia: Ministry of Defence. Retrieved April 11 2010 from http://www.mod.gov.rs/lat/dokumenta/strategije/strategije.php

Reuter, C. (2007, September 12). Allahs zornige jünger. *Stern,* 38, pp. 38–44.

Reuters. (2011, April 11). Court rules against Arizona immigration law. *Reuters.* Retrieved from http://www.reuters.com/article/2011/04/11/us-usa-immigration-arizona-idUSTRE73A54420110411

Ribot, J. (2009). Vulnerability does not fall from the sky: Toward multiscale, pro-poor climate policy. In R. Mearns & A. Norton (Eds.), *Social dimensions of climate change* (pp. 47–74). Washington, DC: The World Bank.

Rich, A. (1979). *On lies, secrets and silence: Selected prose, 1966–1978.* New York, NY: Norton.

Richards, C. (2008). The substance of Polynesian voyaging. *World Archaeology, 40,* 206–223.

Richardson, J. E., & Franklin, B. (2003). Dear Editor: Race, readers' letters and the local press. *Political Quarterly, 74,* 184–192.

Ritter, J. A., & Leibowitz, M. (2009). Press councils: The answer to our first amendment dilemma. In E. Barendt (Ed.). *Freedom of the press.* Farnham, UK, & Burlington, VT: Ashgate Publishing. (Original work published 1974)

Rorty, R. (1989). *Contingency, irony, solidarity.* Cambridge, UK: Cambridge University Press.

Rose, G. (2001). *Visual methodologies: An introduction to the interpretation of visual materials.* London, UK: Sage Publications.

Roy, P., & Connell, J. (1991). Climatic change and the future of atoll states. *Journal of Coastal Research, 7,* 1057–1075.

Rubin, J. (2008, September 17). 15 LAPD officers face discipline in May Day melee. *Los Angeles Times,* A1.

Ryan, C. (1991). *Prime time activism: Media strategies for grassroots organizing.* New York: South End Press.

Said, E. (1978). *Orientalism.* New York, NY: Pantheon Books.

Sandvik, K. B. (2010). Unpacking world refugee day: Humanitarian governance and human rights practice? *Journal of Human Rights Practice, 2,* 287–298.

Santa Ana, O. (2006, May 15). Journalists aren't vigilantes, so why do they talk like them? *Hispanic Link Weekly Report, 24*(20).

———(1999). Like an animal I was treated: Anti-immigrant metaphor in U.S. public discourse. *Discourse & Society, 10,* 191–224.

———(2002). *Brown tide rising: Metaphors of Latinos in contemporary U.S. public discourse.* Austin: University of Texas Press.

Santa Ana, O., & Treviño, S. L. with Bailey, M., Bodossian, K., & de Necochea, A. (2007). A May to remember: Adversarial images of immigrants in U.S. newspapers during the 2006 policy debate. *Du Bois Review: Social Science Research on Race, 4,* 207–232.

Santa Ana, O., López L., & Munguía, E. (2010). Framing peace as violence: U.S. television news depictions of the 2007 Los Angeles police attack on immigrant rights marchers. *Aztlán: A Journal of Chicano Studies, 35*(1), 69–101.

Santa Ana, O. with Morán, J., & Sánchez, C. (1998). Awash under a brown tide: Metaphor and immigration in California public and print media discourse. *Aztlán: A Journal of Chicano Studies, 23*(2), 137–176.

Sardar, Z. (1999). *Orientalism.* Buckingham, UK: Open University Press.

Sassen, S. (1999). *Guests and aliens.* New York, NY: The New York Press.

———(2006). *Territory. Authority. Rights. From medieval to global assemblages.* Princeton, NJ, & Oxford, UK: Princeton University Press.

Saxton, A. (2003). I certainly don't want people like that here: The discursive construction of "asylum seekers". *Media International Australia Incorporating Culture and Policy, 109,* 109–120.

Schmidt, U. (2004, May 16). Deutschland wirft kluge köpfe raus. *Frankfurter Allgemeine Zeitung,* p. 42.

Schuster, L. (2003). Asylum seekers: Sangatte and the tunnel. *Parliamentary Affairs, 56,* 506–522.

———(2005). A sledgehammer to crack a nut: Deportation, detention and dispersal in Europe. *Social Policy & Administration, 39,* 606–621.

Shenker, J. (2011, May 8). Aircraft carrier left us to die, say migrants, *Guardian.* Retrieved from http://www.guardian.co.uk/world/2011/may/08/nato-ship-libyan-migrants

Shi, G. (2004). Global illegal immigration. *International Data Information, 5,* 35–40.

Siebert F. S., Peterson T., & Schramm W. (1956). *Four theories of the press.* Chicago, IL: University of Illinois Press.

Silverstone, R. (2007). *Media and morality. On the rise of the mediapolis.* Cambridge, UK: Polity Press.

Sinavaiana, C., & Kauanui, K. (2007). Introduction. *Pacific Studies, 30,* 5–19.

Singer, B. D. (1970). Mass media and communication processes in the Detroit riot of 1967. *Public Opinion Quarterly, 34*, 236–245.

Skeldon, R. (2000). *Myths and realities of Chinese irregular migration.* Geneva, Switzerland: International Organization for Migration.

Skeldon, R. (2004). *China: From exceptional case to global participant.* Retrieved July 15, 2010, from http://www.migrationinformation.org/Profiles/display.cfm?ID=219

Smart, K., Grimshaw, R., McDowell, C., & Crosland, B. (2007). *Reporting asylum: The UK press and the effectiveness of PCC guidelines Jan–March 2005:* ICAR Public Images Partnership for the National Refugee Integration Forum, community and media sub-group, funded by the Immigration and Nationality Directorate, UK Home Office.

Smith, A. D. (1989). The origins of nations, *Ethnic and Racial Studies, 12*, 340–367.

Snyder, T. (2000). Conclusion: The wall around the West. In P. Andreas & T. Snyder (Eds.), *The wall around the West: State borders and immigration controls in North America and Europe* (pp. 219–227). Lanham, MD: Rowman & Littlefield Publishers.

Souter, J. (2011). A culture of disbelief or denial? Critiquing refugee status determination in the United Kingdom. *Oxford Monitor of Forced Migration, 1*, 48–59.

Southern Poverty Law Center. (2002). The puppeteer. *Intelligence Report.* Retrieved November 19, 2009 from www.splcenter.org/intel/intelreport/article.jsp?pid=180

Spannbauer, A. (2003, August 7). Nach der green card bleibt nur die Heirat. *Die Tageszeitung,* p. 8.

Speers, T. (2001). *Novelty or nuisance: Refugees and the British media* (Unpublished MA dissertation). Cardiff University School of Journalism, Media and Cultural Studies, Cardiff, UK.

Speers, T. (2001). Welcome or over-reaction? Refugees and asylum seekers in the Welsh media. Cardiff, UK: Asylum Seekers and Refugees Media Group.

Spivak, G. C. (1988). Can the subaltern speak? In C. Nelson & L. Grossberg (Eds.), *Marxism and the interpretation of culture* (pp. 271–313). Urbana: University of Illinios Press.

Squires, N., & McElroy, D. (2011, April 7). Libya to unleash wave of migrants on Europe, *Daily Telegraph.* Retrieved from http://www.telegraph.co.uk/news/worldnews/africaandindianocean/libya/8435884/Libya-to-unleash-wave-of-migrants-on-Europe.html

Stalker, P. (2001). *International migration.* Oxford, UK: New International Publications in association with Verso.

Steffek, J. (2003). The legitimation of international governance: A discourse approach. *European Journal of International Relations. 9*, 249–75.

Stevenson, N. (2003). *Cultural citizenship: Cosmopolitan questions.* Maidenhead, UK: Open University Press.

Straw, J. (2000, October 2). Interview on the Human Rights Act. *BBC Radio 4, Today Programme.* Retrieved from http://news.bbc.co.uk/olmedia/950000/audio/_952565_jackstraw08_02oct.ram

t'Hart, P., & Tindall, K. (2009). Leadership by the famous: Celebrity as political capital. In J. Kane, J. Patapan, & P. t'Hart (Eds.) *Dispersed leadership in democracies* (pp. 255–278). Oxford, UK: Oxford University Press.

Tacoli, C. (2009). Crisis or adaptation? Migration and climate change in a context of high mobility. *Environment and Urbanization, 21,* 513–525.

Takle, M. (2007). EU citizens: Challenging the notion of German national political community, 199–2005. *International Journal of the Sociology of Law, 35,* 178–191.

Taylor, M. (1987). *Chinese pupils in Britain.* London, UK: National Foundation for Educational Research.

Taylor, P. J. (2003). The State as container: Territorialiy in the modern world-system. In N. Brenner, B. Jessop, M. Jones, & G. MacLeod (Eds.), *State/space: A reader* (pp. 101–113). Malden, MA, Oxford, UK, Carlton, Australia, & Berlin, Germany: Blackwell.

Taylorhome, D. (2000, April 18). Straw ready to send Albanian refugees home. *Daily Express.*

Tazreiter, C. (2003). Asylum-seekers as pariahs in the Australian state security against the few. *Wider Discussion Paper, 19.*

ter Wal, J. (Ed.). (2002). *Racism and cultural diversity in mass media. An overview of research and examples of good practice in the EU member states, 1995–2000. On behalf of the European monitoring centre on racism and xenophobia, Vienna (EUMC).* Retrieved November 9, 2010, from http://fra.europa.eu/fraWebsite/research/publications/publications_per_year/previous_publications/pub_mr_racism_diversity_media_02_en.htm

Terkessidis, M. (2006). Globale kultur in Deutschland. Der lange abschied von der fremdheit. In A. Hepp & R. Winter (Eds.), *Kultur—medien—macht. Cultural Studies und medienanalyse* (3rd ed.) (pp. 311–325). Wiesbaden, Germany: VS Verlag für Sozialwissenschaften.

Thompson, J. (1995). *Media and modernity.* London, UK: Polity.

Thomson, M. (2003). Images of Sangatte: Political representations of asylum seeking in France and the UK. *Sussex Migration Working Paper No. 18*: Sussex, UK: Sussex Centre for Migration Research.

Thornes, J. E. (2008). Cultural climatology and the representation of sky, atmosphere, weather and climate in selected art works of Constable, Monet and Eliasson. *Geoforum, 39,* 570–580.

Threadgold, T., Clifford, S., Arwo, A., Powell, V., Harb, Z., Jiang, X., et al. (2008). *Immigration and inclusion in South Wales.* York, UK: Joseph Rountree Foundation.

Threadgold, T. (2006). Dialogism, voice and global contexts. *Australian Feminist Studies, 21,* 223–244.

————(2009). The media and migration in the United Kingdom 1999 to 2009. In M. P. I. Bertelsmann Stiftung (Ed.), *Migration, public opinion and politics* (pp. 222–206). Gütersloh, Germany: Verlag Bertelsmann Stiftung.

Tibbetts, J. (2001, May 22). High court to decide if suspected terrorists can stay. *Vancouver Sun*, p. A3.

Ticktin, M. (2005). Policing and humanitarianism in France: Immigration and the turn to law as state of exception. *Interventions, 7*, 347–368.

Tomlinson, J. (2011). Beyond connection: Cultural cosmopolitan and ubiquitous media. *International Journal of Cultural Studies, 14*, 347–361.

Torfing, J. (1999). *New theories of discourse: Laclau, Mouffe and Žižek*. Oxford, UK: Blackwell.

Tsoukala, A. (2008a). Boundary-creating processes and the social construction of threat. *Alternatives, 33*, 137–152.

————(2008b). Defining the terrorist threat in the post-September 11 era. In D. Bigo & A. Tsoukala (Eds.) *Terror, insecurity and liberty: Illiberal practices of liberal regimes after 9/11* (pp. 49–99). London, UK: Routledge.

Tuvalu Parliament. (2005, August 1). Motion 31 (P. Solomona, Trans.).

Tyler, I. (2006). Welcome to Britain: The cultural politics of asylum. *European Journal of Cultural Studies, 9*, 185–202.

U.S. National Advisory Commission on Civil Disorders. (1968). *Report of the National Advisory Commission on Civil Disorders*. Washington D.C.: U.S. Government Printing Office. (Original work also published 1968 as *The Kerner report: The 1968 report of the National Advisory Commission on Civil Disorders*. New York, NY: Pantheon).

UJDI. (1990). *Kosovski cvor: dresiti ili seci?—Izvestaj nezavisne komisje*. Belgrade, Serbia: Xronos.

UKBA. (2007). *Securing the UK border: Our vision and strategy for the future*. London, UK: HMSO.

UKBA. (2008). *A strong new force at the border*. London: HMSO.

Ulack, C. (2011, June 23). The Arab Spring's looming refugee crisis. *Foreign Policy*. Retrieved from http://mideast.foreignpolicy.com/posts/2011/06/23/the_arab_spring_s_looming_refugee_cr isis

UNCERD. (2001). *Concluding observations of the Committee on the Elimination of Racial Discrimination: United Kingdom of Great Britain and Northern Ireland*. Office of the High Commissioner for Human Rights.

United Nations Development Programme. (2009). *Human development report 2009. Overcoming barriers: Human mobility and development*. Retrieved July 1, 2010, from http://hdr.undp.org/en/media/HDR_2009_EN_Complete.pdf

UNHCR. (2011, June 20). Angelina Jolie and UNHCR chief Guterres visit boat people on Italian island. *UNHCR News Stories*. Retrieved from http://www.unhcr.org.uk/news-and-views/news-list/news-detail/article/angelina-jolie-and-unhcr-chief-guterres-visit-boat-people-on-italian-island.html

United Nations Development Programme. (2009). *Human development report 2009 L demographic trends total population.* Retrieved July 1, 2010, from http://hdrstats.undp.org/en/indicators/135.html

University of Nottingham. (2009, October 22–23). *The employment of Chinese migrant workers in UK: Issues and solutions.* Nottingham, UK: International Labour Migration Workshop, University of Nottingham. Retrieved July 6, 2010, from http://www.ilo.org/wcmsp5/groups/public/---ed_norm/---declaration/documents/event/wcms_118303.pdf

van Dijk, T. A. (1988a). Semantics of a press panic: The Tamil "invasion." *European Journal of Communication, 3*, 167–187.

———(1988b). *News analysis: Case studies of international and national news in the press.* Hillsdale, NJ: Lawrence Erlbaum Associates.

———(1988c). *News as discourse.* Hillsdale, NJ: Lawrence Erlbaum Associates.

———(1989). Mediating racism: The role of the media in the reproduction of racism. In R. Wodak, *Language, power and ideology: Studies in political discourse* (pp. 199–226). Philadelpha, PA: John Benjamins Publishing Company.

———(1991). *Racism and the press.* London, UK: Routledge.

———(1993a). *Elite discourse and racism.* London, UK: Sage Publications.

———(1993b). Denying racism: Elite discourse and racism. In J. Solomos & J. Wrench (Eds.), *Racism and migration in Western Europe* (pp. 179–193). Oxford, UK: Berg. Retrieved November 9, 2010 from: http://www.discourses.org/OldArticles/Denying%20racism%20-%20Elite%20discourse%20and%20racism.pdf

———(2006). *Racism and the European press. Presentation for the European Commission against Racism and Intolerance (ECRI), Strasbourg, December 16 2006.* Retrieved November 9, 2010 from http://www.discursos.org/unpublished%20articles/Racism%20and%20the%20European%20Press.pdf

van Leeuwen, T. (2001). Semiotics and iconography. In T. van Leeuwen & C. Jewitt (Eds.), *Handbook of visual analysis* (pp. 92–118). London, UK: Sage Publications.

van Zoonen, L. (1994). *Feminist media studies.* London, UK: Sage Publications.

van Zoonen, L., Mihelj, S., & Vis, F. (2010). Fitna, the video battle: How YouTube enables the young to perform their religious and public identities. Loughborough, UK: Department of Social Sciences, Loughborough University. Retrieved August 13, 2010, from http://www.lboro.ac.uk/departments/ss/research/FITNA/index.html

Vargas, J. A. (2011, June 22). My life as an undocumented immigrant, *New York Times Magazine.* Retrieved from http://www.nytimes.com/2011/06/26/magazine/my-life-as-an-undocumented-immigrant.html?_r=1&ref=magazine&pagewanted=all

Vélez-Ibánez, C. G. (1997). *Border visions: Mexican cultures of the Southwest United States.* Tucson: University of Arizona Press.

Vestergaard A. (2010). Identity, integrity and humanitarian appeal. In L. Chouliaraki & M. Morsing (Eds.). *Media, organisations and identity* (pp. 168–184). London, UK: Palgrave.

Victimology Society in Serbia (VSS). (2004). *Trafficking in people in Serbia.* Belgrade, Serbia: VSS & OSCE.

Vollmer, B. (2008). *Undocumented migration—counting the uncountable, data and trends across Europe—UK report.* Oxford, UK: CLANDESTINO project.

VPRT (Verband Privater Rundfunk & Telemedien) (Ed.). (2007). Stellungnahme des VPRT zum beitrag der privaten rundfunkanbieter zur integration von menschen mit migrationshintergrund. Berlin, Germany: VPRT. Retrieved Nov 9, 2010 from www.vprt.de/get_pdf.php?m=positions&langkey=de&id=12

Waldman, L. (1999, August 24). Refugee system is working just fine. *Toronto Star,* p. 1.

Ward, I. (2002). The *Tampa,* Wedge politics, and a lesson for political journalism. *Australian Journalism Review, 24,* 21–39.

Warner, K., Ehrhart, C., de Sherbinin, A., Adamo, S., & Chai-Onn, T. (2009). *In search of shelter: Mapping the effects of climate change on human migration and displacement.* Atlanta, GA: Care International.

Watson, G. (2011, March 31). Berlusconi pledges to clear Lampedusa in two or three days, *Corriere Della Sera.* Retrieved from http://www.corriere.it/International/english/articoli/2011/03/31/clear-lampedusa.shtml

Watson, J. (1977). *Between two cultures.* Oxford, UK: Basil Blackwell.

Way, T. (2009). *Trauma narratives and the discursive construction of alterity.* Paper presented at Refugees: Lives Pushed to the Margins, 6th Annual Forced Migration Student Conference, University of East London, April 25, 2009, London, UK.

WDR (Westdeutscher Rundfunk) (Ed.). (2004). *Integration und kulturelle vielfalt. Viel erreicht—noch mehr zu leisten.* Köln, Germany. Retrieved November 9, 2010 from www.migration-boell.de/downloads/diversity/WDR-Integration_0104d.pdf

Weber, L., & Bowling, B. (2004). Policing migration: A framework for investigating the regulation of global mobility. *Policing and Society, 14,* 195–212.

Weber, L., & Gelsthorpe, L. (2000). Deciding to detain: How decisions to detain asylum seekers are made at ports of entry. Cambridge, UK: Institute of Criminology, University of Cambridge.

Weber, M. (1948 [1918]). Politics as a vocation. In H. H. Gerth & C. W. Mills (Eds.), *From Max Weber: Essays in sociology* (pp. 71–128). London, UK: Routledge & Kegan Paul.

Weikert, E. (2004, May 5). Helfer atmen durch. *Tageszeitung,* p. 22.

Wengeler, M. (2000). Von "belastungen", "wirtschaftlichem nutzen" und "politischen zielen." Die öffentliche einwanderungsdiskussion in Deutschland, Österreich und der Schweiz anfang der 1970s. In T. Niehr & K. Böke (Eds.) *Einwanderungsdiskurse: Vergleichende diskurslinguistische studien,* (pp. 135–157). Wiesbaden, Germany: Westdeutscher Verlag.

Wengeler, M. (2003). Topos und diskurs: Begründung einer argumentationsanalytischen methode und ihre anwendung auf den migrationsdiskurs (1960–1985). Tübingen, Germany: Niemeyer.

Wetherell, M., & Potter, J. (1992). *Mapping the language of racism.* New York, NY: Columbia University Press.

Whincup, T. (2007). TE WA: The social significance of the traditional canoes of Kiribati. *Shima: The International Journal of Research into Island Cultures, 1,* 43–45.

Wimmer R. D., & Dominick J. R. (2006). *Mass media research: An introduction* (8th ed.). Belmont, CA: Thomson Wadsworth.

Wodak, R., & Meyer, M. (2001). *Methods of critical discourse analysis.* London, UK: Sage Publications.

Wodak, R. (2001). The discourse-historical approach. In R. Wodak & M. Meyer (Eds.) *Methods of critical discourse analysis.* (pp. 63–94). London, UK: Sage.

Wodak, R., de Cillia, R., Reisigl, M., & Liebhart, K. (1999). *The discursive construction of national identity.* (A. Hirsch and R. Mitten, Trans.). Edinburgh, UK: Edinburgh University Press.

Wolfsfeld, G. (2004) *Media and the path to peace.* Cambridge, UK: Cambridge University Press.

Wood, H. (2003). Cultural studies for Oceania. *The Contemporary Pacific, 15,* 340–374.

Wooding, D. (2001, April 26). Stowaway detectors. *Sun.*

World Bank. (2008). *Global development finance: The role of international banking.* Washington, DC: The International Bank for Reconstruction and Development & The World Bank.

Xinhua Net. (2010, May 24). *Fence closed to prevent corrupt officials from fleeing out of China.* Retrieved July 9, 2010, from http://news.xinhuanet.com/legal/2010-05/24/c_12133760.htm

Young, M., & Wilmott, P. (1957). *Family and kinship in East London.* London, UK: Routledge & Kegan Paul.

Yuval-Davis, N., Anthias, F., & Kofman, E. (2005). Secure borders and safe haven and the gendered politics of belonging: Beyond social cohesion. *Ethnic and Racial Studies, 28,* 513–535.

Zambonini, G. (2009). Medien und integration. Der ARD-weg: Vom "gastarbeiter" programm zur querschnittsaufgabe. In Arbeitsgemeinschaft der öffentlich-rechtlichen rundfunkanstalten der Bundesrepublik Deutschland (ARD) (Ed.), *ARD Jahrbuch 2009* (pp. 87–94). Hamburg, Germany: Hans-Bredow Institut.

ZDF (Zweites Deutsches Fernsehen) Hauptabteilung Kommunikation (Ed.). (2007). Die darstellung von migration und integration in den ZDF programmen. Status quo und perspektiven. Mainz, Germany. Retrieved November 9, 2010 from http://www.unternehmen.zdf.de/

fieadmin/files/Download_Dokumente/DD_Das_ZDF/Migration_und_Integration_im_ZDF
-Programm.pdf

ZDF (Zweites Deutsches Fernsehen) Intendant (Ed.). (2008). *Selbstverpflichtungserklärung des ZDF 2009–2010*. Mainz, Germany. Retrieved November 9, 2010 from http://www.unternehmen.zdf.de/fileadmin/files/Download_Dokumente/DD_Das_ZDF/Selbstverpflichtungserklaerung_Programm_Perspektiven_2009_2010.pdf

Zhou, Y., & Wang, X.-F. (2004). Features of the modern illegal emigration from China: Case study of illegal migration from Fujian. *Journal of Jinan University, 26*(2), 15–19.

Zhuang, Z-J. (2001). An analysis of illegal border-crossing among Chinese emmigrants from Wenzhou. *Journal of Zhejiang Police College, 4*(66), 29–30.

Zinterer, T. (2004). *Politikwandel durch politikberatung? Die Kanadische Royal Commission on Aboriginal peoples und die Unabhängige Kommission "zuwanderung" im Vergleich*. Wiesbaden, Germany: Verlag für Sozialwissenschaften.

Zurn, M. (2005). Global governance and legitimacy problem. In D. Held & M. Koenig-Archibugi (Eds.). *Global governance and public accountability* (pp. 36–63). Oxford, UK: Blackwell.

Notes on Contributors

Julia Bayer teaches at the Institute of Social and Cultural Anthropology at Munich University, her main research interests are visual and media anthropology. She also trains journalists from different countries and backgrounds in media diversity and conflict-sensitive reporting.

Harald Bauder is academic director of the Ryerson Centre for Immigration and Settlement (RCIS) and an Associate Professor in the Graduate Program in Immigration and Settlement Studies and the Geography Department at Ryerson University in Toronto, Canada. He is author of *Immigration Dialectic: Imagining Community, Economy and Nation* (University of Toronto Press, 2011), *Labor Movement: How Migration Regulates Labor Markets* (Oxford University Press, 2006) and *Work on the West Side: Urban Neighborhoods and the Cultural Exclusion of Youths* (Lexington Books, 2002).

Jelena Bjelica is an independent researcher and journalist in the Balkans. She is author of *On the Trail of Freedom: Human Trafficking in Europe* (Samizdat, 2005), *Prostitution: The Enslavement of Girls from Eastern Europe* (Paris-Méditerranée, 2005) and *Trafficking in Human Beings in the Balkans: Manual for Journalists* (SDC, 2002). Since 2010 she has worked in Afghanistan for the UNODC.

Bolette B. Blaagaard is a research fellow at the Centre for Law, Justice and Journalism at City University, London. She works in the interdisciplinary field of journalism, media and cultural studies and has published in Nordic as well as international journals on issues of Nordic colonialism, multiculturalism, civil society, cosmopolitanism and new media.

Lilie Chouliaraki is Professor of Media and Communications at the LSE. Her research focuses on mediated public discourses from an ethical and political perspective. She has published widely on the relationship between media, ethics and public life, as well as on discourse analysis, corporate communication and youth culture and pedagogy. She is author of *The Spectatorship of Suffering* (Sage, 2006) and *Media and Violence: Virtue and the Ethics of Public Life* (Polity Press, forthcoming).

Carol Farbotko is a cultural geographer with research interests in climate change. Her work focuses on analysing changing meanings of people and places meaning in a warming world, particularly in the Pacific region.

Bernhard Gross is a Senior Lecturer in journalism at the University of the West of England, Bristol. He has an MA in Newspaper Journalism from Syracuse University, USA, and is working on his PhD at Cardiff University, UK. A former journalist, he has been focussing his academic research on media representations of migration as well as discourses of the nation on television news.

Janet Harris has worked on major series such as *40 Minutes* (BBC2), the BAFTA winning series *Sarajevo: Street Under Siege; Modern Times* (BBC2) and the Grierson Award winning, *The System* (BBC2). She has directed programmes for series such as *Soldiers to Be* (BBC1), the Bafta nominated, *Welcome to Britain* (BBC1) and *Fighting the War* (BBC2); *Saddam's Iraq* (ITV); *Soldier, Father, Daughter, Son* (BBC1); *Spy* (BBC4) and *The Queen's Cavalry* (BBC1). She is currently completing her PhD at Cardiff University on the documentary and news coverage of the British military in Iraq 2004-2009.

Xinyi Jiang has a BA and MA in English literature and PhD in Media and Cultural Studies. She has taught English and journalism and conducted research on immigration, health, science and technology. This chapter is based on her PhD thesis about Fujianese migration in the UK. She now works for the University of Dundee.

Xiaoying Liu is a professor with the Institute of International Journalism, Communication University of China. His research interests include international communication, journalism history and economy of communications. He recently published a monograph *International Journalism: Ontology, Methods and Functions* (Beijing: China Radio & Television Publishing House, 2010). He is currently examining international communication power of China Central Television (CCTV).

Kerry Moore is a Lecturer at Cardiff University, School of Journalism, Media and Cultural Studies (JOMEC). Her research focuses upon migration, issues of cultural identity and media and political discourses of racism. She is currently working on a monograph entitled *Racialised Crises: Asylum, Ethnicity and the Media* (Ashgate, forthcoming, 2013).

Otto Santa Ana is Associate Professor in UCLA's Department of Chicana & Chicano Studies. As a sociolinguist, he put together a widely-used anthology, *Tongue-Tied,* on the speech of minority school children and linguistic ideology of American adults. As a critical discourse analyst, he studies mass media's role in societal inequity. His forthcoming book, *Juan in a Hundred* is a comprehensives study of the visual semiotics of contemporary network television news about Latinos. Santa Ana is now writing about mass media comedy.

Terry Threadgold is Professor of Communication and Cultural Studies (JOMEC) and Pro Vice Chancellor, Staff and Diversity, Cardiff University. Her book, *Feminist Poetics: Poeisis, Performance, Histories* (Routledge, 1997), was a study of race, nation and identity in Australian literature, media and popular culture. Her research on UK media coverage of asylum and refugee issues between 1999 and 2009 is well known. She published *Shoot First and Ask Questions Later: Media Coverage of the 2003 Iraq War* (Peter Lang, 2006) with Justin Lewis, Nick Mosdell and Rod Brookes. Her report for Joseph Rowntree, *Immigration and Inclusion in South Wales* was published in 2008.

Yan Wu lectures in the Department of Political and Cultural Studies, Swansea University, UK. Her research interests include media and the public sphere, new media and citizen journalism, media and migration, and the global communication. She writes bilingually. Her recent publications include a book chapter on climate change as a media discourse in China (Peter Lang, 2009) and a journal article on the web presence of women during the global economic downturn in China (*Feminist Media Studies,* 2009).

Xiangqin Zeng lectures in the English Department, School of International Studies, Communication University of China. Her research interests include international communication and journalism. She recently published 'Women Image in Canadian Media' in *Mirror Image and the Other* (Press of Communication University of China Press, 2009). She is currently examining how advertisements target children in China and the rationales for legislative protection.

Index

Simon Cottle, *General Editor*

From climate change to the war on terror, financial meltdowns to forced migrations, pandemics to world poverty, and humanitarian disasters to the denial of human rights, these and other crises represent the dark side of our globalized planet. They are endemic to the contemporary global world and so too are they highly dependent on the world's media.

Each of the specially commissioned books in the *Global Crises and the Media* series examines the media's role, representation, and responsibility in covering major global crises. They show how the media can enter into their constitution, enacting them on the public stage and thereby helping to shape their future trajectory around the world. Each book provides a sophisticated and empirically engaged understanding of the topic in order to invigorate the wider academic study and public debate about the most pressing and historically unprecedented global crises of our time.

For further information about the series and submitting manuscripts, please contact:

Dr. Simon Cottle
Cardiff School of Journalism
Cardiff University, Room 1.28
The Bute Building, King Edward VII Ave.
Cardiff CF10 3NB
United Kingdom
CottleS@cardiff.ac.uk

To order other books in this series, please contact our Customer Service Department at:

(800) 770-LANG (within the U.S.)
(212) 647-7706 (outside the U.S.)
(212) 647-7707 FAX

Or browse online by series at:

www.peterlang.com